CONSTRUCTION LAW SERIES

CONSTRUCTION INDUSTRY FORMBOOK

SECOND EDITION

James Acret
of the
Los Angeles Bar

SHEPARD'S/McGRAW-HILL, INC.
P.O. Box 35300
Colorado Springs, CO 80935-3530

McGRAW-HILL, INC.

New York • St. Louis • San Francisco • Auckland • Bogotá
Caracas • Colorado Springs • Hamburg • Lisbon • London
Madrid • Mexico • Milan • Montreal • New Delhi
Panama • Paris • San Juan • São Paulo • Singapore
Sydney • Tokyo • Toronto

Copyright © 1979, 1981, 1982, 1984, 1985, 1986, 1987, 1989, 1990 by McGraw-Hill, Inc. All rights reserved. Printed in the United States of America. Except as permitted under the United States Copyright Act of 1976, no part of this publication may be reproduced or distributed in any form or by any means, or stored in a data base or retrieval system, without the prior written permission of the publisher.

Revised edition of *Construction Industry Formbook* by Robert F. Cushman, Michael S. Simon, and McNeill Stokes (McGraw-Hill, Inc 1979).

Information has been obtained by Shepard's/McGraw-Hill, Inc. from sources believed to be reliable. However, because of the possibility of human or mechanical error by our sources, Shepard's/McGraw-Hill, Inc., or other, Shepard's/McGraw-Hill, Inc. does not guarantee the accuracy, adequacy, or completeness of any information and is not responsible for any errors or omissions or for the results obtained from use of such information.

The Sponsoring Editor for this book was Wendy Bliss and the Legal Editor was Dale Agthe.

ISBN 0-07-172276-9
CIFR2

Shepard's Construction Law Series

Architects and Engineers, Second Edition
California Construction Law Manual, Third Edition
Construction Law Digests
Construction Arbitration Handbook
Construction Litigation Handbook
Florida Construction Law Manual, Second Edition
Illinois Construction Law: Manual and Forms
Texas Construction Law Manual

This work is affectionately dedicated
by the author to his sons —

Douglas, Craig, Clayton, Darryl, and Jimmy

Acknowledgments

The author gratefully acknowledges the assistance of Tom Wogan in producing this work.

Contents

Summary

1 **Conventional Prime Contracts: Stipulated Sum, and Cost Plus**

2 **Design-Build Concept**

3 **Construction Management Contract**

4 **Contracts Between Owner and Architect**

5 **Agreements Between Contractor and Architect**

6 **Subcontract**

7 **Design-Build Subcontracts**

8 **Purchase Orders**

9 **Joint Venture Agreements**

   Index

Detailed

1 Conventional Prime Contracts: Stipulated Sum, and Cost Plus

Introduction to Prime Contracts

- §1.01 Definition
- §1.02 Stipulated Sum Contract
- §1.03 Cost Plus Contract
- §1.04 Cost Plus Contract with Guaranteed Maximum Price
- §1.05 "Split Savings" Contract
- §1.06 Design-Build Contract
- §1.07 Fast Track Contract
- §1.08 Construction Management Contract

AIA Document A101 - Stipulated Sum

- §1.09 General Comment
- §1.10 Document A101 First Page
- §1.11 Comment: Article 3.1 Date of Commencement
- §1.12 Comment: Article 3.2 Substantial Completion
- §1.13 Comment: Article 5.3 Applications for Payment
- §1.14 Comment: Article 5.4 Schedule of Values
- §1.15 Comment: Article 5.6.1 Retention
- §1.16 Comment: Article 5.7 Progress Payments
- §1.17 Comment: Article 6 Final Payment
- §1.18 Comment: Article 9.1.3 Contract Documents
- §1.19 Comment: Article 9.1.7 Signatures

AIA Document A111 - Cost Plus Contract

- §1.20 General Comment
- §1.21 Comment: Article 3.1 Relationship of the Parties
- §1.22 Comment: Article 5.1 Contract Sum
- §1.23 Comment: Article 5.2.1 Guaranteed Maximum Price

§1.24 Comment: Article 5.2.2 Alternates
§1.25 Comment: Article 5.2.3 Unit Prices
§1.26 Comment: Article 6 Changes in the Work

Addendum to AIA Document A111

§1.27 General Comment

    FORM 1-1 Addendum to AIA Document A111 - Standard Form of Agreement

AIA Document A201 - General Conditions

§1.28 General Comment

    FORM 1-2 Supplementary General Conditions [Favors Interests of Contractor] (with Comments)

    FORM 1-3 Supplementary General Conditions [Favors Interests of Owner] (with Comments)

Prime Contract - Stipulated Sum - Short Form [Favors Interests of Contractor]

§1.29 General Comment

    FORM 1-4 Prime Contract - Stipulated Sum

Prime Contract - Cost Plus Percentage - Guaranteed Maximum Cost [Favors Interests of Owner]

§1.30 General Comment

    FORM 1-5 Prime Contract - Cost Plus Percentage

Proposal and Prime Contract - Short Form - Stipulated Sum - Small Project

§1.31 General Comment

    FORM 1-6 Proposal and Prime Contract - Short Form - Stipulated Sum

Alternate Prime Contract Provisions

§1.32 General Comment
    FORM 1-7 Alternate Prime Contract Provisions

AIA Document A107 - Abbreviated Form of Agreement between Owner and Contractor

§1.33 General Comment
    FORM 1-8 Supplementary General Conditions - AIA Document A107 [Favors Interests of Contractor] (with Comments)
    FORM 1-9 Supplementary General Conditions - AIA Document A107 [Favors Interests of Owner] (with Comments)

2 Design-Build Concept

Introduction to Design-Build Concepts

§2.01 The Design-Build Concept
§2.02 The Evolution of the Design-Build Concept
§2.03 Disadvantages of Design-Build From the Owners Point of View
§2.04 Advantages of Design-Build From the Owners Point of View
§2.05 The Design-Build Process
§2.06 Some Practical Attributes of Design-Build

AGC Document No. 415 - Design-Build Agreement - Lump Sum

§2.07 General Comment
    FORM 2-1 AGC Docment No. 415 - Standard Form of Design-Build Agreement and General Conditions between Owner and Contractor (Where the Basis of Compensation Is a Lump Sum) (1986)

FORM 2-2 Supplementary General Conditions [Favors Interests of Owner] (with Comments)

AGC Document No. 410 - Design-Build Agreement - Guaranteed Maximum

§2.08 General Comment

FORM 2-3 AGC Document No. 410 - Standard Form of Design-Build Agreement and General Conditions between Owner and Contractor (Provides a Guaranteed Maximum Price) (1982)

FORM 2-4 Supplementary General Conditions [Favors Interests of Owner] (with Comments)

§2.09 Clarifications to AGC Documents Nos. 410 and 415

FORM 2-5 Letter of Intent to Award Design-Build Contract (with Comment)

3 Construction Management Contract

Introduction to Construction Management Contracts

§3.01 General Comment

AGC Document No. 500 - Construction Management Agreement - Guaranteed Maximum Price

FORM 3-1 AGC Document No. 500 - Standard Form of Agreement between Owners and Construction Manager (Guaranteed Maximum Price Option) (1980)

> FORM 3-2 Modifications to Construction Management Agreement [Favors Interests of Owner] (with Comments)

AGC Document No. 501 - Amendment to Owner-Construction Manager Contract

§3.02 General Comment

> FORM 3-3 AGC Document No. 501 - Amendment to Owner-Construction Manager Contract (1977)

AGC Document No. 520 - Gneral Conditions for Trade Contractors

§3.03 General Comment

> FORM 3-4 AGC Document No. 520 - General Conditions for Trade Contractors under Construction Management Agreements (1980)
>
> FORM 3-5 Modifications to General Conditions for Trade Contractors [Favors Interests of Trade Contractor] (with Comments)

4 Contracts Between Owner and Architect

Introduction to Owner/Architects Agreements

§4.01 General Comments

Architect/Owner Agreements

> FORM 4-1 Agreement between Owner and Architect for the Provision of Architectural Services
>
> FORM 4-2 Alternate and Optional Contract Provisions

AIA Document B141 - Standard Form of Agreement between Owner and Architect

§4.02 General Comments

　　FORM 4-3 Modifications to Owner/Architect Agreement [Favors Interests of Owner] (with Comments)

5 Agreements Between Contractor and Architect

Introduction to Contractor/Architect Agreements

§5.01 General Comments

AGC Document No. 420 - Agreement between Contractor and Architect

§5.02 General Comments

　　FORM 5-1 AGC Document No. 420 - Standard Form of Agreement between Contractor and Architect

Revisions to AGC Document No. 420 - Agreement between Contractor and Architect

§5.03 General Comments

　　FORM 5-2 Revisions to AGC Document No. 420 - Agreement between Contractor and Architect (with Comments)

6 Subcontract

Introduction to Subcontract Forms

§6.01 General Comments

§6.02 Forms Drafted by the Author

Subcontract - Long Form [Favors Interests of Prime Contractor]

§6.03 General Comments

　　FORM 6-1 Subcontract - Long Form [Favors Interests of Prime Contractor]

Subcontract - Short Form

§6.04 General Comments
    FORM 6-2 Subcontract - Short Form

Proposal and Subcontract

§6.05 General Comments
    FORM 6-3 Proposal and Subcontract

Alternate Subcontract Provisions

§6.06 General Comments
    FORM 6-4 Alternate Subcontract Provisions

AGC Document No. 600 - Subcontract

§6.07 General Comments
    FORM 6-5 AGC Document No. 600 - Subcontract for Building Construction (1984)
§6.08 Comment: Article 3.2 Schedule
§6.09 Comment: Article 5.2.2 Retainage/Security
§6.10 Comment: Article 5.3 Claims Relating to Contractor
§6.11 Comment: Article 5.3.4 Final Payment Delay
§6.12 Comment: Article 12.1 Indemnification
§6.13 Comment: Article 13.5 Waiver of Rights

AGC Document No. 603 - Subcontract (Short Form)

§6.14 General Comments
    FORM 6-7 AGC Document No. 603 - Subcontract (Short Form) (1987)

AGC Standard Form 605 - Standard Subbid Proposal

§6.15 General Comments
    FORM 6-8 AGC Standard Form 605 - Standard Subbid Proposal

7 Design-Build Subcontracts

Introduction to Design-Build Subcontracts

§7.01 General Comments

AGC Document No. 450 - Standard Design-Build Subcontract - Subcontractor Not Providing Design

§7.02 General Comments

> FORM 7-1 AGC Document No. 450 - Standard Design-Build Subcontract Agreement with Subcontractor Not Providing Design (1983)

AGC Document No. 450-1 - Standard Design-Build Subcontract - Subcontractor Providing Design

§7.03 General Comments

> FORM 7-2 AGC Document No. 450-1 - Standard Design-Build Agreement with Subcontractor Providing Design (1983)

AGC Document No. 430 - Conditions between Contractor and Subcontractor for Design-Build

§7.04 General Comments

> FORM 7-3 AGC Document No. 430 - Conditions between Contractor and Subcontractor for Design-Build (1982)

Revisions to AGC Document No. 430

§7.05 General Comment

> FORM 7-4 Revisions to AGC Document No. 430 (with Comments)

8 Purchase Orders

Introduction to Purchase Orders

§8.01 Purchase Orders in the Construction Industry

§8.02 Special Rules for Commercial Transactions

Purchase Order Forms

§8.03 General Comments

    FORM 8-1 Short Form Purchase Order

    FORM 8-2 Long Form Purchase Order

Alternate Purchase Order Provisions

§8.04 General Comments

    FORM 8-3 Alternate Purchase Order Provisions

Alternate Purchase Order Forms

    FORM 8-4 Short Form Purchase Order - Another Version

    FORM 8-5 Short Form Purchase Order - Another Version

    FORM 8-6 Long Form Purchase Order - Another Version

9 Joint Venture Agreements

Introduction to Joint Venture Agreements

§9.01 General Comments
§9.02 Rights and Responsibilities
§9.03 Interests of Parties
§9.04 Control of Operations
§9.05 Contributions and Financing
§9.06 Employees of the Joint Venture
§9.07 Insurance

Joint Venture Agreements

    FORM 9-1 Joint Venture Agreement

    FORM 9-2 Joint Venture Agreement - Another Version

Index

Conventional Prime Contracts: Stipulated Sum, and Cost Plus

1

Introduction to Prime Contracts

§1.01 Definition
§1.02 Stipulated Sum Contract
§1.03 Cost Plus Contract
§1.04 Cost Plus Contract with Guaranteed Maximum Price
§1.05 "Split Savings" Contract
§1.06 Design-Build Contract
§1.07 Fast Track Contract
§1.08 Construction Management Contract

AIA Document A101 - Stipulated Sum

§1.09 General Comment
§1.10 Document A101 First Page
§1.11 Comment: Article 3.1 Date of Commencement
§1.12 Comment: Article 3.2 Substantial Completion
§1.13 Comment: Article 5.3 Applications for Payment
§1.14 Comment: Article 5.4 Schedule of Values
§1.15 Comment: Article 5.6.1 Retention
§1.16 Comment: Article 5.7 Progress Payments
§1.17 Comment: Article 6 Final Payment
§1.18 Comment: Article 9.1.3 Contract Documents
§1.19 Comment: Article 9.1.7 Signatures

AIA Document A111 - Cost Plus Contract

§1.20 General Comment
§1.21 Comment: Article 3.1 Relationship of the Parties
§1.22 Comment: Article 5.1 Contract Sum
§1.23 Comment: Article 5.2.1 Guaranteed Maximum Price
§1.24 Comment: Article 5.2.2 Alternates

§1.25 Comment: Article 5.2.3 Unit Prices
§1.26 Comment: Article 6 Changes in the Work

Addendum to AIA Document A111

§1.27 General Comment
      FORM 1-1   Addendum to AIA Document A111-Standard Form of Agreement

AIA Document A201 - General Conditions

§1.28 General Comment
      FORM 1-2   Supplementary General Conditions [Favors Interests of Contractor] (with Comments)
      FORM 1-3   Supplementary General Conditions [Favors Interests of Owner] (with Comments)

Prime Contract - Stipulated Sum - Short Form [Favors Interests of Contractor]

§1.29 General Comment
      FORM 1-4   Prime Contract - Stipulated Sum

Prime Contract - Cost Plus Percentage - Guaranteed Maximum Cost [Favors Interests of Owner]

§1.30 General Comment
      FORM 1-5   Prime Contract - Cost Plus Percentage

Proposal and Prime Contract - Short Form - Stipulated Sum - Small Project

§1.31 General Comment
      FORM 1-6   Proposal and Prime Contract - Short Form - Stipulated Sum

Alternate Prime Contract Provisions

§1.32 General Comment
      FORM 1-7   Alternate Prime Contract Provisions

AIA Document A107 - Abbreviated Form of Agreement between Owner and Contractor

§1.33 General Comment
      FORM 1-8   Supplementary General Conditions - AIA Document A107 [Favors Interests of Contractor] (with Comments)
      FORM 1-9   Supplementary General Conditions - AIA Document A107 [Favors Interests of Owner] (with Comments)

Introduction to Prime Contracts

§1.01 Definition

By definition a prime contract is a contract between an owner and a general contractor. As with most forms of construction contract, it is subject to almost infinite variation. The most typical pattern is for the owner to employ a prime general contractor which in turn employs subcontractors. The subcontractors may themselves employ sub-subcontractors of one or more tiers.

The amount of work to be performed by the general contractor with its own forces is not necessarily disclosed in the prime contract document. Some general contractors supply only a management team so that the actual construction work is performed by subcontractors. Some general contractors perform all work with their own forces. Between these two extremes may be found every conceivable allocation of work between the general contractor and subcontractors. In a common pattern, the general contractor performs rough and finish carpentry and concrete work with its own forces while all other work is performed by subcontractors.

In another common pattern, a general contractor is the owner of the project and therefore subcontracts themselves become *prime* contracts in the sense that they are contracts between a contractor and the project owner. The general contractor who is also the owner of the project is usually referred to as a **developer,** or may also be called an **owner-builder.** Subcontractors to owner-builders may be referred to as **trade contractors.**

§1.02 Stipulated Sum Contract

The most common form of prime contract is for a stipulated sum. This form of contract may be preferred by an owner because it permits the owner to budget for a known amount of money to be spent in exchange for a completed project. On the other hand, the "stipulated sum" is often overrun because of construction changes that increase the scope and cost of the work. It seems almost inevitable that the owner of a construction project will change the scope of work in one way or another as the job progresses. This often occurs simply because the owner could not truly visualize the elements of the project from a study of the drawings and specifications. It may also occur because of changing, or unanticipated, requirements of public agencies. Or changes may be required because of omissions or inaccuracies in the construction documents prepared by the architect. Construction changes are so frequent, and so necessary, that one of the most important provisions of the prime contract documents relates to change orders. The owner needs to reserve the right to require the contractor to change the work, and when changes are ordered, a means must be provided for equitably adjusting the contract price.

§1.03 Cost Plus Contract

As may be inferred from its name, the general contractor under a cost plus contract is reimbursed its costs plus an amount of money to compensate for overhead and profit. The drafter of a cost plus contract will need to pay special attention to the definition of the word **cost.** The contractor is reimbursed for costs periodically, usually monthly. Overhead and profit may be computed as a percentage of cost, or as a stipulated fixed fee. A disadvantage to the owner of selecting cost plus a percentage of costs as a formula for compensation is that this type of contract produces an incentive for the contractor to spend more so as to increase the amount of the fee. Consideration of this fact may induce the owner to select **cost plus a fixed fee** as the appropriate formula. When the contract price is cost plus a fixed fee, however, a method must be provided for increasing the fee when the scope of the work is increased, and for decreasing the fee when the scope of the work is reduced.

§1.04 Cost Plus Contract with Guaranteed Maximum Price

A form of contract that combines, from the owner's point of view, the advantages of the stipulated sum contract with the advantages of the cost plus contract is **cost plus with a guaranteed max.** Here the contractor's compensation is measured by cost plus either a percentage or a fixed fee, but with a guaranteed maximum overall price including the costs and the fee. Here again, however, provision must be made to increase or decrease the guaranteed maximum price when the scope of the work is changed by additions to or deletions from the work required by the contract documents.

§1.05 "Split Savings" Contract

A form of contract particularly favored by owners is cost plus with a guaranteed maximum price, with a provision that any savings under the guaranteed maximum price will be split between the owner and the contractor. The contractor's share of savings then acts as an incentive to economize. The contractor may be awarded 50 per cent or less of the savings depending on the owner's views as to the effectiveness of the incentive.

§1.06 Design-Build Contract

In a design-building contract, the contractor takes responsibility for designing the project. In most states, licensed contractors and subcontractors are authorized by law to design certain structures that they build. More complicated structures require the services of architects and engineers, and in such cases contractors may employ architects and engineers to provide the necessary design. Under a design-build contract, however, the owner holds the contractor responsible for design regardless of whether the contractor performs design services with its own employees or through contracts with architects and engineers.

The design-build formula has two great practical advantages: (1) design-build contractors and their subcontractors are usually very familiar with the methods that can be employed to enhance efficiency and economy in construction, and (2) when the contractor is responsible for design, there can be no complaining about, or claims arising out of, contentions that the drawings are inadequate or allegations that the architect or engineer delayed or disrupted the contractor's work. Because of this feature, the design-build system is by far the most effective strategy that an owner can follow in order to reduce and eliminate construction disputes.

The disadvantage to design-build is that the owner loses the protection afforded to the owner by an independent architect or engineer who designs and inspects the project with the primary mission of protecting the interests of the owner. An architect/engineer employed by a contractor is compensated by, and reports to, the contractor rather than the owner. The contractor may be tempted to cheapen the job to increase the contractor's profits by taking short cuts that degrade the quality of the project without becoming immediately obvious to the owner.

§1.07 Fast Track Contract

An owner who has a large investment in property held for construction is highly motivated to convert the unprotected non-productive bare real estate to something that produces income. The carrying costs for real estate are considerable, and probably run in the neighborhood of 15 per cent per annum of the value of the unimproved real estate when the losses associated with lost opportunity are taken into account. Owners may have other practical reasons to need to expedite construction of a project. For example, economies associated with a new warehouse may save thousands of dollars in expenses every day. Under such circumstances, **fast track** construction may become attractive. This means that the contractor will start building as soon as the foundation plans are ready and a foundation permit is issued, regardless of the fact that the architect/engineer has not finished designing the project. As construction proceeds, then, the architect/engineer barely keeps ahead of the contractor. The contractor will probably charge a premium for such work because confusion, delays, and misunderstandings are inevitable. (These risks are much easier for the design-build contractor to accept, since such a contractor controls the design.)

When it employs the fast track system, the owner accepts the fact that the cost of construction will be increased, on the theory that such increased costs will be more than offset by the savings experienced by accelerating the completion of the project and thus hastening the day when the project will produce cash flow.

§1.08 Construction Management Contract

In the 1950s, architects and engineers experienced significant malpractice claims, and to avoid them they began to recede from their responsibilities of inspecting and supervising the work. The very word **architect** is derived from Greek words that mean **master builder.** Modern architects eschew the role of master builder for that of master designer. This strategy has been effective to reduce liability, but has left some owners at a loss for competent management and supervision of their construction projects. Into this void has stepped the professional construction management company, which is sometimes a licensed architect/engineer, but more often is a licensed contractor. The construction manager serves the same function as many general contractors by supplying nothing more to the job than a management team, which receives bids from subcontractors, selects subcontractors, negotiates and awards subcontracts, orders materials, deals with architects/engineers, inspects the job, processes change orders, processes payment requests, schedules the job, and coordinates the work. Subcontracts, however, are signed in the name of the owner and not in the name of the construction manager.

AIA Document A101 - Stipulated Sum

§1.09 General Comment

The American Institute of Architects (AIA) Documents referred to in this text are the property of, and may be purchased from, The American Institute of Architects, 1735 New York Avenue, N.W., Washington, D.C. 20006.

The A101 is the AIA Standard Form of Agreement for a Lump Sum, Fixed Price Contract, and is perhaps the most frequently used of AIA forms of agreement.

Another AIA form of agreement, Document A111, may be used for cost plus contracts.

Others forms of fixed price and cost plus contracts, written by the author, appear at §§1.29-1.31.

The contract sum may be set either by negotiation or by a process of competitive bidding. In practice, competitive bidding a private work is often followed by negotiations with two or more of the lowest bidders. Negotiations often include revisions to the contract documents that may be suggested by a prospective contractor in order to increase quality or reduce cost.

AIA Document A101 is designed to be used in conjunction with the General Conditions, AIA Document A201.

The user of this or any other construction form should consult special state laws that may impose requirements on the content of construction contracts. For example, in many states the law requires that the contract include the contractor's license number. Some states also require that the contract include references to or warnings about the mechanic's lien law.

Consumer protection legislation in many states applies to contracts with homeowners. State legislation, for example, may give the homeowner a *cooling off period* to rescind the contract. Some states control finance charges that can be extracted from a homeowner for home improvements. When finance charges are imposed on a home building contract with a consumer, federal truth in lending requirements apply.

Comments to AIA Document A101 will be found at §§1.10-1.19.

§1.10 Document A101 First Page

Note that the 1987 edition of AIA Document A101 does not merely refer to, but actually incorporates by reference the 1987 edition of AIA Document 201 (the General Conditions of the Contract for Construction). If you do not intend to incorporate Form A201, this language must be stricken.

The contractor's license number should be displayed along with the name of the contractor.

Construction Lender: If the construction lender is to be referred to in the contract documents, the construction lender should be identified on this first page. Review the construction loan agreement to see whether it requires any special provisions to be inserted into the prime contract.

§1.11 Comment: Article 3.1 Date of Commencement

Notice that the date of commencement specified here is the date from which the contract time is figured. If the contractor has already started work, the early start date may be used if appropriate. If the date when the contractor will be able to start work is unknown, provide that the date will be fixed in a notice to proceed delivered by owner to contractor.

Mechanic's lien claims usually take their priority from the date of commencement of a work of improvement. Construction lenders usually require that the mortgage or deed of trust that secures the construction loan take priority over mechanics' liens. Therefore, it is especially important for the contractor to avoid commencement of work, delivery of materials to the jobsite, erection of a power pole, clearing and grubbing, erection of a construction fence, delivery of a job shack, or anything else that might give the appearance of a commencement of work before the owner has had a chance to record the construction loan.

§1.12 Comment: Article 3.2 Substantial Completion

Note that the term **substantial completion** is defined in the General Conditions.

Consider whether a liquidated damages provision should be used. If the contractor delays the completion of the project, the owner will suffer damages that are usually measured by the reasonable rental value of the project. It often occurs, whether by design or inadvertence, that the daily liquidated damages provided for by a construction contract are less than the daily rental value would be. For example, the daily rental value of a 500 room hotel could be

$50,000. Therefore, the contractor gets a break if the daily liquidated damages are specified to be less than that amount, and the owner would receive a windfall if they were more.

The parties may want to use Article 3.2 as a space for providing that the contractor will be entitled to a bonus for early completion.

It should also be considered that if the owner delays the contractor in the completion of the work, the contractor will suffer damages. Therefore, a daily rate of liquidated damages for owner's delay of contractor may be inserted at this point.

§1.13 Comment: Article 5.3 Applications for Payment

Here the question first arises as to whether the architect will be involved in **supervision, inspection, observation of construction,** and processing of payment requests. Owners sometimes omit the architect from the payment process to save expense or to retain more control over payments.

Be very careful to assure that the payment schedule agrees with the payment provisions that are specified in the construction loan agreement.

It is often provided that payments are subject to approval by construction lender.

§1.14 Comment: Article 5.4 Schedule of Values

Great care should be taken in preparation of the schedule of values, with the contractor usually attempting to move payments as close as possible to the **front end** of the contract and the owner seeking to make sure that the contractor does not *front load* the payment schedule. The ultimate result of heavy *front loading* would be for the contractor to remove all profit from the job at the early stages, and therefore lack any economic motivation for continuing with the work.

§1.15 Comment: Article 5.6.1 Retention

The retention or **retainage** is usually 10 per cent, often reduced to 5 per cent after the contractor has satisfactorily completed one-half of the work. It may be provided that retention will be released early for the "early trades" (such as excavation and grading), since early subcontractors may be unwilling to wait until the end of the entire project for their money. It is also sometimes provided that monies expended by the contractor for materials are not subject to retention, since materials dealers are seldom willing to allow a retention to be withheld.

§1.16 Comment: Article 5.7 Progress Payments

Here, the owner may wish to provide for reduction of progress payments because of backcharges for defective work.

§1.17 Comment: Article 6 Final Payment

In most states the retention is not paid until 35 days after notice of completion. A notice of completion is not a contract document, but a document recorded in the County Recorder's office which starts the time limit running for recording mechanics' liens. If the time for recording mechanics' liens is 30 days after notice of completion, as it is in many states, then the title company will check for mechanics' liens on the 31st or 32nd day after recording notice of completion, and notify the owner of any pending lien claims. The owner can then take any pending lien claims into account in determining the amount of the final payment.

§1.18 Comment: Article 9.1.3 Contract Documents

It is good practice for owner and contractor to initial every page of the contract documents, including specifications and geotechnical reports, and every sheet of plans in existence at the time the contract is executed.

Before making a soils report or geotechnical report a part of the contract documents, check to see whether it conflicts with other provisions. If there are such conflicts, it may be appropriate to refer to the soils report or geotechnical report but not incorporate it into the contract documents.

§1.19 Comment: Article 9.1.7 Signatures

The contractor should include its contractor's license number under the signature space.

AIA Document A111 - Cost Plus Contract

§1.20 General Comment

AIA Document A111 is a very popular form of contract that can be used according to several different patterns. Under one pattern it may be used as a cost plus contract, with the contractor's compensation measured by a percentage of cost or by a fixed fee added to cost. It may also be used as a cost plus contract with a guaranteed maximum price. It is also sometimes provided that in the event the total cost of the project including the contractor's fee is less than the guaranteed maximum price, the contractor is entitled to be paid a percentage of the savings.

§1.21 Comment: Article 3.1 Relationship of the Parties

This paragraph provides that there is a relationship of trust and confidence established by the agreement and accepted by the contractor. The special nature of the relationship of trust and confidence arises because of the cost plus nature of the work. Contractor has an obligation to perform the work with the financial interests of the owner in mind, in an efficient and professional manner. The contractor may wish to revise this paragraph to provide that the owner, as well as the contractor, accepts the relationship of trust and confidence.

§1.22 Comment: Article 5.1 Contract Sum

The contractor's fee is usually expressed either as a lump sum or as a percentage of the cost of the work. If the fee is expressed as a percentage of the cost of the work, the amount of the fee automatically increases (or decreases) as the cost of the work increases (or decreases). If, however, the contractor's fee is a lump sum, then it will be desirable to provide a method for adjusting the amount of the fee if the guaranteed maximum price is increased or decreased. The most common system is to provide that the contractor's fee will be increased by a percentage of the amount by which the guaranteed maximum price is increased by changes in the work. If the fee is to be reduced by deletions of the work, the amount of the reduction is usually a smaller percentage than the amount of the increase in the fee resulting from an increase in the scope of the work. This is because the contractor must usually expend considerable administration and supervision to coordinate deletions from the work.

§1.23 Comment: Article 5.2.1 Guaranteed Maximum Price

If the contractor is to be paid a share of any savings under the guaranteed maximum price, the amount is to be inserted here. The share of savings awarded to the contractor is usually between 25 and 50 per cent.

§1.24 Comment: Article 5.2.2 Alternates

If the contract documents contain alternates, then it is necessary to list those that have been agreed to by the contractor and the owner and have therefore been taken into account in fixing the guaranteed maximum price. If other alternates are accepted later on, then the guaranteed maximum price will accordingly be revised.

§1.25 Comment: Article 5.2.3 Unit Prices

Although a guaranteed maximum price has been agreed to, the owner may also wish to have the additional protection that can be gained by inserting unit prices, such as dollars per cubic yard for excavation, dollars per cubic yard for compacted fill, dollars per linear foot for conduit and wire, or dollars per square foot for paving.

The guaranteed maximum price usually includes a specified quantity, and if the quantity increases or decreases above the amount specified, then the guaranteed maximum price is accordingly increased or decreased.

§1.26 Comment: Article 6 Changes in the Work

Experience shows that when both parties agree that a directive issued by the architect or by the owner constitutes a change in the work, the parties can usually negotiate a fair price for the change order. Many disputes, arise, however, because the owner and the contractor do not agree as to the scope of the work required by the contract documents. If the owner orders the contractor to perform work that the contractor believes is beyond the scope of the work required by the contract, the contractor will expect to negotiate extra compensation for it. If, however, the owner or the architect believes that the work is within the scope of the work described by the contract documents, the owner will refuse to pay additional compensation.

The owner may wish to require the contractor to continue performance despite a dispute as to the scope of the work, and resolve the issue by negotiation, arbitration, or litigation. The contractor, on the other hand, would wish to retain the right to stop work in the event of a substantial disagreement as to the scope of the work.

Addendum to AIA Document A111

§1.27 General Comment

The following addendum revises many of the printed contract provisions in such a way as to protect the interests of the owner.

FORM 1-1   Addendum to AIA Document A111 - Standard Form of Agreement

ADDENDUM TO STANDARD FORM OF AGREEMENT BETWEEN OWNER AND CONTRACTOR

¶1. This Addendum modifies the Standard Form of Agreement Between Owner and Contractor (AIA Document A111, 1987 Edition) entered into between _____, as Owner, and _____, as Contractor, in connection with the _____ Project identified therein.

¶2. The Owner and the Contractor hereby agree to supplement, modify, and supersede the Standard Form of Agreement as follows:

¶3. **First:** At Sub-paragraph 2.1, delete the words: "except to the extent specifically indicated in the Contract Documents to be the responsibility of others, or as follows:".

¶4. **Second:** The following Sub-paragraphs are added:

2.2 Except as expressly provided for herein to the contrary, the Contractor at its sole cost, risk and expense shall construct, equip, provide, purchase, pay for and furnish all of the Work in accordance with the Contract Documents and governmental codes and regulations as they apply to performance of the Work. The Work shall include the following items:

2.2.1 The foundation, structure, and all other improvements, facilities and services as described in the Contract Documents.

2.2.2 All materials, supplies, apparatuses, appliances, equipment, fixtures, tools, implements, facilities, labor, supervision, transportation, utilities, storage, and all other services as and when required for or in connection with the performance of the Work.

2.2.3 Providing and maintaining a sufficient construction office on the Project site for the Contractor's use and for the use of the Architect and the Owner's representatives (sufficiency to be determined by the Owner); erection of street barricades, providing of necessary Project security; if necessary, removing and replacing fire hydrants, street signs, street lights, and traffic lights; removal of abandoned utilities and any required relocation of existing utilities; all insurance required by the Contract Documents; paying for all required building permits; payment of all sales, use and other taxes applicable to the Work.

2.2.4 Providing all sanitary facilities, drinking water, temporary lighting, temporary protection, construction water, temporary or permanent power and distribution lines, grades and layout, temporary heating, continuous clean-up, final clean up so that the Work is ready for tenant occupancy, communications, operation of hoisting equipment during and after normal working hours and normal working days if such operation is required for the prompt and efficient performance of the Work. The use of hoisting equipment shall be scheduled through and under the control of the Contractor.

2.2.5 Providing all work called for in the Contract Documents and governmental codes and regulations, and all items necessary, incidental, required by, or fairly implied from the Contract Documents as necessary to provide Owner with a complete and operating building. Items need not be specifically listed in the schedule of values portion of the Contract Documents, or elsewhere in the Contract Documents, in order to be deemed items within the scope of the Work. It is understood that the Contractor is better qualified to list exclusions than the Owner is to list inclusions, therefore any item that is not specifically excluded from the scope of the Work is to be considered a part of the Work.

¶5. Third: Delete Sub-paragraph 4.2 and add the following Sub-paragraphs:

4.2 The Contractor shall achieve Substantial Completion of the entire Work within _____ (__) consecutive calendar days following the commencement date identified in Subparagraph 4.1 above. In the event of delay in the Work beyond the reasonable control of Contractor resulting from conduct or lack of conduct by the Owner or the Architect, or their consultants, representatives, officers, agents or employees; or delay by the Owner in making the site available, or in furnishing any items required to be furnished to the Contractor by Owner pursuant to the Contract Documents; or delay caused by (i) extraordinary conditions of weather for the area and time of year, (ii) war or national conflicts or priorities arising therefrom, (iii) fires beyond the reasonable control of the Contractor, (iv) strikes or other labor disruptions, except for the first five working days of any strike or labor disruption, or (v) earthquakes and other natural disasters, damage from which is beyond the reasonable control of the Contractor; and for no other cause or causes, the Contractor shall be entitled to a reasonable extension of time only and only by the amount of time Contractor is actually delayed thereby in the performance of the Work, provided notice is given as hereinafter provided. Contractor shall not be entitled to any extension of time unless the Contractor notifies the Owner in writing within five days of the commencement of each such delay. The Contractor shall not be entitled to, and hereby waives any and all claim to, increased compensation for, or damages which it may suffer from, any such delay, or any other delay, and the Contractor further waives any and all claim to increased compensation or damages for any disruption, interference, or loss of efficiency or productivity caused by the Owner, the Architect, or their consultants, representatives, officers, agents, or employees. Further, the Contractor agrees that the terms set forth in this Subparagraph 4.2 shall be incorporated into all subcontracts entered into by the Contractor in connection with the Work, and the Contractor shall indemnify and defend Owner and Architect against any and all claims by the Contractor's subcontractors and subcontractors of any tier for additional compensation or damages resulting from any delay, disruption, interference, impact, or loss of efficiency or productivity caused or allegedly caused by Owner, Architect, or their consultants, representatives, officers, agents, or employees, or resulting from any other cause, including, but not limited to, the causes enumerated above.

4.3 No extension of time shall be granted unless the Contractor shall prove to the Owner that the delay in completion of the Work was caused specifically by a delay in a portion of the Work that was on the critical path of the construction schedule.

4.4 The Contractor recognizes it is imperative that the Work proceed uninterrupted and shall endeavor to prevent and shall promptly cure any work stoppage caused by any labor or jurisdictional disputes arising out of the assignment of work to be performed by the Contractor or its Subcontractors or Subcontractors of any tier.

4.5 The completion time contemplated by this Agreement anticipates a certain number of lost days due to normal weather conditions. Only unusual or extreme weather conditions for the time of year will be considered as justification for a delay in completion of the Work.

¶6. **Fourth:** The following sentence is added at the end of Subparagraph 5.2.1:

The difference, if any, by which the Guaranteed Maximum Price exceeds the Cost of the Work plus the Contractor's Fee shall be defined as "Savings". The Contractor shall be paid twenty-five per cent (25%) of the Savings at the time of final payment.

¶7. **Fifth:** Sub-paragraphs 6.1.1 through 6.3.1, inclusive, are annuled and the following Sub-paragraphs are added:

6.1 The Owner, without nullifying any portion of the Contract Documents, may make as many changes in the Work or to the Project as it desires, either to decrease, increase, or modify the Work issuing Change Orders and Construction Change Directives. A Change Order is a written instrument prepared by the Architect and signed by the Owner, the Contractor, and the Architect, stating their agreement upon all of the following: (1) a Change in the Work, (2) the amount of the adjustment in the Guaranteed Maximum Price, if any, and (3) the adjustment in the Contract Time, if any. A Construction Change Directive is a written order prepared by the Architect and signed by the Owner and the Architect, directing a Change in the Work and stating a proposed basis for adjustment, if any, in the Guaranteed Maximum Price or Contract Time, or both. The amount to be paid to the Contractor shall, where applicable, be increased or decreased in the manner hereinafter set forth; provided, however, that if the Contractor should proceed with a Change in the Work upon on an oral order, by whomsoever given, proceeding on such basis shall constitute a waiver by the Contractor of any claim for additional compensation for the work so performed. Upon receipt of a Change Order or Construction Change Directive, the Contractor shall promptly proceed with the Change in the Work and all Changes in the Work shall be performed in accordance with the Contract Documents. Notwithstanding any disagreement the Contractor may have with any item contained in a Construction Change Directive, the Contractor shall promptly and properly proceed with the Change in the Work identified therein, but the Contractor shall have the right to dispute the propriety of the Construction Change Directive or any part thereof upon completion of the Work.

6.2 If a Change in the Work results in an increase in the Guaranteed Maximum Price, the Owner shall have the right to pay the increase on a lump sum basis, a unit price basis, or a time and material basis.

6.3 If the Owner elects to have the Change in the Work performed on a lump sum basis, its election shall be based on a lump sum proposal which shall be submitted by the Contractor to the Owner within ten (10) days of the Owner's request therefor (but the Owner's request for a lump sum proposal shall not be deemed an election by the Owner to have the Change in the Work performed on a lump sum basis). The Contractor's proposal shall be itemized and segregated by labor and materials for the various components of the Change in the Work (no aggregate labor total will be acceptable) and shall be accompanied by signed proposals of any Subcontractors or Sub-subcontractors who will perform any portion of the Change in the Work and of any persons who will furnish materials or equipment for incorporation therein.

6.4 The portion of the lump sum proposal relating to labor, whether by the Contractor's forces or the forces of any of its Subcontractors, shall include reasonably anticipated gross wages of jobsite labor, including foremen, who will be directly involved in the Change in the Work (for such time as they will be so involved), plus payroll costs (including Social Security, state unemployment insurance taxes, and fringe benefits) and up to _____ per cent (__%) of gross wages (but not payroll costs) to compensate for overhead and profit as applicable (said overhead and profit to include all management and supervision, except foremen).

6.5 The portion of the lump sum proposal relating to materials may include the reasonably anticipated direct costs to the Contractor or to any of its Subcontractors of materials to be purchased for incorporation in the Change in the Work, plus transportation and applicable sales or use taxes and up to _____ per cent (__%) of said direct material costs as overhead and profit for the Contractor or any such Subcontractor, and may further include the Contractor's or any of its Subcontractor's reasonably anticipated rental costs in connection with the Change in the Work (either actual rates or discounted local published rates). If any of the items included in the lump sum proposal are covered by unit prices contained in the Contract Documents, the Owner may, if it requires the Change in the Work to be performed on a lump sum basis, elect to use unit prices for such items, in which event an appropriate deduction in the lump sum amount shall be made prior to the application of any allowed overhead and profit percentages. No overhead and profit shall be applied to any such unit prices.

6.6 If the Owner elects to have the Change in the Work performed on a unit price basis, its election shall be based on either the unit prices established in the Contract Documents, if any, or on a unit price proposal which shall be submitted by the Contractor to the Owner within five (5) days of the Owner's request therefor (but the Owner's request for a unit price proposal shall not be deemed an election by the Owner to have the Change in the Work performed on a unit price basis). The Contractor's proposal shall itemize the quantities of each item of the Change in the Work for which there is an applicable unit price contained in the Contract Documents.

6.7 Nothing contained herein shall preclude the Owner from requesting a lump sum proposal and a unit price proposal at the same time with respect to the same Change in the Work, in which event the Contractor shall submit both.

6.8 If the Owner elects to have the Change in the Work performed on a time and material basis, the same shall be performed, by the Contractor and its Subcontractors, at actual direct labor cost through working foremen plus direct cost of materials and equipment plus _____ per cent (__%) of gross wages of jobsite labor and direct material costs and _____ per cent (__%) of equipment costs (other than small tools) to compensate for overhead, supervision, and profit. The Contractor shall submit to the Owner daily time, equipment, and material tickets for Changes in the Work.

6.9 The Owner shall have no obligation or liability on account of a Change in the Work except as specifically provided in this Article 6. Overhead and profit, as allowed under this Article 6, shall be deemed to cover all costs and expenses of any nature whatsoever, including without limitation those for general condition items such as clean-up, protection, supervision, estimating, field operations, small tools, security and jobsite operating costs, which the Contractor or any of its Subcontractors may incur in the performance of or in connection with a Change in the Work.

6.10 If a Change in the Work shall result in a decrease in the Work, then the Guaranteed Maximum Price will be decreased by (1) an amount equal to the actual cost of such decreased work or, (2) the established unit price cost of such work, whichever the Owner chooses; plus _____ per cent (__ per cent) of the actual cost of unit price. Contract Time will be reduced by the length of time fairly attributable to such decrease in the Work.

6.11 If the Change in the Work will result in an extension or contraction of the Contract Time, and the parties are unable to agree as to the number of days by which the time for performance will be extended or contracted, then the matter shall be submitted to the Architect for determination.

6.12 If the Owner and the Contractor disagree as to the scope of Work to be performed under the Contract Documents, or if any dispute should arise between the Owner and the Contractor with respect to an increase or decrease in the Guaranteed Maximum Price, or with respect to an expansion or contraction of the Contract Time, or if any dispute should arise between the Owner and the Contractor with respect to any other right or obligation arising under or relating to the Contract Documents or the performance of the Work, the Contractor shall promptly and diligently perform the Work, including any Change in the Work, as required by the Owner, and the Contractor will not slow or stop the progress of the Work or the Project or any Change in the Work.

¶8. **Sixth:** At Subparagraph 7.1.4.1, insert the following words at the beginning of the first sentence:

> To the extent not otherwise expressly excluded elsewhere in the Contract Documents,

¶9. **Seventh:** At Subparagraph 7.1.4.2, insert the following words at the beginning of the first sentence:

> To the extent not otherwise expressly excluded elsewhere in the Contract Documents,

¶10. **Eighth:** At Subparagraph 7.2.1., add the following words at the end of the existing sentence:

> to the extent the emergency is not the result of the negligence or fault, to any degree, of the Contractor or the negligence or fault, to any degree, or responsibility of any Subcontractor to the Contractor.

¶11. **Ninth:** Delete Subparagraph 7.2.2.

¶12. **Tenth:** Delete Subparagraph 7.2.3.

¶13. **Eleventh:** Delete Subparagraph 7.2.4.

¶14. **Twelfth:** At Subparagraph 8.1.6, delete the words "Except as provided in Subparagraph 7.2.2 through 7.2.4 and Paragraph 13.5 of this Agreement,".

¶15. **Thirteenth:** The following Subparagraph 8.1.9 is added:

> Funds distributed to any employee that are part of a company profit sharing plan, or bonuses, or incentive payments of any kind.

¶16. **Fourteenth:** In Subparagraph 12.5.1, add the words "and Owner" after the words "the Architect" in the last two sentences.

¶17. **Fifteenth:** The following Sub-paragraphs are added:

14.3.1 Notwithstanding the fact that a dispute, controversy or question shall have arisen in the interpretation of any provision of this Contract, the performance of any work, the delivery of any material, the payment of any disputed monies to the Contractor, the value of any Change Order or Construction Change Directive, the scope of work to be performed by the Contractor under this Contract, or otherwise, the Contractor agrees that it will not directly or indirectly stop or delay the Work or any part of the Work to be performed or any work required under any Change Order or Construction Change Directive, as required under this Contract or as ordered by the Owner, or stop or delay the delivery of any materials to be delivered, as required under this Contract or as ordered by the Owner. Contractor further agrees that it will not rescind this Contract in the event of any such dispute, or otherwise, but will continue to diligently prosecute the Work, including work reflected in any Change Order and Construction Change Directive, as directed by the Owner to completion.

¶18. **Sixteenth:** The following Subparagraph 14.3.2 is added:

The Contractor understands that the Project will be financed by a construction lender and, then, by a permanent lender. The Owner may assign any of its rights under this Contract to the construction lender and the Contractor hereby consents to any such transfer provided no such assignment shall relieve the Owner of any of its obligations under this Contract, unless agreed to in writing by the Contractor. The Contractor shall execute any certificates, lien waivers, releases, receipts, and other documents as may be reasonably required by the construction lender or permanent lender including a subordination of its mechanic's lien rights to the construction lender's and permanent lender's mortgage or deed of trust. The construction lender for the Project will be:

_____
_____
_____
_____

¶19. **Seventeenth:** The following Subparagraph 14.3.3 is added:

The Contractor agrees to execute and deliver and to have each of its Subcontractors execute and deliver to the Owner, at such times and from time to time as the Owner may request, a written assignment of subcontracts and Subcontractor's consent to such assignment in a form to be prepared by the Owner. Such assignments and consents to assignment, if implemented, shall require the Contractor, with the Subcontractor's consent, to assign to the Owner all of the Contractor's right, title, and interest in and to all such subcontracts. In no event, however, shall there be deemed to be a contractual relationship between the Owner and any Subcontractor, or any obligation on the part of the Owner to any Subcontractor to make payments with respect to any of the subcontracts assigned thereby, except for services, if any, performed after the Owner's exercise of its rights pursuant to this Subparagraph 14.3.3.

¶20. **Eighteenth:** The following Subparagraph 14.3.4 is added:

Captions appearing in the Contract are descriptive only and for convenience in reference. Should there be any conflict between any such caption and any Article, Paragraph or Subparagraph at the head of which it appears, the Article, Paragraph, or Subparagraph and not such caption shall control and govern the construction of this Contract.

¶21. **Nineteenth:** The following Subparagraph 14.3.5 is added:

Both the Owner and the Contractor shall be deemed to have participated in the drafting of the Contract, and, accordingly, no ambiguity contained within the Contract shall be construed against any party hereto.

¶22. **Twentieth:** Delete Paragraphs 15.1 through 15.4, inclusive, and replace them with the following:

15.1 If the Contractor shall fail to commence the Work in accordance with the provisions of this Contract, fail to prosecute the Work, or any work reflected in a Change Order of Construction Change Directive, to completion thereof in a diligent, efficient, workmanlike, skillful, and careful manner, and in accordance with the provisions of the Contract Documents, fail to use an adequate amount or quality of personnel or equipment to complete the Project without delay, fail to perform any of its obligations under the Contract Documents, fail to make prompt payments to its Subcontractors, material suppliers, and laborers; the Owner shall have the right after giving the Contractor five (5) days written notice thereof, and if such default is not cured in said five (5) days, to (i) terminate Contractor's performance under this Contract, and (ii) take possession of and use all or any part of the Contractor's materials, equipment, supplies and other property of every kind used by the Contractor in performance of the Work and the Project, and to use such property in the manner it deems desirable to complete the Project including engaging the services of other parties. Any such action by the Owner shall not be deemed a waiver of any other right or remedy of the Owner under the Contract Documents or under the law. If, after exercising such remedy, the cost to the Owner in the performance of the balance of the Work is in excess of that portion of the Guaranteed Maximum Price which theretofore has not been paid to the Contractor hereunder, the Contractor shall be liable and shall reimburse the Owner for such excess. Reimbursement of such excess amount shall be in addition to any and all other damages resulting from the Owner's termination of the Contractor under this Paragraph 15.1.

15.2 The Owner shall have the right to terminate this Contract without cause and for the convenience of the Owner at any time by giving the Contractor ten (10) days written notice thereof. Upon receipt of such notice, the Contractor shall promptly demobilize and terminate performance of the Work and Contractor shall perform such acts as may be necessary to preserve and protect the Project. Upon such termination the Owner shall pay to the Contractor (i) all retainages, if any, previously retained by the Owner; (ii) a sum of money equal to the cost of all work properly and timely performed by the Contractor for which payments have not previously been made; and (iii) the pro rata portion of the Contractor's Fee applicable to the Work performed by the Contractor up to the time of termination; and the Contractor will assign to Owner and Owner shall assume the obligations of the Contractor under all of its subcontracts and purchase orders covering the unperformed parts of the Work. Such termination without cause will be in consideration of the payments referred to above, plus payment to the Contractor by the Owner of the sum of One Thousand Dollars ($1,000.00).

¶23. **Twenty-First:** Following Subparagraph 16.1.7, add the following:

(1) Addendum to Standard Form of Agreement Between Owner and Architect (AIA Document A111, 1987 Edition), dated _____, 1990.

(2) Addendum to General Conditions of the Contract for Construction (AIA Document A201, 1987 Edition), dated _____, 1990.

DATED:

OWNER   CONTRACTOR

BY: _____   BY: _____

Its: _____   Its: _____

AIA Document A201 - General Conditions

§1.28 General Comment

The AIA General Conditions are the central feature of the AIA Construction Contract Documents. The General Conditions have been revised many times over the years, most recently in 1987. The 1987 revision has been roundly criticized in some quarters as establishing excessively complicated requirements for written notices and processing of claims. A diagrammatic representation of the claims process is found at page 4 of the Instruction Sheet.

The change order process is also complicated. According to the diagrammatic representation on Page 4 of the Instruction Sheet, change order processing may include 23 different steps, as many as 15 of which steps may apply to the processing of a single change order.

The AIA Document A201 has the weaknesses of its strengths, and the vices of its virtues. The strength of the document is that it gives carefully considered and fully described treatment to most of the issues and problems that may arise during the construction of a major project. The weakness of the document is a reflection of its strength: for some purposes and to people of some temperaments it appears prolix, confusing, and complicated.

As with most AIA contract documents, Document A201 gives good protection to the interests of the architect.

The AIA General Conditions are frequently amended by their users, sometimes radically. Amendments should be made with care so as to avoid ambiguities, or conflict with other portions of the document. Examples of addenda that amend AIA Document A201 will be found at **FORMS 1-2 & 1-3.**

FORM 1-2 Supplementary General Conditions [Favors Interests of Contractor] (with Comments)

Document A201 "General Conditions of the Contract for Construction" is amended as follows:

¶1. **First:** Sub-paragraph 1.1.2. Strike the fourth sentence dealing with third-party beneficiary contracts.

> Comment: Some cases have held that the contractor may be a third-party beneficiary to the contract between the architect and the owner. Such a rule is beneficial to the contractor because it enables the contractor to enforce the architect's obligations to do such things as to provide proper drawings and specifications and to expedite processing of shop drawings. The deleted sentence would negate third-party beneficiary rights.

¶2. **Second:** Sub-paragraph 2.3.1. Add the following:

Owner will exercise the right to stop work only if contractor's performance deviates from the requirements of the contract documents in a material way that is damaging to the interests of the owner. Work will be ordered stopped only in areas of material deviation.

Comment: Stopping the work is a drastic remedy which should be exercised with restraint.

¶3. Third: Sub-paragraph 3.2.2. Strike the words "before commencing activities" from the first sentence.

Comment: Contractor should not be required to take all field measurements and verify all field conditions before commencing work.

¶4. Fourth: Sub-paragraph 3.3.3. Paragraph 3.3.3 is annulled.

Comment: If contractor performs per the architect's instructions and approvals, contractor should be able to assert this as a defense to the owner's claims of breach of contract. Eliminating this paragraph does not mean that the contractor would always be protected by following instructions of the architect, but would at least allow contractor to assert the architect's instructions as a defense in a proper case.

¶5. Fifth: Sub-paragraph 3.12.4. Paragraph 3.12.4 is annulled.

Comment: This paragraph wrongly infers that the contractor should not rely on architect's approval of shop drawings as defining proper performance of the work.

¶6. Sixth: Sub-paragraph 3.12.8. Sub-paragraph 3.12.8 is annulled, and replaced as follows:

3.12.8 Contractor shall inform architect in writing of shop drawings, product data, samples and other similar submittals that deviate from the requirements of the contract documents.

Comment: Contractor should be able to rely on architect's approvals of shop drawings, product data, samples, and other submittals.

¶7. Seventh: Sub-paragraph 3.17.1. The last sentence of Sub-paragraph 3.17.1 is annulled.

Comment: Contractor should not be responsible for reviewing the architect's plans to determine whether they infringe a patent.

¶8. Eighth: Sub-paragraph 3.18.1. The words "architect, architect's consultants" are stricken from the first sentence of Paragraph 3.18.1.

Comment: Contractor should not be required to indemnify architect and its consultants against claims that arise in part from the negligence or wrongdoing of the architect or its consultants.

¶9. **Ninth:** Sub-paragraph 3.18.3. Sub-paragraph 3.18.3 is annulled.

Comment: This follows from the amendment to Paragraph 3.18.1.

¶10. **Tenth:** Sub-paragraph 4.2.6. The last sentence of Sub-paragraph 4.2.6 is annulled.

Comment: If the architect wrongfully rejects contractor's work, architect should be responsible.

¶11. **Eleventh:** Sub-paragraph 4.2.11. The following sentences are added to Sub-paragraph 4.2.11:

Architect will promptly respond to requests for information as to the meaning, intent, and coordination of the drawings and specifications. Except under special circumstances, normal response time to requests for information should be one working day.

Comment: If the architect utilized 15 days to respond to all requests for information, the operations of the contractor would be disrupted and delayed.

¶12. **Twelfth:** Sub-paragraphs 4.3.1 through 4.3.4, 4.3.6 through 4.3.8.1, 4.3.9 through 4.4.4. Sub-paragraphs 4.3.1 through 4.4.4, inclusive (except for Sub-paragraph 4.3.5 and Sub-paragraph 4.3.8.2), are annulled.

Comment: The written notice requirements are difficult to comply with during construction and compliance tends to poison the relationship among contractor, owner, and architect. Architect decisions on claims tend to be biased in favor of the architect and the owner. It is not practical for contractor and owner to prepare evidence and present it to the architect while the job is going on and while other claims may be arising. Subparagraph 4.3.4 (which requires the contractor to continue work pending dispute resolution) is particularly obnoxious to the contractor, since it might require the contractor to continue work at a time when the owner withholds most or all payments because of disputes.

¶13. Thirteenth: Sub-paragraphs 4.5.1 through 4.5.7. Sub-paragraphs 4.5.1 through 4.5.7, inclusive, are annulled. New Sub-paragraphs 4.5.1 through 4.5.6 are adopted to read as follows:

4.5.1 Arbitration. Any controversy, claim, or dispute arising out of or related to this contract or the interpretation, breach, or performance thereof shall be resolved by arbitration in accordance with the Construction Industry Rules of the American Arbitration Association, and judgment shall be entered on the award. The contractor and all subcontractors and sub-subcontractors, the architect and its consultants, material suppliers to the project, inspectors, construction managers, engineers and consultants involved in any way with the construction of the project and who are involved in any such controversy, claim or dispute may with the permission of the arbitrator voluntarily join in and be bound by the arbitration proceedings, and any such party who has signed a document that refers to or incorporates these General Conditions or who has otherwise agreed in writing to do so shall upon the demand of any other party join in and be bound by the arbitration proceedings.

4.5.2 Attorney's Fees. The arbitrator will award reasonable attorney's fees and costs to the prevailing party or parties.

4.5.3 Remedies. The arbitrator may award any remedy that could be awarded by a court, including but not limited to damages for negligence or strict liability, damages for breach of warranty, exemplary and punitive damages, restraining orders, injunctions, receiverships and other provisional remedies.

4.5.4 Ex Parte Award. If a party after due notice fails or refuses to appear at or participate in arbitration hearings, the arbitrator may make an award based on evidence produced by the party or parties who do appear and participate.

4.5.5 Jurisdiction. The jurisdiction of the arbitrator will be determined by the arbitrator.

4.5.6 Federal Arbitration Act. The parties to this contract do not intend by any term of the contract to prevent application of the Federal Arbitration Act to the dispute resolution process under this contract.

Comment: From the contractor's point of view the arbitration provisions of Document A201 contain considerable potential for mischief. Demands for arbitration must be made within 30 days after the written decision of the architect or within a reasonable time, and arbitration claims may be barred by the statute of limitations. A201 prevents joinder of the architect or its employees or consultants except by their written consent. Certain claims, if not included in the demand for arbitration, are waived by the contractor, and the contractor is required to continue work during arbitration even though, under some circumstances, this could mean that the contractor would be required to continue work without adequate progress payments.

A contractor whose dispute with an owner involves work performed by a subcontractor or alleged imperfections in drawings prepared by the architect will need to join the subcontractor and the architect in the arbitration proceedings in order to resolve the entire controversy without resort to litigation.

FORM 1-3   Supplementary General Conditions [Favors Interests of Owner] (with Comments)

Document A201 "General Conditions of the Contract for Construction" is amended as follows:

¶1. **First:**   Sub-paragraph 1.2.2. At line 2, add the following words after "Contractor has":

> thoroughly reviewed and inspected the Drawings, Specifications, all Contract Documents and all other information and documents provided by the Owner to the Contractor,

¶2. **Second:**   Sub-paragraph 1.2.3. The following sentences are added to the end of Sub-paragraph 1.2.3:

> The Contractor has informed the Owner, and hereby represents to the Owner, that it has had extensive experience in constructing projects similar to the Project called for in the Contract Documents, and that it is well acquainted with the components that are properly and customarily included within such a project, including the requirements of state laws, local building codes, local building officials, ASTM's, manufacturers' recommendations, building standards, and trade practices as to the types and quantities of components, items, systems, materials, and methods of construction to be included in the Project in order to produce a first-class Project that will operate with utility and efficiency. The Contractor has included within the Guaranteed Maximum Price all work, materials, equipment and operations that are likely to be required for the Project in accordance with such laws, codes, officials, ASTM's, recommendations, standards, and practices. To the extent, if at all, that the Contract Documents contain ambiguities, discrepancies, errors or omissions, and to the extent, if at all, that there are discrepancies between the Contract Documents and the Project site and surveys (collectively referred to in this Sub-paragraph 1.2.3

as "errors and omissions"), the Contractor hereby waives any claims for additional compensation or damages or additional time resulting from any such errors and omissions to the extent that the Contractor has actually observed, or with the exercise of reasonable care should have observed, those errors and omissions and failed to report them to the Owner and the Architect prior to executing the Agreement.

Comment: Most architects and engineers concede that no set of drawings and specifications can be prepared for a major project that is perfect. Since there will be errors and omissions in the contract documents, the owner here imposes a duty on the contractor to search for errors and omissions and report them to the owner.

¶3. **Third:** Sub-paragraph 2.2.1. Sub-paragraph 2.2.1 is annulled, and replaced as follows:

2.2.1 The Owner, at the request of the Contractor, prior to execution of the Agreement shall furnish or has furnished to the Contractor reasonable evidence that financial arrangements have been made to fulfill the Owner's obligations under the Contract.

Comment: The owner is unwilling to be required to furnish evidence of financial responsibility from time to time during the progress of the work. Technically, the Sub-paragraph is probably surplus, since presumably the contractor would not execute the contract documents unless satisfied as to the owner's financial responsibility. However, the language is retained here as evidence of the intention of the parties before the contract was signed.

¶4. **Fourth:** Sub-paragraph 2.2.5. Add the following:

Owner, however, shall not be required to furnish to the Contractor more than five free copies of such Drawings and Project Manuals.

¶5. **Fifth:** Sub-paragraph 2.3.1. Delete the word "persistently" in line 3.

¶6. **Sixth:** Sub-paragraph 2.4.1. Sub-paragraph 2.4.1 is annulled and replaced as follows:

2.4.1 If the Contractor defaults or neglects to carry out the Work in accordance with the Contract Documents and fails within a seven day period after receipt of written notice from the Owner to commence and continue correction of such default or neglect with diligence and promptness, the Owner may, without prejudice to other remedies the Owner may have, correct such deficiencies. In such case an appropriate Construction Change Directive shall be issued deducting from payments then or thereafter due the Contractor the cost of correcting such deficiencies, including compensation for the Architect's additional services and expenses made necessary by such default, neglect or failure. If payments then or thereafter due the Contractor are not sufficient to cover such amounts, the Contractor shall pay the difference to the Owner.

Comment: This language does away with the second seven day notice, and deletes the requirement that the owner obtain the architect's approval for its action and expenses in correcting defective work.

¶7. **Seventh:** Sub-paragraph 3.2.1. Sub-paragraph 3.2.1 is annulled.

Comment: This material is partly replaced by the revisions to Sub-paragraph 1.2.3.

¶8. **Eighth:** Sub-paragraph 3.7.1. Sub-paragraph 3.7.1 is replaced as follows:

3.7.1 Unless otherwise provided in the Contract Documents, the Contractor shall secure and pay for the building permit and other permits and governmental fees, licenses and inspections necessary for proper execution and completion of the Work.

¶9. **Ninth:** Sub-paragraph 3.7.3. Sub-paragraph 3.7.3 is annulled.

¶10. **Tenth:** Sub-paragraph 3.9.1. Add the following sentence:

The Owner shall have the right, which shall be exercised in a reasonable fashion, to approve and, if necessary, require the replacement of, the superintendent employed by the Contractor.

¶11. **Eleventh:** Sub-paragraph 3.11.1. Add the words "and Owner" after the word "Architect" in line 7.

¶12. **Twelfth:** Sub-paragraph 3.12.5. Add the following sentence:

If Shop Drawings, Product Data, Samples and similar submittals presented to the Architect by the Contractor contain deviations from requirements of the Contract Documents, the Contractor shall, in writing, designate such deviations and designate them as such at the time of submittal.

¶13. **Thirteenth:** Sub-paragraphs 3.18.1, 3.18.2, and 3.18.3. Sub-paragraphs 3.18.1, 3.18.2, and 3.18.3 are annulled and replaced as follows:

3.18.1 The Contractor will indemnify and save harmless the Owner and Architect and their representatives, consultants, officers, agents, servants, employees, and each of them (hereinafter individually and collectively, the "Indemnitees"), from and against any and all claims made or asserted for any damage or injury of any kind or nature whatsoever (including death), to any person or property (including, without limitation, claims for injury to or death of any employee of the Contractor, or subcontractors or suppliers of any tier), which claims result from, arise out of, or occur in connection with the execution of the Work, whether or not such claims are based upon actual or alleged active or passive negligence or wrongdoing of any Indemnitee, except that the Contractor shall not be required to indemnify an Indemnitee against a claim or loss that is the result of the Indemnitee's sole negligence or willful misconduct. Contractor shall indemnify Indemnitees from and against all loss, cost, expense, liability, damage or injury, including legal fees, that Indemnitees may directly or indirectly sustain, suffer or incur as a result thereof, and the Contractor agrees to and does hereby assume on behalf of Indemnitees the defense of any action at law or in equity which may be brought against Indemnitees by reason of such claims, and will pay on behalf of Indemnitees, upon their demand, the amount of any judgment that may be entered against Indemnitees or any of them in any such action. In the event that any such claims, loss, costs, expense, liability, damage or injury arise or are made, asserted or threatened against an Indemnitee for which the insurer of Contractor does not admit coverage, or if the Owner deems such coverage to be inadequate, the Owner shall have the right to withhold from any payments due or to become due to the Contractor an amount sufficient to protect Indemnitees from such claims, loss, costs, expense, liability, damage or injury, including legal fees.

Comment: Indemnity statutes of many states prohibit an owner from requiring a contractor to indemnify the owner against the owner's sole negligence or misconduct.

3.18.2 The obligations of the Contractor under Sub-paragraph 3.18.1 shall not extend to the liability of the Owner's Architect and consultants, or their agents or employees arising out of (1) the preparation or approval of maps, drawings, opinions, reports, surveys, Change Orders, Construction Change Directives, designs or specifications, or (2) the giving of or the failure to give directions or instructions by the Architect, the Architect's consultants, and agents and employees of any of them provided such giving or failure to give is the primary cause of the injury or damage.

3.18.3 The Contractor shall not permit any mechanic's lien or stop notice to be recorded or filed in connection with this Project. If any mechanic's lien is recorded, or stop notice filed, and if the Contractor does not cause such lien or stop notice to be released or discharged (by payment, bonding, or otherwise, and as promptly as possible), the Owner shall have the right (but not the obligation) to pay all sums necessary to obtain such release or discharge and credit all amounts so paid to the Guaranteed Maximum Price. The Owner, at the Owner's discretion, may defend its title against such claims of mechanic's lien, and the Contractor shall indemnify and hold harmless the Owner from all costs and expenses, including attorneys' fees arising out of such liens.

¶14. **Fourteenth:**   Sub-paragraph 4.1.4. Sub-paragraph 4.1.4 is annulled.

¶15. **Fifteenth:**   Sub-paragraph 4.2.8. Sub-paragraph 4.2.8 is annulled, and replaced as follows:

4.2.8 The Architect will prepare Change Orders and Construction Change Directives, and may authorize minor changes in the Work not involving adjustment in the Guaranteed Maximum Price or extension of the Contract Time and not inconsistent with the intent of the Contract Documents. Such minor changes in the Work shall be effected by written order and the Contractor shall carry out such written orders promptly.

¶16. **Sixteenth:**   Sub-paragraph 4.3.2. Sub-paragraph 4.3.2 is replaced as follows:

4.3.2 Decision of Architect. Claims, including those alleging an error or omission by the Architect, shall be referred initially to the Architect for action as provided in Sub-paragraph 4.4. A decision by the Architect as provided in Sub-paragraph 4.4.4 shall be required as a condition precedent to litigation of a Claim between the Contractor and Owner as to all such matters arising prior to the date final payment is due, regardless of (1) whether such matters relate to the execution and progress of the Work or (2) the extent to which the Work has been completed. The decision of the Architect in response to a Claim shall not be a condition precedent to litigation in the event (1) the position of the Architect is vacant, (2) the Architect has failed to render a decision within agreed time limits, (3) the Architect has failed to take action required under Sub-paragraph 4.4.4 within 30 days after the Claim is made, (4) 60 days have passed after the Claim has been referred to the Architect, or (5) the Claim relates to a mechanic's lien.

¶17. **Seventeenth:**   Sub-paragraph 4.3.4. Sub-paragraph 4.3.4 is replaced as follows:

4.3.4 Continuing Contract Performance. Pending final resolution of a Claim, unless otherwise agreed in writing, the Contractor shall proceed diligently with performance of the Contract and the Owner shall continue to make payments in accordance with the Contract Documents to the extent that such payments are undisputed by the Owner.

¶18. Eighteenth: Sub-paragraph 4.4.4. Delete the word "arbitration" and substitute the word "litigation" in line 6.

¶19. Nineteenth: Sub-paragraph 4.5. Sub-paragraphs 4.5.1 through 4.5.7 inclusive, are annulled.

> Comment: Here, the owner has decided to delete the arbitration provisions from the contract in their entirety. The owner may be motivated to delete arbitration by considerations such as the following: (1) the speed of arbitration proceedings may work to the advantage of the contractor; (2) in arbitration proceedings, it may be difficult for the owner to join all parties who are necessary to the complete resolution of the dispute, and under the standard form of AIA contract documents it is impossible to join the architect and its consultants without their specific consent; (3) discovery is usually unavailable in arbitration absent specific agreement of the parties to the contract; (4) the owner may not wish to give up the right to a jury trial.

¶20. Twentieth: Sub-paragraph 5.4.1.1. Delete the words "for cause pursuant to Sub-paragraph 14.2".

¶21. Twenty-First: Sub-paragraph 5.4.2 is annulled.

¶22. Twenty-Second: Sub-paragraph 6.1.1. Delete the words "and waiver of subrogation" at line 7.

¶23. Twenty-Third: Sub-paragraph 6.1.3. Delete the words "and Contract Sum" at line 7.

¶24. Twenty-Fourth: Sub-paragraph 6.2.3 is annulled.

¶25. Twenty-Fifth: Sub-paragraph 8.3.3. Sub-paragraph 8.3.3 is replaced as follows:

> 8.3.3 In the event that the operations of the Contractor are delayed by any act of Owner or Architect, then Contractor will be entitled to apply for an extension of time as provided in Sub-paragraph 8.3.1, but Contractor hereby waives, and shall on no account be entitled to recover, damages for delay, disruption, "impact", loss of efficiency, loss of productivity, or any other similar form of damages or compensation.

> Comment: Courts in most states will enforce a "no damage for delay" clause if the delays are such as may have been within the contemplation of the parties at the time when the contract was executed. Many courts refuse to enforce such a clause when the disruption

or delay is caused by the "active interference" of the owner.

¶26. **Twenty-Sixth:**   Sub-paragraph 9.5.1.7. Delete the word "persistent".

¶27. **Twenty-Seventh:**   Sub-paragraph 9.7.1. At line 6, delete the words "or awarded by arbitration".

¶28. **Twenty-Eighth:**   Sub-paragraphs 9.8.2 and 9.8.3. Sub-paragraphs 9.8.2 and 9.8.3 are annulled. New Sub-paragraph 9.8.2 is adopted as follows:

> 9.8.2 When the Contractor considers that the Work, or a designated portion thereof which is acceptable to the Owner, has achieved Substantial Completion, the Contractor shall prepare for submission to the Architect a punch list of items to be completed or corrected. The failure to include any items on such punch list does not alter the responsibility of the Contractor to complete all Work in accordance with the Contract Documents. When the Architect on the basis of inspection determines that the Work or a designated portion thereof has attained Substantial Completion, the Architect will prepare a Certificate of Substantial Completion which shall establish the Date of Substantial Completion, shall state the responsibilities of the Owner and the Contractor or security, maintenance, heat, utilities, damage to the Work and insurance, and shall fix the time as determined by the Architect and the Owner within which the Contractor shall complete the items listed therein.

¶29. **Twenty-Ninth:**   Sub-paragraph 9.10.1. Sub-paragraph 9.10.1 is deleted.

¶30. **Thirtieth:**   Sub-paragraphs 9.10.2, 9.10.3, and 9.10.4 are annulled and replaced as follows:

> 9.10.2 Subject to the Owner's approval of the Architect's final Certificate for Payment and the actual full compliance with all of the following conditions precedent to final payment, the Contractor shall be entitled to receive as final payment the balance of the Contract Sum, including, if applicable, the Contractor's share of savings calculated as provided in the Agreement.
>
> 9.10.3 The making of final payment shall not constitute a waiver of any claims by the Owner, including, but not limited to, those arising from:
>
> .1 Unsettled liens;
>
> .2 Faulty or defective Work appearing after Substantial Completion;
>
> .3 Failure of the Work to comply with the requirements of the Contract Documents; and
>
> .4 Terms of any guarantees and warranties required by the Contract Documents.

9.10.4 The acceptance of final payment shall constitute a waiver of all claims by the Contractor except those expressly made in writing by the Contractor at the time it submits its final Application for Payment.

9.10.5 Preconditions to the Owner's obligation to make final payment shall be:

.1 Either (a) the passage of five business days following the last date that any mechanic's lien can be properly recorded against the Project or real property, or (b) submission by the Contractor to the Owner of properly completed unconditional waivers and releases of mechanic's lien and stop notice rights executed by the Contractor and all Subcontractors and suppliers of all tiers, with any additional supporting documentation reasonably requested by the Owner, and there shall have been no (i) liens recorded or stop notices filed against the Project or real property which have not been discharged (by bonding or otherwise), or (ii) threats of any claims or lawsuits against the Owner for alleged failure to make payment by the Contractor, or (iii) failure by the Contractor to fulfill any indemnities provided by the Contract.

.2 Upon written request of the Owner or bonding company, the Contractor shall submit, as a condition precedent to final payment, a written report or endorsement from a title insurance company acceptable to the Owner, bonding company and the Owner's construction lender, that no mechanic's lien has been recorded against the real property which has not been discharged and removed, the cost of which report and endorsement shall be included in the Guaranteed Maximum Price.

.3 Submission by the Contractor to the Owner of satisfactory evidence that full payment has been made to all union fringe benefits and into all union trust funds and any and all taxes and insurance for the Project.

.4 Submission by the Contractor to the Owner of an affidavit, sworn to before a Notary Public, stating that all workers and persons employed, all firms supplying the materials, and all Subcontractors upon the Project and all other indebtedness connected with the Work for which the Owner or the Project might in any manner be liable have been paid in full, or will be paid in full from the final payment and that there are no bills outstanding against the Project for either labor or material, except certain items, if any, to be set forth in such affidavit covering disputed claims or other appropriate items.

.5 In the event that any mechanic's liens have been recorded against the Project or the real property or any reason, the Contractor, at the Contractor's expense, shall procure and record a mechanic's lien release bond discharging the lien. Subsequent to the recordation of such release bond, and the discharge of the Owner from any lawsuit to foreclose the mechanic's lien in question, the Owner shall release to the Contractor any funds which have been withheld because of any such lien.

.6 Certification of completion of construction work, including punch list items, and acceptance of the Work by the Architect, the Owner and the Construction Lender.

.7 Submission by the Contractor to the Architect and the Owner of required written guarantees and warranties, properly indexed and placed in a loose leaf binder. Unless provided to the contrary elsewhere in the Contract, and warranties and guarantees shall commence upon making of the final payment.

.8 Submission by the Contractor to the Architect and the Owner of as-built drawings.

.9 Submission by the Contractor to the Owner of a complete list of Subcontractors and principal vendors on the Project, including addresses and telephone numbers.

.10 Submission by the Contractor to the Owner, in an indexed loose leaf binder, of complete installation, operation and maintenance manuals, including all manufacturer's literature, of equipment and materials used in the Work.

.11 Completion by the Owner of any audit permitted under the Contract.

.12 Submission by the Contractor to the Owner, in an indexed loose leaf binder, of all inspection reports, permits and temporary and final certificates of occupancy and licenses necessary for the occupancy of the Project.

.13 Consent of surety, if any, to final payment.

.14 An affidavit that payrolls, bills for materials and equipment, and other indebtedness connected with the Work for which the Owner or the Owner's property might be responsible or encumbered have been paid or otherwise satisfied.

.15 A certificate evidencing that insurance required by the Contract Documents to remain in force after final payment is currently in effect and will not be cancelled or allowed to expire until at least thirty days prior written notice has been given to the Owner.

.16 Any and all other items required pursuant to the Contract Documents.

¶31. **Thirty-First:** Sub-paragraph 10.1.2. Delete the following words from the last sentence: "on which arbitration has not been demanded, or by arbitration under Article 4."

¶32. **Thirty-Second:** Sub-paragraph 10.1.3. The following sentence is added at the end of Sub-paragraph 10.1.3:

The Contractor's consent to perform such work will not be unreasonably withheld.

¶33. Thirty-Third: Sub-paragraph 10.1.4. Sub-paragraph 10.1.4 is annulled.

¶34. Thirty-Fourth: Sub-paragraph 10.2.5. Sub-paragraph 10.2.5 is replaced as follows:

10.2.5 The Contractor shall promptly remedy damage and loss caused in whole or in part by the Contractor, a Subcontractor, a Sub-subcontractor, or anyone directly or indirectly employed by any of them, or anyone for whose acts they may be liable and for which the Contractor is responsible.

¶35. Thirty-Fifth: Sub-paragraph 11.1.1.5. Delete the words "other than to the Work itself".

¶36. Thirty-Sixth: Sub-paragraph 11.1.1.7. Sub-paragraph 11.1.1.7 is replaced as follows:

11.1.1.7 Claims involving contractual liability insurance applicable to the Contractor's obligations under the indemnity provisions of the Contract.

¶37. Thirty-Seventh: Sub-paragraph 11.1.2. Sub-paragraph 11.1.2 is replaced as follows:

11.1.2 The insurance required by Sub-paragraph 11.1.1 shall be written for not less than Ten Million Dollars ($10,000,000), shall be written on an occurrence basis, and shall be maintained without interruption from the date of commencement of the Work until the date of final payment and termination of any coverage required to be maintained after final payment.

¶38. Thirty-Eighth: Sub-paragraph 11.1.3. Add the following:

In addition to Certificates of Insurance, Contractor shall supply a written endorsement to Contractor's general liability insurance policy that names the Owner as an additional insured. The endorsement shall provide that Contractor's liability insurance policy shall be primary, and that any liability insurance of Owner shall be secondary and noncontributory.

¶39. Thirty-Ninth: Sub-paragraph 11.1.4. Sub-paragraph 11.1.4 is amended to read as follows:

11.1.4 Contractor shall require that all Subcontractors of every tier supply Certificates of Insurance evidencing liability insurance that complies with the requirements of Sub-paragraph 11.1.1 with limits according to a schedule of Subcontractor's liability insurance to be submitted by Contractor and approved by Owner. Subcontractors of every tier shall also supply copies of endorsements to their insurance policies naming Owner as an additional named insured as respects the operations of Subcontractor, and providing that the insurance of Subcontractor is primary and the insurance of Owner is secondary and noncontributory.

¶40. **Fortieth:** Sub-paragraphs 11.2 and 11.3. Sub-paragraphs 11.2 and 11.3 are replaced as follows:

11.2 The Owner will purchase, effect and maintain property insurance for all the Work to be performed under this Contract. The policy of insurance shall be a Builder's Risk type on a replacement cost basis, "All-Risk" form, and copies of the policy form to be used will be made available to the Contractor at its request. The policy shall be equal to the full insurable value of the Work. The coverage of the insurance shall not extend to tools and equipment of the Contractor, subcontractors of any tier or property owned by employees of any of them; vehicles of any kind; trees or shrubs or drawings or specifications.

11.3 No other type of insurance than that set forth in Sub-paragraph 11.2 shall be required to be furnished by the Owner. The furnishing of insurance by the Owner shall in no way relieve, nor be construed to relieve, the Contractor or subcontractors of any tier of any responsibility or obligation whatsoever otherwise imposed by this Contract.

Comment: The property insurance provisions of the standard form of AIA Document A201 are established on the premise that in the event of damage to or destruction of the property by fire or other peril covered by the All Risk policy, the proceeds of the insurance will be distributed to the contractor and subcontractors as their interests may appear and the proceeds would then presumably be used for rebuilding the project without additional expense to the owner. As a practical matter, the scheme would be very difficult to work out in practice, and the owner would tend to lose control over the process of construction since money would be delivered to the contractor by the insurance carrier rather than by the owner under the contract documents progressively, according to the progress of construction. As a practical matter, it must also be assumed that the construction lender, also an additional insured under the All Risk policy, would be likely to claim the proceeds of insurance in satisfaction of the construction loan. This would leave the owner and contractor and subcontractors all without funds to proceed with construction.

The premise of the substituted property insurance provisions is that contractor and subcontractors themselves would procure builder's risk insurance to cover their insurable interest in the partially completed project, that each subcontractor and contractor would then collect the proceeds of insurance and use it for rebuilding to the point of completion at which damage or destruction occurred.

Such an arrangement can result in a windfall to the owner, since the owner's construction loan may be paid off, or partially paid off, by the owner's insurance while the cost of rebuilding is paid by the contractor's insurance at no expense to the owner. Such a stacking of insurance coverage will naturally increase the overall insurance premium paid for the project, and the contractor's insurance premium will presumably be passed on to the owner, and therefore the owner will have paid for the apparent "windfall".

¶41. **Forty-First:**   Sub-paragraph 13.6. Sub-paragraph 13.6 is annulled.

¶42. **Forty-Second:**   Sub-paragraph 13.7. Sub-paragraph 13.7 is annulled.

¶43. **Forty-Third:**   Sub-paragraphs 14.1.1 through 14.1.3. Sub-paragraphs 14.1.1 through 14.1.3 are annulled.

Prime Contract - Stipulated Sum - Short Form
[Favors Interests of Contractor]

§1.29   General Comment

As a general rule, it is true that the shorter forms of prime contract are likely to favor the interests of the contractor rather than the interests of the owner. It may even be argued with some force that a contractor is generally better off working on a handshake than with a written contract.

Both of these propositions are true because the contractor's main interest in pursuing a construction project is to receive equitable compensation for work performed. The **handshake** deal protects this interest of the contractor because, under a legal doctrine entitled *quantum meruit,* a contractor who supplies construction services to an owner is entitled to be paid what those services are worth. Therefore, a contractor would usually be better off to work on a handshake than to sign a lengthy contract filled with provisions that are inserted there to protect the interests of the owner.

It does not take very many paragraphs to write a contract favoring the interests of contractor. This next form, then, is such a contract. It may be modified by adding clauses that may be found in **FORM 1-7**, "Alternate Prime Contract Provisions".

The reader is cautioned that in many states a prime contract for construction or remodeling of a home must be in writing and comply with statutory requirements. Before entering into a consumer contract for home building or remodeling, parties should consult a lawyer to be certain that the requirements of any state consumer protection statute are fulfilled.

FORM 1-4 Prime Contract - Stipulated Sum

**Prime Contract - Stipulated Sum - Short Form
[Favors Interests of Contractor]**

¶1. This Contract is between _____
("Owner") and _____ ("Contractor").
The Contractor will construct, on behalf of the Owner, a project consisting of
_____ .
The project is located at _____ .

¶2. Scope of the Work: Contractor will furnish all labor, equipment, materials, scaffolding, building permits, sales taxes, hoisting, transportation, supervision, coordination, communication, shop drawings and storage to complete in a first-class and workmanlike manner the following work:
_____
_____
_____
_____
_____
_____
_____
_____
_____

¶3. Boundaries: Owner will supply Contractor with a legal description of the property, and if requested by Contractor, Owner will supply Contractor with a survey and boundary stakes by a licensed land surveyor.

¶4. Contract, Drawings and Specifications: The project will be constructed according to drawings and specifications which have been initialed by the parties and which are hereby made a part of this Contract. The contract, drawings and specifications are intended to supplement each other. In case of conflict, however, the specifications shall control the drawings, and the provisions of the contract control both.

¶5. Time for Completion of Work: Within ten days after the execution of this Contract, Owner will have the jobsite ready for commencement of construction, and shall give Contractor written notice to commence work. Contractor shall commence work within ten days after such notice, and shall complete the work within _____ calendar days after commencement, subject to permissible delays.

¶6. Building Permits, Charges and Exactions: Contractor will provide and pay for all necessary building permits. Owner will pay bonds, assessments, hookup charges, school fees, financing fees, facility fees, and exactions of utilities and public agencies that are imposed to pay facilities costs.

¶7. Labor and Material: The Contractor shall pay all valid charges for labor and material incurred by Contractor and used in the construction of the project. Contractor is excused from this obligation for bills received in any period during which the Owner is in arrears in making progress payments to Contractor. No waiver or release of mechanic's lien given by Contractor shall be binding until all payments due to the Contractor when the release was executed have been made.

¶8. Payment: For all services performed by Contractor, Owner will pay Contractor the contract price of $_____. Contractor will submit to Owner, on or before the last day of each month, an application for payment showing the percentage of completion of the various portions of the work according to a schedule of values supplied by Contractor and agreed to by Owner. On or before the 10th day of the month, Owner will pay Contractor 90 per cent of the value of the work completed and materials suitably stored at the site during the previous month. If payments are made through a construction lender, the Owner represents that the construction loan fund is sufficient to pay the contract price, and Owner will do everything possible to expedite all payments from the construction lender. Owner hereby irrevocably authorizes the construction lender to make all payments directly to Contractor.

¶9. Final Payment: The final payment will be due ten days after substantial completion of the project. If corrective or repair work of a minor nature remains to be accomplished by the Contractor after the project is ready for occupancy, the Contractor will perform such work expeditiously and the Owner will not withhold payment pending the completion of such minor work. If major items of corrective or repair work remain after the substantial completion of the project, the cost of which aggregates more than 1 per cent of the contract price, Owner, pending completion of such work, after payment of the retention, may withhold payment of a sufficient amount to pay for the completion of such work.

¶10. Reduction of, and Payment of, Retention: After 50 per cent of the contract has been performed, Owner will pay Contractor 95 per cent of the amount of each application for payment, reducing the retention to 5 per cent. Owner will promptly sign and record a Notice of Completion when the project is complete. The retention will be paid to Contractor 35 days after the Notice of Completion is recorded.

¶11. Extra Work: Should Owner, construction lender, or any public agency or inspector direct any deletion from, or modification of or addition to, the work covered by this Contract, the cost shall be added to or deducted from the contract price. In the case of extra work, the Contractor will be paid 15 per cent for its overhead and 7½ per cent for profit. Payments for extra work will be made as extra work progresses, concurrently with progress payments. Orders for extra work should be made in writing, with the price agreed to in advance, but the Contractor is entitled to be paid for extra work, whether the extra work order is reduced to writing or not.

¶12. Allowances: If the contract price includes allowances, and the cost of performing the work covered by an allowance is either greater or less than the allowance, then the contract price shall be increased or decreased accordingly. Unless otherwise requested by Owner in writing, Contractor shall use its judgment in accomplishing work covered by an allowance. If the Owner requests that work covered by an allowance be accomplished in such a way that the cost will exceed the allowance, the Contractor will comply with Owner's request provided that Owner provides for the additional cost in advance.

¶13. Insurance by Owner: Owner will procure at its own expense and before the commencement of work hereunder "all risk" insurance with course of construction, theft, vandalism and malicious mischief endorsements attached, the insurance to be in a sum at least equal to the contract price. The insurance will name the Contractor and its Subcontractors as additional insureds and will be written to protect Owner, Contractor and subcontractors as their interests may appear. Should Owner fail to procure such insurance, Contractor may do so at the expense of Owner, but is not required to do so. Owner and Contractor waive rights of subrogation against each other to the extent that any loss is covered by valid and collectible insurance. If the project is destroyed or damaged by accident, disaster, or calamity such as fire, storm, flood, landslide, subsidence, or earthquake, work done by Contractor in rebuilding or restoring the project shall be paid for by Owner as extra work.

¶14. Contractor's Insurance: Contractor and its subcontractors of every tier will provide Owner the following insurance, along with Certificates of Insurance:

(a) Comprehensive general liability insurance, in standard form, with limits of $500,000 for bodily injury for each occurrence and in the aggregate, and limits of $500,000 for property damage for each occurrence and in the aggregate;

(b) Automobile liability insurance in comprehensive form, including coverage for owned, hired, and non-owned automobiles, with limits of $500,000 for each occurrence and in the aggregate;

(c) Workers' compensation insurance in statutory form.

¶15. Completion and Occupancy: Owner will not occupy the project until construction has been completed, except with the consent of Contractor. Contractor may use such force as is necessary to deny occupancy of the project by Owner until Contractor has received all payments due and until Notice of Completion has been recorded.

¶16. Default: If Owner should default in any of its obligations under this Contract, Contractor may recover, as damages, either the reasonable value of the work performed by Contractor, or the balance of the contract price plus any other damages sustained as a result of Owner's default. If, after signing this Contract, Owner refuses to permit Contractor to proceed with the construction of the project, Owner realizes Contractor would suffer damages including loss of profit which Contractor would otherwise have made on the project. It would be difficult and impractical to determine the amount of such damages, and it is therefore agreed that, in the event of such default, Owner will pay Contractor _____ per cent of the contract price as liquidated damages.

¶17. Delay: Contractor shall be excused for delay in completion of the contract caused by acts of God, acts of the Owner, inclement weather, labor trouble, acts of public agencies, inspectors, or public utilities, extra work, failure of the Owner to make progress payments promptly, or other contingencies unforeseen by Contractor and beyond the reasonable control of Contractor.

¶18. Right to Stop Work: Contractor shall have the right to stop work if payments are not made when due under this Contract, and may keep the job idle until all payments have been received.

¶19. Concealed Conditions: If Contractor should encounter concealed conditions that were not reasonably anticipated by Contractor, such as rock, concrete, or structures, Contractor will call such conditions to the attention of Owner immediately, and the contract price will be accordingly adjusted for such extra work.

¶20. Cleanup: At all times during the progress of the work, and upon completion of the work, Contractor will clean up the jobsite and remove debris and surplus material. The jobsite will be kept in a neat and broom-clean condition.

¶21. Arbitration: Any controversy arising out of this Contract or the performance thereof shall be decided by arbitration in accordance with the Construction Industry Rules of the American Arbitration Association, and judgment may be entered on the award. The arbitration proceeding will include subcontractors, material suppliers, equipment renters, construction lender, architect, designer, engineer, and all other parties to the construction process who have signed any document incorporating or referring to this arbitration agreement. Should any party refuse or neglect to appear at and participate in arbitration proceedings after due notice, the arbitration will make an award based on evidence introduced by the parties who do appear and participate. The arbitrator shall award the prevailing party or parties reasonable compensation for the time, expense, and trouble of arbitration, including arbitration fees, attorney's fees, and executive and administrative fees. Without waiving its right to demand arbitration under this Contract, any party may apply to the court for attachment, injunction, declaratory relief, or other provisional or summary remedy that may not be available in arbitration. Each party will permit all other parties to examine and copy its records that are relevant to the dispute, and the arbitrator is empowered to enforce this agreement for inspection and copying of records.

¶22. <u>Limitations:</u> No action of any character arising out of or related to this Contract or the performance thereof shall be commenced by either party against the other more than two years after the completion or cessation of work under this Contract.

¶23. <u>Attorney's Fees:</u> In the event of litigation arising out of this Contract or the performance thereof, the court will award reasonable attorney's fees to the prevailing party.

¶24. <u>Assignment:</u> Neither party may assign this Contract, or the proceeds thereof, without written consent of the other party.

¶25. <u>Binding on Successors:</u> All of the provisions of this Contract will be binding on the assignees, successors, parent companies, and subsidiary companies of both parties. If either party is acquired by a corporation through purchase, merger, or consolidation, the provisions of this Contract will be binding on the successor or surviving corporation.

DATED: _____

_____ , Owner   _____ , Contractor

By_____   By_____
   (Signature)   (Signature)

Contractor's License No:
_____

Prime Contract - Cost Plus Percentage - Guaranteed Maximum Cost [Favors Interests of Owner]

§1.30 General Comment

This prime contract form favors the interests of the owner to a relatively moderate degree. It assumes that the architect will participate in the construction process by supervision, inspection, or observation of construction and will issue certificates for payment in response to applications for payment submitted by the contractor.

This form may be modified by adding or substituting alternate prime contract provisions as may be found in **FORM 1-7**.

This contract can be converted to a **cost plus a fixed fee** contract by substituting appropriate paragraphs to be found in **FORM 1-7**.

FORM 1-5 Prime Contract - Cost Plus Percentage

PRIME CONTRACT
BETWEEN OWNER AND CONTRACTOR
COST PLUS A PERCENTAGE WITH GUARANTEED
MAXIMUM

¶1. This Contract is between _____
("Owner") and _____ ("Contractor").
The Architect is _____
("Architect). Contractor will construct, on behalf of Owner, a project consisting of _____
The project is located at _____ .

¶2. <u>Scope of the Work:</u> Contractor will furnish all labor, equipment, materials, transportation, communication, scaffolding, hoisting, supervision, coordination, building permits, sales taxes, shop drawings, and samples to complete in a workmanlike manner the following work:
_____
_____
_____

¶3. <u>Investigation by Contractor:</u> Contractor has thoroughly investigated the jobsite, the contract documents, as well as the building codes, laws, and regulations that are applicable to the work. The Guaranteed Maximum Cost includes all work, as shown on the drawings and as specified, needed to provide a finished, complete and operating facility.

¶4. <u>Contract Documents:</u> The following documents, construed together and in a complimentary manner, form the contract:
_____
_____
_____

Work called for on the drawings and not mentioned in the specifications, or vice versa, shall be performed as though set forth in both. If Contractor should perceive an error, omission, or conflict in the contract documents, it will promptly notify the Architect in writing. The Architect will promptly resolve conflicts, errors, and omissions by issuing written instructions, which Contractor will promptly follow. If Contractor proceeds with work based on error, omission, or conflict in the contract documents, without instructions from the Architect, it will be at the risk and expense of Contractor.

¶5. Construction Loan Agreement: Contractor will execute any documents reasonably requested by the construction or permanent lender, including the assignment, in whole or in part, of this Contract.

¶6. Relationship of Trust: This Contract is based on a relationship of trust and confidence between Contractor and Owner. Contractor will utilize its skills and experience to promptly provide a complete and operating project at the lowest cost that is consistent with trade practice and the quality standards established by the contract documents.

¶7. Contractor's License: The Contractor is properly licensed to perform the work called for by the contract documents, and will remain so during the performance of the work.

¶8. Time for Completion: Contractor will commence work within three days after the execution of this Contract, and, subject to excusable delays, will achieve substantial completion of the work in _____ calendar days.

¶9. Progress Schedule: Within 10 days after the execution of this Contract, Contractor shall submit a progress schedule for Owner's approval. The progress schedule will be revised, from time to time, to reflect job conditions and so as to provide for the completion of the project within the number of working days permitted by this Contract.

¶10. Time is of the Essence: Time is of the essence of this contract.

¶11. Cost of the Work: Owner will pay Contractor for the Cost of the Work, which is defined as all costs reasonably and properly incurred in the performance of the work, including wages paid for direct labor, contributions applicable to Contractor's payroll, fringe benefits, payroll taxes, contributions for unemployment, social security, disability, and similar payments and assessments, salaries of clerical and supervisory and other personnel stationed at the jobsite or in the field and employed in the construction of the project, travel and subsistence, the cost of materials, supplies, and equipment incorporated or consumed the work, the cost of subcontracts, the cost of temporary facilities and hand tools consumed in the performance of the work, reasonable equipment rental charges whether the equipment is owned by, or rented to Contractor, power, utility, and telephone charges, permit fees, sales and use taxes incurred about the work, premiums for bonds and insurance that Contractor is required by the contract documents to maintain, cleanup costs, the professional fees of consultants, engineers, designers, or schedulers employed by Contractor to facilitate or expedite the work, and all other costs properly and reasonably incurred in the performance of the work. Discounts and rebates, and the salvage value of tools and equipment consumed in the work, shall not be included in the Cost of the Work. The Owner shall not reimburse the Contractor for any costs incurred before _____.

¶12. Contractor's Fee: The Owner will pay the Contractor's fee, which shall be the Cost of the Work multiplied by _____ per cent. The Contractor's fee shall be paid monthly in proportion to the percentage of completion of the work.

¶13. Guaranteed Maximum Cost: The guaranteed maximum Cost of the Work, including the Contractor's fee, is $_____.

¶14. Overtime: If Owner determines, with the concurrence of Architect, that Contractor has failed to advance the work with sufficient expedition to complete the project in the number of calendar days permitted by the Contract, then Owner may order Contractor to work overtime at Contractor's expense. Premium overtime hourly wage rates and other expenses directly caused by overtime work will not be reimbursed to Contractor by Owner as a Cost of the Work.

¶15. Costs Not to be Paid: Owner will not pay Contractor for the cost of salaries paid to Contractor's home office personnel or any of Contractor's other home office expenses. Owner will not compensate Contractor for costs incurred because of the negligence, fault, or wrongdoing of Contractor, its agents or employees.

¶16. Change Orders: The Owner may issue written change orders to Contractor requiring Contractor to add to, change, or delete from the scope of the work, and the Guaranteed Maximum Cost will be adjusted accordingly. Within 20 days after the issuance of a proposed change order, Contractor will quote, in writing, the price of the change. The quote will be supported by a detailed estimate. If Owner agrees to the proposed price, it will issue the change order and the Guaranteed Maximum Cost will be adjusted accordingly. If Owner does not agree to the price quoted by Contractor, it may issue the change order with no price, and the amount by which the Guaranteed Maximum Cost is to be adjusted will be determined by arbitration. If Owner requires Contractor to perform work that Contractor contends is outside the scope of the work required by the contract documents, Contractor will notify Owner, in writing, of its contention, and will promptly proceed to perform the work. The dispute as to the scope of the work will be decided by arbitration. Contractor shall be paid for changes in the work its percentage fee as defined herein based on the Cost of the Work as defined herein. The amount to be subtracted from the Guaranteed Maximum Cost due to deletions from the scope of the work will be determined by subtracting the Cost of the Work deleted, as defined herein, plus percentage fee as defined herein.

¶17. Applications for Payment: On or before the 10th day of each month, Contractor will submit to Architect an Application for Payment, showing in detail, and with such backup as the Architect may require, the Cost of the Work for the preceding calendar month. The Application for Payment will be broken down

§1.30 COST PLUS PERCENTAGE PRIME CONTRACT   45

between the various divisions of the work, and will include the Contractor's estimated percentage of completion of each division of the work. The Application for Payment will include a computation of the amount of Contractor's fee.

¶18.   Releases: Before Owner makes any progress payment to Contractor, Contractor will supply properly executed mechanic's lien releases, in form satisfactory to Owner, acknowledging payment for all work, equipment and materials supplied to the project before the end of the month preceding the month for which application for payment is made.

¶19.   Certificate for Payment: Architect will issue its Certificate for Payment not more than seven days after receipt of the Application for Payment, and Owner will make payment to Contractor in accordance with the Certificate for Payment no later than 10 days after submission of the Application for Payment to Architect. Owner will withhold a 10 per cent retention until 35 days after completion of the project.

¶20.   Punch List: Owner will pay the retention to Contractor despite minor items remaining to be completed or corrected, consisting in value of not more than one-half of one per cent of the Guaranteed Maximum Cost. Architect will estimate the cost of correcting minor items, and Owner will withhold from Contractor 200 per cent of the estimated cost until all such items have been completed or corrected.

¶21.   Inspection and Testing: Contractor will facilitate all inspection and testing called for by Architect or by the contract documents, and if necessary will, at its own expense, uncover the work so that it is available for inspection and testing. Contractor will pay for retesting required because of work that fails to comply with the requirements of the contract documents Owner will pay for testing that shows Contractor's work to comply with the requirements of the Contract Documents.

¶22.   Audit: Owner may at all times review and audit Contractor's cost accounting records and other job records and Contractor will afford Owner reasonable facilities for such audits. Contractor shall preserve all job records for at least seven years after the completion of the project.

¶23.   Discounts for Prompt Payment: Cash discounts for prompt payment shall accrue to Contractor unless Owner has deposited funds with Contractor with which to make such payments, in which case such discounts shall accrue to Owner.

¶24.   Contractor's and Subcontractor's Insurance: Contractor and its subcontractors of every tier will provide Owner the following insurance, and will deliver to Owner the following Certificates of Insurance and Endorsements issued by insurance companies authorized to write business in this state:

(a) Liability Insurance: Comprehensive general liability insurance, in broad form, including coverage for completed operations, liability assumed by contract, underground hazard, collapse hazard, and explosion. The policy limits shall be not less than $1,000,000 for each occurrence and in the aggregate for bodily injury and $1,000,000 for each occurrence and in the aggregate for property damage. The Certificate of Insurance and the Endorsement to the policy will designate Owner as an additional insured, and will provide that the insurance is primary. The Certificate will provide that the policy may not be cancelled or modified without 30 days prior written notice to Owner.

(b) Automobile Liability: Automobile Liability in comprehensive form including insurance for owned, non-owned, and hired automobiles, trucks and other licensed motor vehicles utilized by Contractor in connection with the work. The policy limits will not be less than $1,000,000 for bodily injury and $1,000,000 for property damage. The Certificate of Insurance will provide that the insurance may not be cancelled or modified without 30 days prior written notice to Owner.

(c) Workers' Compensation Insurance: Workers' Compensation Insurance shall be in statutory form. The Certificate of Insurance will provide that the insurance may not be cancelled without 30 days prior written notice to Owner.

¶25. Owner's Insurance: Owner will provide builder's risk insurance, in "all risk" form, to include the interests of Owner, Contractor, subcontractors and sub-subcontractors. Contractor, its subcontractors and sub-subcontractors shall be named insureds. Owner, Contractor, subcontractors and sub-subcontractors waive rights against each other to recover for damages or loss caused by fire or other perils that are covered by such insurance, or any other insurance, to the extent that such insurance or other insurance is valid and collectible.

¶26. Indemnity: Contractor will indemnity Owner and save it harmless from all claims, liability, loss, and expense, including attorney's fees, asserted or incurred as a result of the fault, negligence, or wrongdoing of Contractor, its agents, employees, or subcontractors or persons acting under them. Contractor shall provide indemnity if Owner is partly at fault, but shall not provide indemnity for claims, liability, loss or expense caused wholly by Owner, or by the sole negligence of Owner.

¶27. Attorney's Fees: In the event of litigation between the parties to this contract, the court will award reasonable attorney's fees to the prevailing party.

¶28. Default by Contractor: If Contractor fails to expeditiously advance the project, or installs work that does not comply with the requirements of the contract documents, or fails to promptly pay for work or materials supplied to the project, or is guilty of any other material default, Owner may: (1) suspend payment, or (2) by written notice to Contractor, terminate Contractor's right to perform all or any portion of the work. Contractor will pay Owner all damages sustained as a result of default by Contractor. If Owner terminates Contractor's right to perform work, Owner may have the work performed by others and charge the cost to Contractor.

¶29. Delay: Contractor will be excused for delay caused by inclement weather, labor disputes, acts of public agencies, acts of Owner or Architect, or other events beyond the reasonable expectation and control of Contractor. Contractor will be entitled to extensions of time for such delay only upon written application to Owner within 10 days after commencement of the delay. Contractor understands that Owner will suffer damages if Owner is unable to occupy the finished project on time, and Contractor will reimburse Owner for all such damages.

¶30. Unanticipated Concealed Conditions: In the event that Contractor encounters adverse concealed conditions that could not reasonably have been anticipated, the Guaranteed Maximum Cost will be equitably adjusted, and the cost of dealing with such unanticipated conditions will become a Cost of the Work.

¶31. Destruction of the Work: If the project should be destroyed by fire or other peril for which Owner is required to provide insurance under these contract documents, Contractor will be paid for its work based on the Cost of the Work plus its fee as limited by the percentage of completion of the project multiplied by the Guaranteed Maximum Cost, and Contractor's work will terminate. If the project is partially destroyed by such a peril (that is, if less than 50 per cent of the value of the work performed by Contractor is destroyed), the Guaranteed Maximum Cost and time for performance will be equitably adjusted, and Contractor will promptly rebuild and complete the project.

¶32. Cleanup: Contractor will keep the job in a neat and clean condition at all times, and will leave the project in a broom-clean condition.

¶33. Arbitration: Any dispute arising out of or related to the performance of the work or the interpretation of this contract, shall be decided by arbitration in accordance with the Construction Industry Rules of the American Arbitration Association, and judgment may be entered on the award. The Architect, the Architect's consultants, subcontractors, sub-subcontractors, suppliers, and construction lender will all be bound by this arbitration clause and will participate in the arbitration proceedings if they have signed a document that incorporates or refers to this arbitration clause.

Any party, without waiving the right to arbitrate the controversy, may apply to the court for provisional relief, writs, attachments or injunctions that may not be available in arbitration. The arbitrator will award reasonable attorney's fees to the prevailing party or parties. All parties will allow all other parties to inspect and copy their job records, and such other books and records as may be ordered by the arbitrator. The arbitrator may issue interlocutory awards enforcing the right to inspect books and records. The arbitrator may award any form of interlocutory and permanent relief that could be awarded by a court.

¶34. <u>Successors and Assigns:</u> This Contract, or the proceeds thereof, may not be assigned by either party without the written consent of the other party. The provisions of this Contract are binding on the parent, subsidiary, and successor companies to Owner and Contractor, and upon the surviving corporation in the event of merger or acquisition.

¶35. <u>Warranty:</u> Contractor guarantees that all workmanship, equipment, and materials will be of specified quality, suited to the intended purpose, and free of defects for a period of one year after the substantial completion of the project. Contractor will promptly correct any such defect at no expense to Owner. Contractor will assign and deliver to Owner all guarantees and warranties of equipment manufacturers and material suppliers that are applicable to portions of the work.

¶36. <u>Subcontracts:</u> Subcontractors will be subject to the approval of Owner, which approval Owner will not unreasonably withhold. If Owner disapproves a subcontractor after the guaranteed maximum price has been established, Owner will pay any increase in cost that is caused by such disapproval. No subcontract will be awarded on a "cost plus" basis unless Owner has approved, in writing, all the terms and conditions of the subcontract.

¶37. <u>No Other Agreement:</u> This Contract, with the contract documents incorporated herein, is the entire agreement between the parties. No oral or written communications or negotiations that occurred before the execution of the Contract will be considered to be a part of the agreement. The Contract can be modified only by a written document signed by both parties, or by a Change Order issued by the Owner.

DATED: _____

_____ , Owner   _____ , Contractor

By_____   By_____
   (Signature)   (Signature)

                                                     Contractor's License No:
                                                     _____

I have read this Contract and am
aware of the duties which are to
be performed by the Architect.

_____ , Architect

By _____

Proposal and Prime Contract - Short Form - Stipulated Sum - Small Project

§1.31 General Comment

This is an extremely short form of Proposal and Prime Contract that favors the interests of the contractor not so much by what is included as by what is omitted. The typical owner would wish to augment this form of contract by adding many of the alternate prime contract provisions that are designed to protect the interest of the owner and as may be found in **FORM 1-7**.

The reader is cautioned that many states have adopted consumer protection statutes that apply to construction contracts entered into by consumers of housing for the construction or remodeling of homes or dwelling units. A lawyer should be consulted in order to be certain that any such state consumer protection statutes have been properly considered and their requirements fulfilled.

FORM 1-6   Proposal and Prime Contract - Short Form Stipulated Sum

Proposal and Prime Contract - Short Form - Stipulated Sum - Small Project

¶1. This Proposal is made by _____ , ("Contractor") to _____ ("Owner"). When accepted by Owner, it will become a contract for the construction of
_____
_____
_____

¶2. Description of the Work: Contractor will furnish all labor, materials and equipment to complete the project in a good, expeditious, workmanlike and substantial manner. The project will be constructed according to plans and specifications that have been examined and identified by Owner. Owner will locate and point out boundary lines to Contractor, and will provide a boundary survey by a licensed surveyor if requested by the Contractor.

¶3. Payment: Owner will pay Contractor the sum of $_____ in monthly installments proportional to the percentage of completion of the project. At the end of each month, Contractor will submit an application for payment to be paid by Owner by the 10th day of the following month. From each payment, Owner will withhold a 10 per cent retention, which will be paid to Contractor 35 days after the completion of the project. Contractor will deliver mechanic's lien releases to Owner with every application for payment, signed by all persons who could claim mechanic's lien rights on the project, and releasing all claims for work or materials supplied through the end of the month preceding the month covered by the application for payment.

¶4. <u>Changes in the Work:</u> Owner may require Contractor to change the work, and the contract price will be increased or decreased to equitably compensate Contractor or Owner for increases or decreases in the work. Changes will be made in writing, if possible, and the amount of the increase or decrease will be agreed to in advance.

¶5. <u>Damage to the Project and Insurance:</u> If the project is destroyed, or if more than 25 per cent of the value of the project is damaged by fire, flood, or other peril, Owner will pay Contractor the reasonable value, measured by the contract price, of work performed, and the obligations of each party under this Contract shall terminate. If less than 25 per cent of the value of the project is damaged through no fault of Contractor, then Owner will pay Contractor equitable compensation, including reasonable overhead and profit, for the cost of rebuilding. Owner will carry builder's risk insurance to protect the Owner and Contractor against damage to or destruction of the work, and each party waives any right to recover compensation from the other party because of damage to or destruction of the work to the extent that such damage or destruction is covered by valid and collectable insurance. Contractor will maintain comprehensive general liability insurance in force, with policy limits of not less than $500,000, at all times during the progress of the work.

¶6. <u>Cleanup:</u> Upon completion of the work, Contractor will remove debris and surplus material from the project and will leave it in a neat and broom-clean condition.

¶7. <u>Arbitration:</u> Any controversy between the parties arising out of the construction of the project will be decided by arbitration in accordance with the Construction Industry Rules of the American Arbitration Association, and judgment will be entered on the award. Should a party fail to participate in arbitration proceedings after due notice, the arbitrator will decide the controversy in accordance with evidence presented by the party who does participate. The arbitrator will award reasonable attorney's fees to the prevailing party. In the event of court proceedings, the court shall award reasonable attorney's fees to the prevailing party.

DATED: _____

_____, Contractor _____, Owner

By_____   By_____
   (Signature)   (Signature)

Contractor's License No:
_____

Alternate Prime Contract Provisions

§1.32 General Comment

These alternate provisions are designed to fit grammatically and syntactically with the immediately preceding forms found in §§1.29, 1.30, and 1.31. They are arranged in alphabetical order. Many favor the interests of one party over the other.

The reader may be interested in knowing that the word **contract** is derived from the Latin expression *contrahere*, translated to draw together. In fidelity to that etymology, most construction contracts are indeed drawn together from different sources such as the standard forms issued by professional and trade associations, forms used by competitors, and sources such as the present work.

In drawing together a form of contract, the reader is cautioned to be certain that the various provisions harmonize with and complement each other.

FORM 1-7   Alternate Prime Contract Provisions

**Alternate
Prime Contract Provisions
(Provisions are in Alphabetical Order)**

¶1. Acceleration: If Owner requires Contractor to accelerate the work, either by accelerating the schedule or by refusing to grant extensions of time to which Contractor is entitled, then Owner will reimburse Contractor for costs of acceleration, including overtime pay, double shifting, oversized crews, and special equipment.

¶2. Alternates: Owner will notify Contractor as to its selection of alternates in sufficient time to enable Contractor to efficiently schedule the delivery of materials and the scheduling of the work. Alternates will be designated in writing, and the contract price will be appropriately adjusted.

¶3. Alternates: Owner will inform Contractor of its selection of alternates in writing, and the guaranteed maximum cost will be adjusted accordingly.

¶4. Arbitration: If the parties become involved in a dispute arising out of or connected with the work performed under this Contract or the interpretation thereof, the dispute will be settled by arbitration in accordance with the Construction Industry Rules of the American Arbitration Association, and judgment will be entered on the award. The arbitrator will award attorney's fees to the prevailing party. If a party after due notice fails to appear at and participate in the proceedings, the arbitrator will make an award based on evidence presented by the party who does participate.

¶5. Arbitration: In the event of a dispute arising out of or related to the work performed under this Contract, or the interpretation thereof, the dispute will be settled by arbitration under the Construction Industry Rules of the American Arbitration Association, and judgment will be entered on the award. All parties to the construction process, including the architect, the architect's consultants, subcontractors, sub- subcontractors, suppliers, and construction lender are bound by this arbitration agreement if they have signed any document that refers to or incorporates this arbitration agreement. The arbitrator will award reasonable attorney's fees to the prevailing party or parties. If a party after due notice fails to appear at and participate in the proceedings, the arbitrator will make an award based on evidence introduced by the party or parties who do participate. The arbitrator may issue interlocutory awards granting provisional remedies, such as restraining orders, injunctions, writs, and attachments, and the parties may apply to the courts to confirm and enforce such orders without waiving the right to have the dispute determined by arbitration. All parties will make their job records available to all other parties for examination and copying. The arbitrator shall enforce this right to inspect job records.

¶6. Arbitration: Any dispute between the parties to this Contract arising out of or related to the performance of the work or the interpretation of the Contract will be decided by arbitration, and judgment will be entered on the award. A party demanding arbitration shall name its arbitrator, and the other party will name its arbitrator within 10 days thereafter. The two arbitrators will select a neutral arbitrator within 10 days. If the party-appointed arbitrators do not select a neutral arbitrator within 10 days, or if the arbitrator so selected fails to assume the duties of an arbitrator, a neutral arbitrator will be appointed by the court. The award will be effective when it is signed by any two arbitrators. The arbitrators will award reasonable attorney's fees to the prevailing party or parties. This arbitration clause will be binding on the parents, subsidiaries, and principals of the parties. If either party should merge or consolidate, the arbitration clause will bind the surviving corporation.

¶7. Attorney's Fees: In the event of litigation or arbitration, the court or arbitrator will award reasonable attorney's fees to the prevailing party.

¶8. Attorney's Fees: In the event of litigation between the parties, or if a party becomes involved in litigation because of wrongful acts of the other party, the court will award attorney's fees to the prevailing or innocent party. The amount will be such as to compensate the prevailing party for all attorney's fees incurred in good faith.

¶9. Backcharges: Owner may withhold from Contractor 150 per cent of the amount it estimates it would cost to correct any defective work, and may also withhold from Contractor the amount that it reasonably estimates as any damages for delay in the completion of the project.

¶10. Backcharges: Owner may withhold from Contractor amounts it reasonably estimates to be necessary for the correction of defective work and to defray damages for delay in the completion of the project. Owner may backcharge Contractor for any amounts owed by Contractor to Owner on other projects, or amounts arising out of other circumstances.

¶11. Building Permits: Contractor will pay for all building permits that are needed for the performance of the work. Owner will pay all fees, charges, reimbursements, hook-up charges, facility fees, revolving fees, and other exactions of public agencies and utilities for financing the activities of such agencies and utilities.

¶12. Certificate of Construction Lender: Before Contractor commences construction Owner will provide a letter issued by the Construction Lender to the Contractor certifying that funds sufficient to cover the contract price have been set aside in a specific construction loan account to be used for construction of the project.

¶13. Certificates for Payment: The Architect will review Contractor's Applications for Payment, and will issue Certificates for Payment of such amounts as the Architect determines have been earned by the Contractor. Certificates for Payment will be issued by the Architect within three working days after receipt of Applications for Payment and will be paid by Owner in accordance with the Payment Schedule.

¶14. Change Orders: Owner may add to or subtract from the scope of the work, or change the work, by issuing written change orders. Contractor will immediately perform the work as changed, and the contract price will be equitably adjusted. Within 20 days after a change order has been issued, Contractor will present a detailed estimate of the cost of the change, including reasonable overhead and profit, backed up by sub-bids. Based on the estimate, the parties will negotiate the amount by which the contract price is to be adjusted, and agree to that amount in writing. If the parties cannot agree as to the amount of the adjustment, the Contractor will not stop or delay the work, but will proceed with the work as changed, and will supply, along with every Application for Payment, a detailed breakdown of the cost of performing the change. Owner, concurrently with monthly progress payments, will reimburse Contractor for the direct costs of performing the change, without allowance for overhead or profit. The parties will negotiate in good faith to resolve additional amounts owed and the amount owed for overhead and profit, or it will be resolved by arbitration or litigation.

¶15. Change Orders: The Owner may add to, subtract from, or change the scope of the work by written order, and Contractor will promptly comply with such order regardless of any dispute as to pricing, scope of the work, or contract time. For changes in the work, the contract price will be equitably adjusted.

¶16. Change Orders: Owner may issue deductive change orders in writing. Contractor will immediately comply with them, and the contract price will be equitably adjusted. Owner may issue proposed additive change orders, and within 20 days thereafter Contractor will submit a price for the change, supported by a detailed written estimate and sub-bids. The parties will then negotiate the price of the change, which will be incorporated in a written change order signed by both parties. The contract price will be accordingly adjusted. If the parties do not reach agreement as to the price of the change, Owner may order Contractor to proceed with the change, and Contractor will promptly do so. Contractor will not slow or stop the work because of disagreement as to change orders.

¶17. Claims for Damages: If either party should claim damages from the other party for any reason, including delay, interference, default, failure to comply with the requirements of the contract documents, injury, destruction, or otherwise, the party aggrieved shall give the other party a written notice of such claim within 10 days after the circumstances arise that give rise to the claim.

¶18. Claims for Damages: It will be conclusively presumed that each party waives any claim that it might have for damages against the other party unless the party gives written notice to the other party of the circumstances of the claim within 10 days after it obtains knowledge of facts supporting the claim.

¶19. Cleanup: Contractor will continuously clean the jobsite, and keep it in a safe, orderly, neat condition. At the completion of the work, the entire jobsite will be left in a broom-clean condition.

¶20. Commencement of the Work: Contractor will commence work within 10 days after written notice from Owner to do so.

¶21. Commencement of the Work: Within 30 days after the execution of this Contract, Owner will give Contractor written notice to commence work, and Contractor will commence work within 10 days thereafter.

¶22. Commencement of the Work: Contractor will not have any equipment or materials delivered to the jobsite, or commence work of any nature, until Owner has given Contractor written notice to do so. Within three days after written notice, Contractor will commence work on the jobsite, and will continue diligently thereafter, until the completion of the project.

¶23. Compliance With Codes and Laws: In the performance of the work, Contractor will comply with the requirements of all applicable building codes, and other laws and regulations.

¶24. Compliance With Codes and Laws: Contractor represents that it is familiar with and will comply with all applicable building codes and regulations, and other ordinances and laws applicable to the work, and that the contract price includes all costs to be incurred for such compliance.

¶25. Concealed Conditions: If Contractor encounters underground or concealed conditions that were unknown to Contractor before the execution of this Contract and that could not reasonably have been anticipated, the Contract price will be equitably adjusted to compensate Contractor for the cost of dealing with such conditions.

¶26. Concealed Conditions: Contractor has examined the jobsite, the contract documents, and the applicable building codes, laws, and regulations that govern the conduct of the work, and has made such investigation as it deems appropriate. The contract price includes full compensation for all efforts to be expended by Contractor in dealing with any concealed, underground, or unknown conditions.

¶27. Concealed Conditions: If the Contractor encounters rock, underground utilities, debris, ground water, or other concealed and unknown conditions, the Contractor will immediately notify the Owner and will stop work until Contractor and Owner have reached agreement as to equitable compensation to be paid to Contractor for dealing with such conditions.

¶28. Construction Lender: Contractor will execute all documents that are reasonably required by construction lender, including an agreement to the assignment of this Contract in the event of default by the Owner under the construction loan. If the payment schedule attached to the construction loan agreement differs from the payment schedule contained in this Contract, the payment schedule attached to the construction loan agreement shall control. No payment will be made by Owner to Contractor except with the consent of construction lender.

¶29. Construction Lender: The construction lender is _____. Owner represents that the amount set aside for construction under the construction loan agreement is sufficient to pay the contract price, and Owner will increase the amount on deposit with the construction lender sufficiently to pay for any extra work ordered by Owner. Owner authorizes construction lender to make payments directly to Contractor at any time when construction lender is authorized to do so under the construction loan documents.

¶30. Contract Documents are Complementary: The contract documents are complementary, and any item exhibited in one part of the contract documents shall be performed as if required in all parts of the contract documents. In the case of conflict, the higher quality or more stringent requirement will control.

¶31. Contract Documents are Complementary: The contract documents are intended to complement each other, and any item exhibited in one part of the contract documents shall be performed as if required in all parts of the contract documents. Contractor will carefully review the contract documents, and will call Owner's attention to any conflict, omission, or ambiguity, and Owner's decision as to the true meaning of the contract documents shall be final.

¶32. Contract Documents are Complementary: The contract documents are complementary, and will be interpreted so as to give full effect to every contract document requirement. If the Contractor is uncertain as to the true intent and meaning of any provision, it will inform the Architect, whose decision shall be final.

¶33. Contractor's License: Contractor represents that it, and its subcontractors, are properly licensed, and will remain so during the progress of the work.

¶34. Correction of the Work: Contractor will immediately, upon written orders of Owner, correct any defect or deficiency in the work, equipment or materials.

¶35. Cost of Executive Salaries: The cost of the work shall include the cost of Contractor's project manager and Contractor's project engineers and project executives working in the home office, to the extent that they are assigned to the project. Such compensation will be reimbursed based on hours actually devoted to the project.

¶36. Cost Plus a Fixed Fee: In exchange for the full performance of all requirements of the contract documents, Owner will pay Contractor the Cost of the Work plus a fixed fee. The fixed fee will be $_____. For changes in the work ordered by Owner, the amount of the fee and the time for performance of the work will be equitably adjusted.

¶37. Cost Plus a Fixed Fee with Guaranteed Maximum: Owner will pay Contractor the Cost of the Work plus a fixed fee of $_____. The Guaranteed Maximum Cost of the work, including Contractor's fee, shall be $_____. For changes in the work ordered by Owner, the guaranteed maximum cost and the Contractor's fee, and the time for performance of the work, shall be equitably adjusted.

¶38. Cost Plus a Fixed Fee with Guaranteed Maximum: For all work to be performed by Contractor, Owner will pay Contractor the Cost of the Work plus a fixed fee of $_____. The Guaranteed Maximum Cost, including the Cost of the Work and the Contractor's fee, is $_____. For changes in the work ordered by Owner, the cost of the work and the Contractor's fee shall be adjusted as provided in Paragraph _____, "Change Orders."

¶39. Cost Plus a Fixed Fee with Guaranteed Maximum: The compensation to be paid to Contractor by Owner under this Contract will be the Cost of the

Work as defined in Paragraph _____, "Cost of the Work", plus a Fixed Fee of $_____. The Contractor recognizes the relationship of trust and confidence created by this Contract, and will conduct the work efficiently and so as to minimize the Cost of the Work. If the scope of the work is increased by Change Orders under Paragraph _____, "Change Orders", then the Cost of the Work and the Contractor's fee will be adjusted as provided in Paragraph _____, " Change Orders". The Guaranteed Maximum Cost, including Contractor's fee, is $_____.

¶40. Cutting and Patching: Contractor will perform cutting and patching necessary to join the Contractor's work with existing structures and with the work of other contractors so that the finished work will have a smooth, neat, and finished appearance.

¶41. Default: If Owner believes that Contractor has failed to perform any of its obligations under the contract documents, Owner may notify Contractor in writing, and Contractor will immediately correct the default. If Contractor fails to take prompt corrective action, commencing no later than 48 hours after notice of default, and if Contractor shall fail to diligently proceed with corrective action, then Owner may terminate Contractor's right to continue performance, and eject Contractor from the job. Contractor will leave its equipment and materials on the jobsite for use of Owner, and will assign its subcontracts to Owner. Contractor will provide Owner with all information needed by Owner to effect an efficient transition of the work to Owner's staff, or to other contractors selected by Owner.

Owner is under no obligation to eject Contractor from the job, and at the election of Owner, Contractor, although in default, will continue diligently to prosecute the work to completion. Contractor will pay to Owner all damages that may be sustained by Owner because of Contractor's default. Damages shall include compensation for the time and money expended by Owner and its staff occasioned by the default.

¶42. Default: If Contractor fails to carry out any of its obligations under the contract documents, it will pay monetary compensation to Owner to compensate Owner for all damages sustained as a consequence of the default, including compensation for additional administrative time and expense.

¶43. Default: If Contractor fails to diligently and faithfully perform any of its obligations under the contract documents, Owner, upon 48 hours written notice, may eject Contractor from the job, and perform the work itself or have the work performed by others. In such event, Contractor will be entitled to no further payment until the completion of the entire work. The cost of completion by Owner, including reasonable reimbursement for additional executive and administrative expense, shall be charged to Contractor, along with all damages for delay and other damages sustained by Owner as a result of Contractor's default. If the total of such charges and damages, added to the payments made by Owner to Contractor, exceeds the contract price, Contractor will immediately pay the difference to Owner. If the total of such charges, payments, and damages is less than the contract price, the difference will be paid by Owner to Contractor, less a 10 per cent management fee to be retained by Owner.

¶44. Delay in Commencement: If through no fault of Contractor the commencement of work is delayed more than 60 days after the execution of the Contract, Contractor may, by written notice, cancel the Contract.

¶45. Delays and Extensions of Time: If the progress of the work is delayed by inclement weather, flood, earthquake, picketing, boycotts, shortages of materials, or other causes beyond the reasonable control of Contractor, the time for performance of the work shall be extended.

¶46. Delays and Extensions of Time: If Contractor is delayed in the performance of the work by inclement weather, flood, earthquake, strikes, or other force majeure, Contractor will give written notice to Owner within ten days of the commencement of each delay, and Owner will, in writing, extend Contractor's time for the performance of the work.

¶47. Delays and Extensions of Time: Contractor has taken into account inclement weather that is normally likely to occur, and the contract time will not be extended for normal inclement weather. For extraordinary inclement weather, and for earthquake, flood, fire, hostile action, and other causes beyond the control of Contractor, Owner will grant Contractor reasonable extensions of time provided Contractor applies for such extensions of time in writing within ten days after the commencement of each delay. Extensions of time will not be granted for delay to portions of the work unless the delay to such portions of the work necessarily delays the completion date of the entire work. Contractor understands that in the event of delay, Owner will suffer damages, and Contractor will reimburse Owner for all damages suffered by Owner as a result of delay in the occupancy of the project.

¶48. Delays and Extensions of Time: If Contractor is delayed in the progress of the work by inclement weather, fire, flood, picketing, shortage of materials, or other causes that the Architect determines are beyond the reasonable anticipation and control of Contractor, then Contractor will apply, in writing, to Architect for extensions of time. The time for the completion of the Contract will be extended as determined, in writing, by Architect.

¶49. Delays and Extensions of Time: Contractor takes the entire risk of inclement weather, fire, earthquake, and other force majeure. There will be no extensions of time, and Contractor agrees to overcome all obstacles in order to complete the project on schedule. Contractor will provide its own insurance against perils that might cause the Contractor to incur additional expense, and will complete the project in accordance with the schedule.

¶50. Description of the Work: The work to be performed by Contractor (hereafter called "Project"), is described as follows: _____

¶51. Description of the Work: The work is described as follows: _____

¶52. Description of the Work: Contractor will perform, in a first-class workmanlike manner, the following work:

¶53. Description of the Work: Contractor will supply all work, materials, equipment, hoisting, scaffolding, protection, transportation, scheduling, coordination, temporary power, supervision, sales taxes, security and coordination necessary to perform the following work:

¶54. Design by Contractor: This is a design and build Contract. Contractor will employ architects, engineers, and designers needed to design a complete and operating facility in accordance with the Preliminary Drawings, Outline Specifications, and Project Requirements attached hereto. It is understood that Contractor will commence work before the entire design has been completed. Contractor will not, however, commence work on any portion of the project until all necessary building permits have been issued and Owner has approved, in writing, the drawings for that portion of the work.

If Owner changes the Preliminary Drawings or the Outline Specifications or the drawings prepared by Contractor in such a way as to modify the scope of the work reasonably inferable from the contract documents in existence at the time of the execution of this Contract, the cost will be adjusted as provided by Paragraph _____, "Change Orders."

¶55. Destruction of the Work: If more than 50 per cent of the value of the work accomplished by Contractor should be damaged or destroyed by fire, flood, earthquake, or other event that is not the fault of Contractor, or subcontractors of any tier, then the obligations of the parties under this Contract shall terminate when Owner has paid Contractor the value of the work accomplished based on its percentage of completion, and Contractor shall be under no obligation to rebuild.

¶56. Destruction of the Work: In the event the work is damaged or destroyed in whole or in part by fire, earthquake, flood, or other peril, the time for completion of the Contract will be extended, and the Contractor shall rebuild at no expense to Owner. Contractor will carry builder's risk insurance to protect itself and its subcontractors from such risk.

¶57. Destruction of the Work: Owner will provide builder's risk insurance to protect against fire, flood, earthquake, and other perils. In the event of damage to or destruction of the work that is covered by such insurance that is valid and collectible, the time for completion of the work shall be extended, and Contractor shall rebuild the work. The parties will negotiate a fair price to be paid by the Owner to the Contractor for such rebuilding. If the parties cannot agree, Owner will reimburse Contractor for all direct costs, excluding overhead and profit, expended for rebuilding, and the amount of overhead and profit to be paid Contractor will be decided later. Owner, Contractor, and all subcontractors of every tier waive all claims against each other for damage to or destruction of the work to the extent that such damage or destruction is covered by valid and collectible insurance, and the insurance carrier shall not subrogate against Owner, Contractor, or any subcontractor.

¶58. Disputes as to the Scope of the Work: If Owner and Contractor disagree as to the scope of the work required to be performed by Contractor for the contract price, Contractor will promptly and diligently perform the work as required by Owner, and will not slow or stop the progress of the work. Such disputes will be settled after the completion of the work.

¶59. Ejection of Contractor: If Contractor fails to perform any of its obligations under this Contract, Owner may eject Contractor from the job, and have the work performed by others at the expense of Contractor.

¶60. Ejection of Contractor: If Contractor fails to perform any of its obligations under the contract documents, Owner may give Contractor written notice of such default, and Contractor will immediately and diligently correct the default. If Contractor does not commence corrective action within 48 hours after written notice, Owner may eject Contractor from the job and have the work done by others at Contractor's expense.

¶61. Ejection of Contractor: If Contractor fails to perform any of its obligations under the contract documents, Owner may, by written notice, eject Contractor from the job, and have the work finished by others at Contractor's expense. Contractor will reimburse Owner for executive and administrative expense incurred as a result of the default. Contractor will leave its equipment, materials, scaffolding, and tools on the jobsite to be used by Owner in the completion of the work, and will assign its subcontracts to Owner. Contractor will assist Owner in making a smooth and efficient transfer of the work to others.

¶62. Equal Employment Opportunity: Contractor will comply with the affirmative action and equal employment opportunity policies of Owner and with all equal employment opportunity requirements adopted by any governmental authority including the Civil Rights Act of 1964, Executive Orders 11246, 11375 and 11478, and any state fair employment practices act. Contractor will likewise require its subcontractors and suppliers to comply with all equal employment opportunity requirements.

¶63. Exclusions from Cost of the Work: The following items are not included in the cost of the work and shall be paid directly by Owner: architectural and engineering fees, blue prints, utility deposits and connection fees, street and utility assessments, plan check and general building permit fees, costs of environmental impact reports, costs of soil reports, costs of inspection and testing other than as specified in the contract documents to be paid by Contractor, premiums for performance and payment bonds, premiums for fire insurance, all-risk insurance and builder's risk insurance during construction, cost of repair of damage to the project caused by earthquake, loan fees and other financing costs, sales and leasing costs.

¶64. Execution Clause: This Contract is executed and effective this _____ day of _____.

¶65. Execution Clause: This Contract shall not be effective until each party has in its possession a copy signed by the other party. No page of Specifications or sheet of Drawings shall be effective until initialed by both parties.

¶66. Execution Clause: This Contract, when signed by Contractor, may be considered a proposal that will be open for ten days, after which the proposal is automatically terminated.

¶67. Fast Track Contract: This is a fast track contract. Contractor will commence work as soon as drawings and specifications have been prepared for the beginning phases of the work, and will coordinate its operations with the activities of Architect so as to promptly proceed with all portions of the work as drawings are completed. Contractor will constantly advise with Architect as to the stage of progress of the work, and as to phasing of the design and construction process.

¶68. Final Payment: Final payment, less the retention, will be made by Owner to Contractor within ten days after the completion of the project.

¶69. Final Payment: Final payment will be paid by Owner to Contractor within ten days after Architect certifies the Substantial Completion of the project. Architect will determine a reasonable amount to be withheld by Owner as security for correction of defective, and performance of incomplete work. Substantial Completion is defined as the accomplishment of all elements of the work so Owner can enjoy the beneficial occupancy of the entire project. Amounts withheld as security for correction and completion of the work will be paid when the work has been corrected or completed.

¶70. Fringe Benefits: Contractor will pay all fringe benefits incurred under any collective bargaining agreement, and will furnish to Owner and Owner's auditors satisfactory evidence to show these have been paid up to the amount due at the time of any scheduled payment from Owner to Contractor. If Contractor or any subcontractor is listed by the administrative office of any fringe benefit trust as delinquent in payment, whether on this project or other projects, such listing shall be a material breach of this contract. Owner may make payments

62 PRIME CONTRACTS

on behalf of Contractor and deduct the amount from Contractor's earnings. Contractor will indemnify and hold Owner harmless from all fringe benefit claims against Contractor or its subcontractors.

¶71. Guaranteed Maximum Cost: The Guaranteed Maximum Cost of the entire project, including Contractor's fee, is $_____.

¶72. Indemnity: Contractor will indemnify Owner and hold Owner harmless from all claims, liability, loss, expense, and attorney's fees caused by, or alleged by the claimant to be caused by, the fault of Contractor or its subcontractors.

¶73. Indemnity: Contractor will hold Owner and construction lender harmless from, and indemnify them against, all claims, liability, loss and expense including attorney's fees arising out of or connected with the performance of the work. This indemnity agreement will not apply to claims, liabilities or losses proved by final judgment of a court to be the sole fault of Owner or Architect.

¶74. Indemnity: To the fullest extent permitted by law, Contractor will indemnify Owner and hold it harmless from all claims, liability, loss and expense including attorney's fees arising out of or connected with the work if the claim, liability or loss and expense is caused, or alleged by the claimant to be caused, wholly or in part by the fault of Contractor or its subcontractors. Contractor will employ, at Contractor's expense, counsel to be nominated by Owner for consultation and defense under this indemnity agreement.

¶75. Indemnity: Each party will indemnify the other against claims, liability, loss and expense including attorney's fees arising out of the work and caused by the party's fault.

> Comment: Many states have adopted statutes that protect contractors against seemingly unreasonable indemnity clauses. Most such statutes make it unlawful for the owner to require the contractor to indemnify the owner or the architect against the sole negligence or misconduct of the owner or the architect. A lawyer should be consulted as to proper drafting of indemnity provisions so as to comply with statutory requirements.

¶76. Independent Contractor: There is no agency or employment relationship between Owner and Contractor. In performing its duties under this Contract, Contractor acts entirely as an independent contractor.

¶77. Insolvency: If Contractor should become insolvent, Owner may terminate Contractor's right to continue with the work, and employ others to finish the project at Contractor's expense.

¶78. Insolvency: If Owner should become doubtful as to Contractor's solvency or Contractor's financial ability to complete the project, then Contractor will provide Owner's auditors with such information, including financial statements and an examination of the books and records of Contractor, as they deem sufficient to determine Contractor's financial strength. If Owner is of the opinion that Contractor does not have sufficient financial strength to promptly and diligently proceed with the performance of the work, Owner may terminate Contractor's right to perform the work, and may employ others to complete the work at the expense of Contractor.

¶79. Insolvency: If Contractor receives information that leads Contractor to believe that Owner is insolvent, or does not have sufficient financial strength to make progress payments as they come due, Contractor will notify Owner, and Owner will provide Contractor with sufficient financial data, satisfactory to Contractor's auditors, to show that Owner has the resources to pay the contract price. If Owner does not provide such information, Contractor may terminate its performance under this Contract, and Owner will pay to Contractor the reasonable value of its work, as measured by the contract price and the percentage of completion of the work.

¶80. Inspection and Testing: Contractor will make all parts of the work accessible for inspection and testing. Any portion of the work covered up before inspection and testing have taken place will be opened up and replaced at Contractor's expense. Contractor will pay fees for inspection and testing called for by the contract documents. If Owner requires additional inspection and testing, it will be at Owner's expense unless inspection or testing shows a failure by Contractor to comply with the requirements of the contract documents, in which case the expense shall be charged to Contractor.

¶81. Inspection and Testing: Contractor will make all portions of the work available at all times for inspection and testing by Owner's inspectors. Inspection and testing will be at the expense of Owner, except that Contractor will pay for all inspection and testing caused by faulty work, equipment or materials supplied or installed by Contractor.

¶82. Interest: Overdue payments will bear interest at the rate of 1½ per cent per month.

¶83. Interest: Overdue payments will bear interest at the highest rate permitted by law.

¶84. Interest: Overdue payments will bear interest at the legal rate.

¶85. Interest: Overdue payments will bear interest at two points above the prime rate in effect at the time when the payments become due.

¶86. Interest: Overdue payments will bear interest at two points above the prime rate as it may change from time to time during the period when the balance is delinquent.

> Comment: Interest payments of 1½ per cent per month will be held usurious in some states. In other states, usury laws apply only to *loans,* and therefore do not apply to "late payment charges" in a construction contract. The theory here is that usury laws were enacted to prevent an unscrupulous lender from taking advantage of a necessitous debtor in need of money to provide such necessaries as food, clothing and shelter. In some states, courts have upheld late payment charges as liquidated damages.

¶87. Interference by Owner: In the event that Owner interferes with or delays Contractor's work, Contractor will be entitled to an extension of time. An extension of time shall be Contractor's exclusive remedy, and Contractor is not entitled to damages for interference or delay.

¶88. Interference by Owner: If Owner interferes with Contractor's work by not having the jobsite ready, or by excessive change orders, or if Owner or its Contractors or employees about the jobsite impede the progress of the work, Owner will pay reasonable compensation to Contractor for such interference.

¶89. Investigation by Contractor : Contractor has made a complete investigation of the jobsite and its environs, and has carefully reviewed the contract documents, drawings, and specifications, as well as the building codes, zoning laws, and other ordinances, laws and regulations applicable to the project. Owner relies on Contractor's expertise to properly investigate such things.

¶90. Jobsite and Approvals: Owner will at all times make the jobsite available to Contractor, and will secure, before commencement of the work, any change of zone, conditional use permit, variance, or other necessary entitlement. Contractor will provide and pay for building permits.

¶91. Joint Checks: Owner reserves the right to make payments to Contractor in the form of checks payable jointly to Contractor and to any of its subcontractors or suppliers that might have a right to assert a claim of mechanic's lien against Owner's property.

¶92. Liability Insurance: Before commencing work, Contractor and its subcontractors of every tier will deliver to Owner a Certificate of Insurance, signed by hand, showing that Contractor has in force, and Contractor shall have in force, a comprehensive liability insurance policy with broad form property damage, covering liability assumed by contract, completed operations, explosion, collapse, underground hazard, and products liability, affording $1,000,000 in coverage for each occurrence and in the aggregate for property damage, and $1,000,000 in coverage for each occurrence and in the aggregate for bodily injury. The certificate of insurance will name Owner and its subcontractors of every tier as additional insureds, and will provide that Contractor's coverage is primary to any insurance coverage obtained by Owner. The Certificate will provide that the insurance may not be cancelled or modified without 30 days prior written notice to Owner.

¶93. Liability Insurance: Owner has provided a comprehensive general liability insurance policy naming Contractor and its subcontractors of every tier as insured. A copy of the policy is available for inspection by Contractor and subcontractors. The comprehensive liability policy has limits of $1,000,000 for each occurrence and in the aggregate for property damage, and $1,000,000 for each occurrence and in the aggregate for bodily injury. Neither Contractor nor Subcontractors will be reimbursed for premiums for comprehensive general liability insurance.

¶94. Liability Insurance: Each party will provide its own form of comprehensive liability insurance, and Owner, Contractor, and its subcontractors of every tier, will each name the other as additional insureds on their policies. Each will provide to the other a Certificate of Insurance showing the existence of the policy, the fact that the other has been named as an additional insured, and providing that the policy will not be cancelled or modified without 30 days advance written notice to the holder of the Certificate.

¶95. Liquidated Damages: Contractor will pay Owner the sum of $_____ per day for every day of delay in completion of the project.

¶96. Liquidated Damages: Owner will suffer severe damage if it is not able to occupy the project on time. Such damages would be extremely difficult and impractical to precisely compute. The parties therefore agree that, as liquidated damages, and not as a penalty, Contractor will pay Owner the sum of $_____ per day for each day of delay in the completion of the project.

¶97. Liquidated Damages: If the project is finished ahead of schedule, Owner will pay Contractor a bonus of $_____ for each day that the completion of the project is advanced. If the completion of the project is delayed, Owner will suffer damages that would be extremely difficult and impractical to compute, and the parties have therefore bargained for and agree to payment by Contractor to Owner, as liquidated damages, the sum of $_____ for each day of delay in the completion of the project.

¶98. Mechanic's Lien Releases: Before Owner makes any payment to Contractor, Contractor will supply Owner with properly executed mechanic's lien releases, in a form satisfactory to Owner, signed by all persons who could claim mechanic's lien rights on the project, and acknowledging payment for all work, materials and equipment supplied to the project up to ten days before any progress payment is due from Owner to Contractor.

¶99. Mechanic's Lien Rights Waived: Contractor, for itself and on behalf of its subcontractors, waives all mechanic's lien rights that could be asserted against Owner's property.

¶100. Mechanic's Lien Rights Waived: Contractor waives all mechanic's lien rights that it might acquire against Owner's property under this Contract, and will cause its subcontractors of every tier likewise to waive their mechanic's lien rights. Waivers of subcontractors, in form satisfactory to Owner, will be delivered to Owner before the commencement of work by any subcontractor.

¶101. No Damages for Delay: If Contractor is delayed in the progress of the work by any act of Owner, Architect, or Owner's agents or employees, Contractor will be entitled to an extension of the time for completion of the project. An extension of time shall be Contractor's sole remedy, and Contractor will be entitled to no damages for delay.

¶102. No Damages for Delay: If Contractor is delayed in the prosecution of the work by the acts of Owner, or if Owner interferes with Contractor's performance, Contractor will be entitled to an extension of the time for completion of the work, which shall be Contractor's exclusive remedy. Contractor shall not be entitled to damages for delay.

Comment: Courts are reluctant to enforce "no damage for delay" clauses, since their operation is inherently inequitable. It is usually held that the no damage for delay clause will only be enforced as to the types of delays that were reasonably within the contemplation of the parties at the time when the contract was signed, and that such clauses will not protect the owner against the legal consequences of its active interference with the contractor's performance.

¶103. No Oral Agreement: This Contract can be modified only by a written document signed by both parties. No attempt to modify this Contract by an oral agreement shall be recognized.

¶104. No Other Agreement: This contract constitutes the entire agreement of the parties, and no written or oral communication between Owner and Contractor before the time of execution of this contract shall be considered to enlarge, modify, or explain the terms of the contract.

¶105. Notices: Any notice required or permitted by this Contract shall be given by Owner to Contractor in writing at the following address: _____ . Any notice required or permitted by this Contract to be given by Contractor to Owner shall be given in writing at the following address: _____ .

¶106. Offsetting Obligations: Owner may offset against payments required under this Contract any monetary obligation from Contractor to Owner, whether the obligation arises out of this project or otherwise.

> Comment: This clause is merely a restatement of the legal doctrine of setoff, which provides that a defendant in a lawsuit may offset against the plaintiff's claim any claim that the defendant may, in its turn, have against the plaintiff.

¶107. Owner's Right to Stop the Work: In the event that Contractor persistently fails to perform its obligations under the contract documents, Owner may stop the work until Contractor has given Owner satisfactory reasonable assurances that Contractor will properly resume and diligently perform the work.

¶108. Payment No Waiver: Neither the making nor acceptance of any payment will constitute a waiver, by either party, of any prior default by the other party.

¶109. Payment Not Approval: No payment made by Owner to Contractor shall be considered to be evidence of Owner's approval of portions of the work completed by Contractor.

¶110. Payment of Retention: The retention will be paid to Contractor 35 days after recording of the Notice of Completion, provided there are no mechanics' liens of record at that time.

¶111. Payment of Retention: Retention will be paid 35 days after the final completion of the project.

¶112. Payment of Retention: If Owner is satisfied with Contractor's progress when the work is 50 per cent complete, the retention will be reduced from 10 per cent to 5 per cent, and the surplus will be paid by Owner to Contractor at that time. The final retention of 5 per cent will be paid 35 days after completion of the entire project, provided no mechanics' liens have been recorded.

¶113. Payment Schedule: Owner will pay Contractor for work performed during the preceding month on the _____ day of each month.

¶114. Payment Schedule: Owner will pay Contractor on the first day of each month for work completed by Contractor through the 10th day of the preceding month, and on the 15th day of each month for work completed by Contractor through the 25th day of the preceding month.

¶115. Performance and Payment Bond: Contractor will provide a performance bond in the full amount of the contract price to guarantee that Contractor will perform all obligations under this Contract. The bond will incorporate the terms of this Contract, and will provide that no modification, change, or alteration in the terms of the Contract, and no prepayment by Owner to Contractor, will exonerate the bond.

Contractor will also provide a payment bond in the full amount of the contract price to guarantee that Contractor and its subcontractors of every tier will pay all amounts owed to subcontractors, material suppliers, workers, and equipment renters. The identity of surety and forms of bonds are subject to approval by Owner.

¶116. <u>Performance and Payment Bond:</u> If at any time during the progress of the work Owner is in doubt as to the ability of Contractor to properly proceed with and diligently complete the work, Owner may demand that Contractor, within 15 days after the demand, supply Owner with a performance bond and a payment bond. Owner will pay the premium. The performance bond will be in the amount of the value of work remaining to be performed by Contractor, and will provide that no change or modification in the terms of the Contract, and no prepayment by Owner, will exonerate the bond. The paymentbond will guarantee that Contractor and its subcontractors of every tier will pay in full for all work, materials, supplies and equipment furnished to the project.

> Comment: Contractors should be aware that they may experience extreme difficulty in obtaining a performance or payment bond for work already in progress, especially if a dispute has arisen between contractor and owner. Few surety companies would be willing to step into an existing construction dispute by writing a bond to apply to work already in progress.

¶117. <u>Reduction of Retention:</u> When Contractor has completed 50 per cent of the work, Owner will withhold no further retention so that, upon completion of the work, the retention will be 5 per cent.

¶118. <u>Release of Phases:</u> The project is divided into _____ phases. This Contract will only be applicable to Phase I until such time as Owner notifies Contractor, in writing, that a subsequent phase is released for work by Contractor. If Owner is dissatisfied with Contractor's performance, Owner may award subsequent phases of the work to other contractors.

¶119. <u>Requests for Quotes:</u> If Owner contemplates making changes in the work, it will deliver to Contractor a "Request for Quote," describing the items to be added to or subtracted from the Scope of the Work. Contractor will promptly, in writing, and in no event more than ten days after the Request for Quote is received, provide to Owner a price to be added to or subtracted from the contract price for the quoted work. The quote will be supported by a detailed cost breakdown with copies of bids from subcontractors and suppliers.

¶120. <u>Responsibility of Signatory:</u> The person who signs this Contract on behalf of Contractor assumes personal responsibility for the performance of the Contract.

¶121. <u>Responsibility of Signatory:</u> The person who signs this Contract on behalf of Owner assumes personal responsibility for its performance.

¶122. <u>Right to Stop Work:</u> If Owner fails to make any payment when it is due, Contractor may stop the work, and keep the job idle until all amounts earned have been paid.

> Comment: This paragraph states explicitly a proposition that, in the absence of a contrary provision, is inherent in any construction contract: a material breach of contract on one side excuses further performance on the other side. For example, failure of an owner to make a progress payment to a contractor is a material breach of contract and therefore would justify the contractor in stopping work. On the other hand, however, defective or delayed performance by the contractor is itself a material breach of contract and may justify the owner in withholding progress payments. The question becomes: "Which was the first to commit a material breach?"

¶123. <u>Safety:</u> Contractor will implement a safety program for the protection of all persons on the jobsite and in the environs of the work. Contractor will indemnify Owner and hold it harmless against all claims, liability, loss and expense, including attorney's fees, caused by or contributed to by unsafe conduct tolerated by Contractor or its subcontractors of any tier.

¶124. <u>Schedule of Values:</u> Within 15 days after the execution of this Contract, Contractor will supply a Schedule of Values that will break down the contract price into its component parts. The Schedule of Values will accurately reflect the comparative costs of the various portions of the work. If Owner questions the accuracy of any item, Contractor will supply a detailed breakdown of its cost. Percentages of completion will be applied to the Schedule of Values to compute progress payments.

¶125. <u>Scheduling:</u> Within 20 days after the execution of this Contract, Contractor will prepare a project schedule that will show, in graphic form, the Contractor's plan for timely completion of the work. The schedule will show the start and stop dates for the various components of the work, and will separately identify those items that must be completed before other portions of the work can be accomplished. Contractor will exchange scheduling information with subcontractors and suppliers, and will periodically revise the schedule to reflect the actual sequence of events. Contractor will order work, equipment, and materials with sufficient lead time to avoid interruption of the work. Contractor, at its own expense, will employ such overtime as may become necessary for the timely completion of the work.

¶126. Scope of the Work: The contract documents are intended to display a complete and operating facility. All items necessary to produce a complete and operating facility in accordance with trade practice, as displayed on the contract documents, are included within the Scope of the Work.

¶127. Security for Payments: Owner represents that the sum of $_____ has been set aside for construction in the construction loan account held by _____, the construction lender. If the amount set aside for construction in the construction loan account should be reduced, or if it should become insufficient because of change orders, or if for any other reason the amount set aside in the construction loan account is insufficient for completion of the project, Owner shall provide Contractor with adequate security for the balance of payments required for the completion of the work.

¶128. Security for Payments: If it should reasonably appear to Contractor that Owner has insufficient financing or funds for payment of the contract price, Contractor may stop the work until Owner provides Contractor with reasonable security.

¶129. Separate Contracts: Owner will award separate contracts for _____ . Contractor will maintain communication with, and will coordinate its activities with the activities of, separate contractors. In the event of conflict between contractors as to Scope of Work or as to scheduling, Owner will decide such conflict and Owner's decision will be final.

¶130. Separate Contracts: If Owner employs separate contractors to perform any portion or portions of the work, Owner will schedule and coordinate their activities so as to avoid interference with Contractor's work.

¶131. Sharing of Savings: In the event that the sum of the cost of the work plus the Contractor's fee is less than the guaranteed maximum cost, Owner will pay Contractor 50 per cent of the difference.

¶132. Shop Drawings: Contractor will submit shop drawings in ample time to maintain the progress schedule. Shop drawings submitted by subcontractors will be thoroughly reviewed by Contractor, and endorsed "approved" by Contractor before submission to Architect. Shop drawings will be promptly processed by Owner and Architect. The approval of a shop drawing does not authorize any deviation from the requirements of the contract documents unless the deviation is separately marked and clearly identified as a deviation from the contract documents. If Contractor submits shop drawings that deviate from the requirements of the contract documents, Contractor guarantees that such deviation is equivalent in serviceability, quality, and function, and that its useful life and ease of maintenance is at least equal to the item displayed by the contract documents.

¶**133.** Shop Drawings: Contractor and its subcontractors will submit complete and detailed shop drawings in ample time to allow for the orderly progress of the work. Shop drawings will be promptly processed by Owner and Architect. Approval of shop drawings by the Architect or the Owner will not excuse Contractor from strict compliance with the requirements of the contract documents.

¶**134.** Subcontracts: All subcontracts are for the benefit of, and may be enforced directly by, Owner. Except as stated in the preceding sentence, subcontractors have no direct contractual relationship with Owner.

¶**135.** Subcontracts: Subcontracts shall incorporate by reference the provisions of the contract documents that apply to the physical performance of work by subcontractors. This incorporation by reference shall not, however, create any contractual relationship between Owner and subcontractors.

¶**136.** Subcontracts: Contractor will make copies of all subcontracts available for inspection by Owner, including any modifications and change orders applicable to such subcontracts. Contractor will revise any subcontract provision to which Owner has reasonable objection.

¶**137.** Substantial Completion: The work will be deemed substantially complete when Contractor has finished all work called for by the contract documents and the work is ready to be used and occupied by the Owner, even though minor items may remain to be installed, finished, or corrected provided such minor items do not have any appreciable effect on the ability of Owner to utilize the work for its intended purpose.

¶**138.** Substitutions: If Contractor proposes or installs any substitutions for work called for by the contract documents, Contractor guarantees these are equal in quality, function, and appearance to the items called for by the contract documents, and that substitutions are as easily maintained and of equal durability to specified items. Contractor will make no substitutions without the prior written approval of Owner.

¶**139.** Successors and Assigns: Rights and duties under this Contract will not be assigned or delegated without the written consent of the other party. In the event of delegation, the delegator guarantees that the delegates will perform as required by the contract documents. The duties and obligations of this Contract are binding on successors, administrators, executors, and the parent and subsidiary corporations of the parties, and, in the event of consolidation or merger, on the surviving corporation or partnership.

¶**140.** Superintendent: Contractor will employ a competent, experienced full-time superintendent approved by Owner to be present at all times during the progress of the work. On demand of Owner, Contractor will replace the superintendent with a person approved by Owner.

¶141. <u>Survey:</u> Owner will provide Contractor with a boundary survey by a licensed surveyor.

¶142. <u>Survey:</u> Contractor will employ a licensed surveyor to locate the boundaries of the Owner's property, and will accurately locate the buildings and facilities called for by the contract documents.

¶143. <u>Suspension of the Work:</u> In the event of underground obstruction, intervention of public entity, strike, civil unrest, flood, earthquake, or other such event beyond the control of Owner, Owner may suspend the work for a reasonable time. Contractor will promptly resume work when ordered to do so by Owner.

¶144. <u>Taxes:</u> Contractor will pay all sales, use, business license, and other taxes imposed by public authority on account of the work. Owner will pay the taxes imposed on the ownership of real property and fees and exactions of public agencies that are used to finance public improvements.

¶145. <u>Termination for Convenience:</u> At any time by reasonable notice to Contractor, Owner may terminate the accrual of any future obligations under this Contract, and terminate the Contractor's right to continue performance. Such termination will be in consideration of payment to Contractor by Owner of the sum of $1,000.

¶146. <u>Termination for Convenience:</u> Either party may terminate further performance and accrual of further obligations under this Contract for its own convenience, by reasonable written notice, and in consideration of the sum of $1,000 to be paid by the terminating party to the other party.

¶147. <u>Time is of the Essence:</u> Time is of the essence of this Contract.

¶148. <u>Turnkey Project:</u> Contractor will design and build every item, structure, and component necessary to construct a complete and operating facility that is fully ready to be occupied and used by Owner, finished in every respect, with all of its component parts and equipment so installed, arranged, hooked up, energized and balanced that Owner need only turn the key in order to occupy and fully utilize the work.

¶149. <u>Union Contractor:</u> Contractor is, and during hte prosecution of the work will remain, signatory to appropriate collective bargaining agreements with the appropriate unions affiliated with the AFL-CIO and the United Brotherhood of Teamsters.

¶150. <u>Unit Prices:</u> Attached hereto is a "Schedule of Unit Prices" which will apply to compute the compensation to be paid by Owner to Contractor. Unit prices include all compensation to Contractor for labor, materials, subcontracts, equipment, tools, fringes, taxes, overhead, and profit.

¶151. Utilities: Contractor will provide at its own expense all power, water, gas, communication, and other utilities, including temporary utilities, that are used or consumed in the prosecution of the work.

¶152. Value Engineering: Contractor will review all drawings, specifications, and other contract documents with a view to improving quality or serviceability, or reducing price and will propose to Owner appropriate revisions to the contract documents.

¶153. Warranty: Contractor warrants that all materials, facilities, work, and equipment will be free of defects and will operate properly for one year after the substantial completion of the project. Contractor will assemble and transmit to Owner the guarantees and operating instructions of all suppliers, subcontractors, and material suppliers. Contractor will, at its own expense, promptly repair or replace any item found to be defective within one year after substantial completion. This warranty does not excuse Contractor from breaches of contract causing defects that occur or are discovered more than one year after substantial completion of the work.

¶154. Withdrawal of Proposal: This Contract, when signed by Contractor, is a proposal that may be withdrawn by Contractor at any time before Owner has delivered a fully executed copy of the Contract to Contractor.

¶155. Workers' Compensation Insurance: Contractor will maintain in force standard form workers' compensation and employer's liability insurance at all times during the performance of the work.

AIA Document A107 - Abbreviated Form of Agreement between Owner and Contractor

§1.33 General Comment

AIA Document A107 is a lump sum contract form that includes an arbitration clause, but no attorney's fee clause. It includes an abbreviated form of general conditions. Its provisions are similar to those of the 1987 Form of General Conditions (AIA) Document A201), but greatly abbreviated and simplified. The provisions for change orders and extensions of time are much abbreviated, and the complicated claims procedure that many find objectionable is omitted.

FORM 1-8 Supplementary General Conditions - AIA Document A107 [Favors Interests of Contractor] (with Comments)

Document A107 "Abbreviated Form of Agreement Between Owner and Contractor" 1987 Edition, is amended as follows:

¶1. **First:** Sub-paragraph 4.2. The following language is added at the end of Sub-paragraph 4.2:

> Overdue payments shall bear interest at the rate of 1½ per cent above the prime rate of interest customarily charged by commercial banks in the county where the Project is located, the rate of interest to vary from time to time according to changes in the prime rate.

¶2. **Second:** Sub-paragraph 9.5. The following sentence is added to Sub-paragraph 9.5:

> Owner shall pay hookup fees, user fees, school fees, and fees that are levied to reimburse or pay for the cost of public utilities, and infrastructure and fees that are levied to defray the costs imposed on public agencies to provide services to the persons who will utilize or inhabit the Project. Contractor shall pay plan check fees.

Comment: Many public agencies impose heavy fees on construction which may be collected as part of the permit process. These fees are based on the theory that the cost to public agencies of providing infrastructure or services to construction projects or their users should be paid for by the persons who cause the project to be built. Such fees and exactions have more in common with property taxes than building permit fees, and should be paid directly by the owner.

¶3. **Third:** Sub-paragraph 9.11. Sub-paragraph 9.11 is amended to read as follows:

> **9.11** The Contractor shall pay all royalties and license fees, and shall defend and hold the Owner harmless from suits or claims for infringement of patent rights arising out of the use of products that are selected by Contractor; Owner shall defend and hold Contractor harmless from suits or claims for infringement of patent rights arising out of the use of products selected by Owner or Architect.

¶4. **Fourth:** Sub-paragraph 9.12. Sub-paragraph 9.12 is amended to read as follows:

> **9.12** Contractor shall indemnify and hold harmless Owner and its agents and employees from and against claims, damages, losses and expenses including but not limited to attorney's fees arising out of or resulting from the performance of the Work, provided that such claim, damage, loss or expense is attributable to bodily injury or death, or to injury to or destruction of tangible property (other than the Work itself) including loss of use resulting therefrom, but only to the extent caused in whole or in part by negligent acts or omissions of the Contractor, or a subcontractor or the agents or employees of either of them, regardless of whether or not such claim, damage, loss or expense is caused in part by Owner or its agents or employees.

Comment: If the contractor carries adequate liability insurance, this indemnity agreement should be covered by the contractor's insurance policy and actually performed by the contractor's insurance carrier. By adopting this language, the contractor is not required to provide indemnity to the architect or its consultants.

¶5. **Fifth:** Sub-paragraph 9.12.2. Sub-paragraph 9.12.2 is annulled.

Comment: Sub-paragraph 9.12.2 should be annulled only if Sub-paragraph 9.12 is modified as proposed above. Otherwise, Sub-paragraph 9.12.2 should be retained.

¶6. **Sixth:** Sub-paragraph 10.8. Sub-paragraph 10.8 is amended to read as follows:

> **10.8** All disputes arising out of or related to this Contract or the interpretation or performance thereof shall be resolved by arbitration under the Rules of the American Arbitration Association, and judgment may be entered on the award. The Architect and its consultants, subcontractors, and any other person who has signed a document that incorporates this arbitration clause or these General Conditions and who is involved in any such dispute shall, upon the demand of Contractor or Owner, become a party to the arbitration proceedings and be bound by the award. The arbitrator is authorized to decide all disputes between all parties to the arbitration agreement that arise out of or are related to the Work or its performance. The arbitrator shall award reasonable attorney's fees and costs to the prevailing party or parties. If any party after due notice fails to appear at and participate in the arbitration proceedings, the arbitrator shall make an award with reference to such party based on evidence produced by the party or parties who do appear and participate. The arbitrator may grant provisional and interlocutory relief including but not limited to injunctions, restraining orders, and appointment of receivers.

Comment: This arbitration clause permits the architect and its consultants and subcontractors and others concerned with the performance of the project to be joined in arbitration proceedings between contractor and owner. In the event of a dispute that involves a subcontractor's work, it is advantageous to the contractor if the subcontractor may be joined in the proceedings. If the dispute involves work performed by the architect or its consultants, it is advantageous both to the contractor and the owner to be able to join them in the proceedings. This avoids the need for separate litigation or arbitration with subcontractors, or the architect and its consultants, and thereby avoids the possibility of inconsistent judgments or awards.

This arbitration clause makes it impossible for a party to obstruct the proceedings by refusing to participate. Without a provision that an arbitration award may be granted *ex parte,* the parties would need to obtain a court order before the arbitrators would be authorized to proceed in the absence of a party.

The presence of an attorney's fee clause in the arbitration agreement puts some pressure on the parties to negotiate an equitable resolution to claims and disputes.

¶7. **Seventh:** Sub-paragraph 13.4. Sub-paragraph 13.4 is added to read as follows:

13.4 If Contractor and Owner do not reach agreement as to the price of work required by a Change Order or Construction Change Directive, Owner will reimburse Contractor, concurrently with each progress payment, for the actual cost of labor, materials, equipment rental and subcontract work paid or incurred by Contractor in the performance of the Change Order or the Construction Change Directive, and the amount to be paid for overhead and profit will be resolved by negotiation or arbitration. Contractor will supply copies of all payroll documents, bills, invoices, and other backup reasonably required to authenticate the cost of such work, and Owner shall have the right to audit and examine Contractor's books and records with reference thereto.

¶8. **Eighth:** Sub-paragraph 14.3. The following sentence is added to Sub-paragraph 14.3:

Contractor shall be entitled to an extension of time for delays that are beyond the reasonable control of Contractor.

¶9. **Ninth:** Sub-paragraph 15.5. Sub-paragraph 15.5 is annulled.

¶10. **Tenth:** Sub-paragraph 17.7. Sub-paragraph 17.7 is added to read as follows:

17.7 In the event of damage to or destruction of the Work by fire or other peril, whether insured or not, the Owner will reimburse the Contractor, from the costs from the proceeds of insurance or otherwise, for the cost of rebuilding and the contract price will be equitably adjusted so as to provide the Contractor with equitable compensation for the cost of rebuilding with reasonable overhead and profit.

Comment: In many instances the proceeds of insurance will be taken by the mortgagee, or will otherwise be inadequate to compensate the contractor and its subcontractors for the cost of rebuilding. Some perils, such as earthquake or flood, may not be covered by the owner's policy. In any such case, the contractor needs either to procure its own insurance or to provide in the contract for equitable compensation for the cost of rebuilding.

¶11. **Eleventh:** Sub-paragraph 19.1. The following sentence is added to Sub-paragraph 19.1:

This provision shall not be interpreted so as to reduce the arbitration rights and obligations of the parties.

Comment: A choice of law provision such as the one included in the printed form can, in unusual circumstances, be interpreted by courts to impair arbitration rights.

¶12. **Twelfth:** Sub-paragraph 19.3. Sub-paragraph 19.3 is added to read as follows:

19.3 In the event of litigation between Owner and Contractor arising out of this Contract or the performance thereof, the court shall award reasonable attorney's fees and costs to the prevailing party.

¶13. **Thirteenth:** Sub-paragraph 20.2. The following is added to Sub-paragraph 20.2:

Before the Owner terminates the Contract, it will give seven days written notice to the Contractor of the causes for termination and of its intention to terminate the Contract for such causes. If the Contractor commences substantial and effective remedial efforts within seven days after such notice is given, then the seven day notice of termination shall be annulled.

FORM 1-9 Supplementary General Conditions - AIA Document A107 [Favors Interests of Owner] (with Comments)

Document A107 "Abbreviated Form of Agreement Between Owner and Contractor" 1987 Edition, is amended as follows:

¶1. <u>First:</u>   Sub-paragraph 2.2. Add the following language at the end of Sub-paragraph 2.2:

> It is agreed that any delay in the completion of the Project would cause the Owner to suffer damages, but that those damages would be extremely difficult and impracticable to precisely compute, and therefore the parties have agreed that a reasonable measure of such damages is the sum of $_____ per calendar day, which sum the Contractor will pay to the Owner for each day of delay in the substantial completion of the Project that is not excused by an extension of time granted by the Owner under the provisions of this Contract. This amount is estimated by Owner and Contractor to be a reasonable approximation of the Owner's actual damages, and is agreed to as liquidated damages and not as a penalty.

¶2. <u>Second:</u>   Sub-paragraph 7.1. The following sentence is added to the end of Sub-paragraph 7.1:

> In the event of ambiguity, inconsistency, or conflict in the contract documents, the conflict, ambiguity or inconsistency will be resolved by requiring the Contractor to provide items, materials, facilities or equipment of higher quality or superior performance rather than those of lower quality or inferior performance.

¶3. <u>Third:</u>   Sub-paragraph 8.1. The following sentence is added to the end of Sub-paragraph 8.1:

> Owner shall furnish a boundary survey only, and Contractor shall survey and lay out building lines, and shall properly locate the various elements of the Project as required by the Contract Documents.

¶4. <u>Fourth:</u>   Sub-paragraph 9.8. The following is added at the end of Sub-paragraph 9.8:

> If the Contractor proposes substitutions which are accepted by the Owner, the Contractor guarantees that such substitute methods, materials or equipment will meet all of the requirements of the Contract Documents and will perform in a manner in every respect equal to, or superior to, methods, materials or equipment specified.

¶5. **Fifth:** Sub-paragraph 9.12. The following language is added at the end of Sub-paragraph 9.12:

> This indemnity agreement shall include claims, damages, losses and expense attributable to wrongful acts, intentional misconduct, and breaches of contract by Contractor, a Subcontractor or anyone directly or indirectly employed by either of them.

¶6. **Sixth:** Sub-paragraph 10.8. Sub-paragraph 10.8, relating to arbitration, is annulled.

Comment: Although arbitration is a favored method of resolving construction industry disputes, owners may be advised to avoid arbitration according to their particular views of the construction process and their opinions as to types of dispute likely to arise. One problem with the arbitration clause included in AIA Document A107 is the fact that it does not permit the owner to join the architect or the architect's consultants in arbitration proceedings without their written consent. This leaves the owner in a precarious position if a dispute arises in which the contractor or the owner alleges that the architect is responsible for damages sustained by the contractor: the owner may be required by an arbitration award to pay the contractor's damages caused by the architect, but may be required to resort to a separate lawsuit to obtain indemnity from the architect or its consultants. The lawsuit might result in a judgment inconsistent with the arbitration award. Therefore, if arbitration is to be employed as a method of dispute resolution, the owner should insist that the architect and its consultants agree to join in the arbitration if a claim by the contractor involves claims against the architect or its consultants. This provision should then be supported by a complementary provision in the contract between the owner and the architect.

Among the many differences between arbitration and litigation, perhaps the most important is that arbitration is usually faster and much less subject to appeal. Whether or not a party wants a swift decision depends on the type of dispute anticipated. If the owner anticipates that the most likely type of dispute would be a breach of contract or breach of warranty claim against the contractor, that would motivate the owner to opt for arbitration. If on the other hand the most likely type of dispute would be a contractor's claim against the owner for extra work or delay, the owner would perhaps prefer to have the matter resolved in court. For a full discussion see J Acret, *Construction Arbitration Handbook* (Shepards/McGraw Hill, Inc 1985).

¶7. **Seventh:** Sub-paragraph 13.4. Sub-paragraph 13.4 is added to read as follows:

13.4 Contractor agrees to accept the contract sum for all work, materials, equipment and services provided under the Contract, and under no circumstances shall Contractor be entitled to additional compensation in the absence of a Change Order or a Construction Change Directive signed by Owner and Architect. The only person authorized to sign a Change Order or a Construction Change Directive on behalf of the Owner is _____. No other person is authorized to order any change in the Work or authorize any extra compensation to be paid to the Contractor.

¶8. **Eighth:**   Sub-paragraph 13.5. Sub-paragraph 13.5 is added to read as follows:

13.5 In the event of any dispute as to the scope of the work, Change Orders, Construction Change Directives, or in the event of claims by the Contractor for additional compensation because of extra work, delay, interference, or from any other cause, the Contractor agrees that it will not slow or stop the work, but will continue the work in accordance with written instructions from Owner and the dispute will be resolved later.

¶9. **Ninth:**   Sub-paragraph 14.3. Sub-paragraph 14.3 is added to read as follows:

14.3 In the event of delay, inefficiency, impact, lack of productivity caused by Owner or Architect, Contractor shall not be entitled to claim damages or any other form of monetary compensation, but the time for performance of the Contract will be extended as provided in Sub-paragraph 14.3.

¶10. **Tenth:**   Sub-paragraph 16.2. Sub-paragraph 16.2 is annulled.

¶11. **Eleventh:**   Sub-paragraph 17.1. Sub-paragraph 17.1 is amended by adding the following language at the end:

Certificates of insurance will be accompanied by copies of endorsements to the insurance policies, and both the certificates and the endorsements shall name the Owner as an additional insured on the Contractor's liability insurance policies and shall provide that there will be no cancellation or reduction in coverage without 30 days advance written notice by the insurance carrier to the Owner.

¶12. **Twelfth:**   Sub-paragraph 17.2. Sub-paragraph 17.2 is annulled.

¶13. **Thirteenth:**   Sub-paragraph 17.7. Sub-paragraph 17.7 is added to read as follows:

17.7 Contractor recognizes that the property insurance purchased by Owner under this Contract may be inadequate to fully protect the interests of Contractor and Subcontractors in the Project, both because the insurance proceeds may be taken by the mortgagee of the property and because the insurance may not cover damage or loss arising from certain perils, such as earthquake, flood, or damage to the work caused by Contractor or Subcontractors. Contractor and its Subcontractors shall therefore purchase such property insurance as they deem necessary or desirable to protect their interests in the work. In the event of damage to or destruction of the work while it is under construction, Contractor and Subcontractors will rebuild at no expense to Owner, and the compensation of Contractor and Subcontractors for such rebuilding shall be paid, if at all, by such insurance procured by Contractor and Subcontractors to the extent that rebuilding is not paid for by insurance supplied by Owner under this Paragraph.

Comment: As a general rule, in the absence of any other provision, a contractor is required to fulfill its contractual obligation to build the project regardless of whether the project is damaged or destroyed by fire or other casualty. Rebuilding is not excused by the legal doctrine of impossibility, since rebuilding is possible (although expensive). The rule of law, therefore, is that if the contractor intended to be excused from performance by damage to or destruction of the project, such a provision would have been included in the contract.

Design-Build Contract   2

Introduction to Design-Build Concepts

§2.01   The Design-Build Concept
§2.02   The Evolution of the Design-Build Contract
§2.03   Disadvantages of Design-Build From the Owners Point of View
§2.04   Advantages of Design-Build From the Owners Point of View
§2.05   The Design-Build Process
§2.06   Some Practical Attributes of Design-Build

AGC Document No. 415 - Design-Build Agreement - Lump Sum

§2.07   General Comment
   FORM 2-1   AGC Document No. 415 - Standard Form of Design-Build Agreement and General Conditions between Owner and Contractor (Where the Basis of Compensation Is a Lump Sum) (1986)
   FORM 2-2   Supplementary General Conditions [Favors Interests of Owner] (with Comments)

AGC Document No. 410 - Design-Build Agreement - Guaranteed Maximum

§2.08   General Comment
   FORM 2-3   AGC Document No. 410 - Standard Form of Design-Build Agreement and General Conditions between Owner and Contractor (Provides a Guaranteed Maximum Price) (1982)
   FORM 2-4   Supplementary General Conditions [Favors Interests of Owner] (with Comments)
§2.09   Clarifications to AGC Documents Nos. 410 and 415
   FORM 2-5   Letter of Intent to Award Design-Build Contract (with Comment)

Introduction to Design-Build Concepts

§2.01 The Design-Build Concept

It is conventional for the owner to employ an architect or an engineer to prepare drawings, specifications, and other contract documents, and then to employ a contractor to perform the work as it is laid out and defined by those documents. This triangular relationship, however, is not eternal. The owner, by electing to go "design-build", can convert the triangle into a straight line between owner and contractor.

In design-build, the contractor, and not the owner, employs the architect or engineer or both. In a variation, the contractor may employ an architect who in turn employs an engineer, or a number of engineers, as consultants to handle various responsibilities; for example, structural engineering, mechanical engineering, soils investigations, soils reports, and like responsibilities.

Variations are of course possible. For example, an owner may employ surveyors and soils engineers, and at the same time enter into a design-build contract with a prime contractor who in turn may employ the project architect.

The design-build contract is a product of evolution and seems destined to become more popular. Many architects view the concept askance because it interferes with, or may virtually destroy, the traditional relationship between architect and client. The client, rather than being the owner, becomes the contractor. The design-build relationship may also be seen by an architect to unfavorably revise the traditional pecking order in which the contractor is seen in a position inferior to the owner and architect, and indeed, the architect's position may be seen as superior to that of the owner and contractor both. Most architects did not go to school to *work for contractors.*

To pass upon such matters is beyond the competence or courage of this humble author. It must be said, nevertheless, that the best way for an owner to prevent construction disputes from arising, the best way to avoid litigation or arbitration, or, being in it, to win, is to employ the design-build pattern.

§2.02 The Evolution of the Design-Build Contract

The word *architect* descends from Greek and Latin roots. *Tectere* means *to build.* The prefix *archi-* occurs in architype, archangel, and arch-enemy to give a few examples, and means *the first* or *the greatest.* Thus, architect once meant *master builder.* In a few cases, the architect still fulfills the function of master builder, but more commonly the architect now serves as a *master designer* and the contractor does the building. This evolution has been accelerated by legal developments. Before the second world war, architects were seldom accused of malpractice. Since then, malpractice claims have become very common. Therefore, the cost of malpractice insurance has multiplied to such an extent that many architects and engineers *go bare,* which is to say, they forego insurance against claims of errors, omissions, and malpractice.

As malpractice claims became more common and expensive, the errors and omissions insurance carriers became influential in giving advice as to methods for avoiding liability and correctly pointed out that much liability could be avoided by minimizing jobsite activity. Therefore, architects and engineers who once performed work, and then supervised it, reduced their activities to inspection and, finally, mere observation. Inspection and testing laboratories have partly filled the vacuum this created, and contractors and construction managers have occupied some of the territory thus made vacant by architects and engineers.

From the point of view of the architect observing this history, although much was gained, much was lost. By reducing jobsite activity, architects and engineers lost the opportunity to prevent problems from arising and to have the opportunity to correct some problems at an early stage.

Looking at it from an owner's point of view, much was lost and nothing was gained. As architects and engineers devoted more energy to design and less to supervision and inspection, the owner lost the protection afforded by the architect's expert participation in the construction process without gaining anything (or perhaps losing something) on the design side. It is probably true that design suffers when architects stay off the jobsite, because it becomes more difficult to learn from, or even learn about, mistakes.

Therefore, as architects have backed away from the jobsite owners have had less to lose by adopting design-build. Nevertheless, design-build has its disadvantages.

§2.03 Disadvantages of Design-Build From the Owners Point of View

Under the conventional pattern of construction, the architect is employed by the owner and is therefore bound by its duty as well as its financial interests to protect the interests of the owner.

When a contractor works under a fixed price or guaranteed maximum price contract, the contractor has a vital interest in increasing its profit or reducing its loss by operating efficiently and in a cost-effective manner. Opportunities to reduce costs by reducing the quality of materials, equipment, or workmanship arise daily and hourly. If a contractor is inclined to take advantage of such opportunities, the owner who is unsophisticated in matters of construction needs the protection of an architect.

By definition, an architect employed by the owner is a person expert in construction, who, both by contractual duty and natural inclination, will protect the owner against shoddy or inferior construction. By going *db*, or *design-build*, the owner loses this protection.

As has been discussed, the level of protection afforded by the architect in the field is not what it once was, but is still significant.

§2.04 Advantages of Design-Build From the Owner's Point of View

A persistent feature of construction is frequent litigation and arbitration. They are dreadfully costly in time and money, and they drain one's energy and spirits.

When an owner employs an architect to prepare drawings and specifications, and then supplies those drawings and specifications to a contractor, the owner takes legal responsibility for the adequacy of those contract documents. Therefore, in the event of a dispute between owner and contractor, the point that is almost invariably drawn into issue is the adequacy of the drawings and specifications.

Thus, disputes often arise because the contractor misunderstands or is misled by the drawings. Extra work and expense may occur because of inadequate coordination of the various elements of the drawings so that, for example, a duct and a beam are required to occupy the same space in defiance of a fundamental law of physics.

When the owner employs an architect as its agent to supervise, inspect, or observe construction, to process certificates for payment and change orders, and to respond to requests for information from the contractor and subcontractors, the owner assumes legal responsibility for the proper performance of all of these jobsite functions. Many construction disputes arise as to the proper performance of just such duties.

If an owner is unsophisticated and not knowledgeable about the customs, traditions, procedures, vocabulary, and protocols of the construction industry, it is in no position to mediate between contractor and architect, or even to be able to effectively evaluate the contractor's allegations of architectural errors, omissions, and misconduct. Therefore, by employing an architect, the owner establishes relationships that are legally disadvantageous from the point of view of a construction dispute.

On the other hand, if the owner is in a position to require the contractor to employ the architect, everything is changed. *The contractor loses the legal power to hold the owner responsible for errors, real or imagined, made by or alleged against the architect.* The contractor becomes responsible for the adequacy of the drawings and specifications, for proper jobsite supervision, inspection, and observation, and for the processing of change orders and RFIs (requests for information). The owner, therefore, occupies the most legally advantageous possible position: that of a person unsophisticated in the ways of construction. It pays an agreed price for a well-conceived, well-designed, properly-constructed, and fully-functioning work of improvement. When something goes wrong, it does not fall to the owner to decide whether the fault lies with architect or contractor. Whether the fault be with the design or the execution, or partly with both, the legal responsibility belongs to the contractor.

§2.05 The Design-Build Process

A particular owner may or may not have a clear concept of the type of structure or improvement it wants and needs. When a railroad wants to build a grade crossing, it probably has an excellent and highly detailed concept of both the physical and the construction requirements to be attained. On the other hand, when a county needs a jail, or a philharmonic association decides to build a symphony hall, there is a good chance, at the outset at least, that nobody has any fixed idea at all as to the physical properties, layout, materials, and equipment to be supplied. If a furniture company wants to build a warehouse, it may have an excellent idea as to the design, appearance, square footage, volume, and appearance of the structure. Therefore, a warehouse is probably more appropriate as a candidate for design-build than a symphony hall or a prison.

Even a prospective owner of a symphony hall or a prison, however, by diligent study and employment of the appropriate consultants, can develop a well-defined program to include such things as the footprint of the building, the floor plan, layout, types of equipment, power requirements, finishes, textures, materials, structural philosophy, type of roof, type of ceiling, and a myriad of details that define the appearance, function, and quality of the final product. Such elements may then be communicated to the design-build contractor in the form of a program to be attained. The design-build contractor then employs architects and engineers who are properly licensed under local law to perform their functions, and, step by step, creates contract documents that must meet the final approval of the owner before the actual commencement of construction.

The owner of course may, and probably should, employ its own consultants: architects and engineers committed only to protecting the interests of the owner; e.g., reviewing the contract documents as they emerge. When the contract documents meet the approval of the owner, a price is established, the contract is signed, and construction begins.

§2.06 Some Practical Attributes of Design-Build

From the owner's point of view, it may appear that there is the danger of a design-build contractor and an architect making a devil's compact to cheapen the job without passing the savings on to the owner. It is certain that cooperation and early exchange of information between contractor, subcontractors, architect, and engineer will increase efficiency and reduce cost. This is because no architect or engineer is likely to be as well acquainted with the fine points of a particular trade as is the subcontractor who makes a living by following that trade from day to day. The contractor and the subcontractor, cooperating with the architect, are in a good position to recommend the adoption of cost-effective procedures, systems, and materials, and avoid the inclusion of elements or systems that look good on paper but impair construction efficiency. Therefore, the opportunity exists for the owner to realize cost savings through design efficiency.

Problems that do come up during construction may be worked out in the field very easily if the architect is in the control of the contractor; if the architect is not performing the contractor can employ another one. When the architect is employed by the owner, however, an adversarial relationship sometimes develops which increases cost, and raises the question of who should bear that increased cost.

AGC Document No. 415 - Design-Build Agreement - Lump Sum

§2.07 General Comment

The Associated General Contractors of America publishes a standard form of Design-Build Agreement between Owner and Contractor, which includes General Conditions. Under this document, the basis of compensation is a lump sum. Please see **§2.09** for clarification, and **FORM 2-5** for a letter of intent.

FORM 2-1 AGC Document No. 415 - Standard Form of Design-Build Agreement and General Conditions between Owner and Contractor (Where the Basis of Compensation is a Lump Sum) (1986)

AIA copyrighted material has been reproduced with the permission of the American Institute of Architects under license number 90153. Permission expires December 31, 1991.

This document is intended for use as a "consumable" (consumables are further defined by Senate Report 94-473 on the Copyright Act of 1976). This document is not intended to be used as "model language" (language taken from an existing document and incorporated, without attribution, into a newly-created document). Rather, it is a standard form which is intended to be modified by appending separate amendment sheets and/or fill in provided blank spaces.

§2.07 AGC DOCUMENT NO. 415   89

THE ASSOCIATED GENERAL CONTRACTORS

STANDARD FORM OF DESIGN-BUILD AGREEMENT AND GENERAL CONDITIONS BETWEEN OWNER AND CONTRACTOR

(WHERE THE BASIS OF COMPENSATION IS A LUMP SUM)

This Document has important legal and insurance consequences; consultation with an attorney and insurance consultants and carriers is encouraged with respect to its completion or modification.

AGREEMENT

Made this   day of   in the year of Nineteen Hundred

and   BETWEEN   the Owner, and

the Contractor.

For services in connection with the following described Project: (Include complete Project location and scope)

The Owner and the Contractor agree as set forth below:

Certain provisions of this document have been derived, with modifications, from the following documents published by The American Institute of Architects: AIA Document A111, Owner-Contractor Agreement, © 1976; AIA Document A201, General Conditions, ©1976 by The American Institute of Architects. Usage made of AIA language, with the permission of AIA, does not imply AIA endorsement or approval of this document. Further reproduction of copyrighted AIA materials without separate written permission from AIA is prohibited.

AGC DOCUMENT NO. 415 • STANDARD FORM OF DESIGN-BUILD AGREEMENT AND GENERAL CONDITIONS BETWEEN OWNER AND CONTRACTOR (LUMP SUM) • FEBRUARY 1986
© 1986 Associated General Contractors of America

DESIGN-BUILD CONTRACT

INDEX

ARTICLE		PAGE
1	The Construction Team and Extent of Agreement	1
2	Contractor's Responsibilities	1
3	Owner's Responsibilities	3
4	Subcontracts	4
5	Contract Time Schedule	4
6	Lump Sum Price	4
7	Changes in the Project	4
8	Payments to the Contractor	6
9	Insurance, Indemnity and Waiver of Subrogation	7
10	Termination of the Agreement and Owner's Right to Perform Contractor's Obligations	9
11	Assignment and Governing Law	10
12	Miscellaneous Provisions	10
13	Arbitration	11

AGC DOCUMENT NO. 415 • STANDARD FORM OF DESIGN-BUILD AGREEMENT AND GENERAL CONDITIONS BETWEEN OWNER AND CONTRACTOR (LUMP SUM) • FEBRUARY 1986
©1986 Associated General Contractors of America

ARTICLE 1

The Construction Team and Extent of Agreement

1.1 *THE CONSTRUCTION TEAM:* The Contractor, the Owner, and the Architect/Engineer called the "Construction Team" shall work from the beginning of design through construction completion. The services of _____ as the Architect/Engineer will be furnished by the Contractor pursuant to an agreement between the Contractor and the Architect/Engineer.

1.2 *EXTENT OF AGREEMENT:* This Agreement represents the entire agreement between the Owner and the Contractor and supersedes all prior negotiations, representations or agreements. When the Drawings and Specifications are complete, they shall be identified by amendment to this Agreement. This Agreement shall not be superseded by any provisions of the documents for construction and may be amended only by written instrument signed by both Owner and Contractor.

1.3 *DEFINITIONS:* The Project is the total construction to be designed and constructed of which the Work is a part. The Work comprises the completed construction required by the Drawings and Specifications. The term day shall mean calendar day unless otherwise specifically designated.

ARTICLE 2

Contractor's Responsibilities

2.1 Contractor's Services

2.1.1 The Contractor shall be responsible for furnishing the Design and for the Construction of the Project. The Contractor shall develop a design and construction phase schedule and the Owner shall be responsible for prompt decisions and approvals so as to maintain the approved schedule. Any design, engineering, architectural, or other professional service required to be performed under this Agreement shall be performed by duly licensed personnel.

2.1.2 The Contractor shall prepare and the Owner approve a design phase schedule as follows: PHASE 1: Based upon the Owner's Project requirements, schematic Design Studies will be prepared by the Architect/Engineer. These Schematics are for the purpose of assisting the Owner in determining the feasibility of the project. PHASE 2: Upon approval of Schematic Designs and authorization from the Owner to proceed, the Architect/Engineer shall prepare Design Development documents to fix the size and character of the Project as to structural, mechanical and electrical systems, materials and other appropriate essential items in the Project. These Development Documents are the basis for the design and construction of the project. PHASE 3: From approved Design Development Documents the Architect/Engineer will prepare working Drawings and Specifications setting forth in detail the requirements for the construction of the Project, and based upon codes, laws or regulations which have been enacted at the time of their preparation.

2.1.3 The Contractor, the Architect/Engineer and the Owner will work closely together to monitor the design in accordance with prior approvals so as to ensure that the Project can be constructed within the Lump Sum as defined in Article 6. As these working Drawings and Specifications are being completed, the Contractor will keep the Owner advised of the effects of any Owner requested changes on the Contract Time Schedule and/or the Lump Sum. *Construction of the Project shall be in accordance with these Drawings and Specifications as approved by the Owner. The Drawings and Specifications shall remain the property of the Contractor and are not to be used by the Owner on this or other projects without the written consent of the Contractor.*

2.1.4 After the completion of any Phase as set forth in Article 2.1.2, if the Project is no longer feasible from the standpoint of the Owner, the Owner may terminate this Agreement and pay the Contractor pursuant to Article 10.3.1.

2.1.5 The Contractor will assist the Owner in securing permits necessary for the construction of the Project.

92 DESIGN-BUILD CONTRACT

2.2 Responsibilities With Respect to Construction

2.2.1 The Contractor will provide all construction supervision, inspection, labor, materials, tools, construction equipment and subcontracted items necessary for the execution and completion of the Project.

2.2.2 The Contractor will pay all sales, use, gross receipts and similar taxes related to the Work provided by the Contractor which have been legally enacted at the time of execution of this Agreement and for which the Contractor is liable.

2.2.3 The Contractor will prepare and submit for the Owner's approval an estimated progress schedule for the Project. This schedule shall indicate the dates for the starting and completion of the various stages of the design and construction. It shall be revised as required by the conditions of the Work and those conditions and events which are beyond the Contractor's control.

2.2.4 The Contractor shall at all times keep the premises free from the accumulation of waste materials or rubbish caused by his operations. At the completion of the Work, he shall remove all of his waste material and rubbish from and around the Project as well as all his tools, construction equipment, machinery and surplus materials.

2.2.5 The Contractor will give all notices and comply with all laws and ordinances legally enacted at the date of execution of the Agreement, which govern the proper execution of the Work.

2.2.6 The Contractor shall take necessary precautions for the safety of his employees on the Work, and shall comply with all applicable provisions of federal, state and municipal safety laws to prevent accidents or injury to persons on, about or adjacent to the Project site. He shall erect and properly maintain, at all times, as required by the conditions and progress of Work, necessary safeguards for the protection of workmen and the public. It is understood and agreed, however, that the Contractor shall have no responsibility for the elimination or abatement of safety hazards created or otherwise resulting from Work at the job site carried on by other persons or firms directly employed by the Owner as separate contractors or by the Owner's tenants, and the Owner agrees to cause any such separate contractors and tenants to abide by and fully adhere to all applicable provisions of federal, state and municipal safety laws and regulations and to comply with all reasonable requests and directions of the Contractor for the elimination or abatement of any such safety hazards at the job site.

2.2.7 The Contractor shall keep such full and detailed accounts as may be necessary for proper financial management under this Agreement. The system shall be satisfactory to the Owner, who shall be afforded access to all the Contractor's records, books, correspondence, instructions, drawings, receipts, vouchers, memoranda and similar data relating to this Agreement. The Contractor shall preserve all such records for a period of three years after the final payment or longer where required by law.

2.3 Royalties and Patents

2.3.1 The Contractor shall pay all royalties and license fees for materials, methods and systems incorporated in the work. He shall defend all suits or claims for infringement of any patent rights and shall save the Owner harmless from loss on account thereof except when a particular design, process or product is specified by the Owner. In such case the Contractor shall be responsible for such loss only if he has reason to believe that the design, process or product so specified is an infringement of a patent, and fails to give such information promptly to the Owner.

2.4 Warranties and Completion

2.4.1 The Contractor warrants to the Owner that all materials and equipment furnished under this Agreement will be new, unless otherwise specified, and that all Work will be of good quality, free from improper workmanship and defective materials and in conformance with the Drawings and Specifications. The Contractor agrees to correct all Work performed by him under this Agreement which proves to be defective in material and workmanship within a period of one year from the Date of Substantial Completion as defined in Paragraph 5.2, or for such longer periods of time as may be set forth with respect to specific warranties contained in the Specifications. This warranty is expressly in lieu of all other rights and remedies at law or in equity.

2.4.2 The Contractor will secure required certificates of inspection, testing or approval and deliver them to the Owner.

2.4.3 The Contractor will collect all written warranties and equipment manuals and deliver them to the Owner.

2.4.4 The Contractor, with the assistance of the Owner's maintenance personnel, will direct the checkout of utilities and operations of systems and equipment for readiness, and will assist in their initial start-up and testing.

2.5 Additional Services

2.5.1 The Contractor will provide the following additional services upon the request of the Owner. A written agreement between the Owner and Contractor shall define the extent of such additional services and the amount and manner in which the Contractor will be compensated for such additional services.

2.5.2 Services related to investigation, appraisals or evaluations of existing conditions, facilities or equipment, or verification of the accuracy of existing drawings or other Owner-furnished information.

2.5.3 Services related to Owner-furnished equipment, furniture and furnishings which are not a part of this Agreement.

2.5.4 Services for tenant or rental spaces not a part of this Agreement.

2.5.5 Obtaining and training maintenance personnel or negotiating maintenance service contracts.

ARTICLE 3

Owner's Responsibilities

3.1 The Owner shall provide full information regarding his requirements for the Project.

3.2 The Owner shall designate a representative who shall be fully acquainted with the Project, and has authority to approve changes in the scope of the Project, render decisions promptly, and furnish information expeditiously and in time to meet the dates set forth in Subparagraph 2.2.3.

3.3 The Owner shall furnish for the site of the Project all necessary surveys describing the physical characteristics, soils reports and subsurface investigations, legal limitations, utility locations, and a legal description.

3.4 The Owner shall secure and pay for all necessary approvals, easements, assessments and charges required for the construction, use, or occupancy of permanent structures or for permanent changes in existing facilities.

3.5 The Owner shall furnish such legal services as may be necessary for providing the items set forth in Paragraph 3.4, and such auditing services as he may require.

3.6 If the Owner becomes aware of any fault or defect in the Project or non-conformance with the Drawings or Specifications, he shall give prompt written notice thereof to the Contractor.

3.7 The Owner shall provide the insurance for the Project as provided in Paragraph 9.4.

3.8 The Owner shall bear the costs of any bonds that may be required.

3.9 The services and information required by the above paragraphs shall be furnished with reasonable promptness at the Owner's expense and the Contractor shall be entitled to rely upon the accuracy and the completeness thereof.

3.10 The Owner shall furnish reasonable evidence satisfactory to the Contractor, prior to commencing Work and at such future times as may be required, that sufficient funds are available and committed for the entire Cost of the Project. Unless such reasonable evidence is furnished, the Contractor is not required to commence or continue any Work, or may, if such evidence is not presented within a reasonable time, stop Work upon 15 days notice to the Owner. The failure of the Contractor to insist upon the providing of this evidence at any one time shall not be a waiver of the Owner's obligation to make payments pursuant to this Agreement, nor shall it be a waiver of the Contractor's right to request or insist that such evidence be provided at a later date.

3.11 The Owner shall have no contractual obligation to the Contractor's Subcontractors and shall communicate with such Subcontractors only through the Contractor.

ARTICLE 4

Subcontracts

4.1 All portions of the Work that the Contractor does not perform with his own forces shall be performed under subcontracts.

4.2 A Subcontractor is a person or entity who has a direct contract with the Contractor to perform any Work in connection with the Project. The term Subcontractor does not include any separate contractor employed by the Owner or the separate contractors' subcontractors.

4.3 No contractual relationship shall exist between the Owner and any Subcontractor. The Contractor shall be responsible for the management of the Subcontractors in the performance of their Work.

ARTICLE 5

Contract Time Schedule

5.1 The Work to be performed under this Agreement shall be commenced on or about   and shall be substantially completed on or about

5.2 The Date of Substantial Completion of the Project or a designated portion thereof is the date when construction is sufficiently complete in accordance with the Drawings and Specifications so the Owner can occupy or utilize the Project or designated portion thereof for the use for which it is intended. Warranties called for by this Agreement or by the Drawings and Specifications shall commence on the Date of Substantial Completion of the Project or designated portion thereof. This date shall be established by a Certificate of Substantial Completion signed by the Owner and Contractor and shall state their respective responsibilities for security, maintenance, heat, utilities, damage to the Work and insurance. This Certificate shall also list the items to be completed or corrected and fix the time for their completion and correction.

5.3 If the Contractor is delayed at any time in the progress of the Project by any act or neglect of the Owner or by any separate contractor employed by the Owner, or by changes ordered in the Project, or by labor disputes, fire, unusual delay in transportation, adverse weather conditions not reasonably anticipated, unavoidable casualties, or any causes beyond the Contractor's control, or a delay authorized by the Owner pending arbitration, then the Date for Substantial Completion shall be extended by Change Order for the period caused by such delay.

ARTICLE 6

Lump Sum Price

6.1 The Lump Sum price for the Project is ($).

6.2 The Lump Sum is based upon laws, codes, and regulations in existence at the date of its establishment and upon criteria, Drawings, and Specifications as set forth in this agreement.

6.3 The Lump Sum will be modified for delays caused by the Owner and for Changes in the Project, all pursuant to Article 7.

6.4 Allowances

6.4.1 Allowances included in the Lump Sum are as set forth below:

6.4.2 Whenever the cost is more than or less than the Allowance, the Lump Sum shall be adjusted by Change Order as provided in Article 7.

ARTICLE 7

Changes in the Project

7.1 The Owner, without invalidating this Agreement, may order Changes in the Project within the general scope of this Agreement consisting of additions, deletions or other revisions. The Lump Sum, and the Contract Time Schedule shall be adjusted accordingly. All such Changes in the Project shall be authorized by Change Order.

7.1.1 A Change Order is a written order to the Contractor signed by the Owner or his authorized agent and issued after the execution of this Agreement, authorizing a Change in the Project and/or an adjustment in the Lump Sum or the Contract Time Schedule.

7.1.2 The increase or decrease in the Lump Sum resulting from a Change in the Project shall be determined in one or more of the following ways:

7.1.2.1 by mutual acceptance of a lump sum properly itemized and supported by sufficient substantiating data to permit evaluation; or

7.1.2.2 by unit prices stated in this Agreement or subsequently agreed upon; or

7.1.2.3 If none of the methods set forth in articles 7.1.2.1 and 7.1.2.2 is agreed upon, the Contractor shall promptly proceed with the Work required by the Change in the Project provided the Contractor receives a written order to proceed signed by the Owner. The increase in the Lump Sum shall then be determined on the basis of the reasonable costs of such Work and savings of those performing the Work attributed to the Change in the Project including a reasonable increase in the Contractor's overhead and profit. The amount of decrease in the Lum Sum to be allowed by Contractor to the Owner for any deletion or Change in the Project with results in a net decrease in cost will be the amount of the actual net decrease only. When both increases and decreases in costs of the Work are involved in any one Change in the Project, the increase in overhead and profit shall be figured on the basis of the net increase in costs, if any. Under this article and articles 7.1.2.1 and 7.1.2.2, the Contractor shall keep and present, in such form as the Owner may prescribe, an itemized accounting together with appropriate supporting data of the effect on the Lump Sum. The increase or decrease in the Lump Sum under this article and articles 7.1.2.1 and 7.1.2.2 shall be authorized by Change Order signed by the Owner or its authorized agent.

7.1.3 If unit prices are stated in this agreement or subsequently agreed upon, and if the quantities originally contemplated are so changed in a proposed Change Order or as a result of several Change Orders that application of the agreed unit prices to the quantities of Work proposed will cause substantial inequity to the Owner or the Contractor, the applicable unit prices and the Lump Sum shall be equitably adjusted.

7.1.4 Should concealed conditions encountered in the performance of the Work below the surface of the ground or should concealed or unknown conditions in an existing structure be at variance with the conditions indicated by the Drawings, Specifications, or Owner-furnished information or should unknown physical conditions below the surface of the ground or should concealed or unknown conditions in an existing structure of an unusual nature, differing materially from those ordinarily encountered and generally recognized as inherent in work of the character provided for in this Agreement, be encountered, the Lump Sum and the Contract Time Schedule shall be equitably adjusted by Change Order upon claim by either party made within a reasonable time after the first observance of the conditions.

7.2 Claims for Additional Cost or Time

7.2.1 If the Contractor wishes to make a claim for an increase in the Lump Sum or an extension in the Contract Time Schedule, he shall give the Owner written notice thereof within a reasonable time after the occurrence of the event giving rise to such claim. This notice shall be given by the Contractor before proceeding to execute the Work, except in an emergency endangering life or property in which case the Contractor shall act, at his discretion, to prevent threatened damage, injury or loss. Claims arising from delay shall be made within a reasonable time after the delay. Increases based upon design and estimating costs with respect to possible changes requested by the Owner, shall be made within a reasonable time after the decision is made not to proceed with the change. No such claim shall be valid unless so made. If the Owner and the Contractor cannot agree on the amount of the adjustment in the Lump Sum, and the Contract Time Schedule, it shall be determined pursuant to the provisions of Article 13. Any change in the Lump Sum or Contract Time Schedule resulting from such claim shall be authorized by Change Order.

7.3 Minor Changes in the Project

7.3.1 The Owner will have authority to order minor Changes in the Work not involving an adjustment in the Lump Sum or an extension of the Contract Time Schedule and not inconsistent with the intent of the Drawings and Specifications. Such Changes may be effected by written order and shall be binding on the Owner and the Contractor.

7.4 Emergencies

7.4.1 In any emergency affecting the safety of persons or property, the Contractor shall act, at his discretion, to prevent threatened damage, injury or loss. Any increase in the Lump Sum or extension of time claimed by the Contractor on account of emergency work shall be determined as provided in this Article.

ARTICLE 8
Payments to the Contractor

8.1 Payments shall be made by the Owner to the Contractor according to the following procedure:

8.1.1 On or before the _____ day of each month after Work has commenced, the Contractor shall submit to the Owner an Application for Payment in such detail as may be required by the Owner based on the Work completed and materials stored on the site and/or at locations approved by the Owner for the period ending on the _____ day of the month.

8.1.2 Within ten (10) days after his receipt of each monthly Application for Payment, the Owner shall pay directly to the Contractor the appropriate amounts for which Application for Payment is made therein. This payment request shall deduct the aggregate of amounts previously paid by the Owner.

8.1.3 If the Owner should fail to pay the Contractor at the time the payment of any amount becomes due, then the Contractor may, at any time thereafter, upon serving written notice that he will stop Work within seven (7) days after receipt of the notice by the Owner, and after such seven (7) day period, stop the Project until payment of the amount owing has been received. Written notice shall be deemed to have been duly served if sent by certified mail to the last known business address of the Owner.

8.1.4 Payments due but unpaid shall bear interest at the rate of two percentage points above the prime interest rate prevailing from time to time at the location of the Project.

8.2 The Contractor warrants and guarantees that title to all Work, materials and equipment covered by an Application for Payment whether incorporated in the Project or not, will pass to the Owner upon receipt of such payment by the Contractor free and clear of all liens, claims, security interests or encumbrances hereinafter referred to as Liens.

8.3 No Progress Payment nor any partial or entire use or occupancy of the Project by the Owner shall constitute an acceptance of any Work not in accordance with the Drawings and Specifications.

8.4 Final payment constituting the unpaid balance of the Project shall be due and payable when the Project is delivered to the Owner, ready for beneficial occupancy, or when the Owner occupies the Project, whichever event first occurs, provided that the Project be then substantially completed and this Agreement substantially performed. If there should remain minor items to be completed, the Contractor and the Owner shall list such items and the Contractor shall deliver, in writing, his guarantee to complete said items within a reasonable time thereafter. The Owner may retain a sum equal to 150 percent of the estimated cost of completing any unfinished items, provided that said unfinished items are listed separately and the estimated cost of completing any unfinished items is likewise listed separately. Thereafter, the Owner shall pay to the Contractor, monthly, the amount retained for incomplete items as each of said items is completed.

8.5 Before issuance of Final Payment, the Owner may request satisfactory evidence that all payrolls, materials bills and other indebtness connected with the Project have been paid or otherwise satisfied.

8.6 The making of Final Payment shall constitute a waiver of all claims by the Owner except those rising from: unsettled liens; improper workmanship or defective materials appearing within one year after the Date of Substantial Completion; and terms of any special guarantees required by the Drawings and Specifications.

8.7 The acceptance of Final Payment shall constitute a waiver of all claims by the Contractor except those previously made in writing and unsettled.

ARTICLE 9

Insurance, Indemnity and Waiver of Subrogation

9.1 Indemnity

9.1.1 The Contractor agrees to indemnify and hold the Owner harmless from all claims for bodily injury and property damage (other than the Work itself and other property insured under Paragraph 9.4) that may arise from the Contractor's operations under this Agreement.

9.1.2 The Owner shall cause any other contractor who may have a contract with the Owner to perform work in the areas where Work will be performed under this Agreement, to agree to indemnify the Owner and the Contractor and hold them harmless from all claims for bodily injury and property damage (other than property insured under Paragraph 9.4) that may arise from that contractor's operations. Such provisions shall be in a form satisfactory to the Contractor.

9.2 Contractor's Liability Insurance

9.2.1 The Contractor shall purchase and maintain such insurance as will protect him from the claims set forth below which may arise out of or result from the Contractor's operations under this Agreement whether such operations be by himself or by any Subcontractor or by anyone directly or indirectly employed by any of them, or by anyone for whose acts any of them may be liable:

9.2.1.1 Claims under workers' compensation, disability benefit and other similar employee benefit acts which are applicable to the Work to be performed;

9.2.1.2 Claims for damages because of bodily injury, occupational sickness or disease, or death of his employees under any applicable employer's liability law;

9.2.1.3 Claims for damages because of bodily injury, or death of any person other than his employees;

9.2.1.4 Claims for damages insured by usual personal injury liability coverage which are sustained (1) by any person as a result of an offense directly or indirectly related to the employment of such person by the Contractor or (2) by any other person;

9.2.1.5 Claims for damages, other than to the Work itself, because of injury to or destruction of tangible property, including loss of use therefrom;

9.2.1.6 Claims for damages because of bodily injury or death of any person or property damage arising out of the ownership, maintenance or use of any motor vehicle.

9.2.2 The Comprehensive General Liability Insurance shall include premises-operations (including explosion, collapse and underground coverage) elevators, independent contractors, completed operations, and blanket contractual liability on all written contracts, all including broad form property damage coverage.

9.2.3 The Contractor's Comprehensive General and Automobile Liability Insurance, as required by Subparagraphs 9.2.1 and 9.2.2 shall be written for not less than limits of liability as follows:

a. Comprehensive General Liability
   1. Bodily Injury $ _____ Each Occurrence
                                              (Completed Operations)
                            $ _____ Aggregate
   2. Property Damage $ _____ Each Occurrence
                            $ _____ Aggregate
b. Comprehensive Automobile Liability
   1. Bodily Injury $ _____ Each Person
                            $ _____ Each Occurrence
   2. Property Damage $ _____ Each Occurrence

9.2.4 Comprehensive General Liability Insurance may be arranged under a single policy for the full limits required or by a combination of underlying policies with the balance provided by an Excess or Umbrella Liability policy.

9.2.5 The foregoing policies shall contain a provision that coverages afforded under the policies will not be cancelled or not renewed until at least sixty (60) days' prior written notice has been given to the Owner. Certificates of Insurance showing such coverages to be in force shall be filed with the Owner prior to commencement of the Work.

9.3   Owner's Liability Insurance

9.3.1 The Owner shall be responsible for purchasing and maintaining his own liability insurance and, at his option, may purchase and maintain such insurance as will protect him against claims which may arise from operations under this Agreement.

9.4   Insurance to Protect Project

9.4.1 The Owner shall purchase and maintain property insurance in a form acceptable to the Contractor upon the entire Project for the full cost of replacement at the time of any loss. This insurance shall include as named insureds the Owner, the Contractor, Subcontractors and Subsubcontractors and shall insure against loss from the perils of Fire, Extended Coverage, and shall include "All Risk" insurance for physical loss or damage including, without duplication of coverage, at least theft, vandalism, malicious mischief, transit, collapse, flood, earthquake, testing, and damage resulting from defective design, workmanship or material. The Owner will increase limits of coverage, if necessary, to reflect estimated replacement cost. The Owner will be responsible for any co-insurance penalties or deductibles. If the Project covers an addition to or is adjacent to an existing building, the Contractor, Subcontractors and Subsubcontractors shall be named as additional insureds under the Owner's Property Insurance covering such building and its contents.

9.4.1.1 If the Owner finds it necessary to occupy or use a portion or portions of the Project prior to Substantial Completion thereof, such occupany shall not commence prior to a time mutually agreed to by the Owner and the Contractor and to which the insurance company or companies providing the property insurance have consented by endorsement to the policy or policies. This insurance shall not be cancelled or lapsed on account of such partial occupancy. Consent of the Contractor and of the insurance company or companies to such occupancy or use shall not be unreasonably withheld.

9.4.2 The Owner shall purchase and maintain such boiler and machinery insurance as may be required or necessary. This insurance shall include the interests of the Owner, the Contractor, Subcontractors and Subsubcontractors in the Work.

9.4.3 The Owner shall purchase and maintain such insurance as will protect the Owner and the Contractor against loss of use of Owner's property due to those perils insured pursuant to Subparagraph 9.4.1. Such policy will provide coverage for expenses of expediting materials, continuing overhead of the Owner and the Contractor, necessary labor expense including overtime, loss of income by the Owner and other determined exposures. Exposures of the Owner and the Contractor shall be determined by mutual agreement and separate limits of coverage fixed for each item.

9.4.4 The Owner shall file a copy of all policies with the Contractor before an exposure to loss may occur. Copies of any subsequent endorsements will be furnished to the Contractor. The Contractor will be given sixty (60) days notice of cancellation, non-renewal, or any endorsements restricting or reducing coverage. If the Owner does not intend to purchase such insurance, he shall inform the Contractor in writing prior to the commencement of the Work. The Contractor may then effect insurance which will protect the interests of himself, the Subcontractors and their Subsubcontractors in the Project, the cost of which shall be added to the Lump Sum by Change Order. If the Contractor is damaged by failure of the Owner to purchase or maintain such insurance or to so notify the Contractor, the Owner shall bear all reasonable costs properly attributable thereto.

9.5   Property Insurance Loss Adjustment

9.5.1 Any insured loss shall be adjusted with the Owner and the Contractor and made payable to the Owner and Contractor as trustees for the insureds, as their interests may appear, subject to any applicable mortgagee clause.

9.5.2 Upon the occurrence of an insured loss, monies received will be deposited in a separate account and the trustees shall make distribution in accordance with the agreement of the parties in interest, or in the absence of such agreement, in accordance with an arbitration award pursuant to Article 13. If the trustees are unable to agree between themselves on the settlement of the loss, such dispute shall also be submitted to arbitration pursuant to Article 13.

9.6   Waiver of Subrogation

9.6.1 The Owner and Contractor waive all rights against each other, the Architect/Engineer, Subcontractors and Subsubcontractors for damages caused by perils covered by insurance provided under Paragraph 9.4, except such rights as they may have to the proceeds of such insurance held by the Owner and Contractor as trustees. The Contractor shall require similar waivers from all Subcontractors and Subsubcontractors.

9.6.2 The Owner and Contractor waive all rights against each other and the Architect/Engineer, Subcontractors and Subsubcontractors for loss or damage to any equipment used in connection with the Project which loss is covered by any property insurance. The Contractor shall require similar waivers from all Subcontractors and Subsubcontractors.

9.6.3 The Owner waives subrogation against the Contractor, Architect/Engineer, Subcontractors, and Subsubcontractors on all property and consequential loss policies carried by the Owner on adjacent properties and under property and consequential loss policies purchased for the Project after its completion.

9.6.4 If the policies of insurance referred to in this Paragraph require an endorsement to provide for continued coverage where there is a waiver of subrogation, the owners of such policies will cause them to be so endorsed.

ARTICLE 10

TERMINATION OF THE AGREEMENT AND OWNER'S RIGHT TO PERFORM CONTRACTOR'S OBLIGATIONS

10.1   Termination by the Contractor

10.1.1 If the Project is stopped for a period of thirty (30) days under an order of any court or other public authority having jurisdiction, or as a result of an act of government, such as a declaration of a national emergency making materials unavailable, through no act or fault of the Contractor or if the Project should be stopped for a period of thirty (30) days by the Contractor for the Owner's failure to make payment thereon, then the Contractor may, upon seven days' written notice to the Owner, terminate this Agreement and recover from the Owner payment for all Work executed, the Lump Sum earned to date, and for any proven loss sustained upon any materials, equipment, tools, construction equipment and machinery, including reasonable profit and damages.

10.2 Owner's Right to Perform Contractor's Obligations and Termination by the Owner for Cause

10.2.1 If the Contractor fails to perform any of his obligations under this Agreement, including any obligation he assumes to perform Work with his own forces, the Owner may, after seven days' written notice, during which period the Contractor fails to perform such obligation, make good such deficiencies. The Lump Sum, if any, shall be reduced by the cost to the Owner of making good such deficiencies.

10.2.2 If the Contractor is adjudged a bankrupt, or if he makes a general assignment for the benefit of his creditors, or if a receiver is appointed on account of his insolvency, or if he persistently or repeatedly refuses or fails, except in cases for which extension of time is provided, to supply enough properly skilled workmen or proper materials, or if he fails to make proper payment to Subcontractors or for materials or labor, or persistently disregards laws, ordinances, rules, regulations or orders of any public authority having jurisdiction, or otherwise is guilty of a substantial violation of a provision of this Agreement, then the Owner may, without prejudice to any right or remedy and after giving the Contractor and his surety, if any, seven (7) days' written notice, during which period the Contractor fails to cure the violation, terminate the employment of the Contractor and take possession of the site and of all materials, equipment, tools, construction equipment and machinery thereon owned by the Contractor and may finish the Work by whatever reasonable method he may deem expedient. In such case, the Contractor shall not be entitled to receive any further payment until the Work is finished nor shall he be relieved from his obligations assumed under Article 6.

10.3 Termination by Owner Without Cause

10.3.1 If the Owner terminates the Agreement other than pursuant to 10.2.2, he shall pay the Contractor the total of: (a.) Costs incurred by the Contractor in performing the Project, including initial costs and preparatory expenses; (b.) Costs incurred in settling and paying termination claims under terminated subcontracts; (c.) Accounting, legal, clerical and other expenses incurred as a result of the termination; (d.) Storage, transportation, demobilization and other costs incurred for the preservation, protection or disposition of material and equipment on the Project; (e.) Any other necessary and reasonable costs incurred by the Contractor as a result of the Owner's termination of this Agreement; (f.) Overhead at ten percent (10%) of the total amount of (a.) thurogh (e.) above; profit at ten percent (10%) of the total amount of (a) through (f) above, as adjusted pursuant to Articles 6 and 7. In calculating the amount due the Contractor under this clause, a deduction shall be made for all payments to the Contractor under this Agreement.

ARTICLE 11

Assignment and Governing Law

11.1 Neither the Owner nor the Contractor shall assign his interest in this Agreement without the written consent of the other except as to the assignment of proceeds.

11.2 This Agreement shall be governed by the law in effect at the location of this Project.

ARTICLE 12

Miscellaneous Provisions

§2.07 AGC DOCUMENT NO. 415   101

ARTICLE 13

Arbitration

13.1 *AGREEMENT TO ARBITRATE:* All claims, disputes and matters in question arising out of, or relating to this Agreement or the breach thereof, except for claims which have been waived by the making or acceptance of final payment, and the claims described in Article 13.7, shall be decided by arbitration in accordance with the Construction Industry Arbitration Rules of the American Arbitration Association then in effect unless the parties mutually agree otherwise. This agreement to arbitrate shall be specifically enforceable under the prevailing arbitration law.

13.2 *NOTICE OF DEMAND:* Notice of the demand for arbitration shall be filed in writing with the other party to this Agreement and with the American Arbitration Association. The demand for arbitration shall be made within a reasonable time after written notice of the claim, dispute or other matter in question has been given, and in no event shall it be made after the date of final acceptance of the Work by the Owner or when institution of legal or equitable proceedings based on such claim, dispute or other matter in-question would be barred by the applicable statute of limitations, whichever shall first occur. The location of the arbitration proceedings shall be the city of the Contractor's headquarters or _____
_____

13.3 *AWARD:* The award rendered by the arbitrator(s) shall be final and judgment may be entered upon it in accordance with applicable law in any court having jurisdiction.

13.4 *WORK CONTINUATION AND PAYMENT:* Unless otherwise agreed in writing, the Contractor shall carry on the Work and maintain the Schedule of Work pending arbitration, and, if so, the Owner shall continue to make payments in accordance with this Agreement.

13.5 *NO LIMITATION OF RIGHTS OR REMEDIES:* Nothing in this Article shall limit any rights or remedies not expressly waived by the Contractor which the Contractor may have under lien laws or payment bonds.

13.6 *SAME ARBITRATORS:* To the maximum extent permitted by law, all claims which are related to or dependent upon each other, shall be heard by the same arbitrator or arbitrators even through the parties are not the same.

13.7 *EXCEPTIONS:* This agreement to arbitrate shall not apply to any claim of contribution or indemnity asserted by one party to this Agreement against the other party and arising out of any action brought in a state or federal court or in arbitration by a person who is under no obligation to arbitrate the subject matter of such action with either of the parties hereto. In any dispute arising over the application of this Article 13.7, the question of arbitrability shall be decided by the appropriate court and not by arbitration.

Attest: _____   Owner: _____

Attest: _____   Contractor: _____

FORM 2-2 Supplementary General Conditions [Favors Interests of Owner] (with Comments)

AGC Document No. 415: Design-Build Agreement is amended as follows:

¶1. First: Article 2.1.4. Article 2.1.4 is annulled and the following language is substituted:

> The Contractor will keep the Owner continuously informed as to the development of the design concepts and as to Contractor's progress in performing its responsibilities under this agreement. Owner, in its sole discretion, may at any time determine that the project is no longer financially feasible, and thereupon may terminate the further performance of this agreement, and shall pay Contractor an amount determined in accordance with Article 10.3.1.

¶2. Second: Article 2.2.1. Add the following language at the end of Article 2.2.1:

> Contractor will provide all planning, design and architectural/engineering services required for the proper design and construction of the project. In fulfilling its obligations under this Article, Contractor or Contractor's Architect shall employ Engineers of the appropriate specialties for proper preparation of the project drawings and specifications, including structural, mechanical, electrical, soils, civil and such other specialties as are reasonably required. All such services shall be performed by appropriately licensed personnel. Contractor takes responsibility for the proper performance of all architectural and engineering services.

> Comment: The basic advantage to the owner of design-build construction is the fact that the contractor takes responsibility for the proper performance of architectural and engineering services. Such services should still, however, be supplied by appropriately qualified and licensed persons employed by the contractor or by the contractor's architect.

¶3. Third: Article 2.2.3. The second sentence of Article 2.2.3 is annulled. The following language is added to Article 2.2.3:

> The Contractor will revise the job schedule from time to time, at least monthly, so as to take into account the actual progress of the work and so as to display the manner in which the work will be scheduled and coordinated for prompt and efficient completion. Revisions to the schedule shall

not affect the obligation of the Contractor to timely complete the Work as provided in Article 5 of this Agreement.

¶4. **Fourth:** **Article 2.2.5.** The following language is added to the end of Article 2.2.5:

Contractor will comply with all laws and ordinances enacted during construction which apply to the Work or to the manner of performance of the Work.

¶5. **Fifth:** **Article 2.2.6.** The last sentence of Article 2.2.6 is annulled, and the following language is added:

If Owner employs separate Contractors, or if Owner allows tenants to occupy the premises while Contractor is performing work, Owner will use reasonable efforts to require separate Contractors and tenants to observe proper safety precautions.

¶6. **Sixth:** **Article 2.4.1.** The last sentence of Article 2.4.1 is annulled, and the following language substituted:

At no expense to Owner, Contractor will correct and repair, at any time when it is discovered, any work, materials or equipment performed or supplied by Contractor that was not performed or supplied in accordance with the contract documents or that was not performed or supplied in a proper, careful and workmanlike manner.

¶7. **Seventh:** **Article 2.5.2.** Article 2.5.2 is annulled.

¶8. **Eighth:** **Article 3.3.** Article 3.3 is amended to read as follows:

The Owner shall furnish access to the project site, and shall supply a boundary survey, if necessary, and a legal description.

¶9. **Ninth:** **Article 3.10.** The following language is added to Article 3.10:

Owner shall not be required to furnish evidence that funds are available for payment of disputed claims.

¶10. **Tenth:** **Article 3.11.** The following language is added to Article 3.11:

Owner shall have no obligation to the Architect/Engineer, or Architects or Engineers employed by Contractor, and shall communicate with them only through Contractor or at meetings where Contractor is represented, except with Contractor's consent.

¶11. **Eleventh:** **Article 6.4.3.** Article 6.4.3 is added to read as follows:

6.4.3 Unless otherwise specified in writing and signed by Owners, allowances are computed based upon the out-of-pocket, direct costs of equipment or materials covered by the allowance. Contractor has allowed, in the contract price, for labor, equipment rental, supervision, overhead and profit allocable to the installation and performance of any item covered by an allowance.

¶12. **Twelfth: Article 7.1.4.** The following language is added to Article 7.1.4:

No adjustment will be made in the contract sum, or the contract time because of conditions that could reasonably be foreseen or anticipated by the Contractor.

¶13. **Thirteenth: Article 7.2.1.** [Parties should evaluate arbitration clause.]

Comment: Article 7.2.1 refers to Article 13, therefore raising the issue of arbitration. The owner should evaluate whether it wishes to utilize arbitration as a dispute resolution mechanism, or allow disputes to be resolved by litigation. The evaluation is a complex one, and the many differences between arbitration and litigation should be evaluated before arriving at a decision. Contractors usually favor arbitration as a method for dispute resolution, because it is usually much faster, and is often less expensive than litigation, and the decisions of an arbitration tribunal are usually not subject to appeal. These considerations, advantageous to the contractor, may be advantageous or disadvantageous to the owner, according to the owner's philosophy and business practice.

One prominent disadvantage of arbitration does not occur in the design-build relationship. This is the difficulty that the owner may have in joining all necessary parties. Since the architect/engineer is employed by the contractor, the contractor is responsible for architectural and engineering errors; thus, the owner is relieved of the need to join the architect/engineer in arbitration proceedings.

¶14. **Fourteenth: Article 8.1.3.** The following language is added to Article 8.1.3:

Contractor will not stop Work if Owner withholds payment because of a legitimate dispute.

¶15. **Fifteenth: Article 8.2.4.** Article 8.1.4 is amended so that the interest rate will be one (1) rather than two (2) percentage points above prime.

¶16. **Sixteenth: Article 8.5.** Article 8.5 is amended by adding the following language:

Before the Owner makes any progress payment, final payment, or pays the retention, Contractor shall supply satisfactory evidence, including mechanic's lien waivers and releases in forms satisfactory to Owner, showing that Contractor has paid for all work, material, equipment, services, and subcontracts that have been at the jobsite through the date for which the payment is made.

¶17. **Seventeenth:** **Article 8.6.** Article 8.6 is annulled.

¶18. **Eighteenth:** **Article 9.1.1.** The parenthetical phrase in Article 9.1.1 "(other than the Work itself and other property insured under Paragraph 9.4)" is annulled.

¶19. **Nineteenth:** **Article 9.2.1.5.** The phrase "other than to the Work itself" is annulled.

¶20. **Twentieth:** **Article 9.2.6.** Article 9.2.6 is added to read as follows:

Before permitting any Subcontractor to commence work on the project, the Contractor shall require the Subcontractor to provide the same insurance as is required to be supplied by Contractor under Article 9.2.1 through 9.2.3, inclusive.

¶21. **Twenty-First:** **Article 9.2.7.** Article 9.2.7 is added.

Before Contractor, or any Subcontractor, commences work on the jobsite it shall deliver to Owner properly executed certificates of insurance and endorsements to its comprehensive liability policies showing that Owner is an additional insured as to claims or damages arising out of or relating to the operations of the insured Contractor or Subcontractor, and that as to such claims, damages, and liability, the insurance of the named Contractor or the named Subcontractor shall be primary to insurance of Owner. The certificates and endorsements shall provide that coverage shall not be terminated or reduced without thirty (30) days written advanced notice to Owner.

Comment: For their favorable impact on construction disputes, these insurance clauses are perhaps the most important in the contract from the owner's point of view. The reason is that many construction defects, such as cracked slabs, cracked drywall, leaking roofs, leaking windows, and damage from settlement or subsidence, are covered by the liability insurance policies of the general contractor and subcontractors. Therefore, it is highly important for the owner to monitor the insurance status of the contractor and subcontractors, and to insist that it receive proper certificates of insurance and endorsements before allowing a contractor or subcontractor to work on the project. Thus, in the unfortunate event of a construction dispute that involves construction defects, insurance money will be there to help resolve the difficulty.

¶22.　Twenty-Second:　Article 9.4. Insurance to Protect Project - Property Insurance.

Comment:　The provisions contained in Article 9.4 of AGC Document No. 415 are such as should never be accepted by a well-advised owner. Under Article 9.4, the owner essentially takes responsibility for any casualty that might occur to the property, including risks that may be essentially uninsurable in some areas of the country, and even including the risk of damage resulting from defective design or improper performance of the contract by the contractor or its subcontractors.

There are three ways for the owner to go. The way to go should be determined only after careful evaluation with the help of a construction insurance consultant.

Option 1: Amend Article 9.4 so as to take responsibility to provide only the insurance that is reasonably available in the market. Insurance against collapse, settlement, flood, earthquake, and property damage resulting from defective design, workmanship, or material is likely unobtainable at a reasonable premium.

Even after such a revision, the parties must face the fact that in the event of a covered loss, the construction lender (under the provisions of the deed of trust or the mortgage securing the construction loan) will probably have the right, which it will probably exercise, to claim all of the insurance proceeds in satisfaction, or partial satisfaction, of the construction loan. If this happens, the parties are left with a fire site and no construction funds until the owner is able to negotiate a new construction loan. Changes in the economy might well make it impossible to obtain a new loan that would provide financing adequate to pay the contract price.

In short, it is not usually possible to revise the contract documents under *Option 1* in such a way as to give full protection to the interests of the owner.

Option 2: Option 2 is to annul Articles 9.4, 9.5, and 9.6. This is a perfectly plausible alternative, but owner and contractor should both be aware of the legal ramifications.

What is the legal effect of damage to or destruction of the project in the absence of a specific provision in the contract? Damage or destruction does not automatically excuse the contractor from performing the contract. This means the contractor must rebuild at its own expense. The legal reasoning behind this outcome is that performance of a contract is excused by impossibility or extreme impracticability. There is nothing impossible or extremely impracticable about rebuilding. It is expensive, but not legally impossible, nor so impracticable as to excuse performance. It is assumed that if the contractor had wanted to guard itself against the obligation to rebuild, it would have so provided in the contract. The contractor has an insurable interest in the continued existence of the project and therefore has the ability to purchase its own insurance to pay the cost of rebuilding. Rather than insist on a clause that would excuse it from rebuilding in the event of damage or destruction, the contractor may purchase insurance to cover itself against that contingency.

Option 3: Option 3 is to specify that the contractor has the obligation to provide its own insurance against damage to or destruction of the project. This makes its very clear that the contractor not only has the obligation to rebuild, but provides the parties with the assurance that a source of funds for rebuilding is available. The disadvantage to this option is that the premium for such insurance is substantial, and the contractor will surely pass the expense of that insurance premium on to the owner. Is it worth it, especially when the construction loan agreement and the mortgage or trust deed that the owner has probably signed requires the owner to provide what is essentially duplicate coverage? The cost is perhaps offset by the fact that the owner could be relieved of both the obligation to repay the construction loan, and also of the obligation to pay the contractor to rebuild the project.

Conclusion. This author's best advice is that the owner carefully consult with a qualified construction insurance expert, and a construction lawyer, so the property insurance provisions will be written in a manner consistent with the insurance that is obtainable under market conditions.

If that is too much trouble or too expensive, then the owner or the contractor will have to take some risks. One way to eliminate the risk to the owner is to annul Articles 9.4.5 and 9.6.

If the contractor will not accept that, then the owner may revise those articles to conform to the realities of the insurance market. Following is *Option 1* language.

¶23. **Twenty-Third:**   Article 9.4.1   Article 9.4.1 is annulled and replaced as follows:

The Owner shall purchase and maintain property insurance insuring the project against fire and other perils in such form as is reasonably available to Owner in the insurance market with loss payable to the construction lender and thereafter to Owner and Contractor as their interests may appear, and Contractor shall be named as an additional insured. Upon the request of Contractor, Owner will deliver a copy of the policy to Contractor so that Contractor, it is so advised, may purchase such additional insurance as Contractor may desire to protect its own insurable interest in the project. At the request of Contractor, Owner will promptly supply copies of endorsements or new policies that may impair or reduce coverage.

¶24. **Twenty-Fourth:** **Article 9.4.1.1.** Article 9.4.1.1 is annulled.

¶25. **Twenty-Fifth:** **Article 9.4.2** Article 9.4.2 is annulled.

¶26. **Twenty-Sixth:** **Article 9.4.3** Article 9.4.3 is annulled.

¶27. **Twenty-Seventh:** **Article 9.4.4** Article 9.4.4 is annulled.

¶28. **Twenty-Eighth:** **Article 9.6.1** Article 9.6.1 is annulled, and replaced as follows:

9.6.1 Owner, Contractor, Architect/Engineer, and Subcontractors of every tier, waive all rights against each other to recover compensation for loses covered by property insurance, but only to the extent that the proceeds of such insurance are actually received to compensate for damages or losses caused by perils covered by insurance provided under Article 9.4.

¶29. **Twenty-Ninth:** **Article 9.6.2** Article 9.6.2 is annulled.

¶30. **Thirtieth:** **Article 9.6.3** Article 9.6.3 is annulled.

¶31. **Thirty-First:** **Article 9.6.4** Article 9.6.4 is annulled.

Comment: Owner should submit the property insurance and waiver of subrogation language to its insurance consultant to obtain assurances that the language employed is consistent with the provisions of policies available, and to obtain a waiver of subrogation endorsement if it is needed.

¶32. **Thirty-Second:** **Article 10.3.1.** Article 10.3.1 is amended by reducing overhead to 8 per cent and reducing profit to 10 per cent.

¶33. **Thirty-Third:** **Article 11.2**   Article 11.2 is annulled.

Comment: This paragraph is usually unnecessary, and it may have unintended results because it has been applied in such a way as to remove certain types of controversies from arbitration. *See Volt Information Sciences, Inc v Board of Trustees of Leland Stanford Junior University,* 489 US 468 (1989).

¶34. **Thirty-Fourth:** **Article 13.1.**   The phrase "except for claims which have been waived by the making or acceptance of final payment" is deleted from Article 13.1.

Comment: Whether or not claims may have been waived by making or acceptance of final payment should be decided by the arbitrators as a part of the arbitration proceeding.

¶35. **Thirty-Fifth:** **Article 13.2.**   Article 13.2 is annulled.

Comment: Whether a party should be barred by lapse of time from making an arbitration claim should be decided by the arbitrators, and the owner should not be barred by acceptance of the work from asserting a claim. The location of arbitration proceedings should be decided by the American Arbitration Association (AAA), based on factors such as the location of the jobsite and the convenience of witnesses rather than being specified to be in the contractor's home town.

¶36. **Thirty-Sixth:** **Article 13.7.**   The last sentence of Article 13.7 is annulled. Article 13.7 is amended by adding the following sentence:

"The exception created by this Article 13.7 shall be applicable only at the written election of the party who asserts the claim that it is entitled to contribution or indemnity, and in the absence of such a written election, claims to contribution and indemnity shall be resolved by arbitration."

Comment: There are circumstances under which entitlement to contribution or indemnity is more properly resolved as a part of an arbitration proceeding in progress to resolve other disputes between the parties.

For general comments as to the advantages and disadvantages of arbitration from an owner's point of view, see **FORM 2-2 ¶13.**

AGC Document No. 410 - Design-Build Agreement - Guaranteed Maximum

§2.08 General Comment

AGC Document No. 410 is a design-build agreement that is similar in many ways to AGC Document No. 415, except that document No. 410 is **cost plus with a guaranteed maximum,** while document No. 415 is a **lump sum** form of contract.

Because a design-build construction contract is almost always signed before the drawings and specifications have been completed, the cost plus format may offer some advantages to the owner, particularly if the owner agrees to split savings with the contractor, thus providing the contractor with an incentive to keep construction costs low.

FORM 2-3 AGC Document No. 410 - Standard Form of Design-Build Agreement and General Conditions between Owner and Contractor (Provides a Guaranteed Maximum Price) (1982)

AIA copyrighted material has been reproduced with the permission of the American Institute of Architects under license number 90153. Permission expires December 31, 1991.

This document is intended for use as a "consumable" (consumables are further defined by Senate Report 94-473 on the Copyright Act of 1976). This document is not intended to be used as "model language" (language taken from an existing document and incorporated, without attribution, into a newly-created document). Rather, it is a standard form which is intended to be modified by appending separate amendment sheets and/or fill in provided blank spaces.

112   DESIGN-BUILD CONTRACT

THE ASSOCIATED GENERAL CONTRACTORS

STANDARD FORM OF DESIGN-BUILD AGREEMENT AND GENERAL CONDITIONS BETWEEN OWNER AND CONTRACTOR

This Document has important legal and insurance consequences; consultation with an attorney and insurance consultants and carriers is encouraged with respect to its completion or modification.

AGREEMENT

Made this   day of   in the year of Nineteen Hundred and

BETWEEN

the Owner, and

the Contractor.

For services in connection with the following described Project: (Include complete Project location and scope)

The Owner and the Contractor agree as set forth below:

Certain provisions of this document have been derived, with modifications, from the following documents published by The American Institute of Architechts: AIA Document A111, Owner-Contractor Agreement, ©1978; AIA Document A201 General Conditions, ©1976 by The American Institute of Architects. Usage made of AIA language, with the permission of AIA, does not imply AIA endorsement or approval of this document. Further reproduction of copyrighted AIA materials without separate written permission from AIA is prohibited.

AGC DOCUMENT NO. 410   STANDARD FORM OF DESIGN-BUILD AGREEMENT AND GENERAL CONDITIONS BETWEEN OWNER AND CONTRACTOR • JANUARY 1982
©1982 Associated General Contractors of America

INDEX

ARTICLE		PAGE
1	The Construction Team and Extent of Agreement	1
2	Contractor's Responsibilities	1
3	Owner's Responsibilities	3
4	Subcontracts	3
5	Contract Time Schedule	4
6	Guaranteed Maximum Price	4
7	Contractor's Fee	4
8	Cost of the Project	5
9	Changes in the Project	6
10	Discounts	8
11	Payments to the Contractor	8
12	Insurance, Indemnity and Waiver of Subrogation	9
13	Termination of the Agreement and Owner's Right to Perform Contractor's Obligations	11
14	Assignment and Governing Law	12
15	Miscellaneous Provisions	12
16	Arbitration	12

AGC DOCUMENT NO. 410 • STANDARD FORM OF DESIGN-BUILD AGREEMENT AND GENERAL CONDITIONS BETWEEN OWNER AND CONTRACTOR • JANUARY 1982
©1982 Associated General Contractors of America

ARTICLE 1

The Construction Team and Extent of Agreement

THE CONTRACTOR accepts the relationship of trust and confidence established between him and the Owner by this Agreement. He agrees to furnish the architectural, engineering and construction services set forth herein and agrees to furnish efficient business administration and superintendence, and to use his best efforts to complete the Project in the best and soundest way and in the most expeditious and economical manner consistent with the interests of the Owner.

1.1 *The Construction Team:* The Contractor, the Owner, and the Architect/Engineer called the "Construction Team" shall work from the beginning of design through construction completion. The services of   , as the Architect/Engineer, will be furnished by the Contractor pursuant to an agreement between the Contractor and the Architect/Engineer.

1.2 *Extent of Agreement:* This Agreement represents the entire agreement between the Owner and the Contractor and supersedes all prior negotiations, representations or agreements. When the Drawings and Specifications are complete, they shall be identified by amendment to this Agreement. This Agreement shall not be superseded by any provisions of the documents for construction and may be amended only by written instrument signed by both Owner and Contractor.

1.3 *Definitions:* The Project is the total construction to be designed and constructed of which the Work is a part. The Work comprises the completed construction required by the Drawings and Specifications. The term day shall mean calendar day unless otherwise specifically designated.

ARTICLE 2

Contractor's Responsibilities

2.1 Contractor's Services

2.1.1 The Contractor shall be responsible for furnishing the Design and for the construction of the Project. The Owner and Contractor shall develop a design and construction phase schedule and the Owner shall be responsible for prompt decisions and approvals so as to maintain the approved schedule.

2.1.2 The Owner and Contractor shall develop a design phase schedule. *PHASE 1:* Based upon the Owner's Project requirements, schematic Design Studies will be prepared by the Architect/Engineer. These Schematics are for the purpose of assisting the Owner in determining the feasibility of the Project. *PHASE 2:* Upon approval of Schematic Designs and authorization from the Owner to proceed, the Architect/Engineer shall prepare Design Development Documents to fix the size and character of the Project as to structural, mechanical and electrical systems, materials and other appropriate essential items in the Project. These Development Documents are the basis to establish a Guaranteed Maximum Price for the design and construction of the Project. *PHASE 3:* From approved Design Development Documents the Architect/Engineer will prepare working Drawings and Specifications setting forth in detail the requirements for the construction of the Project, and based upon codes, laws or regulations which have been enacted at the time of their preparation. These Working Drawings and Specifications will be used to confirm the Guaranteed Maximum Price. Construction of the Project shall be in accordance with these Drawings and Specifications as approved by the Owner. The Drawings and Specifications shall remain the property of the Contractor and are not to be used by the Owner on other projects without the written consent of the Contractor. If the working Drawings and Specifications have not been completed and a Guaranteed Maximum Price has been established prior to the completion of the working Drawings and Specifications, the Contractor, the Architect/Engineer and the Owner will work closely together to monitor the design in accordance with prior approvals so as to ensure that the Project can be constructed within the Guaranteed Maximum Price. As these working Drawings and Specifications are being completed, the Contractor will keep the Owner advised of the effects of any Owner requested changes on the Contract Time Schedule and/or the Guaranteed Maximum Price.

2.1.3 The Contractor will assist the Owner in securing permits necessary for the construction of the Project.

2.2 Responsibilities With Respect to Construction

2.2.1 The Contractor will provide all construction supervision, inspection, labor, materials, tools, construction equipment and subcontracted items necessary for the execution and completion of the Project.

2.2.2 The Contractor will pay all sales, use, gross receipts and similar taxes related to the Work provided by the Contractor which have been legally enacted at the time of execution of this Agreement and for which the Contractor is liable.

2.2.3 The Contractor will prepare and submit for the Owner's approval an estimated progress schedule for the Project. This schedule shall indicate the dates for the starting and completion of the various stages of the design and construction. It shall be revised as required by the conditions of the Work and those conditions and events which are beyond the Contractor's control.

2.2.4 The Contractor shall at all times keep the premises free from the accumulation of waste materials or rubbish caused by his operations. At the completion of the Work, he shall remove all of his waste material and rubbish from and around the Project as well as all his tools, construction equipment, machinery and surplus materials.

2.2.5 The Contractor will give all notices and comply with all laws and ordinances legally enacted at the date of execution of the Agreement, which govern the proper execution of the Work.

2.2.6 The Contractor shall take necessary precautions for the safety of his employees on the Work, and shall comply with all applicable provisions of federal, state and municipal safety laws to prevent accidents or injury to persons on, about or adjacent to the Project site. He shall erect and properly maintain, at all times, as required by the conditions and progress of Work, necessary safeguards for the protection of workmen and the public. It is understood and agreed, however, that the Contractor shall have no responsibility for the elimination or abatement of safety hazards created or otherwise resulting from Work at the job site carried on by other persons or firms directly employed by the Owner as separate contractors or by the Owner's tenants, and the Owner agrees to cause any such separate contractors and tenants to abide by and fully adhere to all applicable provisions of federal, state and municipal safety laws and regulations and to comply with all reasonable requests and directions of the Contractor for the elimination or abatement of any such safety hazards at the job site.

2.2.7 The Contractor shall keep such full and detailed accounts as may be necessary for proper financial management under this Agreement. The system shall be satisfactory to the Owner, who shall be afforded access to all the Contractor's records, books, correspondence, instructions, drawings, receipts, vouchers, memoranda and similar data relating to this Agreement. The Contractor shall preserve all such records for a period of three years after the final payment or longer where required by law.

2.3 Royalties and Patents

2.3.1 The Contractor shall pay all royalties and license fees for materials, methods and systems incorporated in the work. He shall defend all suits or claims for infringement of any patent rights and shall save the Owner harmless from loss on account thereof except when a particular design, process or product is specified by the Owner. In such case the Contractor shall be responsible for such loss only if he has reason to believe that the design, process or product so specified is an infringement of a patent, and fails to give such information promptly to the Owner.

2.4 Warranties and Completion

2.4.1 The Contractor warrants to the Owner that all materials and equipment furnished under this Agreement will be new, unless otherwise specified, and that all Work will be of good quality, free from improper workmanship and defective materials and in conformance with the Drawings and Specifications. The Contractor agrees to correct all Work performed by him under this Agreement which proves to be defective in material and workmanship within a period of one year from the Date of Substantial Completion as defined in Paragraph 5.2, or for such longer periods of time as may be set forth with respect to specific warranties contained in the Specifications.

2.4.2 The Contractor will secure required certificates of inspection, testing or approval and deliver them to the Owner.

2.4.3 The Contractor will collect all written warranties and equipment manuals and deliver them to the Owner.

116   DESIGN-BUILD CONTRACT

2.4.4 The Contractor with the assistance of the Owner's maintenance personnel, will direct the checkout of utilities and operations of systems and equipment for readiness, and will assist in their initial start-up and testing.

2.5 Additional Services

2.5.1 The Contractor will provide the following additional services upon the request of the Owner. A written agreement between the Owner and Contractor shall define the extent of such additional services and the amount and manner in which the Contractor will be compensated for such additional services.

2.5.2 Services related to investigation, appraisals or evaluations of existing conditions, facilities or equipment, or verification of the accuracy of existing drawings or other Owner-furnished information.

2.5.3 Services related to Owner-furnished equipment, furniture and furnishings which are not a part of this Agreement.

2.5.4 Services for tenant or rental spaces not a part of this Agreement.

2.5.5 Obtaining and training maintenance personnel or negotiating maintenance service contracts.

ARTICLE 3

Owner's Responsibilities

3.1 The Owner shall provide full information regarding his requirements for the Project.

3.2 The Owner shall designate a representative who shall be fully acquainted with the Project, and has authority to approve changes in the scope of the Project, render decisions promptly, and furnish information expeditiously and in time to meet the dates set forth in Subparagraph 2.2.3.

3.3 The Owner shall furnish for the site of the Project all necessary surveys describing the physical characteristics, soils reports and subsurface investigations, legal limitations, utility locations, and a legal description.

3.4 The Owner shall secure and pay for necessary approvals, easements, assessments and charges required for the construction, use, or occupancy of permanent structures or for permanent changes in existing facilities.

3.5 The Owner shall furnish such legal services as may be necessary for providing the items set forth in Paragraph 3.4, and such auditing services as he may require.

3.6 If the Owner becomes aware of any fault or defect in the Project or non-conformance with the Drawings or Specifications, he shall give prompt written notice thereof to the Contractor.

3.7 The Owner shall provide the insurance for the Project as provided in Paragraph 12.4.

3.8 The Owner shall bear the costs of any bonds that may be required.

3.9 The services and information required by the above paragraphs shall be furnished with reasonable promptness at the Owner's expense and the Contractor shall be entitled to rely upon the accuracy and the completeness thereof.

3.10 The Owner shall furnish reasonable evidence satisfactory to the Contractor, prior to commencing Work and at such future times as may be required, that sufficient funds are available and committed for the entire Cost of the Project. Unless such reasonable evidence is furnished, the Contractor is not required to commence or continue any Work, or may, if such evidence is not presented within a reasonable time, stop Work upon 15 days notice to the Owner. The failure of the Contractor to insist upon the providing of this evidence at any one time shall not be a waiver of the Owner's obligation to make payments pursuant to this Agreement nor shall it be a waiver of the Contractor's right to request or insist that such evidence be provided at a later date.

3.11 The Owner shall have no contractual obligation to the Contractor's Subcontractors and shall communicate with such Subcontractors only through the Contractor.

ARTICLE 4

Subcontracts

4.1 All portions of the Work that the Contractor does not perform with his own forces shall be performed under subcontracts.

4.2 A Subcontractor is a person or entity who has a direct contract with the Contractor to perform any Work in connection with the Project. The term Subcontractor does not include any separate contractor employed by the Owner or the separate contractors' subcontractors.

4.3 No contractual relationship shall exist between the Owner and any Subcontractor. The Contractor shall be responsible for the management of the Subcontractors in the performance of their Work.

ARTICLE 5

Contract Time Schedule

5.1 The Work to be performed under this Agreement shall be commenced on or about   and shall be substantially completed on or about

5.2 The Date of Substantial Completion of the Project or a designated portion thereof is the date when construction is sufficiently complete in accordance with the Drawings and Specifications so the Owner can occupy or utilize the Project or designated portion thereof for the use for which it is intended. Warranties called for by this Agreement or by the Drawings and Specifications shall commence on the Date of Substantial Completion of the Project or designated portion thereof. This date shall be established by a Certificate of Substantial Completion signed by the Owner and Contractor and shall state their respective responsibilities for security, maintenance, heat, utilities, damage to the Work and insurance. This Certificate shall also list the items to be completed or corrected and fix the time for their completion and correction.

5.3 If the Contractor is delayed at any time in the progress of the Project by any act or neglect of the Owner or by any separate contractor employed by the Owner or by changes ordered in the Project, or by labor disputes, fire, unusual delay in transportation, adverse weather conditions not reasonably anticipatable, unavoidable casualties, or any causes beyond the Contractor's control, or a delay authorized by the Owner pending arbitration, then the Date for Substantial Completion shall be extended by Change Order for the period of time caused by such delay.

ARTICLE 6

Guaranteed Maximum Price

6.1 The Contractor guarantees that the maximum price to the Owner for the Cost of the Project as set forth in Article 8, and the Contractor's Fee as set forth in Article 7, will not exceed
Dollars ($), which sum shall be called the Guaranteed Maximum Price.

6.2 The Guaranteed Maximum Price is based upon laws, codes, and regulations in existence at the date of its establishment and upon criteria, Drawings, and Specifications as set forth below:

6.3 The Guaranteed Maximum Price will be modified for delays caused by the Owner and for Changes in the Project, all pursuant to Article 9.

6.4 Allowances included in the Guaranteed Maximum Price are as set forth below:

6.5 Whenever the cost is more than or less than the Allowance, the Guaranteed Maximum Price shall be adjusted by Change Order.

ARTICLE 7

Contractor's Fee

7.1 In consideration of the performance of the Agreement, the Owner agrees to pay to the Contractor in current funds as compensation for his services a Fee as follows:

7.2 Adjustment in Fee shall be made as follows:

7.2.1 For Changes in the Project as provided in Article 9, the Contractor's Fee shall be adjusted as follows:

7.2.2 For delays in the Project not the responsibility of the Contractor, there will be an equitable adjustment in the fee to compensate the Contractor for his increased expenses.

7.2.3 In the event the Cost of the Project plus the Contractor's Fee shall be less than the Guaranteed Maximum Price as adjusted by Change Orders, the resulting savings will be shared by the Owner and the Contractor as follows:

7.2.4 The Contractor shall be paid an additional fee in the same proportion as set forth in 7.2.1 if the Contractor is placed in charge of managing the replacement of insured or uninsured loss.

7.3 The Contractor shall be paid monthly that part of his Fee proportionate to the percentage of Work completed, the balance, if any, to be paid at the time of final payment.

7.4 Included in the Contractor's Fee are the following:

7.4.1 Salaries or other compensation of the Contractor's employees at the principal office and branch offices, except employees listed in Subparagraph 8.2.3.

7.4.2 General operating expenses of the Contractor's principal and branch offices other than the field office.

7.4.3 Any part of the Contractor's capital expenses, including interest on the Contractor's capital employed for the Project.

7.4.4 Overhead or general expenses of any kind, except as may be expressly included in Article 8.

7.4.5 Costs in excess of the Guaranteed Maximum Price.

ARTICLE 8

Cost of the Project

8.1 The term Cost of the Project shall mean costs necessarily incurred in the design and construction of the Project and shall include the items set forth below in this Article. The Owner agrees to pay the Contractor for the Cost of the Project as defined in this Article. Such payment shall be in addition to the Contractor's Fee stipulated in Article 7.

8.2. Cost Items

8.2.1 All architectural, engineering and consulting fees and expenses incurred in designing and constructing the Project.

8.2.2 Wages paid for labor in the direct employ of the Contractor in the performance of the Work under applicable collective bargaining agreements, or under a salary or wage schedule agreed upon by the Owner and the Contractor, and including such welfare or other benefits, if any, as may be payable with respect thereto.

8.2.3 Salaries of Contractor's employees when stationed at the field office, in whatever capacity employed, employees engaged on the road expediting the production or transportation of material and equipment and employees from the main or branch office performing the functions listed below:

8.2.4 Cost of all employee benefits and taxes for such items as unemployment compensation and social security, insofar as such cost is based on wages, salaries, or other remuneration paid to employees of the Contractor and included in the Cost of the Project under Subparagraphs 8.2.1, 8.2.2 and 8.2.3.

8.2.5 Reasonable transportation, traveling and hotel and moving expenses of the Contractor or of his officers or employees incurred in discharge of duties connected with the Project.

8.2.6 Cost of all materials, supplies and equipment incorporated in the Project, including costs of transportation and storage thereof.

8.2.7 Payments made by the Contractor to Subcontractors for Work performed pursuant to contract under this Agreement.

8.2.8 Cost, including transportation and maintenance, of all materials, supplies, equipment, temporary facilities and hand tools not owned by the workmen, which are employed or consumed in the performance of the Work, and cost less salvage value on such items used, but not consumed, which remain the property of the Contractor.

8.2.9 Rental charges of all necessary machinery and equipment, exclusive of hand tools, used at the site of the Work, whether rented from the Contractor or others, including installations, repairs and replacements, dismantling, removal, costs of lubrication, transportation and delivery costs thereof, at rental charges consistent with those prevailing in the area.

8.2.10 Cost of the premiums for all insurance which the Contractor is required to procure by this Agreement or is deemed necessary by the Contractor.

8.2.11 Sales, use, gross receipts or similar taxes related to the Project, imposed by any governmental authority, and for which the Contractor is liable.

8.2.12 Permit fees, licenses, tests, royalties, damages for infringement of patents and costs of defending suits therefor for which the Contractor is responsible under Subparagraph 2.3.1 and deposits lost for causes other than the Contractor's negligence.

8.2.13 Losses, expenses or damages to the extent not compensated by insurance or otherwise (including settlement made with the written approval of the Owner), and the cost of corrective work.

8.2.14 Minor expenses such as telegrams, long-distance telephone calls, telephone service at the site, expressage, and similar petty cash items in connection with the Project.

8.2.15 Cost of removal of all debris.

8.2.16 Costs incurred due to an emergency affecting the safety of persons and property.

8.2.17 Cost of data processing services required in the performance of the services outlined in Article 2.

8.2.18 Legal costs reasonably and properly resulting from prosecution of the Project for the Owner.

8.2.19 All costs directly incurred in the performance of the Project and not included in the Contractor's Fee as set forth in Paragraph 7.4

120 **DESIGN-BUILD CONTRACT**

ARTICLE 9

Changes in the Project

9.1 The Owner, without invalidating this Agreement, may order Changes in the Project within the general scope of this Agreement consisting of additions, deletions or other revisions, the Guaranteed Maximum Price, if established, the Contractor's Fee, and the Contract Time Schedule being adjusted accordingly. All such Changes in the Project shall be authorized by Change Order.

9.1.1 A Change Order is a written order to the Contractor signed by the Owner or his authorized agent and issued after the execution of this Agreement, authorizing a Change in the Project and/or an adjustment in the Guaranteed Maximum Price, the Contractor's Fee or the Contract Time Schedule. Each adjustment in the Guaranteed Maximum Price resulting from a Change Order shall clearly separate the amount attributable to the Cost of the Project and the Contractor's Fee.

9.1.2 The increase or decrease in the Guaranteed Maximum Price resulting from a Change in the Project shall be determined in one or more of the following ways:

9.1.2.1 by mutual acceptance of a lump sum properly itemized and supported by sufficient substantiating data to permit evaluation; or

9.1.2.2 by unit prices stated in this Agreement or subsequently agreed upon; or

9.1.2.3 by cost to be determined as defined in Article 8 and a mutual acceptable fixed or percentage fee; or

9.1.2.4 by the method provided in Subparagraph 9.1.3.

9.1.3 If none of the methods set forth in Clauses 9.1.2.1 through 9.1.2.3 is agreed upon, the Contractor, provided he receives a written order signed by the Owner, shall promptly proceed with the Work involved. The cost of such Work shall then be determined on the basis of the reasonable expenditures and savings of those performing the Work attributed to the change, including, in the case of an increase in the Guaranteed Maximum Price, a reasonable increase in the Contractor's Fee. In such case, and also under Clauses 9.1.2.3 and 9.1.2.4 above, the Contractor shall keep and present, in such form as the Owner may prescribe, an itemized accounting together with appropriate supporting data of the increase in the Cost of the Project as outlined in Article 8. The amount of decrease in the Guaranteed Maximum Price to be allowed by the Contractor to the Owner for any deletion or change which results in a net decrease in cost will be the amount of the actual net decrease. When both additions and credits are involved in any one change, the increase in Fee shall be figured on the basis of net increase, if any.

9.1.4 If unit prices are stated in this Agreement or subsequently agreed upon, and if the quantities originally contemplated are so changed in a proposed Change Order or as a result of several Change Orders that application of the agreed unit prices to the quantities of Work proposed will cause substantial inequity to the Owner or the Contractor, the applicable unit prices and the Guaranteed Maximum Price shall be equitably adjusted.

9.1.5 Should concealed conditions encountered in the performance of the Work below the surface of the ground or should concealed or unknown conditions in an existing structure be at variance with the conditions indicated by the Drawings, Specifications, or Owner-furnished information or should unknown physical conditions below the surface of the ground or should concealed or unknown conditions in an existing structure of an unusual nature, differing materially from those ordinarily encountered and generally recognized as inherent in work of the character provided for in this Agreement, be encountered, the Guaranteed Maximum Price and the Contract Time Schedule shall be equitably adjusted by Change Order upon claim by either party made within a reasonable time after the first observance of the conditions.

9.2 Claims for Additional Cost or Time

9.2.1 If the Contractor wishes to make a claim for an increase in the Guaranteed Maximum Price, or increase in his Fee or an extension in the Contract Time Schedule, he shall give the Owner written notice thereof within a reasonable time after the occurrence of the event giving rise to such claim. This notice shall be given by the Contractor before proceeding to execute the Work, except in an emergency endangering life or property in which case the Contractor shall act, at his discretion, to prevent threatened damage, injury or loss. Claims arising from delay shall be made within a reasonable time after the delay. Increases based upon design and estimating costs with respect to possible changes requested by the Owner, shall be made within a reasonable time after the decision is made not to proceed with the change. No such claim shall be valid unless so made. If the Owner and the Contractor cannot agree on the amount of the adjustment in the Guaranteed Maximum Price, the Contractor's Fee or Contract Time Schedule, it shall be determined pursuant to the provisions of Article 16. Any change in the Guaranteed Maximum Price, the Contractor's Fee or Contract Time Schedule resulting from such claim shall be authorized by Change Order.

9.3 Minor Changes in the Project

9.3.1 The Owner will have authority to order minor Changes in the Work not involving an adjustment in the Guaranteed Maximum Price or an extension of the Contract Time Schedule and not inconsistent with the intent of the Drawings and Specifications. Such Changes may be effected by written order and shall be binding on the Owner and the Contractor.

9.4 Emergencies

9.4.1 In any emergency affecting the safety of persons or property, the Contractor shall act, at his discretion, to prevent threatened damage, injury or loss. Any increase in the Guaranteed Maximum Price or extension of time claimed by the Contractor on account of emergency work shall be determined as provided in this Article.

ARTICLE 10

Discounts

All discounts for prompt payment shall accrue to the Owner to the extent the Cost of the Project is paid directly by the Owner or from a fund made available by the Owner to the Contractor for such payments. To the extent the Cost of the Project is paid with funds of the Contractor, all cash discounts shall accrue to the Contractor. All trade discounts, rebates and refunds, and all returns from sale of surplus materials and equipment, shall be credited to the Cost of the Project.

ARTICLE 11

Payments to the Contractor

11.1 Payments shall be made by the Owner to the Contractor according to the following procedure:

11.1.1 On or before the _____ day of each month after Work has commenced, the Contractor shall submit to the Owner an Application for Payment in such detail as may be required by the Owner based on the Work completed and materials stored on the site and/or at locations approved by the Owner along with a proportionate amount of the Contractor's Fee for the period ending on the _____ day of the month.

11.1.2 Within ten (10) days after his receipt of each monthly Application for Payment, the Owner shall pay directly to the Contractor the appropriate amounts for which Application for Payment is made therein. This payment request shall deduct the aggregate of amounts previously paid by the Owner.

11.1.3 If the Owner should fail to pay the Contractor at the time the payment of any amount becomes due, then the Contractor may, at any time thereafter, upon serving written notice that he will stop Work within five (5) days after receipt of the notice by the Owner, and after such five (5) day period, stop the Project until payment of the amount owing has been received. Written notice shall be deemed to have been duly served if sent by certified mail to the last business address known to him who gives the notice.

11.1.4 Payments due but unpaid shall bear interest at the rate the Owner is paying on his construction loan or at the legal rate, whichever is higher.

11.2 The Contractor warrants and guarantees that title to all Work, materials and equipment covered by an Application for Payment whether incorporated in the Project or not, will pass to the Owner upon receipt of such payment by the Contractor free and clear of all liens, claims, security interests or encumbrances hereinafter referred to as Liens.

11.3 No Progress Payment nor any partial or entire use or occupancy of the Project by the Owner shall constitute an acceptance of any Work not in accordance with the Drawings and Specifications.

122 DESIGN-BUILD CONTRACT

11.4 Final payment constituting the unpaid balance of the Cost of the Project and the Contractor's Fee shall be due and payable when the Project is delivered to the Owner, ready for beneficial occupancy, or when the Owner occupies the Project, whichever event first occurs, provided that the Project be then substantially completed and this Agreement substantially performed. If there should remain minor items to be completed, the Contractor and the Owner shall list such items and the Contractor shall deliver, in writing, his guarantee to complete said items within a reasonable time thereafter. The Owner may retain a sum equal to 150% of the estimated cost of completing any unfinished items, provided that said unfinished items are listed separately and the estimated cost of completing any unfinished items is likewise listed separately. Thereafter, the Owner shall pay to the Contractor, monthly, the amount retained for incomplete items as each of said items is completed.

11.5 Before issuance of Final Payment, the Owner may request satisfactory evidence that all payrolls, materials bills and other indebtedness connected with the Project have been paid or otherwise satisfied.

11.6 The making of Final Payment shall constitute a waiver of all claims by the Owner except those rising from:

11.6.1. Unsettled Liens.

11.6.2 Improper workmanship or defective materials appearing within one year after the Date of Substantial Completion.

11.6.3 Failure of the Work to comply with the Drawings and Specifications.

11.6.4 Terms of any special guarantees required by the Drawings and Specifications.

11.7 The acceptance of Final Payment shall constitute a waiver of all claims by the Contractor except those previously made in writing and unsettled.

ARTICLE 12
Insurance, Indemnity and Waiver of Subrogation

12.1 Indemnity

12.1.1 The Contractor agrees to indemnify and hold the Owner harmless from all claims for bodily injury and property damage (other than the Work itself and other property insured under Paragraph 12.4) that may arise from the Contractor's operations under this Agreement.

12.1.2 The Owner shall cause any other contractor who may have a contract with the Owner to perform work in the areas where Work will be performed under this Agreement, to agree to indemnify the Owner and the Contractor and hold them harmless from all claims for bodily injury and property damage (other than property insured under Paragraph 12.4) that may arise from that contractor's operations. Such provisions shall be in a form satisfactory to the Contractor.

12.2 Contractor's Liability Insurance

12.2.1 The Contractor shall purchase and maintain such insurance as will protect him from the claims set forth below which may arise out of or result from the Contractor's operations under this Agreement whether such operations be by himself or by any Subcontractor or by anyone directly or indirectly employed by any of them, or by anyone for whose acts any of them may be liable:

12.2.1.1 Claims under workers' compensation, disability benefit and other similar employee benefit acts which are applicable to the Work to be performed.

12.2.1.2 Claims for damages because of bodily injury, occupational sickness or disease, or death of his employees under any applicable employer's liability law.

12.2.1.3 Claims for damages because of bodily injury, or death of any person other than his employees.

12.2.1.4 Claims for damages insured by usual personal injury liability coverage which are sustained (1) by any person as a result of an offense directly or indirectly related to the employment of such person by the Contractor or (2) by any other person.

12.2.1.5 Claims for damages, other than to the Work itself, because of injury to or destruction of tangible property, including loss of use therefrom.

12.2.1.6 Claims for damages because of bodily injury or death of any person or property damage arising out of the ownership, maintenance or use of any motor vehicle.

12.2.2 The Comprehensive General Liability Insurance shall include premises-operations (including explosion, collapse and underground coverage) elevators, independent contractors, completed operations, and blanket contractual liability on all written contracts, all including broad form property damage coverage.

12.2.3 The Contractor's Comprehensive General and Automobile Liability Insurance, as required by Subparagraphs 12.2.1 and 12.2.2 shall be written for not less than limits of liability as follows:

a. Comprehensive General Liability
   1. Bodily Injury -$_____ Each Occurrence
                      (Completed Operations)
                     $_____ Aggregate

   2. Property Damage -$_____ Each Occurrence
                       $_____ Aggregate

b. Comprehensive Automobile Liability
   1. Bodily Injury -$_____ Each Person
                     -$_____ Each Occurrence

   2. Property Damage -$_____ Each Occurrence

12.2.4 Comprehensive General Liability Insurance may be arranged under a single policy for the full limits required or by a combination of underlying policies with the balance provided by an Excess or Umbrella Liability policy.

12.2.5 The foregoing policies shall contain a provision that coverages afforded under the policies will not be cancelled or not renewed until at least sixty (60) days' prior written notice has been given to the Owner. Certificates of Insurance showing such coverages to be in force shall be filed with the Owner prior to commencement of the Work.

12.3 Owner's Liability Insurance

12.3.1 The Owner shall be responsible for purchasing and maintaining his own liability insurance and, at his option, may purchase and maintain such insurance as will protect him against claims which may arise from operations under this Agreement.

12.4 Insurance to Protect Project

12.4.1 The Owner shall purchase and maintain property insurance in a form acceptable to the Contractor upon the entire Project for the full cost of replacement as the time of any loss. This insurance shall include as named insureds the Owner, the Contractor, Subcontractors and Subsubcontractors and shall insure against loss from the perils of Fire, Extended Coverage, and shall include "All Risk" insurance for physical loss or damage including, without duplication of coverage, at least theft, vandalism, malicious mischief, transit, collapse, flood, earthquake, testing, and damage resulting from defective design, workmanship or material. The Owner will increase limits of coverage, if necessary, to reflect estimated replacement cost. The Owner will be responsible for any co-insurance penalties or deductibles. If the Project covers an addition to or is adjacent to an existing building, the Contractor, Subcontractors and Subsubcontractors shall be named as additional insureds under the Owner's Property Insurance covering such building and its contents.

12.4.1.1 If the Owner finds it necessary to occupy or use a portion or portions of the Project prior to Substantial Completion thereof, such occupancy shall not commence prior to a time mutually agreed to by the Owner and the Contractor and to which the insurance company or companies providing the property insurance have consented by endorsement to the policy or policies. This insurance shall not be cancelled or lapsed on account of such partial occupancy. Consent of the Contractor and of the insurance company or companies to such occupancy or use shall not be unreasonably withheld.

12.4.2 The Owner shall purchase and maintain such boiler and machinery insurance as may be required or necessary. This insurance shall include the interests of the Owner, the Contractor, Subcontractors and Subsubcontractors in the Work.

12.4.3 The Owner shall purchase and maintain such insurance as will protect the Owner and the Contractor against loss of use of Owner's property due to those perils insured pursuant to Subparagraph 12.4.1. Such policy will provide coverage for expediting expenses of materials, continuing overhead of the Owner and the Contractor, necessary labor expense including overtime, loss of income by the Owner and other determined exposures. Exposures of the Owner and the Contractor shall be determined by mutual agreement and separate limits of coverage fixed for each item.

12.4.4 The Owner shall file a copy of all policies with the Contractor before an exposure to loss may occur. Copies of any subsequent endorsements will be furnished to the Contractor. The Contractor will be given sixty (60) days notice of cancellation, non-renewal, or any endorsements restricting or reducing coverage. If the Owner does not intend to purchase such insurance, he shall inform the Contractor in writing prior to the commencement of the Work. The Contractor may then effect insurance which will protect the interest of himself, the Subcontractors and their Subsubcontractors in the Project, the cost of which shall be a Cost of the Project pursuant to Article 8, and the Guaranteed Maximum Price shall be increased by Change Order. If the Contractor is damaged by failure of the Owner to purchase or maintain such insurance or to so notify the Contractor, the Owner shall bear all reasonable costs properly attributable thereto.

12.5 Property Insurance Loss Adjustment

12.5.1 Any insured loss shall be adjusted with the Owner and the Contractor and made payable to the Owner and Contractor as trustees for the insureds, as their interests may appear, subject to any applicable mortgagee clause.

12.5.2 Upon the occurrence of an insured loss, monies received will be deposited in a separate account and the trustees shall make distribution in accordance with the agreement of the parties in interest, or in the absence of such agreement, in accordance with an arbitration award pursuant to Article 16. If the trustees are unable to agree between themselves on the settlement of the loss, such dispute shall also be submitted to arbitration pursuant to Article 16.

12.6 Waiver of Subrogation

12.6.1 The Owner and Contractor waive all rights against each other, the Architect/Engineer, Subcontractors and Subsubcontractors for damages caused by perils covered by insurance provided under Paragraph 12.4, except such rights as they may have to the proceeds of such insurance held by the Owner and Contractor as trustees. The Contractor shall require similar waivers from all Subcontractors and Subsubcontractors.

12.6.2 The Owner and Contractor waive all rights against each other and the Architect/Engineer, Subcontractors and Subsubcontractors for loss or damage to any equipment used in connection with the Project which loss is covered by any property insurance. The Contractor shall require similar waivers from all Subcontractors and Subsubcontractors.

12.6.3 The Owner waives subrogation against the Contractor, Architect/Engineer, Subcontractors, and Subsubcontractors on all property and consequential loss policies carried by the Owner on adjacent properties and under property and consequential loss policies purchased for the Project after its completion.

12.6.4 If the policies of insurance referred to in this Paragraph require an endorsement to provide for continued coverage where there is a wavier of subrogation, the owners of such policies will cause them to be so endorsed.

ARTICLE 13

Termination of the Agreement And Owner's Right to Perform Contractor's Obligations

13.1 Termination by the Contractor

13.1.1 If the Project is stopped for a period of thirty (30) days under an order of any court or other public authority having jurisdiction, or as a result of an act of government, such as a declaration of a national emergency making materials unavailable, through no act or fault of the Contractor or if the Project should be stopped for a period of thirty (30) days by the Contractor for the Owner's failure to make payment thereon, then the Contractor may, upon seven days' written notice to the Owner, terminate this Agreement and recover from the Owner payment for all Work executed, the Contractor's Fee earned to date, and for any proven loss sustained upon any materials, equipment, tools, construction equipment and machinery, including reasonable profit and damages.

13.2 Owner's Right to Perform Contractor's Obligations and Termination by the Owner for Cause

13.2.1 If the Contractor fails to perform any of his obligations under this Agreement, including any obligation he assumes to perform Work with his own forces, the Owner may, after seven days' written notice, during which period the Contractor fails to perform such obligation, make good such deficiencies. The Guaranteed Maximum Price, if any, shall be reduced by the cost to the Owner of making good such deficiencies.

13.2.2 If the Contractor is adjudged a bankrupt, or if he makes a general assignment for the benefit of his creditors, or if a receiver is appointed on account of his insolvency, or if he persistently or repeatedly refuses or fails, except in cases for which extension of time is provided, to supply enough properly skilled workmen or proper materials, or if he fails to make proper payment to Subcontractors or for materials or labor, or persistently disregards laws, ordinances, rules, regulations or orders of any public authority having jurisdiction, or otherwise is guilty of a substantial violation of a provision of this Agreement, then the Owner may, without prejudice to any right or remedy and after giving the Contractor and his surety, if any, seven (7) days' written notice, during which period the Contractor fails to cure the violation, terminate the employment of the Contractor and take possession of the site and of all materials, equipment, tools, construction equipment and machinery thereon owned by the Contractor and may finish the Work by whatever reasonable method he may deem expedient. In such case, the Contractor shall not be entitled to receive any further payment until the Work is finished nor shall he be relieved from his obligations assumed under Article 6.

13.3 Termination by Owner Without Cause

13.3.1 If the Owner terminates the Agreement other than pursuant to Article 13.2.2, he shall reimburse the Contractor for any unpaid Cost of the Project due him under Article 8, plus the unpaid balance of the Contractor's Fee. If the Contractor's Fee is based upon a percentage of the Cost of the Project, the Fee shall be calculated upon the adjusted Guaranteed Maximum Cost, if any, otherwise to a reasonable estimated Cost of the Project when completed. The Owner shall also pay to the Contractor fair compensation, either by purchase or rental at the election of the Owner, for any equipment retained. In case of such termination of this Agreement the Owner shall further assume and become liable for obligations, commitments and unsettled claims that the Contractor has previously undertaken or incurred in good faith in connection with said Work. The Contractor shall, as a condition of receiving the payments referred to in this Article 13, execute and deliver such papers and take all such steps, including the legal assignment of his contractual rights, as the Owner may require for the purpose of fully vesting in the Owner the rights and benefits of the Contractor under such obligations or commitments.

ARTICLE 14

Assignment and Governing Law

14.1 Neither the Owner nor the Contractor shall assign his interest in this Agreement without the written consent of the other except as to the assignment of proceeds.

14.2 This Agreement shall be governed by the law in effect at the location of this Project.

126 DESIGN-BUILD CONTRACT

ARTICLE 15

Miscellaneous Provisions

ARTICLE 16

Arbitration

16.1 All claims, disputes and other matters in question arising out of, or relating to, this Agreement or the breach thereof, except with respect to the Architect/Engineer's decision on matters relating to artistic effect, and except for claims which have been waived by the making or acceptance of Final Payment shall be decided by arbitration in accordance with the Construction Industry Arbitration Rules of the American Arbitration Association then obtaining unless the parties mutually agree otherwise. This agreement to arbitrate shall be specifically enforceable under the prevailing arbitration law.

16.2 Notice of the demand for arbitration shall be filed in writing with the other party to this Agreement and with the American Arbitration Association. The demand for arbitration shall be made within a reasonable time after the claim, dispute or other matter in question has arisen, and in no event shall it be made when institution of legal or equitable proceedings based on such claim, dispute or other matter in question would be barred by the applicable statute of limitations.

16.3 The award rendered by the arbitrators shall be final and judgment may be entered upon it in accordance with applicable law in any court having jurisdiction thereof.

16.4 Unless otherwise agreed in writing, the Contractor shall carry on the Work and maintain the Contract Time Schedule during any arbitration proceedings and the Owner shall continue to make payments in accordance with this Agreement.

16.5 All claims which are related to or dependent upon each other shall be heard by the same arbitrator or arbitrators, even though the parties are not the same, unless a specific contract prohibits such consolidation.

16.6 These provisions relating to mandatory arbitration shall not be applicable to a claim asserted in an action in a state or federal court by a person who is under no obligation to arbitrate such claim with either of the parties to this Agreement insofar as the parties to this Agreement may desire to assert any rights of indemnity or contribution with respect to the subject matter of such action.

This Agreement entered into as of the day and year first written above.

ATTEST: OWNER:

ATTEST: CONTRACTOR:

FORM 2-4 Supplementary General Conditions [Favors Interest of Owner] (with Comments)

AGC Document No. 410 Design-Build Agreement is amended as follows:

¶1. <u>First:</u> **Article 1.2** The last sentence of Article 1.2 is annulled.

> Comment: The parties would normally expect that the provisions of the contract documents that are negotiated to implement the design-build agreement would modify or supercede that agreement in the event of inconsistency or conflict.

¶2. <u>Second:</u> **Article 2.1.2** The following sentence is added at the end of Article 2.1.2:

> It is understood that Contractor is responsible for engineering and design, and that, with the consent of Owner, Contractor may employ additional Architects and Engineers, or may replace Architect/Engineer so long as Contractor does not employ any person who is reasonably objectionable to Owner.

¶3. <u>Third:</u> **Article 2.2.4** *See* §2.1.2.

¶4. <u>Fourth:</u> **Article 2.2.6** *See* §2.1.6.

¶5. <u>Fifth:</u> **Article 2.4.1** The following sentence is added to Article 2.4.1:

> Contractor remains responsible for the compliance of all equipment, materials, and workmanship with the requirements of the contract documents, regardless of whether such non-compliance manifests itself or is discovered within one year after substantial completion, or later.

¶6. <u>Sixth:</u> **Article 2.5.2** *See* **FORM 2-2** ¶7

¶7. <u>Seventh:</u> **Article 3.3** *See* **FORM 2-2** ¶8

¶8. <u>Eighth:</u> **Article 3.10** *See* **FORM 2-2** ¶9

¶9. <u>Ninth:</u> **Article 3.11** *See* **FORM 2-2** ¶10

¶10. <u>Tenth:</u> **Article 7.2.4** Article 7.2.4. is annulled.

¶11. <u>Eleventh:</u> **Article 8.2.10** The phrase "or is deemed necessary by the Contractor" is stricken from Article 8.2.10.

¶12. **Twelfth:** **Article 8.2.13** The following sentence is added to Article 8.2.13:

> The Cost of the Project does not include losses, expenses or damages caused by the negligence, fault, or misconduct of Contractor or a Subcontractor of any tier.

¶13. **Thirteenth:** **Article 8.2.17** Article 8.2.17 is annulled.

¶14. **Fourteenth:** **Article 8.2.18** Article 8.2.18 is annulled.

¶15. **Fifteenth:** **Article 8.2.19** Article 8.2.19 is annulled.

¶16. **Sixteenth:** *See* **FORM 2-2** ¶12.

¶17. **Seventeenth:** *See* **FORM 2-2** ¶16.

¶18. **Eighteenth:** **Article 11.6** Article 11.6 is annulled.

¶19. **Nineteenth:** **Article 11.6.1** Article 11.6.1 is annulled.

¶20. **Twentieth:** **Article 11.6.2** Article 11.6.2 is annulled.

¶21. **Twenty-First:** **Article 11.6.3** Article 11.6.3 is annulled.

¶22. **Twenty-Second:** **Article 11.6.4** Article 11.6.4 is annulled.

¶23. **Twenty-Third:** **Article 12.1.1** *See* **FORM 2-2** ¶18.

¶24. **Twenty-Fourth:** **Article 12.2.1.5** *See* **FORM 2-2** ¶19.

¶25. **Twenty-Fifth:** **Article 12.2.6.** Article 12.2.6 is added. *See* **FORM 2-2** ¶20.

¶26. **Twenty-Sixth:** **Article 12.2.7.** Article 12.2.7 is added. *See* **FORM 2-2** ¶21.

¶27. **Twenty-Seventh:** **Article 12.4** *See* **FORM 2-2** ¶22.

¶28. **Twenty-Eighth:** **Article 12.4.1** *See* **FORM 2-2** ¶23.

¶29. **Twenty-Ninth:** **Article 12.4.1.1** *See* **FORM 2-2** ¶24.

¶30. **Thirtieth:** **Article 12.4.2** *See* **FORM 2-2** ¶25.

¶31. **Thirty-First:** **Article 12.4.3** *See* **FORM 2-2** ¶26.

¶32. **Thirty-Second:** Article 12.4.4 *See* FORM 2-2 ¶27.

¶33. **Thirty-Third:** Article 12.6.1 *See* FORM 2-2 ¶28.

¶34. **Thirty-Fourth:** Article 12.6.2 *See* FORM 2-2 ¶29.

¶35. **Thirty-Fifth:** Article 12.6.3 *See* FORM 2-2 ¶30.

¶36. **Thirty-Sixth:** Article 12.6.4 *See* FORM 2-2 ¶31.

¶37. **Thirty-Seventh:** Article 13.3.1 *See* FORM 2-2 ¶32.

¶38. **Thirth-Eighth:** Article 14.2 *See* FORM 2-2 ¶33.

¶39. **Thirty-Ninth:** Article 16.1 Article 16.1 is amended to read as follows:

All claims, disputes and other matters in question arising out of, or relating to, this agreement or the breach or interpretation thereof shall be decided by arbitration in accordance with the Construction Industry Arbitration Rules of the American Arbitration Association, and judgment may be entered on the award.

¶40. **Fourtieth:** Article 16.2 Article 16.2 is annulled.

¶41. **Forty-First:** Article 16.5 Article 16.5 is annulled.

¶42. **Forty-Second:** Article 16.6 *See* FORM 2-2 ¶34.

§2.09 Clarifications to AGC Documents Nos. 410 and 415

AGC Documents Nos. 410 and 415 seem to assume that the parties have agreed on a lump sum price or a guaranteed maximum cost before the contract is signed. It may not be possible, though, for the parties to agree to the price until after the drawings and specifications have been partially prepared so the contractor can obtain sub-bids and also make a reasonable estimate of the cost of work to be done by the contractor's own forces. The process by which the contractor obtains the design on the project usually includes submissions of designs and bids by **design-build subcontractors.**

A contractor may be reluctant to expend the cost of designing a project without assurance that those costs will be reimbursed if the owner elects to abandon the project or employ another contractor. Likewise, an owner may be reluctant to sign a fixed price contract until the drawings and specifications have advanced to such a point as to fairly describe the project.

An instrument that may be used to bridge the gap is a **letter of intent** such as the following:

FORM 2-5 Letter of Intent to Award Design-Build Contract (with Comment)

LETTER OF INTENT TO AWARD DESIGN-BUILD CONTRACT
[LETTER FROM CONTRACTOR TO OWNER]

You have indicated Your intention to award to Our Company a contract to design and build a _____ Project located at _____ at a contract price that will be determined as soon as the construction documents are sufficiently complete to enable us to make a reasonable estimate of construction costs. The general nature of the Project is described in the preliminary sketches and outline specifications that are attached to this letter and identified as follows:

_____
_____ .

Based upon Your execution of this letter of intent, We shall employ licensed Architects, Engineers, and Design-Build Subcontractors, and shall furnish the services of Our Staff in preparing sketches, drawings, layouts, and outline specifications to more fully define, identify, and display the essential characteristics of the project and its equipment, materials, systems, appearance, function and layout.

By signing a copy of this letter, You agree to meet with Our Project Manager and the Design Personnel employed by Our Company at reasonable times to review Our efforts and guide Us in such a way that the design will be in accordance with Your desires as to cost, function, and aesthetics.

When the design development documents are sufficiently complete, which We anticipate will be in approximately sixty (60) days, You intend to sign a contract with Us under which, in exchange for a fixed lump sum contract price, We shall agree to complete the design and build the project according to a mutually agreeable schedule.

You have the right to terminate Our performance under this letter of intent at any time, and thereupon shall be obliged to pay Us an amount as stated below. All of the design development documents that We have prepared until the time of termination, along with Subcontractor bids and estimates, and the estimates of our Own Estimating Department will be turned over to You, and You may use them for any purpose provided that You have paid Us the actual cost of their preparation, plus a coordination and design fee equal to 15 per cent of such costs. An accounting of such costs will be delivered to You and You shall have the right to audit our books and records that pertain to such costs.

As earnest money, You have deposited the sum of $_____ to be applied to the payment of costs and fees, if You should decide to terminate Our performance. Any excess deposit will be refunded to You or You will promptly pay to Us the amount by which the costs and fees may exceed the deposit.

> Comment: A pure "letter of intent" is unenforceable in many states, because it does not evidence a contract, but merely an intention to enter into a contract. However, the letter of intent displayed above is an enforceable contract, since it is supported by consideration on both sides and evidences at least a contract for design services, even though it is arguably no more than a manifestation of intention to enter into a future contract for the construction of the project.

The ingenious contractor should have little difficulty adapting this suggested letter of intent format to its own operations.

Construction Management Contract 3

Introduction to Construction Management Contracts

§3.01 General Comment

AGC Document No. 500 - Construction Management Agreement - Guaranteed Maximum Price

    FORM 3-1   AGC Document No. 500 - Standard Form of Agreement between Owner and Construction Manager (Guaranteed Maximum Price Option) (1980)

    FORM 3-2   Modifications to Construction Management Agreement [Favors Interests of Owner] (with Comments)

AGC Document No. 501 - Amendment to Owner-Construction Manager Contract

§3.02 General Comment

    FORM 3-3   AGC Document No. 501 - Amendment to Owner-Construction Manager Contract (1977)

AGC Document No. 520 - General Conditions for Trade Contractors

§3.03 General Comment

    FORM 3-4   AGC Document No. 520 - General Conditions for Trade Contractors under Construction Management Agreements (1980)

    FORM 3-5   Modifications to General Conditions for Trade Contractors [Favors Interests of Trade Contractor] (with Comments)

Introduction to Construction Management Contracts

§3.01 General Comment

AGC Document No. 500 introduces the construction management concept. Document No. 500 allows for the establishment of a **guaranteed maximum price.**

This form of agreement contemplates that the owner will employ an architect/engineer, and that the construction manager will contract with trade contractors. An option is provided in Article 4.3 that the trade contracts may be established directly between the owner and the trade contractor, at the option of the owner.

From the owner's point of view, it would usually be preferable for the trade contractors to sign directly with the construction manager rather than with the owner, since the construction manager thereby becomes responsible for the performance of the trade contractors.

Since this form of contract is published by the Associated General Contractors, as would be expected, it provides adequate protection of the interests of the contractor.

Amendments that look to protection of the interests of the owner will be found beginning at ¶1 of **FORM 3-2.**

Notice that, in Article 1.1, the construction manager is unabashedly designated the party who "shall provide leadership" to the construction team, which consists of construction manager, owner, and architect/engineer. Thus the contractor, rather than the architect, assumes the legendary position of *master builder.*

To the owner, the great advantage of the construction management concept embodied in AGC Document No. 500 is that the contractor becomes deeply involved in planning, scheduling, and budgeting from the very beginning of design. The obvious difference between construction management and design-build, as exemplified by Chapter Two, is that under the construction management scenario, the architect/engineer is employed by the owner rather than by the contractor.

Article 2.1.4 specifically provides that the construction manager does not assume any of the architect/engineer's responsibilities for design. This deprives the owner of the **single responsible party** advantage of design-build that is referred to in **§2.04.**.

However, since the contractor is very actively involved during the design and budgeting phase of the project, the project should benefit from the contractor's special knowledge of local conditions, public agency requirements, types of materials and equipment that are available and their cost, effective scheduling and sequencing techniques, efficient methods of construction, and the availability of specialized consultants and trade contractors.

AGC Document No. 500 - Construction Management Agreement - Guaranteed Maximum Price

FORM 3-1 AGC Document No. 500 - Standard Form of Agreement between Owner and Construction Manager (Guaranteed Maximum Price Option) (1980)

AIA copyrighted material has been reproduced with the permission of the American Institute of Architects under license number 90153. Permission expires December 31, 1991.

This document is intended for use as a "consumable" (consumables are further defined by Senate Report 94-473 on the Copyright Act of 1976). This document is not intended to be used as "model language" (language taken from an existing document and incorporated, without attribution, into a newly-created document). Rather, it is a standard form which is intended to be modified by appending separate amendment sheets and/or fill in provided blank spaces.

§3.01 AGC DOCUMENT NO. 500   135

THE ASSOCIATED GENERAL CONTRACTORS

STANDARD FORM OF AGREEMENT BETWEEN OWNER AND CONSTRUCTION MANAGER

(GUARANTEED MAXIMUM PRICE OPTION)

(See AGC Document No. 500 for Establishing the Guaranteed Maximum Price)

This Document has important legal and insurance consequences; consultation with an attorney is encouraged with respect to its completion or modification.

AGREEMENT

Made this   day of   in the year of Nineteen Hundred and

BETWEEN   the Owner, and

the Construction Manager.

For services in connection with the following described Project: (Include complete Project location and scope)

The Architect/Engineer for the Project is

The Owner and the Construction Manager agree as set forth below:

Certain provisions of this document have been derived, with modifications, from the following documents published by The American Institute of Architects: AIA Document A111, Owner Contractor Agreement, © 1974, AIA Document A201, General Conditions, © 1976, AIA Document B801, Owner Construction Manager Agreement, © 1973, by The American Institute of Architects. Usage made of AIA language, with the permission of AIA, does not apply AIA endorsement or approval of this document. Further reproduction of copyrighted AIA materials without separate written permission from AIA is prohibited.

AGC DOCUMENT NO. 500   •   OWNER CONSTRUCTION MANAGER AGREEMENT   •   JULY 1980
© 1980 Associated General Contractors of America

CONSTRUCTION MANAGEMENT CONTRACT

TABLE OF CONTENTS

ARTICLES	PAGE
1 The Construction Team and Extent of Agreement	1
2 Construction Manager's Services	1
3 The Owner's Responsibilities	4
4 Trade Contracts	5
5 Schedule	5
6 Guaranteed Maximum Price	6
7 Construction Manager's Fee	6
8 Cost of the Project	7
9 Changes in the Project	8
10 Discounts	9
11 Payments to the Construction Manager	10
12 Insurance, Indemnity and Waiver of Subrogation	10
13 Termination of the Agreement and Owner's Right to Perform Construction Manager's Obligations	13
14 Assignment and Governing Law	14
15 Miscellaneous Provisions	14
16 Arbitration	14

ARTICLE 1

The Construction Team and Extent of Agreement

The CONSTRUCTION MANAGER accepts the relationship of trust and confidence established between him and the Owner by this Agreement. He covenants with the Owner to furnish his best skill and judgment and to cooperate with the Architect/Engineer in furthering the interests of the Owner. He agrees to furnish efficient business administration and superintendence and to use his best efforts to complete the Project in an expeditious and economical manner consistent with the interest of the Owner.

1.1 *The Construction Team:* The Construction Manager, the Owner, and the Architect/Engineer called the "Construction Team" shall work from the beginning of design through construction completion. The Construction Manager shall provide leadership to the Construction Team on all matters relating to construction.

1.2 *Extent of Agreement:* This Agreement represents the entire agreement between the Owner and the Construction Manager and supersedes all prior negotiations, representations or agreements. When Drawings and Specifications are complete, they shall be identified by amendment to this Agreement. This Agreement shall not be superseded by any provisions of the documents for construction and may be amended only by written instrument signed by both the Owner and the Construction Manager.

1.3 *Definitions:* The Project is the total construction to be performed under this Agreement. The Work is that part of the construction that the Construction Manager is to perform with his own forces or that part of the construction that a particular Trade Contractor is to perform. The term day shall mean calendar day unless otherwise specifically designated.

ARTICLE 2

Construction Manager's Services

The Construction Manager will perform the following services under this Agreement in each of the two phases described below.

2.1 Design Phase

2.1.1 *Consultation During Project Development:* Schedule and attend regular meetings with the Architect/Engineer during the development of conceptual and preliminary design to advise on site use and improvements, selection of materials, building systems and equipment. Provide recommendations on construction feasibility, availability of materials and labor, time requirements for installation and construction, and factors related to cost including costs of alternative designs or materials, preliminary budgets, and possible economies.

2.1.2 *Scheduling:* Develop a Project Time Schedule that coordinates and integrates the Architect/Engineer's design efforts with construction schedules. Update the Project Time Schedule incorporating a detailed schedule for the construction operations of the Project, including realistic activity sequences and durations, allocation of labor and materials, processing of shop drawings and samples, and delivery of products requiring long lead-time procurement. Include the Owner's occupancy requirements showing portions of the Project having occupancy priority.

2.1.3 *Project Construction Budget:* Prepare a Project budget as soon as major Project requirements have been identified, and update periodically for the Owner's approval. Prepare an estimate based on a quantity survey of Drawings and Specifications at the end of the schematic design phase for approval by the Owner as the Project Construction Budget. Update and refine this estimate for the Owner's approval as the development of the Drawings and Specifications proceeds, and advise the Owner and the Architect/Engineer if it appears that the Project Construction Budget will not be met and make recommendations for corrective action.

2.1.4 *Coordination of Contract Documents:* Review the Drawings and Specifications as they are being prepared, recommending alternative solutions whenever design details affect construction feasibility or schedules without, however, assuming any of the Architect/Engineer's responsibilities for design.

138 CONSTRUCTION MANAGEMENT CONTRACT

2.1.5 *Construction Planning:* Recommend for purchase and expedite the procurement of long-lead items to ensure their delivery by the required dates.

2.1.5.1 Make recommendations to the Owner and the Architect/Engineer regarding the division of Work in the Drawings and Specifications to facilitate the bidding and awarding of Trade Contracts, allowing for phased construction taking into consideration such factors as time of performance, availability of labor, overlapping trade jurisdictions, and provisions for temporary facilities.

2.1.5.2 Review the Drawings and Specifications with the Architect/Engineer to eliminate areas of conflict and overlapping in the Work to be performed by the various Trade Contractors and prepare prequalification criteria for bidders.

2.1.5.3 Develop Trade Contractor interest in the Project and as working Drawings and Specifications are completed, take competitive bids on the Work of the various Trade Contractors. After analyzing the bids, either award contracts or recommend to the Owner that such contracts be awarded.

2.1.6 *Equal Employment Opportunity:* Determine applicable requirements for equal emloyment opportunity programs for inclusion in Project bidding documents.

2.2 Construction Phase

2.2.1 *Project Control:* Monitor the Work of the Trade Contractors and coordinate the Work with the activities and responsibilities of the Owner, Architect/Engineer and Construction Manager to complete the Project in accordance with the Owner's objectives of cost, time and quality.

2.2.1.1 Maintain a competent full-time staff at the Project site to coordinate and provide general direction of the Work and progress of the Trade Contractors on the Project.

2.2.1.2 Establish on-site organization and lines of authority in order to carry out the overall plans of the Construction Team.

2.2.1.3 Establish procedures for coordination among the Owner, Architect/Engineer, Trade Contractors and Construction Manager with respect to all aspects of the Project and implement such procedures.

2.2.1.4 Schedule and conduct progress meetings at which Trade Contractors, Owner, Architect/Engineer and Construction Manager can discuss jointly such matters as procedures, progress, problems and scheduling.

2.2.1.5 Provide regular monitoring of the schedule as construction progresses. Identify potential variances between scheduled and probable completion dates. Review schedule for Work not started or incomplete and recommend to the Owner and Trade Contractors adjustments in the schedule to meet the probable completion date. Provide summary reports of each monitoring and document all changes in schedule.

2.2.1.6 Determine the adequacy of the Trade Contractors' personnel and equipment and the availability of materials and supplies to meet the schedule. Recommend courses of action to the Owner when requirements of a Trade Contract are not being met.

2.2.2 *Physical Construction:* Provide all supervision, labor, materials, construction equipment, tools and subcontract items which are necessary for the completion of the Project which are not provided by either the Trade Contractors or the Owner. To the extent that the Construction Manager performs any Work with his own forces, he shall, with respect to such Work, perform in accordance with the Plans and Specifications and in accordance with the procedure applicable to the Project.

2.2.3 *Cost Control:* Develop and monitor an effective system of Project cost control. Revise and refine the initially approved Project Construction Budget, incorporate approved changes as they occur, and develop cash flow reports and forecasts as needed. Identify variances between actual and budgeted or estimated costs and advise Owner and Architect/Engineer whenever projected cost exceeds budgets or estimates.

2.2.3.1 Maintain cost accounting records on authorized Work performed under unit costs, actual costs for labor and material, or other bases requiring accounting records. Afford the Owner access to these records and preserve them for a period of three (3) years after final payment.

2.2.4 *Change Orders:* Develop and implement a system for the preparation, review and processing of Change Orders. Recommend necessary or desirable change to the Owner and the Architect/Engineer, review requests for changes, submit recommendations to the Owner and the Architect/Engineer, and assist in negotiating Change Orders.

2.2.5 *Payments to Trade Contractors:* Develop and implement a procedure for the review, processing and payment of applications by Trade Contractors for progress and final payments.

2.2.6 *Permits and Fees:* Assist the Owner and Architect/Engineer in obtaining all building permits and special permits for permanent improvements, excluding permits for inspection or temporary facilities required to be obtained directly by the various Trade Contractors. Assist in obtaining approvals from all the authorities having jurisdiction.

2.2.7 *Owner's Consultants:* If required, assist the Owner in selecting and retaining professional services of a surveyor, testing laboratories and special consultants, and coordinate these services, without assuming any responsibility or liability of or for these consultants.

2.2.8 *Inspection:* Inspect the Work of Trade Contractors for defects and deficiencies in the Work without assuming any of the Architect/Engineer's responsibilities for inspection.

2.2.8.1 Review the safety programs of each of the Trade Contractors and make appropriate recommendations. In making such recommendations and carrying out such reviews, he shall not be required to make exhaustive or continuous inspections to check safety precautions and programs in connection with the Project. The performance of such services by the Construction Manager shall not relieve the Trade Contractors of their responsibilities for the safety of persons and property, and for compliance with all federal, state and local statutes, rules, regulations and orders applicable to the conduct of the Work.

2.2.9 *Document Interpretation:* Refer all questions for interpretation of the documents prepared by the Architect/Engineer to the Architect/Engineer.

2.2.10 *Shop Drawings and Samples:* In collaboration with the Architect/Engineer, establish and implement procedures for expediting the processing and approval of shop drawings and samples.

2.2.11 *Reports and Project Site Documents:* Record the progress of the Project. Submit written progress reports to the Owner and the Architect/Engineer including information on the Trade Contractors' Work, and the percentage of completion. Keep a daily log available to the Owner and the Architect/Engineer.

2.2.11.1 Maintain at the Project site, on a current basis: records of all necessary Contracts, Drawings, samples, purchases, materials, equipment, maintenance and operating manuals and instructions, and other construction related documents, including all revisions. Obtain data from Trade Contractors and maintain a current set of record Drawings, Specifications and operating manuals. At the completion of the Project, deliver all such records to the Owner.

2.2.12 *Substantial Completion:* Determine Substantial Completion of the Work or designated portions thereof and prepare for the Architect/Engineer a list of incomplete or unsatisfactory items and a schedule for their completion.

2.2.13 *Start-Up:* With the Owner's maintenance personnel, direct the checkout of utilities, operations systems and equipment for readiness and assist in their initial start-up and testing by the Trade Contractors.

2.2.14 *Final Completion:* Determine final completion and provide written notice to the Owner and Architect/Engineer that the Work is ready for final inspection. Secure and transmit to the Architect/Engineer required guarantees, affidavits, releases, bonds and waivers. Turn over to the Owner all keys, manuals, record drawings and maintenance stocks.

2.2.15 *Warranty:* Where any Work is performed by the Construction Manager's own forces or by Trade Contractors under contract with the Construction Manager, the Construction Manager shall warrant that all materials and equipment included in such Work will be new, unless otherwise specified, and that such Work will be of good quality, free from improper workmanship and defective materials and in conformance with the Drawings and Specifications. With respect to the same Work, the

140 CONSTRUCTION MANAGEMENT CONTRACT

Construction Manager further agrees to correct all Work defective in material and workmanship for a period of one year from the Date of Substantial Completion or for such longer periods of time as may be set forth with respect to specific warranties contained in the trade sections of the Specifications. The Construction Manager shall collect and deliver to the Owner any specific written warranties given by others.

2.3 Additional Services

2.3.1 At the request of the Owner the Construction Manager will provide the following additional services upon written agreement between the Owner and Construction Manager defining the extent of such additional services and the amount and manner in which the Construction Manager will be compensated for such additional services.

2.3.2 Services related to investigation, appraisals or valuations of existing conditions, facilities or equipment, or verifying the accuracy of existing drawings or other Owner-furnished information.

2.3.3 Services related to Owner-furnished equipment, furniture and furnishings which are not a part of this Agreement.

2.3.4 Services for tenant or rental spaces not a part of this Agreement.

2.3.5 Obtaining or training maintenance personnel or negotiating maintenance service contracts.

ARTICLE 3
Owner's Responsibilities

3.1 The Owner shall provide full information regarding his requirements for the Project.

3.2 The Owner shall designate a representative who shall be fully acquainted with the Project and has authority to issue and approve Project Construction Budgets, issue Change Orders, render decisions promptly and furnish information expeditiously.

3.3 The Owner shall retain an Architect/Engineer for design and to prepare construction documents for the Project. The Architect/Engineer's services, duties and responsibilities are described in the Agreement between the Owner and the Architect/Engineer, a copy of which will be furnished to the Construction Manager. The Agreement between the Owner and the Architect/Engineer shall not be modified without written notification to the Construction Manager.

3.4 The Owner shall furnish for the site of the Project all necessary surveys describing the physical characteristics, soil reports and subsurface investigations, legal limitations, utility locations, and a legal description.

3.5 The Owner shall secure and pay for necessary approvals, easements, assessments and charges required for the construction, use or occupancy of permanent structures or for permanent changes in existing facilities.

3.6 The Owner shall furnish such legal services as may be necessary for providing the items set forth in Paragraph 3.5, and such auditing services as he may require.

3.7 The Construction Manager will be furnished without charge all copies of Drawings and Specifications reasonably necessary for the execution of the Work.

3.8 The Owner shall provide the insurance for the Project as provided in Paragraph 12.4, and shall bear the cost of any bonds required.

3.9 The services, information, surveys and reports required by the above paragraphs or otherwise to be furnished by other consultants employed by the Owner, shall be furnished with reasonable promptness at the Owner's expense and the Construction Manager shall be entitled to rely upon the accuracy and completeness thereof.

3.10 If the Owner becomes aware of any fault or defect in the Project or non-conformance with the Drawings and Specifications, he shall give prompt written notice thereof to the Construction Manager.

3.11 The Owner shall furnish, prior to commencing work and at such future times as may be requested, reasonable evidence satisfactory to the Construction Manager that sufficient funds are available and committed for the entire cost of the Project. Unless such reasonable evidence is furnished, the Construction Manager is not required to commence or continue any Work; or may, if such evidence is not presented within a reasonable time, stop the Project upon 15 days notice to the Owner. The failure of the Construction Manager to insist upon the providing of this evidence at any one time shall not be a waiver of the Owner's obligation to make payments pursuant to this Agreement nor shall it be a waiver of the Construction Manager's right to request or insist that such evidence be provided at a later date.

3.12 The Owner shall communicate with the Trade Contractors only through the Construction Manager.

ARTICLE 4

Trade Contracts

4.1 All portions of the Project that the Construction Manager does not perform with his own forces shall be performed under Trade Contracts. The Construction Manager shall request and receive proposals from Trade Contractors and Trade Contracts will be awarded after the proposals are reviewed by the Architect/Engineer, Construction Manager and Owner.

4.2 If the Owner refuses to accept a Trade Contractor recommended by the Construction Manager, the Construction Manager shall recommend an acceptable substitute and the Guaranteed Maximum Price if applicable shall be increased or decreased by the difference in cost occasioned by such substitution and an appropriate Change Order shall be issued.

4.3 Unless otherwise directed by the Owner, Trade Contracts will be between the Construction Manager and the Trade Contractors. Whether the Trade Contracts are with the Construction Manager or the Owner, the form of the Trade Contracts including the General and Supplementary Conditions shall be satisfactory to the Construction Manager.

4.4 The Construction Manager shall be responsible to the Owner for the acts and omissions of his agents and employees, Trade Contractors performing Work under a contract with the Construction Manager, and such Trade Contractors' agents and employees.

ARTICLE 5

Schedule

5.1 The services to be provided under this Contract shall be in general accordance with the following schedule:

5.2 At the time a Guaranteed Maximum Price is established, as provided for in Article 6, a Date of Substantial Completion of the project shall also be established.

5.3 The Date of Substantial Completion of the Project or a designated portion thereof is the date when construction is sufficiently complete in accordance with the Drawings and Specifications so the Owner can occupy or utilize the Project or designated portion thereof for the use for which it is intended. Warranties called for by this Agreement or by the Drawings and Specifications shall commence on the Date of Substantial Completion of the Project or designated portion thereof.

5.4 If the Construction Manager is delayed at any time in the progress of the Project by any act or neglect of the Owner or the Architect/Engineer or by any employee of either, or by any separate contractor employed by the Owner, or by changes ordered in the Project, or by labor disputes, fire, unusual delay in transportation, adverse weather conditions not reasonably anticipatable, unavoidable casualties or any causes beyond the Construction Manager's control, or by delay authorized by the Owner pending arbitration, the Construction Completion Date shall be extended by Change Order for a reasonable length of time.

ARTICLE 6

Guaranteed Maximum Price

6.1 When the design, Drawings and Specifications are sufficiently complete, the Construction Manager will, if desired by the Owner, establish a Guaranteed Maximum Price, guaranteeing the maximum price to the Owner for the Cost of the Project and the Construction Manager's Fee. Such Guaranteed Maximum Price will be subject to modification for Changes in the Project as provided in Article 9, and for additional costs arising from delays caused by the Owner or the Architect/Engineer.

6.2 When the Construction Manager provides a Guaranteed Maximum Price, the Trade Contracts will either be with the Construction Manager or will contain the necessary provisions to allow the Construction Manager to control the performance of the Work. The Owner will also authorize the Construction Manager to take all steps necessary in the name of the Owner, including arbitration or litigation, to assure that the Trade Contractors perform their contracts in accordance with their terms.

6.3 The Guaranteed Maximum Price will only include those taxes in the Cost of the Project which are legally enacted at the time the Guaranteed Maximum Price is established.

ARTICLE 7

Construction Manager's Fee

7.1 In consideration of the performance of the Contract, the Owner agrees to pay the Construction Manager in current funds as compensation for his services a Construction Manager's Fee as set forth in Subparagraphs 7.1.1 and 7.1.2.

7.1.1 For the performance of the Design Phase services, a fee of which shall be paid monthly, in equal proportions, based on the scheduled Design Phase time.

7.1.2 For work or services performed during the Construction Phase, a fee of which shall be paid proportionately to the ratio the monthly payment for the Cost of the Project bears to the estimated cost. Any balance of this fee shall be paid at the time of final payment.

7.2 Adjustments in Fee shall be made as follows:

7.2.1 For Changes in the Project as provided in Article 9, the Construction Manager's Fee shall be adjusted as follows:

7.2.2 For delays in the Project not the responsibility of the Construction Manager, there will be an equitable adjustment in the fee to compensate the Constructon Manager for his increased expenses.

7.2.3 The Construction Manager shall be paid an additional fee in the same proportion as set forth in 7.2.1 if the Construction Manager is placed in charge of the reconstruction of any insured or uninsured loss.

7.3 Included in the Construction Manager's Fee are the following:

7.3.1 Salaries or other compensation of the Construction Manager's employees at the principal office and branch offices, except employees listed in Subparagraph 8.2.2.

7.3.2 General operating expenses of the Construction Manager's principal and branch offices other than the field office.

7.3.3 Any part of the Construction Manager's capital expenses, including interest on the Construction Manager's capital employed for the project.

7.3.4 Overhead or general expenses of any kind, except as may be expressly included in Article 8.

7.3.5 Costs in excess of the Guaranteed Maximum Price.

ARTICLE 8
Cost of the Project

8.1 The term Cost of the Project shall mean costs necessarily incurred in the Project during either the Design or Construction Phase, and paid by the Construction Manager, or by the Owner if the Owner is directly paying Trade Contractors upon the Construction Manager's approval and direction. Such costs shall include the items set forth below in this Article.

8.1.1 The Owner agrees to pay the Construction Manager for the Cost of the Project as defined in Article 8. Such payment shall be in addition to the Construction Manager's Fee stipulated in Article 7.

8.2 Cost Items

8.2.1 Wages paid for labor in the direct employ of the Construction Manager in the performance of his Work under applicable collective bargaining agreements, or under a salary or wage schedule agreed upon by the Owner and Construction Manager, and including such welfare or other benefits, if any, as may be payable with respect thereto.

8.2.2 Salaries of the Construction Manager's employees when stationed at the field office, in whatever capacity employed, employees engaged on the road in expediting the production or transportation of materials and equipment, and employees in the main or branch office performing the functions listed below.

8.2.3 Cost of all employee benefits and taxes for such items as unemployment compensation and social security, insofar as such cost is based on wages, salaries, or other remuneration paid to employees of the Construction Manager and included in the Cost of the Project under Subparagraphs 8.2.1 and 8.2.2.

8.2.4 Reasonable transportation, traveling, moving, and hotel expenses of the Construction Manager or of his officers or employees incurred in discharge of duties connected with the Project.

8.2.5 Cost of all materials, supplies and equipment incorporated in the Project, including costs of transportation and storage thereof.

8.2.6 Payments made by the Construction Manager or Owner to Trade Contractors for their Work performed pursuant to contract under this Agreement.

8.2.7 Cost, including transportation and maintenance, of all materials, supplies, equipment, temporary facilities and hand tools not owned by the workmen, which are employed or consumed in the performance of the Work, and cost less salvage value on such items used but not consumed which remain the property of the Construciton Manager.

8.2.8 Rental charges of all necessary machinery and equipment, exclusive of hand tools, used at the site of the Project, whether rented from the Construction Manager or other, including installation, repairs and replacements, dismantling, removal, costs of lubrication, transportation and delivery costs thereof, at rental charges consistent with those prevailing in the area.

144 CONSTRUCTION MANAGEMENT CONTRACT

8.2.9 Cost of the premiums for all insurance which the Construction Manager is required to procure by this Agreement or is deemed necessary by the Construction Manager.

8.2.10 Sales, use, gross receipts or similar taxes related to the Project imposed by any governmental authority, and for which the Construction Manager is liable.

8.2.11 Permit fees, licenses, tests, royalties, damages for infringement of patents and costs of defending suits therefor, and deposits lost for causes other than the Construction Manager's negligence. If royalties or losses and damages, including costs of defense, are incurred which arise from a particular design, process, or the product of a particular manufacturer or manufacturers specified by the Owner or Architect/Engineer, and the Construction Manager has no reason to believe there will be infringement of patent rights, such royalties, losses and damages shall be paid by the Owner and not considered as within the Guaranteed Maximum Price.

8.2.12 Losses, expenses or damages to the extent not compensated by insurance or otherwise (including settlement made with the written approval of the Owner).

8.2.13 The cost of corrective work subject, however, to the Guaranteed Maximum Price.

8.2.14 Minor expenses such as telegrams, long-distance telephone calls, telephone service at the site, expressage, and similar petty cash items in connection with the Project.

8.2.15 Cost of removal of all debris.

8.2.16 Cost incurred due to an emergency affecting the safety of persons and property.

8.2.17 Cost of data processing services required in the performance of the services outlined in Article 2.

8.2.18 Legal costs reasonably and properly resulting from prosecution of the Project for the Owner.

8.2.19 All costs directly incurred in the performance of the Project and not included in the Construction Manager's Fee as set forth in Paragraph 7.3.

ARTICLE 9
Changes in the Project

9.1 The Owner, without invalidating this Agreement, may order Changes in the Project within the general scope of this Agreement consisting of additions, deletions or other revisions, the Guaranteed Maximum Price, if established, the Construction Manager's Fee and the Construction Completion Date being adjusted accordingly. All such Changes in the Project shall be authorized by Change Order.

9.1.1 A Change Order is a written order to the Construction Manager signed by the Owner or his authorized agent issued after the execution of this Agreement, authorizing a Change in the Project or the method or manner of performance and/or an adjustment in the Guaranteed Maximum Price, the Construction Manager's Fee, or the Construction Completion Date. Each adjustment in the Guaranteed Maximum Price resulting from a Change Order shall clearly separate the amount attributable to the Cost of the Project and the Construction Manager's Fee.

9.1.2 The increase or decrease in the Guaranteed Maximum Price resulting from a Chance in the Project shall be determined in one or more of the following ways:

.1 by mutual acceptance of a lump sum properly itemized and supported by sufficient substantiating data to permit evaluation;

.2 by unit prices stated in the Agreement or subsequently agreed upon;

.3 by cost as defined in Article 8 and a mutually acceptable fixed or percentage fee; or

.4 by the method provided in Subparagraph 9.1.3.

9.1.3 If none of the methods set forth in Clauses 9.1.2.1 through 9.1.2.3 is agreed upon, the Construction Manager, provided he receives a written order signed by the Owner, shall promptly proceed with the Work involved. The cost of such Work shall then be determined on the basis of the reasonable expenditures and savings of those performing the Work attributed to the change, including, in the case of an increase in the Guaranteed Maximum Price, a reasonable increase in the Construction Manager's Fee. In such case, and also under Clauses 9.1.2.3 and 9.1.2.4 above, the Construction Manager shall keep and present, in such form as the Owner may prescribe, an itemized accounting together with appropriate supporting data of the increase in the Cost of the Project as outlined in Article 8. The amount of decrease in the Guaranteed Maximum Price to be allowed by the Construction Manager to the Owner for any deletion or change which results in a net decrease in cost will be the amount of the actual net decrease. When both additions and credits are involved in any one change, the increase in Fee shall be figured on the basis of net increase, if any.

9.1.4 If unit prices are stated in the Agreement or subsequently agreed upon, and if the quantities originally contemplated are so changed in a proposed Change Order or as a result of several Change Orders that application of the agreed unit prices to the quantities of Work proposed will cause substantial inequity to the Owner or the Construction Manager, the applicable unit prices and Guaranteed Maximum Price shall be equitably adjusted.

9.1.5 Should concealed conditions encountered in the performance of the Work below the surface of the ground or should concealed or unknown conditions in an existing structure be at variance with the conditions indicated by the Drawings, Specifications, or Owner-furnished information or should unknown physical conditions below the surface of the ground or should concealed or unknown conditions in an existing structure of an unusual nature, differing materially from those ordinarily encountered and generally recognized as inherent in work of the character provided for in this Agreement, be encountered, the Guaranteed Maximum Price and the Construction Completion Date shall be equitably adjusted by Change Order upon claim by either party made within a reasonable time after the first observance of the conditions.

9.2 Claims for Additional Cost or Time

9.2.1 If the Construction Manager wishes to make a claim for an increase in the Guaranteed Maximum Price, an increase in his fee, or an extension in the Construction Completion Date, he shall give the Owner written notice thereof within a reasonable time after the occurrence of the event giving rise to such claim. This notice shall be given by the Construction Manager before proceeding to execute any Work, except in an emergency endangering life or property in which case the Construction Manager shall act, at his discretion, to prevent threatened damage, injury or loss. Claims arising from delay shall be made within a reasonable time after the delay. No such claim shall be valid unless so made. If the Owner and the Construction Manager cannot agree on the amount of the adjustment in the Guaranteed Maximum Price, Construction Manager's Fee or Construction Completion Date, it shall be determined pursuant to the provisions of Article 16. Any change in the Guaranteed Maximum Price, Construction Manager's Fee or Construction Completion Date resulting from such claim shall be authorized by Change Order.

9.3. Minor Changes in the Project

9.3.1 The Architect/Engineer will have authority to order minor Changes in the Project not involving an adjustment in the Guaranteed Maximum Price or an extension of the Construction Completion Date and not inconsistent with the intent of the Drawings and Specifications. Such Changes may be effected by written order and shall be binding on the Owner and the Construction Manager.

9.4 Emergencies

9.4.1 In any emergency affecting the safety of persons or property, the Construction Manager shall act, at his discretion, to prevent threatened damage, injury or loss. Any increase in the Guaranteed Maximum Price or extension of time claimed by the Construction Manager on account of emergency work shall be determined as provided in this Article.

ARTICLE 10

Discounts

All discounts for prompt payment shall accrue to the Owner to the extent the Cost of the Project is paid directly by the

146 CONSTRUCTION MANAGEMENT CONTRACT

Owner or from a fund made available by the Owner to the Construction Manager for such payments. To the extent the Cost of the Project is paid with funds of the Construction Manager, all cash discounts shall accrue to the Construction Manager. All trade discounts, rebates and refunds, and all returns from sale of surplus materials and equipment, shall be credited to the Cost of the Project.

ARTICLE 11

Payments to the Construction Manager

11.1 The Construction Manager shall submit monthly to the Owner a statement, sworn to if required, showing in detail all moneys paid out, costs accumulated or costs incurred on account of the Cost of the Project during the previous month and the amount of the Construction Manager's Fee due as provided in Article 7. Payment by the Owner to the Construction Manager of the statement amount shall be made within ten (10) days after it is submitted.

11.2 . Final payment constituting the unpaid balance of the Cost of the Project and the Construction Manager's Fee shall be due and payable when the Project is delivered to the Owner, ready for beneficial occupancy, or when the Owner occupies the Project, whichever event first occurs, provided that the Project be then substantially completed and this Agreement substantially performed. If there should remain minor items to be completed, the Construction Manager and Architect/Engineer shall list such items and the Construction Manager shall deliver, in writing, his unconditional promise to complete said items within a reasonable time thereafter. The Owner may retain a sum equal to 150% of the estimated cost of completing any unfinished items, provided that said unfinished items are listed separately and the estimated cost of completing any unfinished items likewise listed separately. Thereafter, Owner shall pay to Construction Manager, monthly, the amount retained for incomplete items as each of said items is completed.

11.3 The Construction Manager shall promptly pay all the amounts due Trade Contractors or other persons with whom he has a contract upon receipt of any payment from the Owner, the application for which includes amounts due such Trade Contractor or other persons. Before issuance of final payment, the Construction Manager shall submit satisfactory evidence that all payrolls, materials bills and other indebtedness connected with the Project have been paid or otherwise satisfied.

11.4 If the Owner should fail to pay the Construction Manager within seven (7) days after the time the payment of any amount becomes due, then the Construction Manager may, upon seven (7) additional days' written notice to the Owner and the Architect/Engineer, stop the Project until payment of the amount owing has been received.

11.5 Payments due but unpaid shall bear interest at the rate the Owner is paying on his construction loan or at the legal rate, whichever is higher.

ARTICLE 12

Insurance, Indemnity and Waiver of Subrogation

12.1 Indemnity

12.1.1 The Construction Manager agrees to indemnify and hold the Owner harmless from all claims for bodily injury and property damage (other than the Work itself and other property insured under Paragraph 12.4) that may arise from the Construction Manager's operations under this Agreement.

12.1.2 The Owner shall cause any other contractor who may have a contract with the Owner to perform construction or installation work in the areas where Work will be performed under this Agreement, to agree to indemnify the Owner and the Construction Manager and hold them harmless from all claims for bodily injury and property damage (other, than property insured under Paragraph 12.4) that may arise from that contractor's operations. Such provisions shall be in a form satisfactory to the Construction Manager.

12.2 Construction Manager's Liability Insurance

12.2.1 The Construction Manager shall purchase and maintain such insurance as will protect him from the claims set forth below which may arise out of or result from the Construction Manager's operations under this Agreement whether such operations be by himself or by any Trade Contractor or by anyone directly or indirectly employed by any of them, or by anyone for whose acts any of them may be liable:

12.2.1.1 Claims under workers' compensation, disability benefit and other similar employee benefit acts which are applicable to the Work to be performed.

12.2.1.2 Claims for damages because of bodily injury, occupational sickness or disease, or death of his employees under any applicable employer's liability law.

12.2.1.3 Claims for damages because of bodily injury, death of any person other than his employees.

12.2.1.4 Claims for damages insured by usual personal injury liability coverage which are sustained (1) by any person as a result of an offense directly or indirectly related to the employment of such person by the Construction Manager or (2) by any other person.

12.2.1.5 Claims for damages, other than to the Work itself, because of injury to or destruction of tangible property, including loss of use therefrom.

12.2.1.6 Claims for damages because of bodily injury or death of any person or property damage arising out of the ownership, maintenance or use of any motor vehicle.

12.2.2 The Construction Manager's Comprehensive General Liability Insurance shall include premises – operations (including explosion, collapse and underground coverage) elevators, independent contractors, completed operations, and blanket contractual liability on all written contracts, all including broad form property damage coverage.

12.2.3 The Construction Manager's Comprehensive General and Automobile Liability Insurance, as required by Subparagraphs 12.2.1 and 12.2.2 shall be written for not less than limits of liability as follows:

a. Comprehensive General Liability
   1. Personal Injury $_____ Each Occurrence
                              $_____ Aggregate
                                              (Completed Operations)

   2. Property Damage $_____ Each Occurrence
                              $_____ Aggregate

b. Comprehensive Automobile Liability
   1. Bodily Injury $_____ Each Person
                              $_____ Each Occurrence

   2. Property Damage $_____ Each Occurrence

12.2.4 Comprehensive General Liability Insurance may be arranged under a single policy for the full limits required or by a combination of underlying policies with the balance provided by an Excess or Umbrella Liability policy.

12.2.5 The foregoing policies shall contain a provision that coverages afforded under the policies will not be cancelled or not renewed until at least sixty (60) days' prior written notice has been given to the Owner. Certificates of Insurance showing such coverages to be in Force shall be filed with the Owner prior to commencement of the Work.

12.3 Owner's Liability Insurance

12.3.1 The Owner shall be responsible for purchasing and maintaining his own liability insurance and, at his option, may purchase and maintain such insurance as will protect him against claims which may arise from operations under this Agreement.

12.4 Insurance to Protect Project

12.4.1 The Owner shall purchase and maintain property insurance in a form acceptable to the Construction Manager upon the entire Project for the full cost of replacement as of the time of any loss. This insurance shall include as named insureds the Owner, the Construction Manager, Trade Contractors and their Trade Subcontractors and shall insure against loss from the perils of Fire, Extended Coverage, and shall include "All Risk" insurance for physical loss or damage including, without duplication of coverage, at least theft, vandalism, malicious mischief, transit, collapse, flood, earthquake, testing, and damage resulting from defective design, workmanship or material. The Owner will increase limits of coverage, if necessary, to reflect estimated replacement cost. The Owner will be responsible for any co-insurance penalties or deductibles. If the Project covers an addition to or is adjacent to an existing building, the Construction Manager, Trade Contractors and their Trade Subcontractors shall be named as additional insureds under the Owner's Property Insurance covering such building and its contents.

12.4.1.1 If the Owner finds it necessary to occupy or use a portion or portions of the Project prior to Substantial Completion thereof, such occupancy shall not commence prior to a time mutually agreed to by the Owner and Construction Manager and to which the insurance company or companies providing the property insurance have consented by endorsement to the policy or policies. This insurance shall not be cancelled or lapsed on account of such partial occupancy. Consent of the Construction Manager and of the insurance company or companies to such occupancy or use shall not be unreasonably withheld.

12.4.2 The Owner shall purchase and maintain such boiler and machinery insurance as may be required or necessary. This insurance shall include the interests of the Owner, the Construction Manager, Trade Contractors and their Trade Subcontractors in the Work.

12.4.3 The Owner shall purchase and maintain such insurance as will protect the Owner and Construction Manager against loss of use of Owner's property due to those perils insured pursuant to Subparagraph 12.4.1. Such policy will provide coverage for expediting expenses of materials, continuing overhead of the Owner and Construction Manager, necessary labor expense including overtime, loss of income by the Owner and other determined exposures. Exposures of the Owner and the Construction Manager shall be determined by mutual agreement and separate limits of coverage fixed for each item.

12.4.4 The Owner shall file a copy of all policies with the Construction Manager before an exposure to loss may occur. Copies of any subsequent endorsements will be furnished to the Construction Manager. The Construction Manager will be given sixty (60) days notice of cancellation, non-renewal, or any endorsements restricting or reducing coverage. If the Owner does not intend to purchase such insurance, he shall inform the Construction Manager in writing prior to the commencement of the Work. The Construction Manager may then effect insurance which will protect the interest of himself, the Trade Contractors and their Trade Subcontractors in the Project, the cost of which shall be a Cost of the Project pursuant to Article 8, and the Guaranteed Maximum Price shall be increased by Change Order. If the Construction Manager is damaged by failure of the Owner to purchase or maintain such insurance or to so notify the Construction Manager, the Owner shall bear all reasonable costs properly attributable thereto.

12.5 Property Insurance Loss Adjustment

12.5.1 Any insured loss shall be adjusted with the Owner and the Construction Manager and made payable to the Owner and Construction Manager as trustees for the insureds, as their interests may appear, subject to any applicable mortgagee clause.

12.5.2 Upon the occurrence of an insured loss, monies received will be deposited in a separate account and the trustees shall make distribution in accordance with the agreement of the parties in interest, or in the absence of such agreement, in accordance with an arbitration award pursuant to Article 16. If the trustees are unable to agree on the settlement of the loss, such dispute shall also be submitted to arbitration pursuant to Article 16.

12.6 Waiver of Subrogation

12.6.1 The Owner and Construction Manager waive all rights against each other, the Architect/Engineer, Trade Contractors, and their Trade Subcontractors for damages caused by perils covered by insurance provided under Paragraph 12.4, except such rights as they may have to the proceeds of such insurance held by the Owner and Construction Manager as trustees. The Construction Manager shall require similar waivers from all Trade Contractors and their Trade Subcontractors.

12.6.2   The Owner and Construction Manager waive all rights against each other and the Architect/Engineer, Trade Contractors and their Trade Subcontractors for loss or damage to any equipment used in connection with the Project and covered by any property insurance. The Construction Manager shall require similar waivers from all Trade Contractors and their Trade Subcontractors.

12.6.3   The Owner waives subrogation against the Construction Manager, Architect/Engineer, Trade Contractors, and their Trade Subcontractors on all property and consequential loss policies carried by the Owner on adjacent properties and under property and consequential loss policies purchased for the Project after its completion.

12.6.4   If the policies of insurance referred to in this Paragraph require an endorsement to provide for continued coverage where there is a waiver of subrogation, the owners of such policies will cause them to be so endorsed.

ARTICLE 13

Termination of the Agreement and Owner's
Right to Perform Construction Manager's Obligations

13.1   Termination by the Construction Manager

13.1.1   If the Project, in whole or substantial part, is stopped for a period of thirty days under an order of any court or other public authority having jurisdiction, or as a result of an act of government, such as a declaration of a national emergency making materials unavailable, through no act or fault of the Construction Manager, or if the Project should be stopped for a period of thirty days by the Construction Manager for the Owner's failure to make payment thereon, then the Construction Manager may, upon seven days' written notice to the Owner and the Architect/Engineer, terminate this Agreement and recover from the Owner payment for all work executed, the Construction Manager's Fee earned to date, and for any proven loss sustained upon any materials, equipment, tools, construction equipment and machinery, cancellation charges on existing obligations of the Construction Manager, and a reasonable profit.

13.2   Owner's Right to Perform Construction Manager's Obligations and Termination by the Owner for Cause

13.2.1   If the Construction Manager fails to perform any of his obligations under this Agreement including any obligation he assumes to perform Work with his own forces, the Owner may, after seven days' written notice during which period the Construction Manager fails to perform such obligation, make good such deficiencies. The Guaranteed Maximum Price, if any, shall be reduced by the cost to the Owner of making good such deficiencies.

13.2.2   If the Construction Manager is adjudged a bankrupt, or if he makes a general assignment for the benefit of his creditors, or if a receiver is appointed on account of his insolvency, or if he persistently or repeatedly refuses or fails, except in cases for which extension of time is provided, to supply enough properly skilled workmen or proper materials, or if he fails to make proper payment to Trade Contractors or for materials or labor, or persistently disregards laws, ordinances, rules, regulations or orders of any public authority having jurisdiction, or otherwise is guilty of a substantial violation of a provision of the Agreement, then the Owner may, without prejudice to any right or remedy and after giving the Construction Manager and his surety, if any, seven days' written notice, during which period the Construction Manager fails to cure the violation, terminate the employment of the Construction Manager and take possession of the site and of all materials, equipment, tools, construction equipment and machinery thereon owned by the Construction Manager and may finish the Project by whatever reasonable method he may deem expedient. In such case, the Construction Manager shall not be entitled to receive any further payment until the Project is finished nor shall he be relieved from his obligations assumed under Article 6.

13.3   Termination by Owner Without Cause

13.3.1   If the Owner terminates this Agreement other than pursuant to Subparagraph 13.2.2 or Subparagraph 13.3.2, he shall reimburse the Construction Manager for any unpaid Cost of the Project due him under Article 8, plus (1) the unpaid balance of the Fee computed upon the Cost of the Project to the date of termination at the rate of the percentage named in Subparagraph 7.2.1 or if the Construction Manager's Fee be stated as a fixed sum, such an amount as will increase the payment on account of his fee to a sum which bears the same ratio to the said fixed sum as the Cost of the Project at the time of termination bears to the adjusted Guaranteed Maximum Price, if any, otherwise to a reasonable estimated Cost of the Project when completed. The Owner shall also pay to the Construction Manager fair compensation, either by purchase or rental at the election of the Owner, for any equipment retained. In case of such termination of the Agreement the Owner shall further assume and become liable for obligations, commitments and unsettled claims that the Construction Manager has previously undertaken or incurred in good faith in connection with said Project. The Construction Manager shall, as a condition of receiving the payments referred to in this Article 13, execute and deliver all such papers and take all such steps, including the legal assignment of his contractual rights, as the Owner may require for the purpose of fully vesting in him the rights and benefits of the Construction Manager under such obligations or commitments.

13.3.2 After the completion of the Design Phase, if the final cost estimates make the Project no longer feasible from the standpoint of the Owner, the Owner may terminate this Agreement and pay the Construction Manager his Fee in accordance with Subparagraph 7.1.1 plus any costs incurred pursuant to Article 9.

ARTICLE 14

Assignment and Governing Law

14.1 Neither the Owner nor the Construction Manager shall assign his interest in this Agreement without the written consent of the other except as to the assignment of proceeds.

14.2 This Agreement shall be governed by the law of the place where the Project is located.

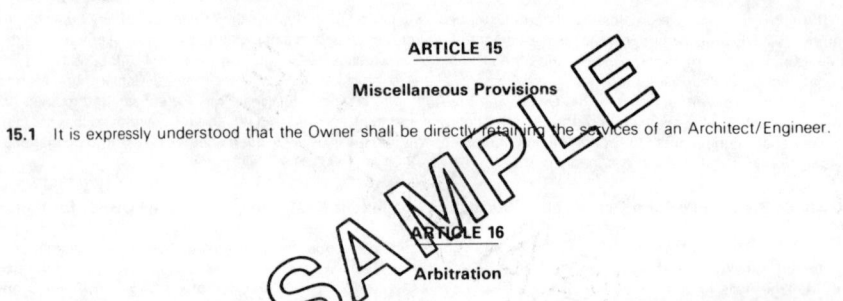

ARTICLE 15

Miscellaneous Provisions

15.1 It is expressly understood that the Owner shall be directly retaining the services of an Architect/Engineer.

ARTICLE 16

Arbitration

16.1 All claims, disputes and other matters in questions arising out of, or relating to, this Agreement or the breach thereof, except with respect to the Architect/Engineer's decision on matters relating to artistic effect, and except for claims which have been waived by the making or acceptance of final payment shall be decided by arbitration in accordance with the Construction Industry Arbitration Rules of the American Arbitration Association then obtaining unless the parties mutually agree otherwise. This Agreement to arbitrate shall be specifically enforceable under the prevailing arbitration law.

16.2 Notice of the demand for arbitration shall be filed in writing with the other party to this Agreement and with the American Arbitration Association. The demand for arbitration shall be made within a reasonable time after the claim, dispute or other matter in question has arisen, and in no event shall it be made after the date when institution of legal or equitable proceedings based on such claim, dispute or other matter in question would be barred by the applicable statute of limitations.

16.3 The award rendered by the arbitrators shall be final and judgment may be entered upon it in accordance with applicable law in any court having jurisdiction thereof.

16.4 Unless otherwise agreed in writing, the Construction Manager shall carry on the Work and maintain the Contract Completion Date during any arbitration proceedings, and the Owner shall continue to make payments in accordance with this Agreement.

16.5 All claims which are related to or dependent upon each other, shall be heard by the same arbitrator or arbitrators even though the parties are not the same unless a specific contract prohibits such consolidation.

§3.01 AGC DOCUMENT NO. 500   151

This Agreement executed the day and year first written above.

ATTEST: OWNER:

ATTEST: CONSTRUCTION MANAGER:

FORM 3-2 Modifications to Construction Management Agreement [Favors Interests of Owner] (with Comments)

The Standard Form of Agreement Between Owner and Construction Manager (Guaranteed Maximum Price Option), AGC Document No. 500, is modified as follows:

¶1. <u>First:</u> **Article 2.1.7.** Article 2.1.7 is added to read as follows:

> **2.1.7 Design-Build Trade Contractors:** With the consent of Owner and the cooperation of Architect/Engineer, Construction Manager will employ design-build Trade Contractors where it would advance the interests of the Project to do so.

¶2. <u>Second:</u> **Article 2.2.3.1.** Contractor will preserve records for a period of five years, rather than three years, after final payment.

¶3. <u>Third:</u> **Article 2.2.8.** Article 2.2.8 is revised to read as follows:

> **2.2.8 Inspection:** At least daily inspect the Work of Trade Contractors for defects and deficiencies in the Work, and require Trade Contractors to promptly perform necessary corrections.

¶4. <u>Fourth:</u> **Article 2.2.8.1.** The first two sentences of Article 2.2.8.1 are revised to read as follows:

> **2.2.8.2** Review the safety programs of each of the Trade Contractors and make appropriate recommendations. In the process of making inspections, Construction Manager shall check the job for adherence to sound safety procedures, and will use its best efforts to enforce safety-discipline upon all jobsite personnel.

¶5. <u>Fifth:</u> **Article 2.2.15.** The following language is added to Article 2.2.15:

> The designation of the period of one year as a warranty period does not relieve Construction Manager or any Trade Contractor of obligations to perform the Work as required by the Contract Documents.

Comment: Parties sometimes confuse the concepts of *one-year warranty* and *statute of limitations.* The purpose of a warranty is to require the contractor to correct deficiencies even if they do not arise out of a breach of contract. If a contractor is guilty of a breach of contract, for example, by failing to follow drawings or specifications, then the contractor is responsible for that breach even if the condition does not manifest itself or is not discovered for more than one year after completion of the project. After a latent construction defect becomes manifest, then the statute of limitations comes into play, and requires the owner to file an action against the contractor within a specified period of time. The amount of time varies from state to state, but in the case of a written contract an action for breach must usually be filed within three to five years after its manifestation. Most states have also enacted so-called *statutes of repose*. Statutes of repose cut off a cause of action for latent construction defects after a specified number of years from the completion of the project. The number of years varies from state to state, but in most states, after from six to ten years from completion of the project, an owner's cause of action for construction defects is cut off, whether the defect has manifested itself or not.

¶6. **Sixth:** **Article 3.4.** The following language is added to the end of Article 3.4:

Construction Manager will advise Owner as to the types of surveys and investigations that should be procured, and will assist Owner in locating existing utilities.

¶7. **Seventh:** **Article 3.9.** The following language is added at the end of Article 3.9:

The Construction Manager will promptly review information, surveys, and reports furnished by Owner, and will inform Owner if they appear to be inaccurate or incomplete.

¶8. **Eighth:** **Article 7.2.2.** The following language is added at the end of Article 7.2.2:

Construction Manager will take responsibility for delays caused by Trade Contractors.

¶9. **Ninth:** **Article 8.2.9.** Article 8.2.9 is amended by deleting the words "or is deemed necessary by the Construction Manager".

¶10. **Tenth:** **Article 8.2.13.** The following language is added to Article 8.2.13:

Owner will not reimburse costs incurred because of the negligence, breach of contract, or other misconduct of Construction Manager.

¶11. **Eleventh:** **Article 8.2.19.** The following language is added to Article 8.2.19:

Owner will not reimburse costs incurred because of the negligence, breach of contract, or other misconduct of Construction Manager.

¶12. <u>Twelfth:</u> **Article 11.6.** Article 11.6 is added to read as follows:

11.6 Along with each Application for Payment, Construction Manager will submit mechanic's lien releases properly executed by all Subcontractors and Suppliers who have the right to claim mechanics' liens. The form of such releases shall be subject to the approval of Owner. The effectiveness of releases may be conditioned upon payment, and in such instances, the Owner may issue checks payable jointly to Construction Manager and the potential mechanic's lien claimant.

¶13. <u>Thirteenth:</u> **Article 12.1.1.** The parenthetical phrase "(other than the Work itself and other property insured under Paragraph 12.4)" is deleted. The following sentence is added to Article 12.1.1:

This indemnity agreement is subject to the waiver of subrogation provisions contained in Article 12.6.

¶14. <u>Fourteenth:</u> **Article 12.1.2.** The parenthetical phrase "(other than property insured under Paragraph 12.4)" is deleted from Article 12.1.2.

¶15. <u>Fifteenth:</u> **Article 12.2.1.4.** Article 12.2.1.4 is annulled.

Comment: The term *personal injury,* as it is used in the insurance industry, refers to claims for libel and slander, advertising liability, and such other esoteric claims as are often included under an *umbrella* policy. Since the owner must reimburse the contractor for premiums paid for insurance required by the contract, and the owner gains little advantage from such coverage, it should not be required.

¶16. <u>Sixteenth:</u> **Article 12.2.1.5.** The words "other than to the Work itself" are stricken from Article 12.2.1.5.

Comment: The construction manager should obtain a broad form endorsement to its general liability policy, and, under such a broad form endorsement, damage caused by the construction manager to work performed by trade contractors is usually covered. This form of insurance is particularly important for the construction manager to provide in the event of disputes that concern construction defects, since most construction defects are, in fact, a form of property damage that is covered by general liability insurance under the broad form endorsement. It is highly beneficial both for the construction manager and for the owner that this insurance should be provided, since it provides a source of payment for many construction defects that might otherwise be extracted from the construction manager or a trade contractor as backcharges.

¶17. **Seventeenth:** Article 12.2.2. The following language is added to Article 12.2.2:

The Construction Manager's comprehensive general liability insurance shall also include coverage for liability assumed by contract, including coverage for liability assumed under the indemnity provisions of Article 12.1.

¶18. **Eighteenth:** Article 12.2.3. In Article 12.2.3, the phrase "personal injury" is replaced by the words "bodily injury".

¶19. **Nineteenth:** Article 12.2.6. Article 12.2.6 is added to read as follows:

12.2.6 The Contractor's comprehensive general liability policy and comprehensive automobile liability policy shall be endorsed so as to name Owner as an additional insured as to claims arising out of the operations of Construction Manager, and the endorsement will provide that as to such claims, Construction Manager's insurance policy shall be primary to any liability insurance of Owner.

¶20. **Twentieth:** Article 12.4. Article 12.4, including Article 12.4.1 through 12.4.4, is annulled.

Comment: The parties should understand that under most circumstances, in the event a construction project is damaged or destroyed by fire or other casualty, the contractor will be required to rebuild at no expense to the owner, unless the contract otherwise provides. This is a reflection of the common law doctrine of *impossibility of performance* of a contract, which holds that the performance of a contract is only excused by natural impossibility. In some states this doctrine has been modified so that *extreme impracticability* excuses performance of a contract. However, the destruction of a construction project does not make it impossible to rebuild, or extremely impracticable: it is merely extremely expensive.

Both the contractor and the owner have an insurable interest in the continued existence of the project. When the property insurance provisions of the contract are annulled, as they are in this example, then it becomes the responsibility of the contractor and the owner each to provide insurance covering its insurable interest in the continued existence of the project. This would mean, in most cases, that in the event of an insured loss, the construction lender would have the right under provisions in the mortgage or deed of trust to take the proceeds of the insurance and use them to pay off the balance of the construction loan. This would leave the owner without funds to pay for reconstruction, but the contractor's property insurance (usually called builder's risk insurance) would pay the contractor for the cost of rebuilding. This means that two premiums are paid for two insurance policies, but it also would result in value received by the owner in the event of a loss, since the owner's construction loan would be paid off and the contractor's insurance would pay the cost of rebuilding.

For an explanation of other options available to owner and contractor, and appropriate contractual language, see **FORM 2-2 ¶22.**

¶21. Twenty-First: Article 12.5. Article 12.5 (12.5.1 and 12.5.2) is annulled in its entirety.

¶22. Twenty-Second: Article 12.6. Article 12.6 (12.6.1 through 12.6.4) is annulled in its entirety.

¶23. Twenty-Third: Article 16. Arbitration.

Comment: Many contractors, owners, and lawyers have fixed opinions about arbitration, and will decide whether to include or exclude arbitration provisions based on those opinions.

For those whose minds have not closed, whether to include an arbitration clause in a contract is a decision that should be made only after many factors have been weighed.

Every factor in the decision whether or not to arbitrate has a different weight, but the most important of all is whether, in the event of a dispute, a party expects to be *right* or *wrong,* or, to put it another way, whether a party expects to *win* or *lose.* A party who expects to win a dispute should usually choose arbitration. A party with a good possibility of losing should choose litigation. This is because arbitration is faster, and less appealable. These factors favor the winning party.

Contractors and owners will usually have at least a plausible ability to forecast whether they are likely to win or lose construction disputes depending on their track records and their philosophies of doing business. The decision as to whether or not to include an arbitration clause in the contract follows from these considerations.

For a discussion of some other factors, see **§2.04.**

AGC Document No. 501 - Amendment to Owner-Construction Manager Contract

§3.02 General Comment

This agreement provides for exercising the **guaranteed maximum price option** of AGC Document No. 500.

FORM 3-3 AGC Document No. 501 - Amendment to Owner-Construction Manager Contract (1977)

THE ASSOCIATED GENERAL CONTRACTORS

AMENDMENT TO OWNER-CONSTRUCTION MANAGER CONTRACT

SAMPLE

Pursuant to Article 6 of the original Agreement, AGC form No. 500, dated _____

between _____ (Owner)

and _____ (the Construction Manager),

for _____ (the Project),

the Owner desires to fix a Guaranteed Maximum Price for the Project and the Construction Manager agrees that the design, plans and specifications are sufficiently complete for such purpose. Therefore, the Owner and Construction Manager agree as set forth below.

ARTICLE I

Guaranteed Maximum Price

The Construction Manager's Guaranteed Maximum Price for the Project, including the Cost of the Work as defined in Article 8 and the Construction Manager's Fee as defined in Article 7 is _____ Dollars ($ _____). This price is for the performance of the Work in accordance with the documents listed and attached to this Amendment and marked Amendment Exhibit A.

(OPTIONAL SAVINGS CLAUSE) It is further agreed that if, upon completion of the work, the actual cost of the work plus the Construction Manager's Fee is less than the Guaranteed Maximum Price as set forth herein and as adjusted by approved change orders that the Owner agrees to pay to the Construction Manager an amount equal to _____% of such savings, as additional compensation.

AGC DOCUMENT NO 501 • AMENDMENT TO OWNER CONSTRUCTION MANAGER CONTRACT • JUNE 1977
©ASSOCIATED GENERAL CONTRACTORS OF AMERICA 1977

§3.02 AGC DOCUMENT NO. 501   159

ARTICLE II

Time Schedule

The Construction Completion date established by this Amendment is:

ATTEST:

_____

OWNER:

By: _____

Date: _____

CONSTRUCTION MANAGER:

_____

ATTEST:

_____

By: _____

Date: _____

AGC DOCUMENT NO 501 • AMENDMENT TO OWNER CONSTRUCTION MANAGER CONTRACT • JUNE 1977
©ASSOCIATED GENERAL CONTRACTORS OF AMERICA 1977

AGC Document No. 520 - General Conditions for Trade Contractors

§3.03 General Comment

These General Conditions are intended to be incorporated into **Trade Contracts (Subcontracts)** entered into by the construction manager or the owner with trade contractors performing under a construction management program.

The General Conditions have been drafted by AGC with a view to protecting the interests of the construction manager and the owner; therefore, the following modifications are suggested for use when the drafter is motivated to give additional protection to the interests of the trade contractor.

FORM 3-4 General Conditions for Trade Contractors under Construction Management Agreements (1980)

AIA copyrighted material has been reproduced with the permission of the American Institute of Architects under license number 90153. Permission expires December 31, 1991.

This document is intended for use as a "consumable" (consumables are further defined by Senate Report 94-473 on the Copyright Act of 1976). This document is not intended to be used as "model language" (language taken from an existing document and incorporated, without attribution, into a newly-created document). Rather, it is a standard form which is intended to be modified by appending separate amendment sheets and/or fill in provided blank spaces.

THE ASSOCIATED GENERAL CONTRACTORS

GENERAL CONDITIONS FOR TRADE CONTRACTORS UNDER CONSTRUCTION MANAGEMENT AGREEMENTS

INSTRUCTIONS FOR CONSTRUCTION MANAGER

1. These conditions primarily govern the obligations of the Trade Contractors and in addition establish the general procedures for the administration of construction. They have been drafted to cover Trade Contracts with either the Owner or the Construction Manager.

2. In all cases your attorney should be consulted to advise you on their use and any modifications.

3. Nothing contained herein is intended to conflict with local, state or federal laws or regulations.

4. It is recommended all insurance matters be reviewed with your insurance consultant and carrier such as implications of errors and omission liability, completed operations, and waiver of subrogation.

5. Each article should be reviewed by the Construction Manager as to the applicability to a given project and contractual conditions.

6. Special conditions and terms for the project or the Trade Contractor Agreements should cover the following:

    - trade contractor retainages
    - payment schedules
    - insurance limits
    - owner's protective insurance if required of trade contractors
    - builder's risk deductible, if any.

7. If the Owner does not provide Builder's Risk Insurance, Paragraph 12.2 will need to be modified.

Certain provisions of this document have been derived, with modifications, from the following document published by The American Institute of Architects: AIA Document A201, General Conditions, © 1976, by The American Institute of Architects. Usage made of AIA language, with the permission of AIA, does not imply AIA endorsement or approval of this document. Further reproduction of copyrighted AIA materials without separate written permission from AIA is prohibited.

AGC DOCUMENT NO. 520 • GENERAL CONDITIONS FOR TRADE CONTRACTORS UNDER CONSTRUCTION MANAGEMENT AGREEMENTS • JULY 1980
© 1980 Associated General Contractors of America

THE ASSOCIATED GENERAL CONTRACTORS

GENERAL CONDITIONS FOR TRADE CONTRACTORS UNDER CONSTRUCTION MANAGEMENT AGREEMENTS

SAMPLE

TABLE OF CONTENTS

ARTICLES		PAGE
1	Contract Documents	1
2	Owner	2
3	Architect/Engineer	2
4	Construction Manager	3
5	Trade Contractors	4
6	Trade Subcontractors	8
7	Separate Trade Contracts	9
8	Miscellaneous Provisions	10
9	Time	11
10	Payments and Completion	12
11	Protection of Persons and Property	15
12	Insurance	16
13	Changes in the Work	18
14	Uncovering and Correction of Work	19
15	Termination of the Contract	20

Certain provisions of this document have been derived, with modifications, from the following document published by The American Institute of Architects: AIA Document A201, General Conditions, © 1976, by The American Institute of Architects. Usage made of AIA language, with the permission of AIA, does not imply AIA endorsement or approval of this document. Further reproduction of copyrighted AIA materials without separate written permission from AIA is prohibited.

AGC DOCUMENT NO. 520 • GENERAL CONDITIONS FOR TRADE CONTRACTORS UNDER CONSTRUCTION MANAGEMENT AGREEMENTS • JULY 1980
© 1980 Associated General Contractors of America

164 CONSTRUCTION MANAGEMENT CONTRACT

ARTICLE 1

CONTRACT DOCUMENTS

1.1 DEFINITIONS

1.1.1 THE CONTRACT DOCUMENTS

The Contract Documents consist of the Agreement between the Owner or Construction Manager, as the case may be, and the Trade Contractor, the Conditions of the Contract (General, Supplementary and other Conditions), the Drawings (and criteria if the drawings are not complete), the Specifications, all Addenda issued prior to execution of the Contract, and all Modifications issued after the execution of the contract. A modification is (1) a written amendment to the Contract signed by both parties, (2) a Change Order, (3) a written interpretation issued by the Architect/Engineer pursuant to Subparagraph 3.2.2, or (4) a written order for a minor change in the Work issued on the Owner's behalf pursuant to Paragraph 13.4. The Contract Documents do not include Bidding or Proposal Documents such as the Advertisement or Invitation To Bid, Requests for Proposals, sample forms, Trade Contractors Bid or Proposal, or portions of Addenda relative to any of these, or any other documents other than those set forth in this subparagraph unless specifically set forth in the Agreement with the Trade Contractor. In the event of an inconsistency between the Agreement and the other Contract Documents, the provisions of the Agreement will control.

1.1.2 THE CONTRACT

The Contract Documents form the Contract with the Trade Contractor. This Contract represents the entire and integrated agreement and supersedes all prior negotiations, representations, or agreements, either written or oral. The Contract may be amended or modified only by a Modification as defined in Subparagraph 1.1.1.

1.1.3 THE WORK

The Work comprises the completed construction performed by the Construction Manager with his own forces or required by a Trade Contractor's contract and includes all labor necessary to produce such construction required of the Construction Manager or a Trade Contractor, and all materials and equipment incorporated or to be incorporated in such construction.

1.1.4 THE PROJECT

The Project is the total construction to be performed under the Agreement between the Owner and Construction Manager of which the Work is a part.

1.2 EXECUTION, CORRELATION AND INTENT

1.2.1 By executing this Agreement, each Trade Contractor represents that he has visited the site, familiarized himself with the local conditions under which the Work is to be performed and correlated his observations with the requirements of the Contract Documents.

1.2.2 The intent of the Contract Documents is to include all items necessary for the proper execution and completion of the Work. The Contract Documents are complementary, and what is required by any one shall be as binding as if required by all. Work not covered in the Contract Documents will not be required unless it is consistent therewith and is reasonably inferable therefrom as being necessary to produce the intended results. Words and abbreviations in the Contract Documents which have well-known technical or trade meanings are used in accordance with such recognized meanings.

1.2.3 The organization of the Specifications into divisions, sections and articles, and the arrangements of Drawings shall not control the Construction Manager in dividing the Work among Trade Contractors or in establishing the extent of Work to be performed by any trade.

1.3 OWNERSHIP AND USE OF DOCUMENTS

1.3.1 Unless otherwise provided in the Contract Documents, the Trade Contractor will be furnished, free of charge, all copies of Drawings and Specifications reasonably necessary for the execution of the Work.

AGC DOCUMENT NO. 520 • GENERAL CONDITIONS FOR TRADE CONTRACTORS UNDER CONSTRUCTION MANAGEMENT AGREEMENTS • JULY 1980

1.3.2 All Drawings, Specifications and copies thereof furnished by the Architect/Engineer are and shall remain his property. They are to be used only with respect to this Project and are not to be used on any other project. With the exception of one contract set for each party, such documents are to be returned or suitably accounted for to the Architect/Engineer on request at the completion of the Work. Submission or distribution to meet official regulatory requirements or for other purposes in connection with the Project is not to be construed as publication in derogation of the Architect/Engineer's common law copyright or other reserved rights.

ARTICLE 2

OWNER

2.1 DEFINITION

2.1.1 The Owner is the person or entity identified as such in the Agreement between the Owner and Construction Manager and is referred to throughout the Contract Documents as if singular in number and masculine in gender. The term Owner means the Owner or his authorized representative.

2.2 INFORMATION AND SERVICES FURNISHED BY THE OWNER

2.2.1 The Owner will furnish all surveys describing the physical characteristics, legal limitations and utility locations for the site of the Project, and a legal description of the site.

2.2.2 Except as provided in Subparagraph 5.7.1 the Owner will secure and pay for necessary approvals, easements, assessments and charges required for the construction, use, or occupancy of permanent structures or for permanent changes in existing facilities.

2.2.3 Information or services under the Owner's control will be furnished by the Owner with reasonable promptness to avoid delay in the orderly progress of the Work.

2.2.4 The Owner shall forward all instructions to the Trade Contractors through the Construction Manager even when the Owner has direct contracts with Trade Contractors.

ARTICLE 3

ARCHITECT/ENGINEER

3.1 DEFINITION

3.1.1 The Architect/Engineer is the person lawfully licensed to practice architecture or engineering or an entity lawfully practicing architecture or engineering and identified as such in the Agreement between the Owner and Construction Manager and is referred to throughout the Contract Documents as if singular in number and masculine in gender. The term Architect/Engineer means the Architect/Engineer or his authorized representative.

3.1.2 Nothing contained in the Contract Documents shall create any contractual relationship between the Architect/Engineer and any Trade Contractor.

3.2 ARCHITECT/ENGINEER'S DUTIES DURING CONSTRUCTION

3.2.1 The Architect/Engineer shall at all times have access to the Work wherever it is in preparation and progress. When directed by the Construction Manager, the Trade Contractor shall provide facilities for such access so the Architect/Engineer may perform his functions under the Contract Documents.

3.2.2 The Architect/Engineer will be the interpreter of the requirements of the Drawings and Specifications. The Architect/Engineer will, within a reasonable time, render such interpretations as are necessary for the proper execution of the progress of the Work.

166 CONSTRUCTION MANAGEMENT CONTRACT

3.2.3 All interpretations of the Architect/Engineer shall be consistent with the intent of and reasonably inferable from the Contract Documents and will be in writing or in the form of drawings. All requests for interpretations shall be directed through the Construction Manager. The Architect/Engineer shall not be liable to the Trade Contractor for the result of any interpretation or decision rendered in good faith in such capacity.

3.2.4 The Architect/Engineer's decisions in matters relating to artistic effect will be final if consistent with the intent of the Contract Documents.

3.2.5 The Architect/Engineer will have authority to reject Work which does not conform to the Contract Documents. Whenever, in his opinion, he considers it necessary or advisable for the implementation of the intent of the Contract Documents, he will have authority to require special inspection or testing of the Work in accordance with Subparagraph 8.7.2 whether or not such Work be then fabricated, installed or completed. However, neither the Architect/Engineer's authority to act under this Subparagraph 3.2.5, nor any decision made by him in good faith either to exercise or not to exercise such authority, shall give rise to any duty or responsibility of the Architect/Engineer to the Trade Contractor, any Trade Subcontractor, any of their agents or employees, or any other person performing any of the Work.

3.2.6 The Architect/Engineer will review and approve or take other appropriate action upon Trade Contractor's submittals such as Shop Drawings, Product Data and Samples, but only for conformance with the design concept of the Work and with the information given in the Contract Documents. Such action shall be taken with reasonable promptness so as to cause no delay. The Architect/Engineer's approval of a specific item shall not indicate approval of an assembly of which the item is a component.

3.2.7 The Architect/Engineer along with the Construction Manager will conduct inspections to determine the dates of Substantial Completion and final completion, will receive and review written warranties and related documents required by the Contract and assembled by the Trade Contractor.

3.2.8 The Architect/Engineer will communicate with the Trade Contractors through the Construction Manager.

ARTICLE 4
CONSTRUCTION MANAGER

4.1 DEFINITION

4.1.1 The Construction Manager is the person or entity who has entered into an agreement with the Owner to serve as Construction Manager and is referred to throughout the Contract Documents as if singular in number and masculine in gender. The term Construction Manager means the Construction Manager acting through his authorized representative.

4.1.2 Whether the Trade Contracts are between the Owner and Trade Contractors, or the Construction Manager and Trade Contractors, it is the intent of these General Conditions to allow the Construction Manager to direct and schedule the performance of all Work and the Trade Contractors are expected to follow all such directions and schedules.

4.2 ADMINISTRATION OF THE CONTRACT

4.2.1 The Construction Manager will provide, as the Owner's authorized representative, the general administration of the Project as herein described.

4.2.2 The Construction Manager will be the Owner's construction representative during construction until final payment and shall have the responsibility to supervise and coordinate the work of all Trade Contractors.

4.2.3 The Construction Manager shall prepare and update all Construction Schedules and shall direct the Work with respect to such schedules.

4.2.4 The Construction Manager shall have the authority to reject Work which does not conform to the Contract Documents and to require any Special Inspection and Testing in accordance with Subparagraph 8.7.2.

4.2.5 The Construction Manager will prepare and issue Change Orders to the Trade Contractors in accordance with Article 13.

4.2.6 The Construction Manager along with the Architect/Engineer will conduct inspections to determine the dates of Substantial Completion and final completion, and will receive and review written warranties and related documents required by the Contract and assembled by the Trade Contractor.

4.2.7 Nothing contained in the Contract Documents between a Trade Contractor and the Owner shall create any contractual relationship between the Construction Manager and any Trade Contractor.

4.3 OWNER'S AND CONSTRUCTION MANAGER'S RIGHT TO STOP WORK

4.3.1 If the Trade Contractor fails to correct defective Work as required by Paragraph 14.2 or persistently fails to carry out the Work in accordance with the Contract Documents, the Construction Manager or the Owner through the Construction Manager may order the Trade Contractor to stop the Work, or any portion thereof, until the cause for such order has been eliminated.

4.3.2 If the Trade Contractor defaults or neglects to carry out the Work in accordance with the Contract Documents and fails within seven days after receipt of written notice from the Construction Manager to commence and continue correction of such default or neglect with diligence and promptness, the Construction Manager may, by written notice, and without prejudice to any other remedy he or the Owner may have, make good such deficiencies. In such case an appropriate Change Order shall be issued deducting from the payments then or thereafter due the Trade Contractor the cost of correcting such deficiencies, including compensation for the Architect/Engineer's and Construction Manager's additional services made necessary by such default, neglect or failure.

ARTICLE 5

TRADE CONTRACTORS

5.1 DEFINITION

5.1.1 A Trade Contractor is the person or entity identified as such in the Agreement between the Owner or Construction Manager and a Trade Contractor and is referred to throughout the Contract Document as if singular in number and masculine in gender. The term Trade Contractor means the Trade Contractor or his authorized representative.

5.1.2 The Agreements with the Trade Contractors may either be with the Owner or with the Construction Manager. These conditions in several instances make reference to obligations and rights of the "Owner or Construction Manager" to cover both possibilities. Such references are only to cover either possibility and such use does not create a joint obligation on the Owner and Construction Manager to the Trade Contractor. The contract obligation with the Trade Contractor is solely with the person or entity with whom he has his Agreement.

5.1.3 If the Trade Contracts are with the Construction Manager, the Trade Contractor assumes toward the Construction Manager all the obligations and responsibilities which the Construction Manager assumes toward the Owner under the Agreement between the Owner and the Construction Manager. A copy of the pertinent parts of this Agreement will be made available on request.

5.2 REVIEW OF CONTRACT DOCUMENTS

5.2.1 The Trade Contractor shall carefully study and compare the Contract Documents and shall at once report to the Construction Manager any error, inconsistency or omission he may or reasonably should discover. The Trade Contractor shall not be liable to the Owner or the Architect/Engineer or the Construction Manager for any damage resulting from any such errors, inconsistencies or omissions.

5.3 SUPERVISION AND CONSTRUCTION PROCEDURES

5.3.1 The Trade Contractor shall supervise and direct the Work, using his best skill and attention. He shall be solely responsible for all construction means, methods, techniques, sequences and procedures and for coordinating all portions of the Work under the Contract subject to the overall coordination of the Construction Manager.

5.3.2 The Trade Contractor shall be responsible to the Owner and the Construction Manager for the acts and omissions of his employees and all his Trade Subcontractors and their agents and employees and other persons performing any of the Work under a contract with the Trade Contractor.

5.3.3 Neither observations nor inspections, tests or approvals by persons other than the Trade Contractor shall relieve the Trade Contractor from his obligations to perform the Work in accordance with the Contract Documents.

5.4 LABOR AND MATERIALS

5.4.1 Unless otherwise specifically provided in the Contract Documents, the Trade Contractor shall provide and pay for all labor, materials, equipment, tools, construction equipment and machinery, transportation, and other facilities and services necessary for the proper execution and completion of the Work.

5.4.2 The Trade Contractor shall at all times enforce strict discipline and good order among his employees and shall not employ on the Work any unfit person or anyone not skilled in the task assigned to him.

5.5 WARRANTY

5.5.1 The Trade Contractor warrants to the Owner and the Construction Manager that all materials and equipment furnished under this Contract will be new unless otherwise specified, and that all Work will be of good quality, free from faults and defects and in conformance with the Contract Documents. All Work not so conforming to these requirements, including substitutions not properly approved and authorized, may be considered defective. If required by the Construction Manager, the Trade Contractor shall furnish satisfactory evidence as to the kind and quality of materials and equipment. This warranty is not limited by the provisions of Paragraph 14.2.

5.6 TAXES

5.6.1 The Trade Contractor shall pay all sales, consumer, use and other similar taxes for the Work or portions thereof provided by the Trade Contractor which are legally enacted at the time bids or proposals are received, whether or not yet effective.

5.7 PERMITS, FEES AND NOTICES

5.7.1 Unless otherwise provided in the Contract Documents, the Trade Contractor shall secure and pay for all permits, governmental fees, licenses and inspections necessary for the proper execution and completion of his Work, which are customarily secured after execution of the contract and which are legally required at the time bids or proposals are received.

5.7.2 The Trade Contractor shall give all notices and comply with all laws, ordinances, rules, regulations and orders of any public authority bearing on the performance of the Work.

5.7.3 Unless otherwise provided in the Contract Documents, it is not the responsibility of the Trade Contractor to make certain that the Contract Documents are in accordance with applicable laws, statutes, building codes and regulations. If the Trade Contractor observes that any of the Contract Documents are at variance therewith in any respect, he shall promptly notify the Construction Manager in writing, and any necessary changes shall be by appropriate Modification.

5.7.4 If the Trade Contractor performs any Work knowing it to be contrary to such laws, ordinances, rules and regulations, and without such notice to the Construction Manager, he shall assume full responsibility therefor and shall bear all costs attributable thereto.

5.8 ALLOWANCES

5.8.1 The Trade Contractor shall include in the Contract Sum as defined in 10.1.1 all allowances stated in the Contract Documents. Items covered by these allowances shall be supplied for such amounts and by such persons as the Construction Manager may direct, but the Trade Contractor will not be required to employ persons against whom he makes a reasonable objection.

5.8.2 Unless otherwise provided in the Contract Documents:

.1 These allowances shall cover the cost to the Trade Contractor, less applicable trade discount, of the materials and equipment required by the allowance delivered at the site, and all applicable taxes.

.2 The Trade Contractor's costs for unloading and handling on the site, labor, installation costs, overhead, profit and other expenses contemplated for the original allowance shall be included in the Contract Sum and not in the allowance.

.3 Whenever the cost is more than or less than the allowance, the Contract Sum shall be adjusted accordingly by Change Order, the amount of which will recognize changes, if any, in handling costs on the site, labor, installation costs, overhead, profit and other expenses.

5.9 SUPERINTENDENT

5.9.1 The Trade Contractor shall employ a competent superintendent and necessary assistants who shall be in attendance at the Project site during the progress of the Work. The superintendent shall be satisfactory to the Construction Manager, and shall not be changed except with the consent of the Construction Manager, unless the superintendent proves to be unsatisfactory to the Trade Contractor or ceases to be in his employ. The superintendent shall represent the Trade Contractor and all communications given to the superintendent shall be as binding as if given to the Trade Contractor. Important communications shall be confirmed in writing. Other communications shall be so confirmed on written request in each case.

5.10 PROGRESS SCHEDULE

5.10.1 The Trade Contractor, immediately after being awarded the Contract, shall prepare and submit for the Construction Manager's information an estimated progress schedule for the Work. The progress schedule shall be related to the entire Project to the extent required by the Contract Documents and shall provide for expeditious and practicable execution of the Work. This schedule shall indicate the dates for the starting and completion of the various stages of construction, shall be revised as required by the conditions of the Work, and shall be subject to the Construction Manager's approval.

5.11 DRAWINGS AND SPECIFICATIONS AT THE SITE

5.11.1 The Trade Contractor shall maintain at the site for the Construction Manager and Architect/Engineer two copies of all Drawings, Specifications, Addenda, Change Orders and other Modifications, in good order and marked currently to record all changes made during construction. These Drawings, marked to record all changes during construction, and approved Shop Drawings, Product Data and Samples shall be delivered to the Construction Manager for the Owner upon completion of the Work.

5.12 SHOP DRAWINGS, PRODUCT DATA AND SAMPLES

5.12.1 Shop Drawings are drawings, diagrams, schedules and other data especially prepared for the Work by the Trade Contractor or any Trade Subcontractor, manufacturer, supplier or distributor to illustrate some portion of the Work.

5.12.2 Product Data are illustrations, standard schedules, performance charts, instructions, brochures, diagrams and other information furnished by the Trade Contractor to ilustrate a material, product or system for some portion of the Work.

5.12.3 Samples are physical examples which illustrate materials, equipment or workmanship and establish standards by which the Work will be judged.

5.12.4 The Trade Contractor shall review, approve and submit through the Construction Manager with reasonable promptness and in such sequence as to cause no delay in the Work or in the work of any separate contractor, all Shop Drawings, Product Data and Samples required by the Contract Documents.

5.12.5 By approving and submitting Shop Drawings, Product Data and Samples, the Trade Contractor represents that he has determined and verified all materials, field measurements, and field construction criteria related thereto, or will do so, and that he has checked and coordinated the information contained within such submittals with the requirements of the Work and of the Contract Documents.

5.12.6 The Construction Manager, if he finds such submittals to be in order, will forward them to the Architect/Engineer. If the Construction Manager finds them not to be complete or in proper form, he may return them to the Trade Contractor for correction or completion.

5.12.7 The Trade Contractor shall not be relieved of responsibility for any deviation from the requirements of the Contract Documents by the Construction Manager's forwarding them to the Architect/Engineer, or by the Architect/Engineer's approval of Shop Drawings, Product Data or Samples under Subparagraph 3.2.6 unless the Trade Contractor has specifically informed the Architect/Engineer and Construction Manager in writing of such deviation at the time of submission and the Architect/Engineer has given written approval to the specific deviation. The Trade Contractor shall not be relieved from responsibility for errors or omissions in the Shop Drawings, Product Data or Samples by the Construction Manager's forwarding or the Architect/Engineer's approval thereof.

5.12.8 The Trade Contractor shall direct specific attention, in writing or on resubmitted Shop Drawings, Product Data or Samples, to revisions other than those requested by the Architect/Engineer or Construction Manager on previous submittals.

5.12.9 No portion of the Work requiring submission of a Shop Drawing, Product Data or Sample shall be commenced until the submittal has been approved by the Architect/Engineer. All such portions of the Work shall be in accordance with approved submittals.

5.13 USE OF SITE

5.13.1 The Trade Contractor shall confine operations at the site to areas designated by the Construction Manager, permitted by law, ordinances, permits and the Contract Documents and shall not unreasonably encumber the site with any materials or equipment.

5.14 CUTTING AND PATCHING OF WORK

5.14.1 The Trade Contractor shall be responsible for all cutting, fitting or patching that may be required to complete the Work or to make its several parts fit together properly. He shall provide protection of existing Work as required.

5.14.2 The Trade Contractor shall not damage or endanger any portion of the Work or the work of the Construction Manager or any separate contractors by cutting, patching or otherwise altering any work, or by excavation. The Trade Contractor shall not cut or otherwise alter the work of the Construction Manager or any separate contractor except with the written consent of the Construction Manager and of such separate contractor. The Trade Contractor shall not unreasonably withhold from the Construction Manager or any separate contractor his consent to cutting or otherwise altering the Work.

5.15 CLEANING UP

5.15.1 The Trade Contractor at all times shall keep the premises free from accumulation of waste materials or rubbish caused by his operations. At the completion of the Work he shall remove all his waste materials and rubbish from and about the Project as well as all his tools, construction equipment, machinery and surplus materials.

5.15.2 If the Trade Contractor fails to clean up, the Construction manager may do so and the cost thereof shall be charged to the Trade Contractor.

5.16 COMMUNICATIONS

5.16.1 The Trade Contractor shall forward all communications to the Owner and Architect/Engineer through the Construction Manager.

5.17 ROYALTIES AND PATENTS

5.17.1 The Trade Contractor shall pay all royalties and license fees. He shall defend all suits or claims for infringement of any patent rights and shall save the Owner and Construction Manager harmless from loss on account thereof, except that the Owner shall be responsible for all such loss when a particular design, process or the product of a particular manufacturer or manufacturers is specified, but if the Trade Contractor has reason to believe that the design, process or product specified is an infringement of a patent, he shall be responsible for such loss unless he promptly gives such information to the Construction Manager.

5.18 INDEMNIFICATION

5.18.1 To the fullest extent permitted by law, the Trade Contractor shall indemnify and hold harmless the Owner, the Construction Manager and the Architect/Engineer and their agents and employees from and against all claims, damages, losses and expenses, including but not limited to attorneys' fees, arising out of or resulting from the performance of the Work, provided that any such claim, damage, loss or expense (1) is attributable to bodily injury, sickness, disease or death, or to injury to or destruction of tangible property (other than the Work itself) including the loss of use resulting therefrom, and (2) is caused in whole or in part by any negligent act or omission of the Trade Contractor, any Trade Subcontractor, anyone directly or indirectly employed by any of them or anyone for whose acts any of them may be liable, regardless of whether or not it is caused in part by a party indemnified hereunder. Such obligation shall not be construed to negate, abridge or otherwise reduce any other right or obligation of indemnity which would otherwise exist as to any party or person described in this Paragraph 5.18.

5.18.2 In any and all claims against the Owner, the Construction Manager or the Architect/Engineer or any of their agents or employees by any employee of the Trade Contractor, any Trade Subcontractor, anyone directly or indirectly employed by any of them or anyone for whose acts any of them may be liable, the indemnification obligation under this Paragraph 5.18 shall not be limited in any way by any limitation on the amount or type of damages, compensation or benefits payable by or for the Trade Contractor or any Trade Subcontractor under workers' or workmen's compensation acts, disability benefit acts or other employee benefit acts.

5.18.3 The obligations of the Trade Contractor under this Paragraph 5.18 shall not extend to the liability of the Architect/Engineer, his agents or employees arising out of (1) the preparation or approval of maps, drawings, opinions, reports, surveys, designs or specifications, or (2) the giving of or the failure to give directions or instructions by the Architect/Engineer, his agents or employees provided such giving or failure to give is the primary cause of the injury or damage.

ARTICLE 6
TRADE SUBCONTRACTORS

6.1 DEFINITION

6.1.1 A Trade Subcontractor is a person or entity who has a direct contract with a Trade Contractor to perform any of the Work at the site. The term Trade Subcontractor is referred to throughout the Contract Documents as if singular in number and masculine in gender and means a Trade Subcontractor or his authorized representative.

6.1.2 A Trade Subcontractor is a person or entity who has a direct or indirect contract with a Trade Subcontractor to perform any of the Work at the site. The term Trade Subsubcontractor is referred to throughout the Contract Documents as if singular in number and masculine in gender and means a Trade Subsubcontractor or an authorized representative thereof.

6.2 AWARD OF TRADE SUBCONTRACTS AND OTHER CONTRACTS FOR PORTIONS OF THE WORK

6.2.1 Unless otherwise required by the Contract Documents or in the Bidding or Proposal Documents, the Trade Contractor shall furnish to the Construction Manager in writing, for acceptance by the Owner and the Construction Manager in writing, the names of the persons or entities (including those who are to furnish materials or equipment fabricated to a special design) proposed for each of the principal portions of the Work. The Construction Manager will promptly reply to the Trade Contractor in writing if either the Owner or the Construction Manager, after due investigation, has reasonable objection to any such proposed person or entity. Failure of the Owner or Construction Manager to reply promptly shall constitute notice of reasonable objection.

6.2.2 The Trade Contractor shall not contract with any such proposed person or entity to whom the Owner or the Construction Manager has made reasonable objection under the provisions of Subparagraph 6.2.1. The Trade Contractor shall not be required to contract with anyone to whom he has a reasonable objection.

6.2.3 If the Owner or Construction Manager refuses to accept any person or entity on a list submitted by the Trade Contractor in response to the requirements of the Contract Documents, the Trade Contractor shall submit an acceptable substitute, however, no increase in the Contract Sum shall be allowed for any such substitution.

6.2.4 The Trade Contractor shall make no substitution for any Trade Subcontractor, person or entity previously selected if the Owner or Construction Manager makes reasonable objection to such substitution.

6.3 TRADE SUBCONTRACTUAL RELATIONS

6.3.1 By an appropriate agreement, written where legally required for validity, the Trade Contractor shall require each Trade Subcontractor, to the extent of the work to be performed by the Trade Subcontractor, to be bound to the Trade Contractor by the terms of the Contract Documents, and to assume toward the Trade Contractor all the obligations and responsibilities which the Trade Contractor, by these Documents, assumes toward the Owner, the Construction Manager, or the Architect/Engineer. Said agreement shall preserve and protect the rights of the Owner, the Construction Manager an the Architect/Engineer under the Contract Documents with respect to the Work to be performed by the Trade Subcontractor so that the subcontracting thereof will not prejudice such rights, and shall allow to the Trade Subcontractor, unless specifically provided otherwise in the Trade Contractor-Trade Subcontractor agreement, the benefit of all rights, remedies and redress against the Trade Contractor that the Trade Contractor, by these Documents, has against the Owner or Construction Manager. Where appropriate, the Trade Contractor shall require each Trade Subcontractor to enter into similar agreements with his Trade Subsubcontractors. The Trade Contractor shall make available to each proposed Trade Subcontractor, prior to the execution of the Trade Subcontract, copies of the Contract Documents to which the Trade Subcontractor will be bound by this Paragraph 6.3, and shall identify to the Trade Subcontractor any terms and conditions of the proposed Trade Subcontract which may be at variance with the Contract Documents. Each Trade Subcontractor shall similarly make copies of such Documents available to his Trade Subsubcontractors.

ARTICLE 7

SEPARATE TRADE CONTRACTS

7.1 MUTUAL RESPONSIBILITY OF TRADE CONTRACTORS

7.1.1 The Trade Contractor shall afford the Construction Manager and other trade contractors reasonable opportunity for the introduction and storage of their materials and equipment and the execution of their work, and shall connect and coordinate his Work with others under the general direction of the Construction Manager.

7.1.2 If any part of the Trade Contractor's Work depends, for proper execution or results, upon the work of the Construction Manager or any separate trade contractor, the Trade Contractor shall, prior to proceeding with the Work, promptly report to the Construction Manager any apparent discrepancies or defects in such work that render it unsuitable for such proper execution and results. Failure of the Trade Contractor so to report shall constitute an acceptance of the other trade contractor's or Construction Manager's work as fit and proper to receive his Work, except as to defects which may subsequently become apparent in such work by others.

7.1.3 Any costs caused by defective or ill-timed work shall be borne by the party responsible thereof.

7.1.4 Should the Trade Contractor wrongfully cause damage to the work or property of the Owner or to other work on the site, the Trade Contractor shall promptly remedy such damage as provided in Subparagraph 11.2.5.

7.1.5 Should the Trade Contractor wrongfully cause damage to the work or property of any separate trade contractor or other contractor, the Trade Contractor shall, upon due notice, promptly attempt to settle with the separate trade contractor or other contractor by agreement, or otherwise resolve the dispute. If such separate trade contractor or other contractor sues the Owner or the Construction Manager or initiates an arbitration proceeding against the Owner or Construction Manager on account of any damage alleged to have been caused by the Trade Contractor, the Owner or Construction Manager shall notify the Trade Contractor who shall defend such proceedings at the Trade Contractor's expense, and if any judgment or award against the Owner or Construction Manager arises therefrom, the Trade Contractor shall pay or satisfy it and shall reimburse the Owner or Construction Manager for all attorney's fees and court or arbitration costs which the Owner or Construction Manager has incurred.

7.2 CONSTRUCTION MANAGER'S RIGHT TO CLEAN UP

7.2.1 If a dispute arises between the separate Trade Contractors as to their responsibility for cleaning up as required by Paragraph 5.15, the Construction Manager may clean up and charge the cost thereof to the Trade Contractors responsible therefor as the Construction Manager shall determine to be just.

ARTICLE 8

MISCELLANEOUS PROVISIONS

8.1 GOVERNING LAW

8.1.1 The Contract shall be governed by the law of the place where the Project is located.

8.2 SUCCESSORS AND ASSIGNS

8.2.1 The Owner or Construction Manager (as the case may be) and the Trade Contractor each binds himself, his partners, successors, assigns and legal representatives to the other party hereto and to the partners, successors, assigns and legal representatives of such other party in respect to all covenants, agreements and obligations contained in the Contract Documents. Neither party to the Contract shall assign the Contract or sublet it as a whole without the written consent of the other.

8.3 WRITTEN NOTICE

8.3.1 Written notice shall be deemed to have been duly served if delivered in person to the individual or member of the firm or entity or to an officer of the corporation for whom it was intended, or if delivered at or sent by registered or certified mail to the last business address known to him who gives the notice.

8.4 CLAIMS FOR DAMAGES

8.4.1 Should either party to the Trade Contract suffer injury or damage to person or property because of any act or omission of the other party or of any of his employees, agents or others for whose acts he is legally liable, claim shall be made in writing to such other party within a reasonable time after the first observance of such injury or damage.

8.5 PERFORMANCE BOND AND LABOR AND MATERIAL PAYMENT BOND

8.5.1 The Owner or Construction Manager shall have the right to require the Trade Contractor to furnish bonds in a form and with a corporate surety acceptable to the Construction Manager covering the faithful performance of the Contract and the payment of all obligations arising thereunder if and as required in the Bidding or Proposal Documents or in the Contract Documents.

8.6 RIGHTS AND REMEDIES

8.6.1 The duties and obligations imposed by the Contract Documents and the rights and remedies available thereunder shall be in addition to and not a limitation of any duties, obligations, rights and remedies otherwise imposed or available by law.

8.6.2 No action or failure to act by the Construction Manager, Architect/Engineer or Trade Contractor shall constitute a waiver of any right or duty afforded any of them under the Contract Documents, nor shall any such action or failure to act constitute an approval of or acquiescence in any breach thereunder, except as may be specifically agreed in writing.

8.7 TESTS

8.7.1 If the Contract Documents, laws, ordinances, rules, regulations or orders of any public authority having jurisdiction require any portion of the Work to be inspected, tested or approved, the Trade Contractor shall give the Construction Manager timely notice of its readiness so the Architect/Engineer and Construction Manager may observe such inspection, testing or approval. The Trade Contractor shall bear all costs of such inspections, tests or approvals unless otherwise provided.

8.7.2 If the Architect/Engineer or Construction Manager determines that any Work requires special inspection, testing or approval which Subparagraph 8.7.1 does not include, he will, through the Construction Manager, instruct the Trade Contractor to order such special inspection, testing or approval and the Trade Contractor shall give notice as in Subparagraph 8.7.1. If such special inspection or testing reveals a failure of the Work to comply with the requirements of the Contract Documents, the Trade Contractor shall bear all costs thereof, inluding compensation for the Architect/Engineer's and Construction Manager's additional services made necessary by such failure. If the Work complies, the Owner or Construction Manager (as the case may be) shall bear such costs and an appropriate Change Order shall be issued.

8.7.3 Required certificates of inspection, testing or approval shall be secured by the Trade Contractor and promptly delivered by him through the Construction Manager to the Architect/Engineer.

8.7.4 If the Architect/Engineer or Construction Manager is to observe the inspections, tests or approvals required by the Contract Documents, he will do so promptly and, where practicable, at the source of supply.

8.8 INTEREST

8.8.1 Payments due and unpaid under the Contract Documents shall bear interest from the date payment is due at such rate upon which the parties may agree in writing or, in the absence thereof, at the legal rate prevailing at the place of the Project.

8.9 ARBITRATION

8.9.1 All claims, disputes and other matters in question arising out of, or relating to this Contract or the breach thereof, except as set forth in Subparagraph 3.2.4 with respect to the Architect/Engineer's decisions on matters relating to artistic effect, and except for claims which have been waived by the making or acceptance of final payment provided by Subparagraphs 10.8.4 and 10.8.5, shall be decided by arbitration in accordance with the Construction Industry Arbitration Rules of the American Arbitration Association then obtaining unless the parties mutually agree otherwise. This agreement to arbitrate shall be specifically enforceable under the prevailing arbitration law. The award rendered by the arbitrators shall be final, and judgment may be entered upon it in accordance with applicable law in any court having jurisdiction thereof.

8.9.2 Notice of the demand for arbitration shall be filed in writing with the other party to the Contract and with the American Arbitration Association. The demand for arbitration shall be made within a reasonble time after the claim, dispute or other matter in question has arisen, and in no event shall it be made after the date when institution of legal or equitable proceedings based on such claim, dispute or other matter in question would be barred by the applicable statute of limitations.

8.9.3 The Trade Contractor shall carry on the Work and maintain the progress schedule during any arbitration proceedings, unless otherwise agreed by him and the Construction Manager in writing.

8.9.4 All claims which are related to or dependent upon each other shall be heard by the same arbitrator or arbitrators even though the parties are not the same unless a specific contract prohibits such consolidation.

ARTICLE 9

TIME

9.1 DEFINITIONS

9.1.1 Unless otherwise provided, the Contract Time is the period of time allotted in the Contract Documents for the Substantial Completion of the Work as defined in Subparagraph 9.1.3 including authorized adjustments thereto.

9.1.2 The date of commencement of the Work is the date established in a notice to proceed. If there is no notice to proceed, it shall be the date of the Trade Contractor Agreement or such other date as may be established therein.

9.1.3 The Date of Substantial Completion of the Work or designated portion thereof is the Date certified by the Architect/Engineer when construction is sufficiently complete, in accordance with the Contract Documents, so the Owner can occupy or utilize the Work or designated portion thereof for the use for which it is intended.

9.1.4 The term day as used in the Contract Documents shall mean calendar day unless otherwise specifically designated.

9.2 PROGRESS AND COMPLETION

9.2.1 All time limits stated in the Contract Documents are of the essence of the Contract.

9.2.2 The Trade Contractor shall begin the Work on the date of commencement as defined in Subparagraph 9.1.2. He shall carry the Work forward expeditiously with adequate forces and shall achieve Substantial Completion within the Contract Time.

9.3 DELAYS AND EXTENSIONS OF TIME

9.3.1 If the Trade Contractor is delayed at any time in the progress of the Work by any act or neglect of the Owner, Construction Manager, or the Architect/Engineer, or by any employee of either, or by any separate contractor employed by the Owner, or by changes ordered in the Work, or by labor disputes, fire, unusual delay in transportation, adverse weather conditions not reasonably anticipatable, unavoidable casualties or any causes beyond the Trade Contractor's control, or by delay authorized by the Owner or Construction Manager pending arbitration, or by any other cause which the Construction Manager determines may justify the delay, then the Contract Time shall be extended by Change Order for such reasonable time as the Construction Manager may determine.

9.3.2 Any claim for extension of time shall be made in writing to the Construction Manager not more than twenty (20) days after the commencement of the delay; otherwise, it shall be waived. In the case of a continuing delay only one claim is necessary. The Trade Contractor shall provide an estimate of the probable effect of such delay on the progress of the Work.

9.3.3 If no agreement is made stating the dates upon which interpretations as set forth in Subparagraph 3.2.2 shall be furnished, then no claim for delay shall be allowed on account of failure to furnish such interpretations until fifteen days after written request is made for them, and not then unless such claim is reasonable.

9.3.4 It shall be recognized by the Trade Contractor that he may reasonably anticipate that as the job progresses, the Construction Manager will be making changes in and updating Construction Schedules pursuant to the authority given him in Subparagraph 4.2.3. Therefore, no claim for an increase in the Contract Sum for either acceleration or delay will be allowed for extensions of time pursuant to this Paragraph 9.3 or for other changes in the Construction Schedules which are of the type ordinarily experienced in projects of similar size and complexity.

9.3.5 This Paragraph 9.3 does not exclude the recovery of damages for delay by either party under other provisions of the Contract Documents.

ARTICLE 10

PAYMENTS AND COMPLETION

10.1 CONTRACT SUM

10.1.1 The Contract Sum is stated in the Agreement between the Owner or Construction Manager and the Trade Contractor including adjustments thereto and is the total amount payable to the Trade Contractor for the performance of the Work under the Contract Documents.

10.2 SCHEDULE OF VALUES

10.2.1 Before the first Application for Payment, the Trade Contractor shall submit to the Construction Manager a schedule of values allocated to the various portions of the Work prepared in such form and supported by such data to substantiate its accuracy as the Construction Manager may require. This schedule, unless objected to by the Construction Manager, shall be used only as a basis for the Trade Contractor's Application for Payment.

10.3 APPLICATIONS FOR PAYMENT

10.3.1 At least ten days before the date for each progress payment established in the Trade Contractor's Agreement, the Trade Contractor shall submit to the Construction Manager an itemized Application for Payment, notarized if required, supported by such data substantiating the Trade Contractor's right to payment as the Owner or the Construction Manager may require and reflecting retainage, if any, as provided elsewhere in the Contract Documents.

176 CONSTRUCTION MANAGEMENT CONTRACT

10.3.2 Unless otherwise provided in the Contract Documents, payments will be made on account of materials or equipment not incorporated in the Work but delivered and suitably stored at the site and, if approved in advance by the Construction Manager, payments may similarly be made for materials or equipment stored at some other location agreed upon in writing. Payments made for materials or equipment stored on or off the site shall be conditioned upon submission by the Trade Contractor of bills of sale or such other procedures satisfactory to the Construction Manager to establish the Owner's title to such materials or equipment or otherwise protect the Owner's interest, including applicable insurance and transportation to the site for those materials and equipment stored off the site.

10.3.3 The Trade Contractor warrants that title to all Work, materials and equipment covered by an Application for Payment will pass to the Owner either by incorporation in the construction or upon the receipt of payment by the Trade Contractor, whichever occurs first, free and clear of all liens, claims, security interests or encumbrances, hereinafter referred to in this Article 10 as "liens;" and that no Work, materials or equipment covered by an Application for Payment will have been acquired by the Trade Contractor, or by any other person performing his Work at the site or furnishing materials and equipment for his Work, subject to an agreement under which an interest therein or an encumbrance thereon is retained by the seller or otherwise imposed by the Trade Contractor or such other person. All Trade Subcontractors and Trade Subsubcontractors agree that title will so pass upon their receipt of payment from the Trade Contractor.

10.4 PROGRESS PAYMENTS

10.4.1 If the Trade Contractor has made Application for Payment as above, the Construction Manager will, with reasonable promptness but not more than seven days after the receipt of the Application, review and process such Application for payment in accordance with the Contract.

10.4.2 No approval of an application for a progress payment, nor any progress payment, nor any partial or entire use or occupancy of the Project by the Owner, shall constitute an acceptance of any Work not in accordance with the Contract Documents.

10.4.3 The Trade Contractor shall promptly pay each Trade Subcontractor upon receipt of payment out of the amount paid to the Trade Contractor on account of such Trade Subcontractor's Work, the amount to which said Trade Subcontractor is entitled, reflecting the percentage actually retained, if any, from payments to the Trade Contractor on account of such Trade Subcontractor's Work. The Trade Contractor shall, by an appropriate agreement with each Trade Subcontractor, also require each Trade Subcontractor to make payments to his Trade Subsubcontractors in a similar manner.

10.5 PAYMENTS WITHHELD

10.5.1 The Construction Manager may decline to approve an Application for Payment if in his opinion the Application is not adequately supported. If the Trade Contractor and Construction Manager cannot agree on a revised amount, the Construction Manager shall process the Application for the amount he deems appropriate. The Construction Manager may also decline to approve any Applications for Payment or, because of subsequently discovered evidence or subsequent inspections, he may nullify in whole or in part any approval previously made to such extent as may be necessary in his opinion because of:

.1 defective work not remedied;

.2 third party claims filed or reasonable evidence indicating probable filing of such claims;

.3 failure of the Trade Contractor to make payments properly to Trade Subcontractors or for labor, materials or equipment;

.4 reasonable evidence that the Work cannot be completed for the unpaid balance of the Contract Sum;

.5 damage to the Construction Manager, the Owner, or another contractor working at the Project;

.6 reasonable evidence that the Work will not be completed within the Contract Time; or

.7 persistent failure to carry out the Work in accordance with the Contract Documents.

10.5.2 When the above grounds in Subparagraph 10.5.1 are removed, payment shall be made for amounts withheld because of them.

10.6 FAILURE OF PAYMENT

10.6.1 If the Trade Contractor is not paid within seven days after any amount is approved for payment by the Construction Manager and has become due and payable, then the Trade Contractor may, upon seven additional days' written notice to the Owner and Construction Manager, stop the Work until payment of the amount owing has been received. The Contract Sum shall be increased by the amount of the Trade Contractor's reasonable costs of shutdown, delay and start up, which shall be effected by appropriate Change Order in accordance with Paragraph 13.3.

10.7 SUBSTANTIAL COMPLETION

10.7.1 When the Trade Contractor considers that the Work, or a designated portion thereof which is acceptable to the Owner, is substantially complete as defined in Subparagraph 9.1.3, the Trade Contractor shall prepare for submission to the Construction Manager a list of items to be completed or corrected. The failure to include any items on such list does not alter the responsibility of the Trade Contractor to complete all Work in accordance with the Contract Documents. When the Construction Manager and Architect/Engineer on the basis of inspection determine that the Work or designated portion thereof is substantially complete, the Architect/Engineer will then prepare a Certificate of Substantial Completion which shall establish the Date of Substantial Completion, shall state the responsibilities of the Owner, the Construction Manager and the Trade Contractor for security, maintenance, heat, utilities, damage to the Work, and insurance, and shall fix the time within which the Trade Contractor shall complete the items listed therein. Warranties required by the Contract Documents shall commence on the Date of Substantial Completion of the Work or designated portion thereof unless otherwise provided in the Certificate of Substantial Completion. The Certificate of Substantial Completion shall be submitted to the Owner, the Construction Manager and the Trade Contractor for their written acceptance of the responsibilities assigned to them in such Certificate.

10.8 FINAL COMPLETION AND FINAL PAYMENT

10.8.1 Upon receipt of written notice that the Work is ready for final inspection and acceptance and upon receipt of a final Application for Payment, the Architect/Engineer and the Construction Manager will promptly make such inspection and, when they find the Work acceptable under the Contract Documents and the Contract fully performed, the Construction Manager will promptly approve final payment.

10.8.2 Neither the final payment nor the remaining retained percentage shall become due until the Trade Contractor submits to the Construction Manager (1) an affidavit that all payrolls, bills for materials and equipment, and other indebtedness connected with the Work for which the Owner or his property might in any way be responsible, have been paid or otherwise satisfied, (2) consent of surety, if any, to final payment, and (3) if required by the Owner, other data establishing payment or satisfaction of all such obligations, such as receipts, releases and waivers of liens arising out of the Contract, to the extent and in such form as may be designated by the Owner. If any Trade Subcontractor refuses to furnish a release or waiver required by the Owner or Construction Manager, the Trade Contractor may furnish a bond satisfactory to the Owner and Construction manager to indemnify them against any such lien. If any such lien remains unsatisfied after all payments are made, the Trade Contractor shall refund to the Owner or Construction Manager all moneys that the latter may be compelled to pay in discharging such lien, including all costs and reasonable attorneys' fees.

10.8.3 If, after Substantial Completion of the Work, final completion thereof is materially delayed through no fault of the Trade Contractor or by the issuance of Change Orders affecting final completion, and the Construction Manager so confirms, the Owner or Construction Manager shall, upon certification by the Construction Manager, and without terminating the Contract, make payment of the balance due for that portion of the Work fully completed and accepted. If the remaining balance for Work not fully completed or corrected is less than the retainage stipulated in the Contract Documents, and if bonds have been furnished as provided in Paragraph 8.5, the written consent of the surety to the payment of the balance due for that portion of the Work fully completed and accepted shall be submitted by the Trade Contractor to the Construction Manager prior to such payment. Such payment shall be made under the terms and conditions governing final payment, except that it shall not constitute a waiver of claims.

10.8.4 The making of final payment shall constitute a waiver of all claims by the Owner or Construction Manager except those arising from:

.1 unsettled liens;

.2 faulty or defective Work appearing after Substantial Completion;

178 CONSTRUCTION MANAGEMENT CONTRACT

.3 failure of the Work to comply with the requirements of the Contract Documents; or

.4 terms of any special warranties required by the Contract Documents.

10.8.5 The acceptance of final payment shall constitute a waiver of all claims by the Trade Contractor except those previously made in writing and identified by the Trade Contractor as unsettled at the time of the Final Application for Payment.

Article 11

PROTECTION OF PERSONS AND PROPERTY

11.1 SAFETY PRECAUTIONS AND PROGRAMS

11.1.1 The Trade Contractor shall be responsible for initiating, maintaining and supervising all safety precautions and programs in connection with the Work.

11.1.2 If the Trade Contractor fails to maintain the safety precautions required by law or directed by the Construction Manager, the Construction Manager may take such steps as necessary and charge the Trade Contractor therefor.

11.1.3 The failure of the Construction Manager to take any such action shall not relieve the Trade Contractor of his obligations in Subparagraph 11.1.1.

11.2 SAFETY OF PERSONS AND PROPERTY

11.2.1 The Trade Contractor shall take all reasonable precautions for the safety of, and shall provide all reasonable protection to prevent damage, injury or loss to:

.1 all employees on the Work and all other persons who may be affected thereby;

.2 all the Work and all materials and equipment to be incorporated therein, whether in storage on or off the site, under the care, custody or control of the Trade Contractor or any of his Trade subcontractors or Trade Subsubcontractors; and

.3 other property at the site or adjacent thereto, including trees, shrubs, lawns, walks, pavements, roadways, structures and utilities not designated for removal, relocation or replacement in the course of construction.

11.2.2 The Trade Contractor shall give all notices and comply with all applicable laws, ordinances, rules, regulations and lawful orders of any public authority bearing on the safety of persons or property or their protection from damage, injury or loss.

11.2.3 The Trade Contractor shall erect and maintain, as required by existing conditions and progress of the Work, all easonable safeguards for safety and protection, including posting danger signs and other warnings against hazards, promulgating safety regulations and notifying owners and users of adjacent utilities. If the Trade Contractor fails to so comply he shall, at the direction of the Construction Manager, remove all forces from the Project without cost or loss to the Owner or Construction Manager, until he is in compliance.

11.2.4 When the use or storage of explosives or other hazardous materials or equipment is necessary for the execution of the Work, the Trade Contractor shall exercise the utmost care and shall carry on such activities under the supervision of properly qualified personnel.

11.2.5 The Trade Contractor shall promptly remedy all damage or loss (other than damage or loss insured under Paragraph 12.2) to any property referred to in Clauses 11.2.1.2 and 11.2.1.3 caused in whole or in part by the Trade Contractor, his Trade Subcontractors, his Trade Subsubcontractors, or anyone directly or indirectly employed by any of them, or by anyone for whose acts any of them may be liable and for which the Trade Contractor is responsible under Clauses 11.2.1.2 and 11.2.1.3, except damage or loss attributable to the acts or omissions of the Owner or Architect/Engineer or anyone directly or indirectly employed by either of them or by anyone for whose acts either of them may be liable, and not attributable to the fault or negligence of the Trade Contractor. The foregoing obligations of the Trade Contractor are in addition to his obligations under Paragraph 5.18.

11.2.6 The Trade Contractor shall designate a responsible member of his organization at the site whose duty shall be the prevention of accidents. This person shall be the Trade Contractor's superintendent unless otherwise designated by the Trade Contractor in writing to the Construction Manager.

11.2.7 The Trade Contractor shall not load or permit any part of the Work to be loaded so as to endanger its safety.

11.3 EMERGENCIES

11.3.1 In any emergency affecting the safety of persons or property, the Trade Contractor shall act, at his discretion, to prevent threatened damage, injury or loss. Any additional compensation or extension of time claimed by the Trade Contractor on account of emergency work shall be determined as provided in Article 13 for Changes in the Work.

ARTICLE 12

INSURANCE

12.1 TRADE CONTRACTOR'S LIABILITY INSURANCE

12.1.1 The Trade Contractor shall purchase and maintain such insurance as will protect him from claims set forth below which may arise out of or result from the Trade Contractor's operations under the Contract, whether such operations be by himself or by any of his Trade Subcontractors or by anyone directly or indirectly employed by any of them, or by anyone for whose acts any of them may be liable:

.1 claims under workers' or workmen's compensation, disability benefit and other similar employee benefit acts which are applicable to the Work to be performed including the "Broad Form" All States" Endorsement;

.2 claims for damages because of bodily injury, occupational sickness or disease, or death of his employees under any employers liability law including, if applicable, those required under maritime or admiralty law for wages, maintenance, and cure;

.3 claims for damages because of bodily injury, sickness or disease, or death of any person other than his employees;

.4 claims for damages insured by usual personal injury liability coverage which are sustained (1) by any person as a result of an offense directly or indirectly related to the employment of such person by the Trade Contractor, or (2) by any other person;

.5 claims for damages other than to the Work itself because of injury to or destruction of tangible property, including loss of use resulting therefrom; and

.6 claims for damages because of bodily injury or death of any person or property damage arising out of the ownership, maintenance or use of any motor vehicle.

12.1.2 The insurance required by Subparagraph 12.1.1 shall be written for not less than any limits of liability specified in the Contract Documents, or required by law, whichever is greater.

12.1.3 The insurance required by Subparagraph 12.1.1 shall include premises-operations (including explosion, collapse and underground coverage), elevators, independent contractors, products and/or completed operations, and contractual liability insurance (on a "blanket basis" designating all written contracts), all including broad form property damage coverage. Liability insurance may be arranged under Comprehensive General Liability policies for the full limits required or by a combination of underlying policies for lesser limits with the remaining limits provided by an excess or Umbrella Liability Policy.

12.1.4 The foregoing policies shall contain a provision that coverages afforded under the policies will not be cancelled until at least sixty days' prior written notice has been given to the Construction Manager. Certificates of Insurance acceptable to the Construction Manager shall be filed with the Construction Manager prior to commencement of the Work. Upon request, the Trade Contractor shall allow the Construction Manager to examine the actual policies.

12.2 PROPERTY INSURANCE AND WAIVER OF SUBROGATION

12.2.1 Unless otherwise provided, the Owner will purchase and maintain property insurance upon the entire Work at the site to the full insurable value thereof. This insurance shall include the interests of the Owner, the Construction Manager, the Trade Contractors, and Trade Subcontractors in the Work and shall insure against the perils of fire and extended coverage, and shall include "all risk" insurance for physical loss or damage.

12.2.2 The Owner will effect and maintain such boiler and machinery insurance as may be necessary and/or required by law. This insurance shall include the interest of the Owner, the Construction Manager, the Trade Contractors, and Trade Subcontractors in the Work.

12.2.3 Any loss insured under Paragraph 12.2 is to be adjusted with the Owner and Construction Manager and made payable to the Owner and Construction Manager as trustees for the insureds, as their interests may appear, subject to the requirements of any applicable mortgagee clause.

12.2.4 The Owner, the Construction Manager, the Architect/Engineer, the Trade Contractors, and the Trade Subcontractors waive all rights against each other and any other contractor or subcontractor engaged in the Project for damages caused by fire or other perils to the extent covered by insurance provided under Paragraph 12.2, or any other property or consequential loss insurance applicable to the Project, equipment used in the Project, or adjacent structures, except such rights as they may have to the proceeds of such insurance. If any policy of insurance requires an endorsement to maintain coverage with such waivers, the owner of such policy will cause the policy to be so endorsed. The Owner will require, by appropriate agreement, written where legally required for validity, similar waivers in favor of the Trade Contractors and Trade Subcontractors by any separate contractor and his subcontractors.

12.2.5 The Owner and Construction Manager shall deposit in a separate account any money received as trustees, and shall distribute it in accordance with such agreement as the parties in interest may reach, or in accordance with an award by arbitration in which case the procedure shall be as provided in Paragraph 8.9. If after such loss no other special agreement is made, replacement of damaged Work shall be covered by an appropriate Change Order.

12.2.6 The Owner and Construction Manager as trustees shall have power to adjust and settle any loss with the insurers unless one of the parties in interest shall object in writing within five days after the occurrence of loss to the Owner's and Construction Manager's exercise of this power, and if such objection be made, arbitrators shall be chosen as provided in Paragraph 8.9. The Owner and Construction Manager as trustees shall, in that case, make settlement with the insurers in accordance with the directions of such arbitrators. If distribution of the insurance proceeds by arbitration is required, the arbitrators will direct such distribution.

12.2.7 If the Owner finds it necessary to occupy or use a portion or portions of the Work prior to Substantial Completion thereof, such occupancy shall not commence prior to a time mutually agreed to by the Owner and Construction Manager and to which the insurance company or companies providing the property insurance have consented by endorsement to the policy or policies. This insurance shall not be cancelled or lapsed on account of such partial occupancy.

ARTICLE 13

CHANGES IN THE WORK

13.1 CHANGE ORDERS

13.1.1 A Change Order is a written order to the Trade Contractor signed by the Owner or Construction Manager, as the case may be, issued after the execution of the Contract, authorizing a Change in the Work or an adjustment in the Contract Sum or the Contract Time. The Contract Sum and the Contract Time may be changed only by Change Order. A Change Order signed by the Trade Contractor indicates his agreement therewith, including the adjustment in the Contract Sum or the Contract Time.

13.1.2 The Owner or Construction Manager, without invalidating the Contract, may order Changes in the Work within the general scope of the Contract consisting of additions, deletions or other revisions, the Contract Sum and the Contract Time being adjusted accordingly. All such changes in the Work shall be authorized by Change Order, and shall be performed under the applicable conditions of the Contract Documents.

13.1.3 The cost or credit to the Owner or Construction Manager resulting from a Change in the Work shall be determined in one or more of the following ways:

.1 by mutual acceptance of a lump sum properly itemized and supported by sufficient substantiating data to permit evaluation; or

.2 by unit prices stated in the Contract Documents or subsequently agreed upon; or

.3 by cost to be determined in a manner agreed upon by the parties and a mutually acceptable fixed or percentage fee; or

.4 by the method provided in Subparagraph 13.1.4.

13.1.4 If none of the methods set forth in Clauses 13.1.3.1, 13.1.3.2 or 13.1.3.3 is agreed upon, the Trade Contractor, provided he receives a written order signed by the Owner or the Construction Manager, shall promptly proceed with the Work involved. The cost of such Work shall be determined by the Construction Manager on the basis of the reasonable expenditures and savings of those performing the Work attributable to the change, including, in the case of an increase in the Contract Sum, a reasonable allowance for overhead and profit. In such case, and also under Clauses 13.1.3.3 and 13.1.3.4 above, the Trade Contractor shall keep and present, in such form as the Construction Manager may prescribe, an itemized accounting together with appropriate supporting data for inclusion in a Change Order. Unless otherwise provided in the Contract Documents, cost shall be limited to the following: cost of materials; including sales tax and cost of delivery; cost of labor, including social security, old age and unemployment insurance, and fringe benefits required by agreement or custom; workers' or workmen's compensation insurance; bond premiums; rental value of equipment and machinery; and the additional costs of supervision and field office personnel directly attributable to the change. Pending final determination of cost, payments on account shall be made as determined by the Construction Manager. The amount of credit to be allowed by the Trade Contractor for any deletion or change which results in a net decrease in the Contract Sum will be the amount of the actual net cost as confirmed by the Construction Manager. When both additions and credits covering related Work or substitutions are involved in any one change, the allowance for overhead and profit shall be figured on the basis of the net increase, if any, with respect to that change.

13.1.5 If unit prices are stated in the Contract Documents or subsequently agreed upon, and if the quantities originally contemplated are so changed in a proposed Change Order that application of the agreed unit prices to the quantities of Work proposed will cause substantial inequity to the Owner, the Construction Manager, or the Trade Contractor, the applicable unit prices shall be equitably adjusted.

13.2 CONCEALED CONDITIONS

13.2.1 Should concealed conditions encountered in the performance of the Work below the surface of the ground or should concealed or unknown conditions in an existing structure be at variance with the conditions indicated by the Contract Documents, or should unknown physical conditions below the surface of the ground or should concealed or unknown conditions in an existing structure of an unusual nature, differing materially from those ordinarily encountered and generally recognized as inherent in work of the character provided for in this Contract, be encountered, the Contract Sum shall be equitably adjusted by Change Order upon claim by either party made within twenty days after the first observance of the conditions.

13.3 CLAIMS FOR ADDITIONAL COST

13.3.1 If the Trade Contractor wishes to make a claim for an increase in the Contract Sum, he shall give the Construction Manager written notice thereof within twenty days after the occurrence of the event giving rise to such claim. This notice shall be given by the Trade Contractor before proceeding to execute the Work, except in an emergency endangering life or property in which case the Trade Contractor shall proceed in accordance with Paragraph 11.3. No such claim shall be valid unless so made. Any change in the Contract Sum resulting from such claim shall be authorized by Change Order.

13.3.2 If the Trade Contractor claims that additional cost is involved because of, but not limited to, (1) any written interpretation issued pursuant to Subparagraph 3.2.2, (2) any order by the Owner or Construction Manager to stop the Work pursuant to Paragraph 4.3 where the Trade Contractor was not at fault, or (3) any written order for a minor change in the Work issued pursuant to Paragraph 13.4, the Trade Contractor shall make such claim as provided in Subparagraph 13.3.1.

182 CONSTRUCTION MANAGEMENT CONTRACT

13.4 MINOR CHANGES IN THE WORK

13.4.1 The Architect/Engineer will have authority to order through the Construction Manager minor changes in the Work not involving an adjustment in the Contract Sum or an extension of the Contract Time and not inconsistent with the intent of the Contract Documents. Such changes shall be effected by written order and such changes shall be binding on the Owner, the Construction Manager, and the Trade Contractor. The Trade Contractor shall carry out such written orders promptly.

ARTICLE 24

UNCOVERING AND CORRECTION OF WORK

14.1 UNCOVERING OF WORK

14.1.1 If any portion of the Work should be covered contrary to the request of the Construction Manager or Architect/Engineer, or to requirements specifically expressed in the Contract Documents, it must, if required in writing by the Construction Manager, be uncovered for their observation and replaced, at the Trade Contractor's expense.

14.1.2 If any other portion of the Work has been covered which neither the Construction Manager nor the Architect/Engineer has specifically requested to observe prior to being covered, the Architect/Engineer or Construction Manager may request to see such Work and it shall be uncovered by the Trade Contractor. If such Work be found in accordance with the Contract Documents, the cost of uncovering and replacement shall, by appropriate Change Order, be charged to the Owner or Construction Manager, as the case may be. If such Work be found not in accordance with the Contract Documents, the Trade Contractor shall pay such costs unless it be found that this condition was caused by a separate trade contractor employed as provided in Article 7, and in that event the separate trade contractor shall be responsible for the payment of such costs.

14.2 CORRECTION OF WORK

14.2.1 The Trade Contractor shall promptly correct all Work rejected by the Architect/Engineer or the Construction Manager as defective or as failing to conform to the Contract Documents whether observed before or after Substantial Completion and whether or not fabricated, installed or completed. The Trade Contractor shall bear all costs of correcting such rejected Work, including compensation for the Architect/Engineer's and/or Construction Manager's additional services made necessary thereby.

14.2.2 If, within one year after the Date of Substantial Completion of Work or designated portion thereof, or within one year after acceptance by the Owner of designated equipment or within such longer period of time as may be prescribed by law or by the terms of any applicable special warranty required by the Contract Documents, any of the Work is found to be defective or not in accordance with the Contract Documents, the Trade Contractor shall correct it promptly after receipt of a written notice from the Owner or Construction Manager to do so unless the Owner or Construction Manager has previously given the Trade Contractor a written acceptance of such condition. This obligation shall survive the termination of the Contract. The Owner or Construction Manager shall give such notice promptly after discovery of the condition.

14.2.3 The Trade Contractor shall remove from the site all portions of the Work which are defective or non-conforming and which have not been corrected under Subparagraphs 5.5.1, 14.2.1 and 14.2.2, unless removal has been waived by the Owner.

14.2.4 If the Trade Contractor fails to correct defective or non-conforming Work as provided in Subparagraphs 5.5.1, 14.2.1 and 14.2.2, the Owner or Construction Manager may correct it in accordance with Subparagraph 4.3.2.

14.2.5 If the Trade Contractor does not proceed with the correction of such defective or non-conforming Work within a reasonable time fixed by written notice from the Construction Manager, the Owner or Construction Manager may remove it and may store the materials or equipment at the expense of the Trade Contractor. If the Trade Contractor does not pay the cost of such removal and storage within ten days thereafter, the Owner or Construction Manager may upon ten additional days' written notice sell such Work at auction or at private sale and shall account for the net proceeds thereof, after deducting all the costs that should have been borne by the Trade Contractor, including compensation for the Construction Manager's additional services made necessary thereby. If such proceeds of sale do not cover all costs which the Trade Contractor should have borne, the difference shall be charged to the Trade Contractor and an appropriate Change Order shall be issued. If the payments then or thereafter due the Trade Contractor are not sufficient to cover such amount, the Trade Contractor shall pay the difference to the Owner or Construction Manager.

AGC DOCUMENT NO. 520 • GENERAL CONDITIONS FOR TRADE CONTRACTORS UNDER CONSTRUCTION MANAGEMENT AGREEMENTS • JULY 1980

14.2.6 The Trade Contractor shall bear the cost of making good all work of the Construction Manager or other contractors destroyed or damaged by such removal or correction.

14.3 ACCEPTANCE OF DEFECTIVE OR NONCONFORMING WORK

14.3.1 If the Owner or Construction Manager prefers to accept defective or non-conforming Work, he may do so instead of requiring its removal and correction, in which case a Change Order will be issued to reflect reduction in the Contract Sum where appropriate and equitable. Such adjustment shall be effected whether or not final payment has been made.

ARTICLE 15

TERMINATION OF THE CONTRACT

15.1 TERMINATION BY THE TRADE CONTRACTOR

15.1.1 If the Work is stopped for a period of thirty days under an order of any court or other public authority having jurisdiction, or as a result of an act of government, such as a declaration of a national emergency making materials unavailable, through no act or fault of the Trade Contractor or a Trade Subcontractor or their agents or employees or any other persons performing any of the Work under a contract with the Trade Contractor, or if the Work should be stopped for a period of thirty days by the Trade Contractor because of a failure to receive payment in accordnace with the Contract, then the Trade Contractor may, upon seven additional days' written notice to the Construction Manager, terminate the Contract and recover from the Owner or Construction Manager, as the case may be, payment for all Work executed and for any proven loss sustained upon any materials, equipment, tools, construction equipment and machinery, including reasonable profit and damages.

15.2 TERMINATION BY THE OWNER OR CONSTRUCTION MANAGER

15.2.1 If the Trade Contractor is adjudged a bankrupt, or if he makes a general assignment for the benefit of his creditors, or if a receiver is appointed on account of his insolvency, or if he persistently or repeatedly refuses or fails, except in cases for which extension of time is provided, to supply enough properly skilled workmen or proper materials, or if he fails to make prompt payment to Trade Contractors or for materials or labor, or persistently disregards laws, ordinances, rules, regulations or orders of any public authority having jurisdiction, or otherwise is guilty of a substantial violation of a provision of the Contract Documents, then the Owner or Construction Manager may, without prejudice to any right or remedy and after giving the Trade Contractor and his surety, if any, seven days' written notice, terminate the employment of the Trade Contractor and take possession of the site and of all materials, equipment, tools, construction equipment and machinery thereon owned by the Trade Contractor and may finish the Work by whatever method he may deem expedient. In such case the Trade Contractor shall not be entitled to receive any further payment until the Work is finished.

15.2.2 If the unpaid balance of the Contract Sum exceeds the costs of finishing the Work, including compensation for the Construction Manager's additional services made necessary thereby, such excess shall be paid to the Trade Contractor. If such costs exceed the unpaid balance, the Trade Contractor shall pay the difference to the Owner or Construction Manager.

FORM 3-5 Modifications to General Conditions for Trade Contractors [Favors Interests of Trade Contractor] (with Comments)

The General Conditions for Trade Contractors under Construction Management Agreements, AGC Document No. 520, is modified as follows:

¶1. <u>First:</u>   Article 3.2.3.   The last sentence of Article 3.2.3 is annulled.

¶2. <u>Second:</u>   Article 3.2.5.   The last sentence of Article 3.2.5 is annulled.

¶3. <u>Third:</u>   Article 6.2.1.   The last sentence of Article 6.2.1 is annulled.

¶4. <u>Fourth:</u>   Article 6.2.3.   The phrase "however, no increase in the Contract Sum shall be allowed for any such substitution" is deleted from Article 6.2.3.

¶5. <u>Fifth:</u>   Article 8.1.1.   Article 8.1.1 is deleted.

> Comment: The inclusion of a governing law clause can have unintended effects on the enforceability of an arbitration agreement. *See Volt Information Sciences, Inc v Board of Trustees of the Leland Stanford Junior University,* 489 US 468 (1989).

¶6. <u>Sixth:</u>   Article 8.9.   For commentaries on the arbitration clause and whether it should be included or excluded from the Contract Documents, see FORM 2-2 §2.04, and FORM 3-2 ¶23.

¶7. <u>Seventh:</u>   Article 12.1.1.4.   Article 12.1.1.4 is annulled.

> Comment: *Personal injury,* in insurance lingo, refers to libel, slander, advertising liability, and the like. It should not be required in a construction contract.

¶8. <u>Eighth:</u>   Article 12.1.1.5.   The words "other than to the Work itself" are deleted from Article 12.1.1.5.

> Comment: The usual form of subcontractor insurance excludes coverage for damage to the subcontractor's work, but not for damage to work performed by other trade contractors or by the general contractor or construction manager.

¶9. <u>Ninth:</u>   Article 12.1.3.   Article 12.1.3 is amended by adding the following sentence:

The comprehensive general liability policy of the Trade Contractor shall include coverage for liability assumed by contract, including the indemnity provisions of this Contract.

¶10. **Tenth: Article 12.1.5.** Article 12.1.5 is added to read as follows:

12.1.5 The Trade Contractor's comprehensive general liability policy shall contain an endorsement naming Construction Manager and Owner as additional insureds, as respects claims and losses arising out of the operations of Trade Contractor, and shall provide that such insurance is primary to liability insurance procured by Construction Manager and Owner. Trade Contractor shall not commence work on the jobsite until a copy of the endorsement has been supplied to Construction Manager.

¶11. **Eleventh: Article 12.2.** Article 12.2 (12.2.1 through 12.2.7) is annulled.

Comment: The factors taken into consideration as to the inclusion or deletion of property insurance provisions are discussed in **FORM 3-2 ¶20.**

Trade contractors, or subcontractors, are in a different legal position from that of a construction manager with respect to the doctrine of impossibility of performance. It is truly physically impossible, for example, for an electrical subcontractor to wire a building that does not exist. Therefore, if the project is destroyed by fire and not rebuilt, the electrical subcontractor would be excused by the doctrine of impossibility from further performance of the work.

If, as recommended above, the construction manager purchases a policy covering its insurable interest in the continued existence of the building, then in the event of an insured loss, the construction manager would receive sufficient funds to rebuild. As a result, the construction manager would have the money to make payments to the electrical subcontractor and other trade contractors.

Therefore, except in unusual circumstances, the trade contractor will not need to purchase property insurance.

Contracts Between Owner and Architect 4

Introduction to Owner/Architect Agreements

§4.01 General Comments

Architect/Owner Agreements

    FORM 4-1   Agreement between Owner and Architect for the Provision of Architectural Services

    FORM 4-2   Alternate and Optional Contract Provisions - Agreement between Owner and Architect - Architectural Services

AIA Document B141 - Standard Form of Agreement between Owner and Architect

§4.02 General Comments

    FORM 4-3   Modifications to Owner/Architect Agreement [Favors Interests of Owner] (with Comments)

Introduction to Owner/Architect Agreements

§4.01 General Comments

The author is indebted to Arthur F. O'Leary, FAIA for consultation and advice as to the following form of agreement.

This agreement contains a broadly worded arbitration clause that permits arbitration of multiple party disputes. All parties who may be involved in a job dispute may be brought into the arbitration proceeding. This eliminates the need for multiple proceedings.

The form includes an attorney's fee clause, as the standard AIA form (AIA Document B141) does not.

This form assumes that owner and contractor will enter into a conventional relationship under which the owner, utilizing the services of an architect, supplies drawings and specifications to the contractor, who agrees to construct the project according to those plans and specifications.

Paragraph 1 emphasizes the importance of communication between owner and architect as to the owner's program. This requires organized thinking on the owner's part. Provision is made for the owner to advise the architect in writing as to budgetary restraints.

Under Paragraph 2, the architect supplies a written preliminary estimate of the cost of constructing the project along with preliminary drawings. It is acknowledged, though, that the preliminary estimate is subject to a substantial margin of error.

Under Paragraph 5, the architect undertakes responsibility for inspection of the project except for intrusive, destructive, chemical, mechanical, and laboratory testing, which are to be performed by inspection agencies employed by the owner.

Paragraph 13 gives the owner an option of paying a 15 per cent surcharge to induce the architect to assume responsibility for errors and omissions.

Architect/Owner Agreements

FORM 4-1 Agreement between Owner and Architect for the Provision of Architectural Services

AGREEMENT BETWEEN OWNER AND ARCHITECT FOR THE PROVISION OF ARCHITECTURAL SERVICES

THIS AGREEMENT is between _____, owner, and _____, architect. The owner has acquired or is in the process of acquiring land described as: _____
_____
_____

Owner wants to develop, on the land, the following project: _____
_____
_____

Owner employs architect to perform, and architect agrees to perform, the following services:

1. <u>Programming and Schematics.</u> Owner will provide architect with programming information, to inform architect as to the use of the structures to be designed and the amount of space needed to be devoted to various purposes, and will supply architect with as much detailed information as possible as to

the characteristics of the project desired by owner. Owner will take the time and trouble to provide architect with specific and detailed information as to the owner's criteria for the project, both economic and aesthetic. Owner will supply architect with all information and documents in owner's possession as to zoning, governmental restrictions, permits, variances, conditional uses, title, surveys, construction financing, recorded covenants, conditions, restrictions, and all other information that is known to owner and would be relevant to the proper performance of architect's duties under this contract. The architect will then propose, for the consideration of owner, a scheme of design as to the location, structure, appearance, and function of the project. Owner will in turn provide architect with detailed reactions to the architect's scheme, and the architect will supply a gross estimate as to the cost of the project. If owner is operating under financing or budget constraints, owner will inform architect of such constraints, in writing, as early as possible. Owner acknowledges that many desirable architectural features are costly and that design requires compromise. Architect will supply owner with schematic drawings that will display the general characteristics, appearance, and dimensions of the project.

2. Preliminary Drawings. After owner and architect have agreed as to the philosophy of design and after owner has approved the schematics, the architect will proceed with preliminary drawings. The purpose of the preliminary drawings is to totally describe the general characteristics of the project as to the size and location of buildings, size and location of rooms and other spaces within the buildings, the general characteristics of the architectural design, the general characteristics of the structural and roof design, and the allocation of interior and exterior functions and spaces. Architect will not proceed with working drawings until owner has approved, in writing, the preliminary drawings. Based on the preliminary drawings, architect will supply owner with a written preliminary estimate of the cost of constructing the project. The preliminary estimate is subject to a substantial margin of error, because of the preliminary nature of the design, cost fluctuations, and the limited sources of cost data that are available to architect. If owner needs a more accurate estimate, owner will employ an independent estimating service to provide detailed information.

3. Working Drawings. Architect will produce working drawings and specifications for the construction of the project. Architect will submit the drawings to all applicable governmental agencies for approval, and will make any corrections that are necessary to obtain all necessary governmental approval. Owner will commit the time that is necessary to carefully and promptly check the drawings and specifications for conformance to owner's aesthetic, functional, and economic requirements. Architect will perform revisions and redesign necessary to meet owner's requirements. If owner requires architect to change drawings that owner has already approved or agreed to, architect's fee will be equitably adjusted.

4. Contracts and Bidding. Architect will consult with Owner as to the various systems available for the employment of a contractor or contractors

for the construction of the project, and will provide appropriate forms of agreement. Owner will provide review of the forms of agreement by a lawyer selected by owner. Architect will advise owner as to the reputations (if known) of contractors and subcontractors who are under consideration. If competitive bidding is to be employed, it will be from a select bid list approved by owner and architect, and bidding and bid opening will be supervised by architect.

5. <u>Inspection and Observation.</u> During the progress of the job, the architect will visit the jobsite at appropriate intervals and observe the progress of the work. The architect's inspection will be as to those features of the project that can be observed without intrusive or destructive techniques. Intrusive, destructive, chemical, mechanical, and laboratory testing will be performed by appropriate agencies employed by owner upon the recommendation of architect. Architect will act as owner's agent, and will deal, as such, with the contractor to protect the interests of owner against deviation from the contract documents or acceptable standards of construction. If architect determines that work performed by the contractor does not comply with the requirements of the contract documents, architect will notify owner and contractor of such deviation in writing, and owner will take such measures as it deems desirable to secure compliance. If legal assistance is needed to obtain proper performance from the prime contractor or subcontractors, owner will employ a lawyer for that purpose.

6. <u>Progress Payments.</u> Architect will recommend documents and an appropriate system for processing progress payments to the contractor, and will issue certificates for payment, as appropriate under the contract documents, based on information obtained by architect by inspection of the progress of the work.

7. <u>Change Orders.</u> Architect will recommend a procedure for processing change orders, will check pricing of change orders, and will recommend appropriate change orders for signature by owner. Owner will avoid dealing directly with the contractor and will process change orders through architect.

8. <u>Job Site Discipline and Safety.</u> Within the constraints of periodic inspection and observation, architect will use its best efforts, as the agent of owner, to require the contractor to maintain a disciplined, orderly, and safe job site. Architect is not, however, responsible for activities that are beyond its control, or that occur when architect is not present on the site, or for activities or conditions that are not reasonably observable by architect when present on the site. If architect determines that the job is being conducted in an unsafe manner, it will inform the contractor and owner in writing, and owner will take such measures as are necessary to require the contractor to proceed safely.

9. <u>Shop Drawings, Submittals, Selections.</u> Architect will process shop drawings and other submittals and will make color and material selections, and will promptly respond to reasonable requests for information from contractor.

10. <u>Completion and Occupancy.</u> When the project is substantially complete, architect will make a detailed inspection, and will prepare a punch list. Architect will determine when the project is substantially complete, and when it is ready for occupancy.

11. <u>Repairs and Warranties.</u> Architect will assist the owner in processing warranty claims, repairs, and corrections, and will use its best efforts, as the agent of the owner, to require contractors, subcontractors, and suppliers to correct improper work and to make good their warranties. If legal action is required to secure corrective or warranty work, owner will employ a lawyer for that purpose.

12. <u>Payment.</u> For the architect's services, owner shall make payments as follows:

　　(a)　<u>Creation of Design Concept and Philosophy.</u> For the creation of the design concept and philosophy, including schematic drawings, owner will pay a retainer fee of $_____ in advance. Upon the completion of the schematic drawings, owner will pay a design fee of $_____.

　　(b)　<u>Working Drawings and Specifications.</u> For the preparation of working drawings and specifications, owner will pay architect, against monthly billings, according to Schedule A which is attached hereto and incorporated herein.

　　(c)　<u>Consultants' Fees.</u> Owner will reimburse architect, monthly as billed, for the fees of consultants employed by architect for mechanical, electrical, and structural services.

　　(d)　<u>Survey, Testing, Reproduction, and Incidentals.</u> Owner will reimburse architect, monthly as billed, for surveying, testing, inspection, reproduction, and incidental fees and expenses incurred by architect, including any moneys laid out by architect for permits, inspections, materials, services, or necessary travel or subsistence.

　　(e)　<u>Bidding, Change Orders, Redesign, and Other Services.</u> For all other services rendered by architect, including services in connection with bidding, rebidding, change orders, redesign, supervision, inspection, warranty, and corrective work, owner will pay architect in accordance with the rates established by Schedule A attached hereto.

　　(f)　<u>Extra Services.</u> If architect provides extra services at the request of owner, architect will bill monthly for such services, which will be compensated by owner on an equitable basis. Examples of extra services are feasibility studies, surveys, appearances before governmental agencies, preparing documents for alternates, providing continuous onsite supervision, interior design, tenant improvements, making revisions requested by owner, providing consultant and testing services, serving as an expert witness, or providing services made necessary by default of the contractor.

13. <u>Errors and Omissions</u>. Architect will use its best efforts to guard against errors or omissions in the performance of its services under this agreement, and will carefully prepare the drawings, contract documents, and instruments of service. Architect will not be responsible for negligence, errors, omissions, mistakes, or breaches of warranty, and the risk of damage from such causes rests with owner. Owner may elect to make architect responsible for negligence, errors, omissions, mistakes, and breaches of warranty that may be committed by architect in exchange for a surcharge of 15 per cent in addition to all of the charges specified in Paragraph 12. The initials of owner and architect at the end of this paragraph indicate owner's election to pay the surcharge and architect's agreement to extend its liability.

☐ ☐
Initials   Initials

14. <u>Disputes.</u> If a dispute should arise between owner and the contractor, architect shall determine the dispute by a written decision. Architect's written decision shall be subject to review by appropriate arbitration or court proceedings. Architect shall give each party an opportunity to produce evidence and argument supporting its side of the dispute.

15. <u>Attorneys' Fees.</u> If architect or owner should become involved in litigation or arbitration proceedings as a result of this agreement, or the construction of the project, the court or arbitration tribunal shall award reasonable attorneys' fees to the party justly entitled thereto.

16. <u>Arbitration</u>. If a dispute should arise between architect and owner relating to this agreement or its performance, it shall be subject to arbitration under the rules of the American Arbitration Association. The contractor and any other party with a direct interest in the dispute may become a party to the arbitration with the permission of the arbitrator. By submitting the dispute to arbitration, the parties do not waive the right to seek provisional remedies from the court, such as restraining orders, attachments, injunctions, and receiverships. The parties authorize the arbitration tribunal to grant equitable, as well as monetary relief. The arbitration tribunal is authorized to award compensation for the time and trouble of arbitration, including arbitration fees, expert witness fees, and attorneys' fees, to the party or parties justly entitled thereto. If a party, after due notice, fails to participate in an arbitration hearing, the tribunal shall decide the dispute in accordance with evidence introduced by the party or parties who do participate.

DATED: _____

OWNER

_____

ARCHITECT

_____

The following contract provisions may be substituted for, or added to, provisions of the preceding form.

FORM 4-2 Alternate and Optional Contract Provisions - Agreement between Owner and Architect - Architectural Services

ALTERNATIVE AND OPTIONAL CONTRACT PROVISIONS

The language of the following paragraphs may be used to replace, or may be used in addition to, provisions of the preceeding form.

Ownership of Drawings
All of the drawings produced by architect under this agreement are supplied for the owner's use in constructing the project only, and are not to be reused for any purpose. Architect shall remain the owner of the drawings, and owner shall not have any ownership interest therein.

Ownership of Drawings
The entire product of the architect's services under this agreement shall become the property of owner. Upon the completion of the project, architect will deliver the tracings for all drawings to owner, and owner shall have the right to use and reuse the tracings as owner sees fit.

As-Built Drawings
During the progress of the project, architect will obtain from the contractor marked prints showing as-built information to show the true location of electrical, mechanical, structural, and architectural features. The architect will revise the tracings to incorporate the as-built information, and will deliver a print of the as-built drawings to the owner.

Reimbursements
Owner will reimburse architect for all expenditures laid out for the project including transportation, long distance telephone, permit fees, reproduction costs, and other similar items. Such items will be reimbursed monthly, plus a 10 per cent handling charge, as billed. Expenditures in excess of $_____ will be paid by owner in advance.

Delay of Project

The fees established by this agreement are based on the assumption that the project will be completed in _____ months. In the event that the completion is delayed, then fees paid for those services rendered after _____, are subject to escalation in accordance with the following formula:

> For services rendered during the year beginning _____, fees will be 110 per cent of those specified in the agreement. Annually, thereafter, the fees specified in the agreement are subject to an additional 10 per cent increase.

Supervision and Progress Reports

Architect will provide continuous jobsite observation, inspection, and supervision, and will use its best efforts to cause the contractor to comply with all the requirements of the contract documents and good trade practice. Architect will provide monthly progress reports to owner as to the progress of the work. Architect will use its best efforts to require contractor to correct any defective work. If the contractor refuses to correct defective work, architect will report such failure, in writing, to owner and contractor.

Meetings and Reports

Architect will convene weekly jobsite meetings to be attended by contractor, subcontractors, and other job site personnel. Architect shall maintain minutes of such meetings, which will be forwarded to owner and contractor. Architect will supply a written job cost progress report to owner each month.

Scheduling

Contractor will prepare a project schedule before the commencement of the work. Architect will monitor the progress of the work for conformance to the schedule. The contractor will revise the schedule at least monthly. Copies of the revisions will be distributed to owner and architect. Architect will use its best efforts to require contractor, subcontractors, and suppliers to comply with the schedule, but will not be responsible for their failure to do so.

Errors and Ommissions Insurance

Throughout the duration of the project, architect shall carry professional liability insurance in a standard form with a company admitted to do insurance business in the State of _____. Such insurance shall be on a project insurance basis, and not on the claims made basis. Owner shall have the right, at any time, to inspect the insurance policy. The insurance shall be written with limits of $_____.

Change Orders

After consultation with owner, architect is authorized to issue written change orders to contractor, and owner will pay for such changes when due.

Architect Independent Contractor
In performing duties under this agreement, the architect shall act as an independent contractor and not as the agent of owner.

> Comment: Courts usually hold that an architect is an independent contractor when he or she prepares contract documents and instruments of service but acts as the agent of the owner in inspecting and supervising job site work. Some cases, however, have found that an architect, supervising job site work, acted as an independent contractor. See §8.03. If evidence shows that the owner exerted actual control of the detailed activities of the architect, the independent contractor language in the contract would not serve to protect the owner from liability.

Impartiality as Between Owner and Contractor
In judging the performance of the work, and in issuing payment certificates, the architect shall favor neither the owner nor the contractor but shall act impartially so that the interests of both the owner and the contractor are protected.

Architect as Arbitrator
If a dispute should arise between the owner and the contractor, the architect shall act as arbitrator of the dispute to the extent that the architect is called upon to do so under the contract documents. In making its decision, the architect shall favor neither the owner nor the contractor but shall decide the dispute impartially in accordance with the evidence presented by the parties.

Payment for Schematic and Preliminary Drawings
For the schematic and preliminary drawings, the architect shall be paid monthly for the time of its personnel working on the project in accordance with the following schedule:

Principal	_____
Associate	_____
Draftsman	_____

The maximum charge for the schematic phase is $_____. The maximum charge for the preliminary phase (excluding schematics) is $_____. Maximum charges exclude reimbursables.

Computation of Charges
For services provided under this agreement, the owner will pay the architect _____ per cent of the hourly rate for the time expended by architect's personnel on the project. The hourly rate consists of salaries or wages plus fringe benefits and contributions including payroll taxes, workers' compensation insurance, liability insurance, pension benefits, and similar contributions and benefits.

AIA Document B141 - Standard Form of Agreement between Owner and Architect

§4.02 General Comments

The American Institute of Architects (AIA) Documents referred to in this text are the property of, and may be purchased from, The American Institute of Architects, 1735 New York Avenue, N.W., Washington, D.C. 20006.

AIA Document B141 is designed to be used in conjunction with the 1987 edition of AIA Document A201, General Conditions of the Contract for Construction. AIA Document B141 explicitly provides that the architect is to provide administration of the contract as set forth in the current edition of AIA Document A201 (Article 2.6.2).

The architect is given the responsibility of keeping the owner advised as to cost estimates during the development of the project. (Articles 2.2.5, 2.3.2, 2.4.3.)

Owner and contractor (perhaps impractically) are required to communicate through the architect. (Article 2.6.8.)

In deciding disputes between owner and contractor, the architect is to endeavor to secure faithful performance on both sides, and is not to show partiality to either. (Articles 2.6.15, 2.6.16.) The architect's decisions on claims and disputes are subject to arbitration. (Article 2.6.19.)

The B141 document imposes some heavy responsibilities on the owner that have often been assumed, at least in part, by the architect. The owner is required to furnish surveys, determine zoning, and locate existing buildings and utilities. (Article 4.5.) The owner must furnish services of a geotechnical engineer when requested by architect, and the services of other consultants reasonably required and requested by the architect. (Articles 4.6, 4.6.1.) The owner must also furnish structural, mechanical, and chemical tests, pollution tests, and tests for hazardous materials. (Article 4.7.)

The arbitration clause prohibits consolidation or joinder of other parties or claims without the written consent of the architect. (Article 7.3.)

The architect has no responsibility to discover hazardous materials. (Article 9.8.)

FORM 4-3 Modifications to Owner/Architect Agreements [Favors Interests of Owner) (with Comments)

¶1. **First: Article 4.5.** The following language is added to Article 4.5:

> The Architect will advise Owner as to all surveys, reports, and information needed for the Project and to be supplied by Owner under this paragraph, and will supervise the acquisition of such information and the preparation of such reports.

> Comment: The average owner needs the architect's help to know what types of surveys, reports, and information are needed for the proper performance of the project work.

¶2. **Second: Article 4.6.**   The following language is added to Article 4.6:

The Architect will assist the Owner in determining what geotechnical services should be obtained, and in the evaluation and interpretation of geotechnical information.

¶3. **Third: Article 4.7.**   The following language is added to Article 4.7:

The Architect will assist the Owner in determining what tests, inspections, and reports are required by law or should be obtained by the Owner because of the particular circumstances of the Project.

Comment: Most owners would not be knowledgeable as to project requirements for hazardous materials and environmental tests and inspections.

¶4. **Fourth: Article 7.3.**   Article 7.3 is replaced as follows:

7.3   If there is an arbitration clause in the Contract between Owner and Contractor, and if claims are made against the Architect by any party to such an arbitration, then arbitration of all claims, disputes, or other matters in question between the parties to this Agreement shall be resolved in accordance with the arbitration provisions of the prime contract, and Architect shall become a party to such arbitration proceedings and shall be bound by the award. In such event, the arbitration provisions of Articles 7.1 and 7.2 will not apply except as to any disputes between the parties to this Agreement that may be totally unrelated to disputes that are subject to arbitration under the arbitration provisions of the prime contract.

Comment: The arbitration provisions of AIA documents have been drafted to help the architect avoid becoming involved as a party to arbitration proceedings between owner and contractor. This is very beneficial to the interests of the architect, who usually has little to gain, but much to lose, from involvement in disputes between owner, contractor, and subcontractors. A party to such a dispute may be tempted to avoid liability by pinning blame on the architect.

It is in the interests of owner, contractor, and subcontractors, however, to be able to resolve all disputes in a single proceeding and to determine, as a part of that proceeding, if the architect is partly responsible for jobsite problems.

Agreements Between Contractor and Architect 5

Introduction to Contractor/Architect Agreements

§5.01 General Comments

AGC Document No. 420 - Agreement between Contractor and Architect

§5.02 General Comments
    FORM 5-1   AGC Document No. 420 - Standard Form of Agreement between Contractor and Architect (1985)

Revisions to AGC Document No. 420 - Agreement between Contractor and Architect

§5.03 General Comments
    FORM 5-2   Revisions to AGC Document No. 420 - Agreement between Contractor and Architect (with Comments)

Introduction to Contractor/Architect Agreements

§5.01 General Comments

The most typical—I had almost said conventional—scenario for a construction dispute finds an owner in a field of fire between a prime contractor and an architect. Such a story unfolds as follows: (1) the job falls behind schedule, (2) the contractor claims that the drawings are inconsistent and need clarification, (3) the architect claims the contractor does not know how to read plans, (4) the owner threatens to assess damages for delay against the contractor, (5) the contractor claims that delay and inefficiency have been caused by poorly coordinated and misleading plans, (6) the contractor and subcontractors begin to demand extra compensation for work beyond the scope of the drawings.

(7) the architect and the owner contend that the alleged extras are within the scope of the work defined by the contract documents. The melancholy story elaborates and escalates from there to a point where, in the construction industry equivalent of nuclear war, the owner ejects the contractor from the job or the contractor abandons the work.

The innocent party in all this may be the owner, who, a true novice in construction matters, came in good faith to the construction industry and followed its established forms and procedures by employing a qualified architect and a reputable contractor. Having done so, should not the owner have been able to safely stand by and enjoy the sights and sounds of its cherished construction project being brought into physical being by the skillful and diligent practitioners of the ancient and honorable businesses, trades, and professions of the construction industry? One would have thought so, but the owner may, to its dismay, discover that it has the legal responsibility to provide the contractor and its subcontractors with proper plans and specifications, and with prompt decisions, clarifications, instructions, and information. Yet, the owner, who is not knowledgeable in the conventions, traditions, and procedures of the construction industry does not have a good way to resolve, or even understand the merits of, such controversies. Such an owner might long to return to bygone centuries when architects performed as true master builders. They not only designed, but built, the great medieval and renaissance monuments, cathedrals, temples, and palaces.

It is for the very reason that the role of master builder places the whole responsibility of construction and design on one party that architects now eschew that role because of the daunting weight of the financial and legal liability that one assuming such a role must carry.

Under the rubric **design-build,** however, the contractor shoulders the weight of that responsibility and potential liability. In AGC Document No. 420 which follows, the architect is employed by the prime contractor who, therefore, becomes legally responsible for job problems whether they are caused by inadequate drawings or otherwise.

AGC Document No. 420 - Agreement between Contractor and Architect

§5.02 General Comments

In the preamble to the agreement, the contractor and architect agree to cooperate in a *relationship of trust.* This relationship of trust has important practical ramifications, if it can be established in reality (as well as on paper). The relationship also has important legal ramifications, if it is not established in reality. Parties dealing in a relationship of trust are entitled to expect candor and full disclosure, each from the other. Each party must fully respect the interests of the other party.

In AGC Document No. 420, the contractor is the leader of the construction team who has the "overall coordination and direction of the Project." (Article

1.1.) The contractor furnishes the program and its budget. (Article 1.1.1.) The architect prepares schematic design documents to fit within that program and budget. (Article 1.1.4.)

The architect prepares construction documents for approval by contractor and owner. (Article 1.1.5.1.) The architect is the interpreter of the requirements of the drawings and specifications. (Article 1.1.6.2.) In a reversal of the usual procedure, the architect only communicates with owner through the contractor. (Article 1.1.6.8.)

It is the contractor who obtains information from the owner regarding the requirements for the project and obtains from the owner soils reports, surveys, and legal description. (Article 2.)

If the architect has a claim against the owner (for example, for delay of the project), the architect makes the claim through the contractor. (Article 3.1.3.) Thus, the architect for such purposes occupies the position of a subcontractor.

Contractor makes progress payments to architect as services are performed. Architect has the right to stop work if the payments are not made when due. (Article 3.2, 3.4.) The Architect is required to furnish evidence of comprehensive general liability insurance and professional liability insurance. (Article 8.)

Architect and contractor indemnify each other against claims arising out of their negligence, errors, or omissions, but the indemnity becomes effective only upon a final determination of legal liability. Indemnity is on a comparative fault basis. In a provision that is perhaps ill-advised (Article 9.4), contractor and architect waive indemnity for losses covered by the contractor's or the architect's insurance. (See **FORM 5-2 ¶10**.)

Disputes are resolved by arbitration. (Article 10.)

FORM 5-1 AGC Document No. 420 - Standard Form of Agreement between Contractor and Architect (1985)

AIA copyrighted material has been reproduced with the permission of the American Institute of Architects under license number 90153. Permission expires December 31, 1991.

This document is intended for use as a "consumable" (consumables are further defined by Senate Report 94-473 on the Copyright Act of 1976). This document is not intended to be used as "model language" (language taken from an existing document and incorporated, without attribution, into a newly-created document). Rather, it is a standard form which is intended to be modified by appending separate amendment sheets and/or fill in provided blank spaces.

THE ASSOCIATED GENERAL CONTRACTORS

STANDARD FORM OF AGREEMENT BETWEEN CONTRACTOR AND ARCHITECT

INSTRUCTIONS TO CONTRACTOR

1. These documents are intended to be used with AGC Document No. 410, Standard Form of Design-Build Agreement and General Conditions Between Owner and Contractor, January, 1982. Nothing contained herein is intended to conflict with local, state or federal laws or regulations. However, in all cases your attorney should be consulted to advise you on their use and any modifications. Care should be taken to assure that all modifications are correlated so the provisions of all documents are consistent.

2. Article 1 covers both the basic service and supplemental services to be performed by the architect. Any of these services which the Contractor does not desire to be performed by the Architect should be eliminated from this Agreement. The Contractor should verify that either he or the Architect includes sufficient funds for the services to be provided to the Owner based on the assumption that the Contractor is providing the Owner with a firm figure, be it lump sum or guaranteed maximum cost, for the Contractor's work and responsibilities.

3. It is recommended that all insurance matters such as the implications of errors and omissions liability, completed operations, and waiver of subrogation be reviewed with your insurance consultant and carrier.

Certain provisions of this document have been derived, with modifications, from the following documents published by The American Institute of Architects: AIA Document B141, Owner-Architect Agreement, ©1977; AIA Document A201, General Conditions, ©1976, by The American Institute of Architects. Usage made of AIA language, with the permission of AIA, does not imply AIA endorsement or approval of this document. Further reproduction of copyrighted AIA materials without separate written permission from AIA is prohibited.

AGC Document No. 420
© 1979 Associated General Contractors of America

CONTRACTOR-ARCHITECT AGREEMENT

January 1985

THE ASSOCIATED GENERAL CONTRACTORS

STANDARD FORM OF AGREEMENT BETWEEN CONTRACTOR AND ARCHITECT

(See AGC Document No. 400 for Preliminary Design-Build Contract; AGC Document No. 410 for Design-Build Agreement and General Conditions)

This Document has important legal consequences; consultation with an attorney is encouraged with respect to its completion or modification.

AGREEMENT
Made as of the _____ day of _____ in the year Nineteen Hundred and _____

BETWEEN

_____ hereinafter referred to as the "Contractor," and _____ hereinafter referred to as the "Architect."

The Contractor has entered into a Contract with _____ hereinafter referred to as the "Owner" for the design and construction of (include description, location and anticipated construction sequencing)

hereinafter referred to as the "Project."

The Contractor and the Architect shall cooperate in carrying out the Project in a relationship of trust and agree as set forth below:

AGC Document No. 420 • CONTRACTOR-ARCHITECT AGREEMENT • January 1985   1

§5.02 AGC DOCUMENT NO. 420   203

THE ASSOCIATED GENERAL CONTRACTORS

STANDARD FORM OF AGREEMENT BETWEEN CONTRACTOR AND ARCHITECT

TABLE OF CONTENTS

ARTICLES	PAGE
1 Architect's Services and Responsibilities	3
2 Contractor's Responsibilities	6
3 Architect's Compensation and Payments	6
4 Changes in the Work	7
5 Contract Time Schedule	7
6 Ownership and Use of Documents	7
7 Termination of Agreement	8
8 Insurance	8
9 Indemnity	9
10 Arbitration	9
11 Extent of Agreement Between Contractor and Architect	10
12 Governing Law	10

Certain provisions of this document have been derived, with modifications, from the following documents published by The American Institute of Architects: AIA Document B141, Owner-Architect Agreement, © 1977; AIA Document A201, General Conditions, © 1976, by The American Institute of Architects. Usage made of AIA language, with the permission of AIA, does not imply AIA endorsement or approval of this document. Further reproduction of copyrighted AIA materials without separate written permission from AIA is prohibited.

204 CONTRACTOR/ARCHITECT AGREEMENTS

ARTICLE 1
ARCHITECT'S SERVICES AND RESPONSIBILITIES

1.1 BASIC SERVICES

The Architect's Basic Services consist of the four phases described in this Paragraph 1.1 and include normal architectural, structural, mechanical and electrical engineering services. These services and those included in Paragraph 1.2 shall be provided in accordance with the Contractor's overall coordination and direction of the Project, including all necessary financial constraints.

Schematic Design Phase

1.1.1 The Architect shall review the program and Project budget furnished by the Contractor to ascertain the requirements of the Project and shall review the understanding of such requirements with the Contractor and the Owner.

1.1.2 The Architect shall review with the Contractor alternative approaches to design and construction of the Project.

1.1.3 Based on the mutually agreed upon program and Project budget requirements, the Architect shall prepare, for approval by the Contractor and the Owner, Schematic Design Documents consisting of drawings and other documents illustrating the scale and relationship of Project components.

Design Development Phase

1.1.4 Based on the approved Schematic Design Documents and any adjustments authorized by the Contractor in the program or Project budget, the Architect shall review with and prepare for approval of the Contractor and the Owner, Design Development Documents consisting of drawings and other documents to fix and describe the size and character of the entire Project as to architectural, structural, mechanical and electrical systems, materials and such other elements as may be appropriate.

Construction Documents Phase

1.1.5.1 Following the Contractor's and the Owner's approval of the Design Development Documents, the Architect shall review with and prepare for approval of the Contractor and the Owner, Construction Documents consisting of Drawings and Specifications for the construction of the Project.

1.1.5.2 The Architect shall assist the Contractor in the preparation of the necessary bidding information, bidding forms, and the General Conditions (AGC Document No. 410) and any other conditions of the contract.

Construction Phase

1.1.6.1 The Architect shall at all times have access to the Work wherever it is in preparation and progress.

1.1.6.2 The Architect shall be the interpreter of the requirements of the Drawings and Specifications. The Architect shall, within a reasonable time, render such interpretations and clarifications as are necessary for the proper execution or progress of the Work.

1.1.6.3 All interpretations of the Architect shall be consistent with the intent of and reasonably inferable from the Drawings and Specifications, and when requested, shall be in written or graphic form.

1.1.6.4 The Architect's decisions in matters relating to artistic effect shall be final if consistent with the intent of the Drawings and Specifications.

1.1.6.5 Whenever the Architect considers it necessary or advisable for the implementation of the intent of the Drawings and Specifications, he shall recommend to the Contractor special inspection or testing of the Work in accordance with the General Conditions whether or not such Work be then fabricated, installed or completed. However, neither the Architect's obligation to recommend action under this Subparagraph nor any decision made by him in good faith, either to make or not to make such recommendation, shall give rise to any duty or responsibility of the Architect to the Owner, any Subcontractor, any Sub-subcontractor, any of their agents or employees, or any other person not a party to this Agreement.

1.1.6.6 The Architect shall review and approve or take other appropriate action upon Contractor's submittals such as Shop Drawings, Product Data and Samples, but only for conformance with the design concept of the Work and with the information given in the Drawings and Specifications. Such action shall be taken with reasonable promptness so as to cause no delay. The Architect's approval of a specific item shall not indicate approval of an assembly of which the item is a component.

1.1.6.7 The Architect with the Contractor shall conduct inspections to determine the dates of Substantial Completion and Final Completion.

1.1.6.8 The Architect shall only communicate with the Owner and the Subcontractors through the Contractor.

1.1.6.9 The Architect shall not have control or charge of and shall not be responsible for construction means, methods, techniques, sequences, or procedures, or for safety precautions or programs in connection with the Work, for the acts or omissions of the Contractor, Subcontractors, or any other person performing any of the Work, or for the failure of any of them to carry out the Work in accordance with the Contract Documents.

1.2 SUPPLEMENTAL SERVICES (Optional: Those which are not applicable should be struck. Those which are accepted should remain.)

1.2.1 The Architect shall investigate existing conditions or facilities, make measured drawings thereof and verify the accuracy of drawings or other information furnished by the Contractor.

1.2.2 The Architect shall prepare a set of reproducible record drawings showing significant changes in the Work made during the construction process, based on marked-up prints, drawings and other data furnished by the Contractor to the Architect.

1.2.3 The Architect shall provide services of the following consultants in addition to those required by Paragraph 1.1 to accomplish Basic Services as follows:

1.2.4 The Architect shall visit the site to perform on site observations and to recommend to the Contractor rejection of Work which does not conform to the Drawings and Specifications, and shall provide the required personnel for such observations, for attendance at job meetings and for other consultation, including all travel expenses as follows:

206 CONTRACTOR/ARCHITECT AGREEMENTS

1.2.5 The Architect shall provide assistance in the utilization of equipment and systems, such as initial start-up or testing, adjusting or balancing, as follows:

1.2.6 The Architect, exercising his professional judgment, shall identify the architectural, structural, mechanical, chemical and other laboratory tests, inspections and reports, to be required, as follows:

1.2.7 The Architect shall pay fees required by governmental authorities having jurisdiction in order to produce the Drawings and Specifications described in the Schematic Design, Design Development, and Construction Document Phases of Basic Services, as follows:

1.2.8 The Architect shall provide the following number of copies of sets of Drawings and Specifications:

Schematic Design Documents: _____ sets
Design Development Documents: _____ sets
Construction Documents: _____ sets
Bulletins: _____ sets

1.2.9 The Architect shall provide interior design and other similar services required for or in connection with the selection, procurement or installation of furniture, furnishings and related equipment, as follows:

1.2.10 The Architect shall provide services for planning tenant or rental spaces, as follows:

1.2.11 The Architect shall provide further supplemental services, as follows: (Include any of the services to be provided by the Architect, such as data processing, photographic production techniques, renderings, models and mock-ups, etc.)

ARTICLE 2

CONTRACTOR'S RESPONSIBILITIES

2.1 The Contractor shall obtain from the Owner full information regarding his requirements for the Project.

2.2 The Contractor shall obtain from the Owner for the site of the Project all necessary surveys describing the physical characteristics, topography, soils reports, and sub-surface investigation, legal limitations, utility locations and a legal description.

2.3 The information required by Paragraph 2.1 and 2.2 shall be furnished with reasonable promptness and the Architect shall be entitled to rely upon the accuracy and the completeness thereof.

2.4 The Contractor shall prepare all budgets, cost estimates and schedules for the Project. The Contractor shall consult with the Architect before establishing the time necessary for the Architect to perform his services and discharge his responsibilities.

2.5 The Contractor shall carefully study and compare the Contract Documents and shall at once report to the Architect any error, inconsistency or omission he may discover.

ARTICLE 3

ARCHITECT'S COMPENSATION AND PAYMENTS

3.1 COMPENSATION

3.1.1 The Contractor shall compensate the Architect for the Basic and Supplemental Services as described in Article 1, including all overhead and expenses including travel expense, on the following basis:

3.1.2 The Contractor shall compensate the Architect for any additional services on the following basis:

3.1.3 If the Contractor makes a claim for an increase in his contract price with the Owner due to delays in the Project and if these delays have resulted in an increase in the Architect's costs, the Architect shall present his delay claim to the Contractor for his approval and for inclusion in the Contractor's claim to the Owner.

PAYMENTS

3.2 The Architect shall submit periodic Applications for Payment, and payment for services shall be made promptly in proportion to services performed. Compensation which is based on a lump sum amount or on a percentage of construction completion, shall not, at the completion of each Phase, exceed the following percentages of the total compensation:

Schematic Design Phase:	_____ %
Design Development Phase:	_____ %
Construction Documents Phase:	_____ %
Construction Phase:	_____ %
Total	_____ %

3.3 The Contractor may decline to approve an Application for Payment if, in his opinion, the Application is not adequately supported. If the Architect and Contractor cannot agree on a revised amount, the Contractor shall make payment for the amount he deems appropriate.

3.4 If the Contractor should fail to pay the Architect at the time the payment of any amount becomes due, then the Architect may, at any time thereafter, upon serving written notice that he will stop work within five (5) days after receipt of the notice by the Contractor, and after such five (5) day period, stop work until payment of the amount owing has been received. Written notice shall be deemed to have been duly served if sent by certified mail to the last business address known to him who gives the notice.

3.5 The acceptance of final payment shall constitute a waiver of all claims by the Architect for compensation for services performed.

ARTICLE 4

CHANGES IN THE WORK

4.1 If the Owner or Contractor requests Changes in the Work in accordance with Contractor's Agreement with the Owner, the Architect shall furnish the Contractor with a firm figure to include in the particular Change Order to cover his compensation with respect to the Change.

4.2 If the Owner does not proceed with a Change in the Work upon receiving its estimated cost, the Architect shall be paid for his services in the absence of a prior contrary Agreement.

ARTICLE 5

CONTRACT TIME SCHEDULE

5.1 The Work to be performed under the Contractor's agreement with the Owner shall be commenced on or about _____ and shall be substantially completed on or about _____

5.2 The Architect shall perform his services and discharge his responsibilities within the time schedule established pursuant to Paragraph 2.4. If he is delayed at any time by any act or neglect of the Contractor or the Owner, or by Change Orders in the Project, or any causes beyond the Architect's control, or a delay authorized by the Contractor pending arbitration, then the time allotted within the schedule for performing his services and discharging his responsibilities shall be extended for the period of such delay.

ARTICLE 6

OWNERSHIP AND USE OF DOCUMENTS

6.1 Drawings and Specifications as instruments of service are and shall remain the property of the Architect whether the Project for which they are prepared is executed or not. The Contractor shall be permitted to retain copies, including reproducible copies, of Drawings and Specifications for information and reference in connection with the Owner's use and occupancy of the Project. The Drawings and Specifications shall not be used on other projects, for additions to this Project, or for completion of this Project by others provided the Architect is not in default under this Agreement, except by agreement in writing and with appropriate compensation to the Architect.

6.2 Submission or distribution to meet official regulatory requirements or for other purposes in connection with the Project is not to be construed as publication in derogation of the Architect's rights.

ARTICLE 7

TERMINATION OF AGREEMENT

7.1 This Agreement may be terminated by either party upon seven (7) days' written notice should the other party fail substantially to perform in accordance with its terms through no fault of the party initiating the termination.

7.2 This Agreement may be terminated by the Contractor upon at least seven (7) days' written notice to the Architect in the event that the Project is permanently abandoned.

7.3 In the event of termination not the fault of the Architect, the Architect shall be compensated for all services performed to the termination date.

ARTICLE 8

INSURANCE

8.1 The Architect shall purchase and maintain such insurance as will protect him from the claims set forth below which may arise out of or result from the Architect's operations under this Agreement whether such operations be by himself or by any of his consultants or by anyone directly or indirectly employed by any of them, or by anyone for whose acts any of them may be liable:

8.1.1 Claims under workers' compensation, disability benefit and other similar employee benefit acts which are applicable to the work to be performed.

8.1.2 Claims for damages because of bodily injury, occupational sickness or disease, or death of his employees and under any applicable employer's liability law with customary limits.

8.1.3 Claims for damages because of bodily injury, or death of any person other than his employees.

8.1.4 Claims for damages insured by usual personal injury liability coverage which are sustained (1) by any person as a result of an offense directly or indirectly related to the employment of such person by the Architect or (2) by any other person.

8.1.5 Claims for damages, other than to the Work itself, because of injury to or destruction of tangible property, including loss of use therefrom.

8.1.6 Claims for damages because of bodily injury or death of any person or property damage arising out of the ownership, maintenance or use of any motor vehicle.

8.2 The Architect's Comprehensive General and Automobile Liability Insurance, as required by Paragraph 8.1 shall be written for not less than limits of liability as follows:

a.	Comprehensive General Liability		
	1. Personal Injury	$_____	Aggregate
	2. Bodily Injury	$_____	Each Occurrence
		$_____	Aggregate
	3. Property Damage	$_____	Each Occurrence
		$_____	Aggregate
b.	Comprehensive Automobile Liability		
	1. Bodily Injury	$_____	Each Person
		$_____	Each Occurrence
	2. Property Damage	$_____	Each Occurrence

8.3 Comprehensive General Liability Insurance may be arranged under a single policy for the full limits required or by a combination of underlying policies with the balance provided by an Excess or Umbrella Liability policy.

8.4 The foregoing policies shall contain a provision that coverages afforded under the policies will not be cancelled or not renewed until at least sixty (60) days' prior written notice has been given to the Contractor. Certificates of Insurance showing such coverages to be in force shall be filed with the Contractor prior to commencement of the Architect's Services.

8.5 The Architect shall furnish the Contractor an appropriate certificate, including any endorsements directly relating to this Project, indentifying the Architect's Professional Liability Insurance Coverage and stipulating amounts of coverage and deductible. Such certificate shall indicate that coverage thereunder will not be cancelled or not renewed until at least thirty (30) days' prior written notice has been given to the Contractor. If the Contractor, on review of the policy stipultations including monetary limits, requires the Architect to modify the current terms or limits, the Architect's compensation will be increased by the premium difference caused by the change and similarly increased on every policy anniversary therafter until completion of the Project or on reversion to the original terms should this occur prior to Final Completion.

8.6 With respect to any equipment or other property used by the Contractor or Architect in connection with the Work, the Contractor and Architect mutually waive their rights of recovery against each other and all Subcontractors and Owners for loss or damage caused or resulting from any peril insured under Equipment or Property policies. With respect to any equipment or property used in connection with the Work by any Subcontractor, the Contractor will require similar waivers to the Architect. If the policies of insurance referred to in this paragraph require an endorsement to provide for continued coverage where there is a waiver of subrogation, the owners of such policies will cause them to be so endorsed.

ARTICLE 9

INDEMNITY

9.1 The Architect shall indemnify the Contractor from all claims and losses arising from negligent acts, errors or omissions of the Architect in the performance of professional services under this agreement, to the extent that the Architect is responsible for such losses on a comparative basis of fault and responsibility between the Architect and the Contractor. The Architect shall have the option to assume the defense of any such claim, without prejudice to any other rights the Architect may have. The failure of the Architect to assume such defense shall not constitute a waiver of any other rights he may have.

9.2 The Contractor shall indemnify the Architect from all claims and losses arising from negligent acts, errors or omissions of the Contractor in the performance of services under this agreement or under the Contractor's agreement with the Owner to the extent that the Contractor is responsible for such losses on a comparative basis of fault and responsibility between the Contractor and the Architect.

9.3 Such indemnification by either party shall become due and owing only upon a final determination of legal liability between the parties under this Article 9.

9.4 The Contractor and Architect waive all rights to indemnification from each other and their agents and employees for claims or losses arising from negligent acts, errors or omissions arising under this agreement for any such claims or losses covered by insurance obtained by the Contractor or Architect, or which covers the project or equipment used on the project. The aforesaid waiver shall not be applicable to subrogation under 9.1 above by the Contractor's Professional Liability Insuror, if any, in the case of design claims, the defense of which was tendered to the Architect within a reasonable time after it arose. It shall also not be applicable to subrogation by the Architect's Professional Liability Insuror, if any, to claims against the Contractor under 9.2 above.

ARTICLE 10

ARBITRATION

10.1 All claims, disputes and other matters in question between the Contractor and the Architect arising out of or relating to either's obligations to the other under this Agreement, shall be decided by arbitration in accordance with the Construction Industry Arbitration Rules of the American Arbitration Association then obtaining except for those specifically excluded in this Article. This agreement to arbitrate is expressly intended to exclude any obligation to arbitrate matters arising under this Project with any person other than the parties to this Agreement and only the Contractor may initiate an arbitration proceeding against the Architect and only the Architect may initiate an arbitration proceeding against the Contractor pursuant to the terms of this Article. This Article is also expressly intended to preclude consolidation of any arbitration proceeding under this Article with any other arbitration proceeding.

10.2 Notice to the demand for arbitration shall be served upon the other party to this Agreement and filed in writing with the American Arbitration Association. The demand for arbitration shall be made within a reasonable time after the claim accrues, or the dispute or other matter in question arises, but in no event shall it be made after the date when institution of legal or equitable proceedings based upon such claim, dispute or other matter in question would be barred by the applicable statute of limitations.

10.3 The award rendered by the arbitrators shall be final and judgment may be entered thereon in accordance with the applicable law in any court having jurisdiction thereof.

10.4 Each party shall proceed with his obligations under this Agreement pending any arbitration proceedings, unless otherwise agreed in writing.

10.5 If a claim is asserted against the Contractor by the Owner, a Subcontractor or other person not a party to this Agreement which is predicated upon alleged errors or omissions in Drawings, Specifications, or other design responsibilities of the Architect, the Contractor shall promptly give notice of such design claim to the Architect and the Architect shall cooperate fully with the Contractor in the defense of such design claim. The Architect shall, if he so elects, have the right to control the defense of such design claim.

10.6 Paragraph 10.5 shall also be applicable in the event a contract claim is made in a court of law or equity and no party to that proceeding seeks to specifically enforce or assert as a defense any existing obligation to arbitrate.

10.7 This Article shall not be applicable to an action for bodily injury or property damage brought by a third party who is under no obligation to arbitrate such claim with either the Contractor or Architect, insofar as either the Contractor or Architect may desire to assert any rights of indemnity or contribution against the other with respect to the subject matter of such action.

ARTICLE 11

EXTENT OF AGREEMENT BETWEEN CONTRACTOR AND ARCHITECT

This Agreement represents the entire agreement between the Contractor and the Architect and supersedes all prior negotiations, representations or agreements.

This Agreement shall not be superseded by any provisions of the documents for construction and may be amended only by written instrument signed by both Contractor and Architect.

ARTICLE 12

GOVERNING LAW

12.1 This Agreement shall be governed by the law in effect at _____

This Agreement entered into as of the day and year first above written.

CONTRACTOR	ARCHITECT
By: _____	By: _____
Title: _____	Title: _____

Revisions to AGC Document No. 420 - Agreement between Contractor and Architect

§5.03 General Comments

Most of the following revisions may be utilized or not, according to the circumstances of a project or according to a party's views as to the adequate protection of its interests.

The author believes that the proposed revisions to Articles 8 and 9 (Insurance and Indemnity) are necessary to avoid losing benefits that might otherwise be secured from the liability insurance policies of the parties.

FORM 5-2   Revisions to AGC Document No. 420 - Agreement between Contractor and Architect (with Comments)

REVISIONS TO AGC DOCUMENT NO. 420 AGREEMENT BETWEEN CONTRACTOR AND ARCHITECT

¶1. **First:** **Article 1.1.6.2.** The following language is added to Article 1.1.6.2:

> In making its interpretations, the Architect shall not favor Contractor, Subcontractor, or Owner, but shall give a fair and reasonable interpretation that takes into account the relative degrees of sophisticated construction industry knowledge possessed by the parties.

Comment: In many cases it is the owner, rather than any other party, that needs to be protected from an unreasonable interpretation of the construction documents. This is because the owner's relative knowledge of construction vocabulary, technique, tradition, and procedure is likely to be much lower than the knowledge of professional members of the construction team. Under the conventional system, the owner employs the architect, and therefore the owner's relative lack of knowledge is offset by the architect's knowledge since the architect, being employed by the owner, naturally is motivated to look to the protection of the owner's interests.

The language suggested above can help protect the owner against a potential unreasonable interpretation.

¶2. **Second:** **Article 1.1.6.8.** Article 1.1.6.8 is annulled.

> Comment: It may be appropriate for the owner to reserve the right to communicate directly with the architect. Direct communication would surely enhance the owner's level of comfort that the architect is sensitive to the owner's concerns and will properly take them into account in developing the owner's program. Increased communication can prevent misunderstandings and disputes.
>
> Direct communication between architect and subcontractors may facilitate the processing of shop drawings and may enable the architect to communicate and discuss subtleties of interpretation.

In another alternative, Article 1.1.6.8 could be revised as follows:

¶3. **Third: Article 1.1.6.8.** The word "Owner" is stricken from Article 1.1.6.8.

> Comment: This revision would allow the architect to communicate directly with the owner, but not subcontractors.

¶4. **Fourth: Article 3.1.3.** Article 3.1.3 is amended by adding the following language:

> This paragraph does not prevent the Architect from claiming compensation from the Contractor in the event that a delay in the Project caused by the Contractor causes damages to the Architect.

¶5. **Fifth: Article 3.5.** The following language is added to Article 3.5:

> Acceptance of final payment does not waive claims previously presented by the Architect to the Contractor in writing.

¶6. **Sixth: Article 8.1.4.** Article 8.1.4 is annulled.

> Comment: *Personal injury* coverage is usually provided as a part of an umbrella policy, and, in the vocabulary of the insurance industry, refers not to *bodily injury* but to libel, slander, advertising liability, unlawful eviction, and other such wrongs. It would therefore be logical to annul Article 8.1.4.

¶7. **Seventh: Article 8.1.5.** The words "other than to the Work itself" are stricken from Article 8.1.5.

> Comment: A broad form of comprehensive general liability insurance usually covers damage to a construction project, or at least damage to those portions of a construction project that were not

built by the insured. Therefore, the contract should be written in such a way as to encourage the architect to purchase the broad form of liability insurance, since coverage would then be available to resolve claims made against the architect because of construction defects.

Most persons, when they think of claims for property damage, tend to think about the type of damage resulting from automobile accidents, overspray of paint, runaway bulldozers, and the like. However, many courts define *property damage* to include the diminution in value of property that results from the presence in the property of defective construction. Thus all sorts of construction defects, under this interpretation, must be paid for by the insurance carrier that provides comprehensive liability insurance to the contractor, subcontractor, supplier, architect, or engineer.

It should be noted, though, that most insurance carriers, when they write comprehensive general liability policies for architects and engineers, exclude from their coverage property damage arising from the performance of professional services. These exclusionary endorsements, though, are sometimes omitted (whether by design or by error), and are sometimes written in restrictive language. For example, one common endorsement excludes coverage for liability caused by the preparation of plans, specifications, or contract documents. Such an endorsement would not exclude coverage for claims against an architect or engineer for faulty inspection.

¶8. **Eighth:** **Article 8.5.** Article 8.5 is revised to read as follows:

8.5 Before commencing work, Architect will supply Contractor with a certificate of insurance showing that Architect carries errors and omissions insurance with limits of not less than $5,000,000 and a deductible of not more than $25,000. The certificate shall be signed by the insurance carrier, and shall provide that the coverage will not be canceled, reduced, or allowed to lapse without 60 days written notice first given to Contractor. If such insurance is on a claims made form, then Architect covenants that it will maintain such insurance in effect for a period of at least six years following the completion of the Project.

Comment: Almost all errors and omissions insurance is now written on a *claims made* basis, which means that the insurance applies only to claims that are first made during the policy period, rather than applying to cover damages that *occurred* during the policy period. Therefore, the contractor needs assurance not only that the architect will maintain insurance during the construction of the project, but for a reasonable period of time after the project is finished.

Most architectural malpractice claims, needless to say, are made for the first time after the completion of the project, rather than during the progress of the work.

Obviously, to provide that the architect must maintain insurance for six years after the close of the project does not address the question of how the contractor should *enforce* that contractual provision. This must be left to the diligence of the contractor and the ingenuity of the contract drafter.

¶9. **Ninth: Article 8.6.** Article 8.6 is revised to read as follows:

8.6 With respect to any construction equipment used by Contractor or Architect in connection with the Work, Contractor and Architect mutually waive their rights against each other to recover damages for injury to, destruction of, or loss of use of such construction equipment caused by accidental physical injury to the equipment, to the extent that such damages are covered by valid and collectable insurance.

Comment: The printed form of Article 8.6 should be deleted because it includes a waiver of claims for damages to *other property* in addition to construction equipment. The contractor should not waive its prospective claims against the architect for damage to property, since a construction defect may be construed as *damage to property*, and the contractor would, therefore, waive its right to make malpractice claims against the architect for construction defects.

¶10. **Tenth: Article 9** - Indemnity.

The provisions of Article 9 appear to this author to be inconsistent in result, and uncertain in their application. The entire Article should either be annulled or redrafted.

The thrust of Articles 9.1 through 9.3 is simply to describe the application of the doctrine of comparative fault and implied equitable indemnity as they already exist in most states, with the modification that the Architect is given the option to assume the defense of claims made against the Contractor because of the Architect's misconduct.

As the party in the superior bargaining position, the Contractor would be better served by an indemnity clause such as the following:

Articles 9.1, 9.2, 9.3, 9.4. Articles 9.1, 9.2, 9.3 and 9.4 are annulled and replaced as follows:

9.1 To the fullest extent permitted by law, Architect will defend and hold the Contractor harmless from and against claims, demands, liability and

loss arising out of the negligence or other misconduct or breach of contract by Architect. This indemnity shall be provided by the Architect even though the Contractor is partly at fault for the claim, demand, liability, or loss, but the Architect will not provide indemnity against claims, demands, liabilities, or losses resulting from the sole negligence of Contractor.

Comment: Article 9.4 should not be used because it could result in a loss of insurance coverage for which premiums would have been paid by contractor and architect.

The type of language utilized in Article 9.4 is sometimes appropriate when applied to property insurance, but would never be appropriately applied to liability insurance.

To have the contractor waive claims against the architect arising out of errors and omissions of the architect that are covered by insurance would be to defeat the very purpose of the insurance.

The architect might well desire to extract from the contractor a waiver of claims against the architect for damage to property caused by the fault of the architect to the extent that the property damage is covered by *property* insurance (rather than by *liability* insurance). Language appropriate to such a purpose follows.

9.4 To the extent that any damage to, injury to, or loss of use of, the Work, is covered by valid and collectible property insurance supplied by Contractor or Owner, Contractor waives all claims for damage or injury to or loss of use of the Work or any part thereof caused by the negligence, breach of contract, or other misconduct of Architect. Contractor will use its best efforts to obtain from the property insurer an endorsement approving this waiver of subrogation.

Comment: The salutary purpose of waivers of indemnity and subrogation is to require losses that are covered by insurance to be paid by the insurance carrier without subrogating against one of the parties to the contract and thereby, as would often be the case, transferring the loss to the liability insurance carrier of that party.

¶11. **Eleventh:** **Article 10.** Arbitration.

Comment: The presence of an arbitration clause in a construction contract confronts the parties with the question of whether it is better to arbitrate or litigate a dispute that might arise under that contract.

Architects, through the AIA Documents, appear to sincerely favor arbitration as a method of resolving construction disputes as long as they do not get dragged into an arbitration between contractor and owner. This is because involvement in a dispute between owner and contractor puts an architect in a position where it usually has nothing to win (the exception being the possibility of recovering unpaid fees) and much to lose. This enables the architect to participate in arbitration as a witness, rather than as a party. Functioning as a witness, the architect may attempt to protect the owner's interests.

It is only if the contractor recovers an award against the owner that the architect may have to face a separate lawsuit or arbitration with the owner to recover indemnity from the architect for losses caused by malpractice of the architect.

Since the AGC form of agreement is one that will be likely be proposed by the contractor for signature by the architect, the contractor will likely elect to retain the arbitration clause, perhaps with a modification to make it clear that all parties with an interest in the project may be joined in the same arbitration proceeding.

Contractors are usually motivated to utilize arbitration on the basic assumption that they are more likely to be claimant than respondent, and thus surely benefit from the undoubted speed and perhaps benefit from the supposed efficiency of arbitration, as opposed to litigation, as the method selected for dispute resolution.

Subcontract 6

Introduction to Subcontract Forms
§6.01 General Comments
§6.02 Forms Drafted by the Author

Subcontract - Long Form [Favors Interests of Prime Contractor]
§6.03 General Comments
    FORM 6-1   Subcontract - Long Form [Favors Interests of Prime Contractor]

Subcontract - Short Form
§6.04 General Comments
    FORM 6-2   Subcontract - Short Form

Proposal and Subcontract
§6.05 General Comments
    FORM 6-3   Proposal and Subcontract

Alternate Subcontract Provisions
§6.06 General Comments
    FORM 6-4   Alternate Subcontract Provisions

AGC Document No. 600 - Subcontract
§6.07 General Comments
    FORM 6-5   AGC Document No. 600 - Subcontract for Building Construction (1984)
§6.08 Comment: Article 3.2 Schedule
§6.09 Comment: Article 5.2.2 Retainage/Security
§6.10 Comment: Article 5.3 Claims Relating to Contractor
§6.11 Comment: Article 5.3.4 Final Payment Delay
§6.12 Comment: Article 12.1 Indemnification

§6.13 Comment: Article 13.5 Waiver of Rights

AGC Document No. 603 - Subcontract (Short Form)

§6.14 General Comments

FORM 6-7   AGC Document No. 603 - Subcontract (Short Form) (1987)

AGC Standard Form 605 - Standard Subbid Proposal

§6.15 General Comments

FORM 6-8   AGC Standard Form 605 - Standard Subbid Proposal

Introduction to Subcontract Forms

§6.01 General Comments

This chapter presents three forms of subcontract drafted by the author, along with an array of special subcontract clauses that may be added to the three basic forms. Also presented are a selection of AGC subcontract and bidding forms.

It appears to be an axiom of the free enterprise system that the party offering to supply goods or services occupies a bargaining position inferior to that of the party who is in a position to pay money for those goods and services. Therefore, in the hierarchy of the construction industry, the owner usually has the leverage to impose favorable contract terms on the prime contractor, and the prime contractor likewise on the subcontractor. The subcontractor, however, cannot always impose favorable purchase order terms on a Fortune 500 equipment or material supplier.

As the ultimate supplier of money, needless to say, banks and savings and loan associations can impose harsh terms on their borrowers, and such terms are frequently encountered in construction loan agreements, trust deeds, mortgages, and continuing guarantees.

Most prime contractors will have **drafted,** or **pulled together,** subcontract documents that are fitted to ameliorate or avoid problems that are a part of the corporate history of that prime contractor. Sometimes it seems that every dispute that has ever been encountered by the management personnel of the contractor is reflected in the subcontract document.

Subcontractors often rightly deem such one-sided forms of contract to be unfair and inequitable, and yet they sign the forms to sell the job.

On the other hand, when market conditions change, if the subcontractor has a very good price or has the effective control of desirable facilities or equipment, the subcontractor may be able to bargain for favorable subcontract terms.

Experienced and sophisticated subcontractors generally bargain subcontract terms, often with success. The terms most frequently bargained about are: terms of payment; retention; indemnity; insurance; and scope of the work.

§6.02 Forms Drafted by the Author

The three subcontract forms drafted by the author are of diminishing length, and, therefore, of diminishing bias. Contractors and subcontractors are often advised not to do work on a handshake. This may not be very good advice. A contractor or a subcontractor would often be better off to work on a handshake than to accept the combination of contract terms offered by the other party.

The primary interest that a contractor or subcontractor has is to be paid for its work. It is usually only one paragraph in a construction contract that provides payment. Most of the other paragraphs, in one way or another, can be used to avoid payment. A **handshake deal,** although it leaves some areas of uncertainty, makes at least one thing clear: the contractor will be paid for its work.

The three subcontract forms are drafted so that they may be modified by adding paragraphs that the user may select from an array of alternate provisions presented in **FORM 6-4.**

Subcontract - Long Form [Favors Interests of Prime Contractor]

§6.03 General Comments

The following form is typical of those encountered in the industry, because it favors the interests of the prime contractor and goes to some lengths to do so. The contractor is given the right to withhold payments from the subcontractor to satisfy claims of contractor arising out of other projects (¶9). Subcontractor may not claim damages for delay (¶11). Subcontractor takes responsibility for compliance with codes and regulations (¶15). Subcontractor must supply a payment and performance bond if demanded by contractor during the progress of the work—contractor pays the premium (¶17). Subcontractor must indemnify contractor even if contractor is negligent, but not against claims caused by the sole negligence of contractor (¶18). Subcontractor must perform change orders and settle the price later if agreement cannot be reached as to the price (¶20). Subcontractor may not stop the work because of disputes (¶23).

FORM 6-1 Subcontract - Long Form [Favors Interests of Prime Contractor]

SUBCONTRACT - LONG FORM
[FAVORS INTERESTS OF PRIME CONTRACTOR]

¶1. This Subcontract is between _____ ("Contractor") and _____ ("Subcontractor"). The project consists of _____. The project is located at _____.

¶2. Scope of the Work: Subcontractor will furnish all labor, equipment, tools, materials, scaffolding, permits, sales and other taxes, hoisting, transportation, supervision, coordination, communication, samples, shop drawings, and storage, to complete in a first-class and workmanlike manner the following work:

_____
_____
_____
_____
_____
_____
_____

¶3. Examination of the Work: Subcontractor has examined the contract documents and the applicable ordinances, rules, regulations, and building codes, and has examined the site of the work and satisfied itself as to all conditions to be encountered in the performance of the work.

¶4. Utilities: Before commencing work, Subcontractor will satisfy itself as to the location of all utilities that may affect or interfere with Subcontractor's work. Subcontractor will fully protect all utilities, and keep them operating at all times.

¶5. Contract Documents: Subcontractor will perform its work in accordance with the contract documents, which are identified as follows:

_____

¶6. Contract Documents Complementary: The contract documents are complementary. Anything required by any portion of the contract documents shall be performed as if it were displayed in all portions of the contract documents. The contract documents will be construed together so as to give effect to every part, but in case of conflict or ambiguity, Subcontractor will bring the conflict or ambiguity to the attention of Contractor as soon as it is discovered, and the decision of Contractor as to the interpretation of the contract documents shall be final.

¶7. Payment: For all services performed by Subcontractor under this Subcontract, Contractor will pay Subcontractor the Subcontract price of $_____. Payments will be made in accordance with the following payment schedule:

_____
_____
_____

¶8. Releases: Applications for payment must be accompanied by labor and material releases properly executed by all laborers, sub-subcontractors, suppliers, and others who might claim mechanic's lien rights on the project. The releases will be in form satisfactory to Contractor and its counsel. Failure to supply proper releases will result in delay of payment.

¶9. Backcharges and Withholds: Contractor may withhold payments from Subcontractor in amounts that are sufficient to protect Contractor against any improper work or damage to the work, and also to protect itself against any claims Contractor may have against Subcontractor arising out of other projects.

¶10. Commencement and Progress: Subcontractor will commence work within three days after telephone or written notice from Contractor to do so, and shall prosecute the work diligently and in accordance with Contractor's progress schedule.

¶11. Extensions of Time: If Subcontractor is delayed in the performance of the work by conditions that could not be foreseen by Subcontractor and that are beyond the reasonable control of Subcontractor, then Contractor will grant Subcontractor a reasonable extension of time, provided that Subcontractor applies in writing for such an extension of time within ten days after the commencement of the delay. Subcontractor will be entitled to no damages or other monetary compensation for delay, even if such delay is caused, or partly caused, by Contractor.

¶12. Time is of the Essence: In the performance of Subcontractor's obligations under this Agreement, time is of the essence. Contractor may, from time to time, issue and change milestones and other scheduling requirements. Subcontractor will comply with Contractor's requirements as to timely performance, and, if necessary, will employ additional crews and work overtime without additional compensation. Subcontractor recognizes that Contractor will incur severe economic loss if the project is not timely completed, and that Subcontractor will be responsible to compensate Contractor for such loss if Subcontractor does not comply with the schedule.

¶13. Quality of Work: Workmanship, equipment, and materials shall be as specified and shall be to the satisfaction of Contractor.

¶14. Contractor's License: Subcontractor represents that it is and will remain properly licensed, and that its subcontractors (if any) are and will remain properly licensed, to perform all work required under this Subcontract.

¶15. Codes and Regulations: Subcontractor represents that it is fully familiar with all ordinances, codes, rules, and regulations that apply to the work, and that Subcontractor will comply with them in performing the work. If there is a conflict between the contract documents and any applicable ordinance, code, rule, or regulation, the Subcontractor will comply with the ordinance, code, rule, or regulation at no increase in price. Subcontractor acknowledges that Contractor relies on Subcontractor's special expert knowledge of the ordinances, codes, rules, and regulations that apply to its trade.

¶16. Permits: Subcontractor will obtain and pay for all special permits that are required for Subcontractor's work.

¶17. Payment and Performance Bond: Upon the request of Contractor, Subcontractor will provide a payment and performance bond issued by a surety admitted to write surety business in the state. Contractor may request the bond at any time during the progress of the work. If it is requested after the contract has been signed by both parties, Contractor will pay the standard premium. Any excess premium will be paid by Subcontractor.

¶18. Indemnity: In the event that Contractor shall have a claim made against it, or become involved in litigation or arbitration, because of claims, damages, injury, or loss arising out of or related to the activities of or the work performed by Subcontractor or its subcontractors, the Subcontractor shall indemnify Contractor against and hold it harmless from all such claims, loss, liability, and expense, including attorney's fees and the executive and administrative expenses of Contractor incurred as a result. This indemnity shall be provided by Subcontractor even if Contractor is partly responsible for the claim, damage, injury, or loss, but Subcontractor shall not provide indemnity for claims or losses caused by the sole negligence or wilful misconduct of Contractor or its employees. This indemnity agreement shall be covered by Subcontractor's comprehensive general liability insurance policies.

¶19. Liability and Workers' Compensation Insurance: Before commencing work on the project, Subcontractor and its subcontractors of every tier will supply to Contractor duly issued certificates of insurance, which name Contractor and Owner as additional insureds, showing in force the following insurance for comprehensive general liability, automobile liability, and workers' compensation:

> (a) Comprehensive general liability policies that are in comprehensive form with a deductible not to exceed $1,000 per occurrence including a broad form comprehensive liability endorsement that includes coverage for liability assumed under any oral or written contract relating to the conduct of Subcontractor's business, including this contract, and also including (1) broad form property damage liability coverage, (2) premises-operations coverage, (3) explosion and collapse hazard coverage, (4) underground hazard coverage, (5) products and completed operations hazard coverage, and (6) independent contractor coverage. The limit of liability shall be not less than $1,000,000 for each occurrence and in the aggregate for bodily injury, and not less than $1,000,000 for each occurrence and in the aggregate for property damage.

(b) Automobile liability policy in comprehensive form affording coverage for owned, hired, and non-owned automobiles. The limits shall be not less than $1,000,000 for bodily injury and property damage combined, $1,000,000 for each occurrence and in the aggregate.

(c) Workers' compensation insurance shall comply with the statutory form.

The liability insurance policies, including comprehensive general liability, automobile liability, and excess liability, shall be endorsed to provide: (1) that Contractor and Owner are additional insureds, (2) that the insurance afforded by the policies shall apply to Contractor as though a separate policy had been issued to Contractor, and (3) that the coverage afforded to Contractor is primary and any other insurance in force for Contractor will be excess and will not contribute to the primary policies.

No work shall be performed by Subcontractor until certificates of insurance have been delivered to Contractor that comply with the requirements of this paragraph. The certificates shall provide that the insurers will give 30 days written notice to Contractor before cancellation of modification of any policy. Upon the modification, expiration, or cancellation of any policy, Subcontractor shall supply to Contractor a new certificate of insurance that complies with the requirements of this paragraph. Subcontractor shall indemnify Contractor and its insurance carriers for any failure to provide Contractor with the insurance required by this paragraph.

¶20. <u>Changes:</u>   Contractor may add to or subtract from the scope of Subcontractor's work by written change order, and the Subcontractor will promptly perform the work as modified. If the Subcontractor contends that a change order results in a net increase in the Subcontractor's cost of performing the work, Subcontractor will promptly, within ten days after the issuance of the change order, provide Contractor with a detailed estimate of the additional cost. The parties will then negotiate an equitable adjustment to the subcontract price. If agreement is not reached as to the amount by which the subcontract price should be adjusted, Subcontractor will comply with the change order, and the amount of the adjustment will be determined later. Change orders must be issued only in writing. The only person with authority to issue change orders is _____ (9) _____. The authorized person may be changed by written notice.

¶21. <u>Substitutions:</u>   If Subcontractor requests or recommends any revisions or substitutions, Subcontractor represents that such revisions or substitutions are equal to the items specified in appearance, capacity, quality, efficiency, and durability, and that the use of such revisions or substitutions will not interfere with the work of Contractor or any other subcontractor.

¶22. <u>Disputes as to Scope of the Work:</u>   If Contractor and Subcontractor should dispute whether any work is within the original scope of Subcontractor's work, Subcontractor will promptly follow the written orders of Contractor as to the performance of the work, and the dispute will be settled later.

¶23. Noninterruption of the Work: Subcontractor will not interrupt or delay its work, because of any dispute with Contractor, but will continue to perform its subcontract work diligently to completion, and will later negotiate in good faith for settlement of the dispute.

¶24. Protection of the Work: Subcontractor will protect the jobsite, the work of Contractor and other subcontractors, and its own work until completion and acceptance of the entire project. Subcontractor will obtain property insurance covering Subcontractor's interest in the work. If Subcontractor's work is damaged or destroyed before it is finally completed and accepted by Contractor, Subcontractor will look to its insurance carrier for compensation, and will promptly commence and diligently proceed to reaccomplish the work at no expense to Contractor.

¶25. Default: In the event of a default by Subcontractor, Contractor may eject Subcontractor from the job by giving 24 hours written notice, and Subcontractor will remove its personnel from the project, leaving all tools, equipment, and material on the jobsite to be used by Contractor to complete Subcontractor's work. Subcontractor will promptly pay to Contractor all damages suffered as a result of the default, including any amount of money to compensate Contractor for executive and administrative expenses caused by the default.

¶26. Cleanup: Subcontractor will continuously clean the jobsite of its debris and excess materials and at the end of each day will leave its working areas in broom-clean condition. If Subcontractor fails to do so, Contractor may perform the cleanup and deduct the cost thereof from Subcontractor's payments.

¶27. Guarantee: Subcontractor guarantees that all work, equipment, and materials supplied by Subcontractor will be as specified and supplied in accordance with the requirements of the contract documents. Promptly upon notification by Contractor, Subcontractor will, for a period of one year after occupancy, at its own expense, service, correct, and repair any defective work, equipment, or materials. If corrective or repair work is required because of a breach of contract by Subcontractor, Subcontractor will perform such work promptly upon notice despite the lapse of more than one year after occupancy.

¶28. Signatures: No contractual obligations are imposed on Contractor by this document until Subcontractor has been supplied with a copy signed by Contractor.

¶29. Proposal Irrevocable: This document, when signed by Subcontractor, becomes a proposal which is irrevocable for 30 days after delivery to Contractor.

226 SUBCONTRACTS

¶30. <u>Assignment and Subcontracting:</u> Subcontractor will not assign the work under this Subcontract, or subcontract any portion of it, without the written consent of Contractor. Subcontractor will not make any assignment of payments to be earned by Subcontractor under this Subcontract.

¶31. <u>No Other Agreement:</u> This subcontract document represents the entire agreement of the parties, and it shall not be modified by any proposal, bid, estimate, conversation, submittal, or other form of communication between Subcontractor and Contractor before the date when this Subcontract is fully executed. This Subcontract cannot be modified by oral agreements, and may be modified only by a writing signed by Contractor.

DATED: _____

By _____   By _____
   (Signature)   (Signature)

Contractor's License No: Contractor's License No:
_____   _____

Subcontract - Short Form

§6.04 General Comments

Subcontractors rightly assume that the longer the subcontract form, the more biased it is likely to be against the interests of the subcontractor.

The following form, although shorter than the preceding form, is still geared to protect the vital interests of the prime contractor, but it does so without imposing undue burdens on the subcontractor.

FORM 6-2 Subcontract - Short Form

**SUBCONTRACT
SHORT FORM**

¶1. This Subcontract is between _____ ("Contractor") and _____ ("Subcontractor"). The project consists of _____. The project is located at _____. The Owner is _____.

¶2. Scope of the Work: Subcontractor will furnish all labor, equipment, tools, materials, transportation, and supervision to complete in a workmanlike manner the following work:

_____
_____
_____
_____
_____

¶3. Contract Documents: Subcontractor will perform its work in accordance with the contract documents, which are identified as follows: _____

¶4. Subcontract Price: Contractor will pay Subcontractor the subcontract price of $_____. Contractor will make monthly progress payments to Subcontractor on or before the 10th day of each month. The amount of each payment will be computed based on the value of work completed during the calendar month and the value of materials and equipment not incorporated in the work but suitably stored at the jobsite. Subcontractor will submit applications for payment on the last day of each month showing the percentage of completion of the various portions of the work, and the value of the work performed and equipment and materials delivered to the jobsite. Payments are subject to a retention of 10 per cent, to be paid 35 days after the completion of the project.

¶5. Releases: With every request for payment, Subcontractor will submit to Contractor mechanic's lien releases sufficient to release all claims for work or materials furnished to Subcontractor through the date of the previous request for payment.

¶6. Responsibility of Subcontractor: The Subcontractor will be bound to the Contractor by the terms of the contract documents and this Subcontract. Subcontractor assumes toward the Contractor all the obligations and responsibilities that the Contractor assumes toward the Owner, so far as such obligations and responsibilities are applicable to this Subcontract.

¶7. Permits: Subcontractor will provide and pay for permits that are required for Subcontractor's performance of the work.

¶8. Scheduling and Progress of the Work: Subcontractor and Contractor will cooperate, under the control and supervision of Contractor, to schedule the work for diligent, efficient, and prompt performance. Each will supply information as to the times when various phases of the work will be accomplished, and the length of time required for each operation. The schedule will be periodically revised and updated to adjust to field conditions. If Subcontractor is unable to adhere to Contractor's schedule because of events that could not reasonably be foreseen and that are beyond Subcontractor's reasonable control, the time for Subcontractor's performance of the work will be equitably adjusted.

¶9. Indemnity: In the event that a claim is made against Owner or Contractor, of if either should become involved in litigation or arbitration because of claims, loss, liability, or expense arising out of the activities of Subcontractor, Subcontractor shall indemnify Owner and Contractor and hold them harmless from such claims, loss, liability, and expense, including attorney's fees.

¶10. Insurance: Before commencing work on the project, Subcontractor and its subcontractors of every tier will supply to Contractor duly issued certificates of insurance, naming Contractor and Owner as additional insureds, showing in force the following insurance for general liability, automobile liability, and workers' compensation:

(a) Comprehensive general liability with limits of not less than $500,000.

(b) Automobile liability in comprehensive form with coverage for owned, hired, and non-owned automobiles, with limits of not less than $500,000.

(c) Workers' compensation insurance in statutory form.

¶11. Safety: Subcontractor will comply with all statutes and regulations that establish safety requirements, and will cooperate with Contractor in the establishment and enforcement of safe working procedures.

¶12. Changes: Contractor may increase or reduce the scope of the work to be performed by Subcontractor by issuing written change orders, and the subcontract price will be equitably increased or decreased. Upon the issuance of a change order, the Subcontractor will promptly quote to Contractor the amount to be added to or subtracted from the subcontract price because of the change. The quote will be supported by a detailed written estimate. Subcontractor will not proceed with the revised scope of the work until Contractor and Subcontractor have executed a written change order that contains the agreed revision to the subcontract price.

¶13. Cleanup: Subcontractor will continuously clean up its work areas, and keep them in a safe and sanitary condition.

¶14. Guarantee: Subcontractor guarantees that all equipment and material supplied by Subcontractor will be of merchantable quality, and that all work performed by Subcontractor will be performed in a workmanlike manner. Subcontractor will, at its own expense, at the request of Contractor or Owner, promptly replace or repair any work, equipment, or materials that fail to function properly for a period of one year after completion of Subcontractor's work.

¶15. Acceptance of Subcontract: This Subcontract, when signed by Subcontractor, constitutes a proposal that will be held open for ten days. Contractor may accept the proposal by signing and returning a copy within ten days.

¶**16.** No Other Agreement: This subcontract document represents the entire agreement of the parties, and it shall not be modified by any proposal, bid, estimate, conversation, submittal, or other form of communication between Subcontractor and Contractor before the date when this Subcontract is fully executed. This Subcontract cannot be modified by oral agreements, and may be modified only by a writing signed by both parties.

DATED: _____

By _____   By _____
                                                            (Signature)   (Signature)

Contractor's License No: Contractor's License No:

Proposal and Subcontract

§6.05 General Comments

A form of **Proposal and Contract** has become popular in many states, as a proposal usually tendered directly to the owner for small jobs. The proposal becomes a contract when signed. Since it is a document usually tendered by a contractor to an unsophisticated owner on a small job without an architect, it usually has terms that are favorable to the contractor.

The following is a form of **Proposal and Subcontract** that has some of those same characteristics.

The subcontractor is given the right to stop work if progress payments are not made promptly (¶8). Subcontractor is entitled to be paid for extra work whether reduced to writing or not (¶12). The form also contains an arbitration clause (¶7).

The user may have noticed that the long form and short form subcontracts do not contain arbitration clauses. From the standpoint of a general contractor, the disadvantages of an arbitration clause in a subcontract form may outweigh the advantages. This is because of the general contractor's special vulnerability to inconsistent awards. The general contractor should have an arbitration clause in its subcontract form only if there is also an arbitration clause in the prime contract form, and the two arbitration clauses are coordinated so that, in the event of a dispute arising out of a subcontractor's work, the owner, the general contractor, the subcontractor, and possibly the architect/engineer may all be required to participate in the arbitration proceedings, and be bound by the award.

In the absence of such coordination, the general contractor runs the risk of losing the arbitration with the subcontractor and also losing the arbitration with the owner. Thus, the prime contractor might be required to pay damages to the owner for subcontractor's work, but fail to recover indemnity from the subcontractor.

If the arbitration clauses, though, are properly coordinated, then if the contractor wins the dispute with the owner it does not have to win as against the subcontractor. On the other hand, if the contractor loses the dispute against the owner, it will probably recover indemnity from the subcontractor.

Arbitration clauses that are appropriate to require all parties to participate may be found at **FORM 6-4 ¶¶2, 3, & 4.**

FORM 6-3 Proposal and Subcontract

PROPOSAL AND SUBCONTRACT

¶1. This Proposal is made by _____ ("Subcontractor") to _____ ("Contractor"). We propose to furnish the work and services designated below for the project designated as _____.

¶2. <u>Scope of the Work:</u> Subcontractor will furnish the following work: ___
_____
_____
_____
_____
_____
_____
_____
_____
_____
_____

¶3. <u>Price:</u> The price for the scope of work designated above is $_____.

¶4. <u>Acceptance of Proposal:</u> This Proposal may be accepted by promptly signing and returning it to Subcontractor. The price quoted is for immediate acceptance, and may be revised if not promptly accepted.

¶5. <u>Payment:</u> Contractor will make progress payments to Subcontractor on or before the 10th day of each month for the value of work completed plus the amount of materials and equipment suitably stored at the jobsite during the previous month. Final payment shall be due 30 days after completion of Subcontractor's work.

¶6. Interest: Any amounts that are not paid when due shall bear interest at the rate of 1½ per cent per month until paid, or the maximum rate permitted by law, whichever is less.

¶7. Arbitration: Any dispute arising out of or related to this Subcontract or the performance of the work shall be resolved by arbitration in accordance with the Construction Industry Rules of the American Arbitration Association, and judgment shall be entered on the award. If a party after due notice fails to appear at and participate in arbitration proceedings, the arbitrator will make an award based on evidence produced by the party who does appear and participate. The arbitrator shall award reasonable attorney's fees to the prevailing party. Either party may apply to court for attachments, injunctive relief, or other remedies or relief that may not be available in arbitration, without waiving the right to arbitrate disputes under this paragraph. This arbitration agreement is binding on the partners, parent companies, and successors to each party, whether by merger, consolidation, acquisition, or otherwise.

¶8. Right to Stop Work: If Contractor fails to make payments when they are due to Subcontractor, Subcontractor may stop work, and remain idle until payments are made current.

¶9. Delay: The parties will cooperate to facilitate the prompt and efficient performance of the work, and neither party will obstruct, interfere with, or delay the work of the other. Both parties will be excused for delay caused by inclement weather, fire, flood, war, shortage of materials, and other causes not reasonably foreseeable and that are beyond reasonable control by the party. If either party, without excuse, interferes with or delays work by the other party, the other party shall be entitled to reasonable compensation for such interference or delay.

¶10. Warranty: All workmanship and materials are guaranteed for a period of one year after completion of the project.

¶11. Facilities: Contractor shall furnish temporary power, suitable storage areas, and sanitary facilities. Subcontractor may utilize Contractor's scaffolding, manlifts, and hoisting facilities.

¶12. Extra Work: Subcontractor will be paid reasonable compensation for any extra work ordered by Contractor. Extra work should be performed only by written change order, and after agreement in writing as to the amount of extra compensation to be paid. If the parties fail to reduce extra work orders to writing, Subcontractor will be paid the reasonable value of the extra work according to commercially reasonable rates as adjusted for difficult or unusual working conditions.

¶13. Materials and Workmanship: All materials supplied by Subcontractor will be of standard trade quality, and workmanship shall be first-class. Subcontractor will keep its work areas clean, and leave the jobsite in a broom-clean condition.

DATED: _____

By _____
   (Signature)

By _____
   (Signature)

Contractor's License No:
_____

Contractor's License No:
_____

Alternate Subcontract Provisions

§6.06 General Comments

These provisions are drafted in such a way that their vocabulary and syntax will fit with the three preceding forms, so the user may utilize those paragraphs found desirable for the intended purpose.

The reader will soon see that the alternate paragraphs (which are arranged in alphabetical order) sometimes favor the interests of the prime contractor, sometimes those of the subcontractor, and in some cases are neutral. Many clauses are presented in two or three different versions. All three arbitration clauses require the subcontractor to participate in arbitration under the prime contract arbitration clause with the owner. Version two requires the subcontractor to supply counsel, evidence, and witnesses at its own expense in any arbitration with the owner (¶3). Version three provides that each party designates an arbitrator, and the arbitrators then select a neutral arbitrator (¶4).

The attorney's fee clauses should be given consideration when preparing any form of subcontract agreement (¶¶5, 6, and 7). The attorney's fee clause will probably be omitted by many prime contractors. Attorney's fee clauses encourage the litigation of sound claims, while they discourage the litigation of unsound ones. Most contractors would prefer not to encourage litigation at all, especially litigation of sound claims against themselves.

FORM 6-4 Alternate Subcontract Provisions

ALTERNATE SUBCONTRACT PROVISIONS

¶1. <u>Alternates:</u> The additive or deductive amounts listed for "alternates" will be added to or subtracted from the subcontract price in accordance with the alternates selected by Owner. If Owner does not select any alternates, there will be no change in the subcontract price.

¶2. *Arbitration:* Any controversy arising out of the performance or nonperformance of the work required by this Subcontract or any sub-subcontract, or the interpretation thereof, is subject to arbitration and judgment may be entered on the award. All sub-subcontractors and material suppliers of Subcontractor are bound by this arbitration provision.

Arbitration shall be in accordance with the arbitration provision contained in the contract between the Contractor and the Owner, when there is such an arbitration provision. Upon the demand of any party, any other party subject to this arbitration agreement shall join in and become a party to and be bound by such arbitration proceedings.

If, because of the objections of other parties or because of the structure of the arbitration clause in the agreement between Contractor and Owner it is not possible for Subcontractor or its subcontractors or suppliers to become parties to the arbitration proceedings, and if Subcontractor's work becomes an issue in arbitration proceedings between Contractor and Owner, then Subcontractor will, at its own expense, supply counsel, evidence, and witnesses to establish Subcontractor's performance of its obligations under this Subcontract. Subcontractor will be bound to Contractor by the award, so far as it applies to Subcontractor's portion of the work, to the same extent that Contractor is bound to Owner by the award.

¶3. *Arbitration:* Any controversy arising out of the performance or nonperformance of the work required by this Subcontract or any sub-subcontract, or the interpretation thereof, is subject to arbitration, and judgment may be entered on the award. All sub-subcontractors and material suppliers to Subcontractor are bound by this arbitration provision.

Arbitration shall be in accordance with the arbitration provision contained in the contract between the Contractor and the Owner, when there is such an arbitration provision. Upon the demand of any party, any other party subject to this arbitration agreement shall join in and become a party to and by bound by such arbitration proceedings.

If, because of the objections of other parties or because of the structure of the arbitration clause in the agreement between Contractor and Owner it is not possible for Subcontractor or its subcontractors or suppliers to become parties to the arbitration proceedings, and if Subcontractor's work becomes an issue in arbitration proceedings between Contractor and Owner, then Subcontractor will, at its own expense, supply counsel, evidence, and witnesses to establish Subcontractor's performance of its obligations to Contractor under this Subcontract. Subcontractor will be bound to Contractor by the award, so far as it applies to Subcontractor's portion of the work, to the same extent that Contractor is bound to Owner by the award.

If there is no arbitration clause in the contract between Contractor and Owner, then arbitration shall be in accordance with the Construction Industry Rules of the American Arbitration Association. Should any party refuse or neglect to appear at or participate in arbitration proceedings after due notice, the arbitrator will decide the controversy in accordance with evidence introduced by the party or parties who do appear. The arbitrator will award reasonable attorney's fees to the prevailing party. Rescission of this Subcontract shall not impair this arbitration agreement.

¶4. <u>Arbitration:</u> Any controversy arising out of Subcontractor's performance of this Subcontract or the interpretation thereof shall be decided by arbitration, and judgment may be entered on the award. Arbitration shall be in accordance with the arbitration clause contained in the contract between Contractor and Owner. If it is able to do so, Subcontractor will become a party to such arbitration proceedings. Otherwise, Subcontractor will supply evidence, witnesses, and counsel, at Subcontractor's expense, to establish Subcontractor's position as to performance of its work, and Subcontractor will be bound to Contractor by the award that is issued in the arbitration proceedings between Contractor and Owner.

If there is no arbitration agreement in effect between Contractor and Owner, then arbitration shall be had before a tribunal of three arbitrators. Each party will designate an arbitrator in writing within ten days after written demand for arbitration by either party. The arbitrators will, within ten days after their selection, designate a neutral arbitrator. The arbitrators will provide the parties with reasonable notice, and parties will be given an opportunity to present their evidence and testimony. An award signed by any two arbitrators will be binding. The arbitrators will award reasonable attorney's fees to the prevailing party.

If the arbitrators selected by the parties fail to designate a neutral arbitrator within ten days, the neutral arbitrator will be appointed by the American Arbitration Association.

¶5. <u>Attorney's Fees:</u> If the Contractor becomes involved in litigation or arbitration proceedings with Subcontractor or any other party arising out of or related to this Subcontract or Subcontractor's performance of the work under this Subcontract, then Subcontractor shall pay Contractor's reasonable attorney's fees.

¶6. <u>Attorney's Fees:</u> If Contractor and Subcontractor become involved in litigation or arbitration as a result of this Subcontract or the performance or nonperformance thereof, then the court or arbitration tribunal shall award reasonable attorney's fees to the prevailing party.

¶7. Attorney's Fees: If either party becomes involved in litigation arising out of this Subcontract or the performance thereof, the court in such litigation, or in a separate suit, shall award attorney's fees to the justly entitled party. The award of attorney's fees shall be such as to fully reimburse all attorney's fees actually incurred in good faith, regardless of the size of the judgment, it being the intention of the parties to fully compensate for all attorney's fees paid or incurred in good faith.

¶8. Backcharges: Subcontractor will promptly pay Contractor for any damage or loss that Contractor may sustain as a result of Subcontractor's performance or failure of performance. If Subcontractor is performing more than one project for Contractor, the Contractor may withhold payment on any project because of backcharges assessed on any other project.

¶9. Building Permits: Subcontractor will provide and pay for all licenses and building permits that are peculiar to Subcontractor's work. Subcontractor shall not, however, be required to pay use fees, hookup charges, sewer or other utility reimbursement fees, or similar charges or exactions that are required as a means of financing public improvements or utilities.

¶10. Change Orders: The subcontract price shall be deemed to be full compensation for all work and materials furnished by Subcontractor whether specifically called for in the contract documents or not, and no additional compensation shall be paid to Subcontractor unless a written change order has been signed by Contractor in advance of the extra work, stating that the work is extra work and designating any additional amounts to be paid.

If Subcontractor contends that any work or materials furnished by Subcontractor should be paid for as extra work, the Subcontractor must give written notice to Contractor to that effect within ten days after the work or materials in question are first furnished. Otherwise, it will be conclusively presumed that the Contractor and Subcontractor have agreed that such work or materials are within the original scope of the work and that no additional compensation will be paid for the extra work.

¶11. Change Orders: All labor and materials furnished by Subcontractor shall be deemed to be included within the subcontract price, even though such labor or materials are not specifically displayed in the contract documents. Contractor may, at any time, in writing, issue change orders to add to or subtract from the work, and Subcontractor shall perform in accordance with such written orders. The subcontract price shall be equitably adjusted. Subcontractor shall submit a detailed written breakdown, and the parties shall promptly agree in writing as to the amount to be added to or deducted from the subcontract price. The computation will be in accordance with unit prices when unit prices are included in the contract documents. Notice of any claim by Subcontractor for extra compensation shall be given within ten days of the occurrence of the event that caused the claim.

If the parties do not agree as to extra compensation claimed by Subcontractor, then Subcontractor shall submit to the project superintendent a daily work report covering the work for which extra compensation is claimed, naming all personnel employed about such work and designating the number of hours expended and the type of work performed. Subcontractor shall promptly supply backup documentation for equipment and materials. Contractor and Subcontractor will negotiate extra compensation based on such documentation and reports.

In the event that the Owner requests a change order that affects Subcontractor's work, the following procedure will be followed: (a) Contractor will send a "request for quote" (RFQ) to Subcontractor; (b) within 20 days Subcontractor will quote a price for the RFQ. The price will be supported with a complete cost breakdown. If the RFE does not affect the Subcontractor's work, the Subcontractor will return it within ten days endorsed "does not apply" and signed by Subcontractor; (c) if Subcontractor fails to submit a price within 20 days, Contractor will determine the price unilaterally, and issue a change order accordingly. Subcontractor will then be bound to such change order.

Upon receipt of a signed change order from the Owner, Contractor will issue an appropriate change order to the Subcontractor.

In the event of a dispute as to pricing a change order, or in the event of a dispute as to the scope of the work required by the contract documents, Subcontractor will promptly proceed with the work as ordered by Contractor, and will not stop or slow the work pending resolution of the dispute.

¶12. Claims for Damages: If either party for any reason claims damages against the other party, prompt written notice of the claim shall be given, no later than ten days after the occurrence of the even that gives rise to the claim.

¶13. Cleanup: Subcontractor will continuously clean the jobsite, and Subcontractor's work areas will be maintained in an orderly condition at all times. Subcontractor will locate its materials and equipment so as to avoid interference with other trades. If Subcontractor fails to perform as required by this paragraph, Contractor may do so at Subcontractor's expense.

¶14. Commencement of the Work: Subcontractor will not deliver any materials to the jobsite or commence work until notified to do so by Contractor. Subcontractor will commence work within three days after written notice from Contractor.

¶15. Compliance With Codes and Laws: In the performance of its work, Subcontractor will comply with all building codes, safety regulations, and all other laws, ordinances, and statutes that apply to the work.

¶16. Concealed Conditions: By executing this Subcontract, Subcontractor represents that it has made a thorough examination of the jobsite and has located and allowed for all conditions, including concealed underground conditions such as rock and utilities, that are to be encountered in the performance of the work. Subcontractor has taken such conditions into account in arriving at the Subcontract price. No additional compensation or extension of time shall be allowed because of concealed or unforeseen conditions about the jobsite.

¶17. Concealed Conditions: In the event that Subcontractor encounters rock, ground water, underground structures or utilities, or other underground conditions unknown to Subcontractor and not reasonably foreseeable by Subcontractor, then Subcontractor shall immediately call Contractor's attention to such concealed conditions in writing. The subcontract time and price will be equitably adjusted in writing to take such concealed conditions into account.

¶18. Conduit Clause: Subcontractor will perform for Contractor all of the obligations that Contractor is required to perform for Owner under the contract documents, to the extent that such obligations relate to Subcontractor's work or are customarily performed by Subcontractor's trade. The work required to be performed by Subcontractor is not confined to any particular portion of the drawings or section of the specifications, but may be scattered throughout the contract documents. In the event of disagreement between Subcontractor and Contractor or any other subcontractor as to the portions of the work required to be performed by Subcontractor, the Contractor will give due consideration to the contentions of all subcontractors. The orders of Contractor shall be followed and the decision of Contractor shall be final.

¶19. Construction Lender: In performing its work, Subcontractor shall meet all requirements of the construction lender. If the construction lender's payment schedule differs from the payment schedule contained in the contract documents, the construction lender's payment schedule shall control. In the event of a default under the Owner's construction loan agreement, Subcontractor will continue with the work at the request of construction lender provided that construction lender will pay Subcontractor, in accordance with the subcontract price, for all work performed by Subcontractor at the request of construction lender.

¶20. Contract Documents Complementary: The contract documents are complementary, and work displayed in one portion of the contract documents will be performed as though displayed in all portions of the contract documents.

¶21. Contractor's License: Subcontractor represents to Contractor and Owner that Subcontractor and its subcontractors are properly licensed to perform the work called for under this Subcontract, and will remain so throughout the duration of the project.

¶22. Contractor's License: Contractor and Subcontractor represent that they are properly licensed to perform their work on this project, and will remain so until the completion of work. Subcontractor represents that its subcontractors, if any, are likewise properly licensed, and will likewise remain so.

¶23. Contractor's Right to do Subcontractor's Work: If Subcontractor fails to supply sufficient forces, equipment or materials to advance the work according to Contractor's schedule, then Contractor may use its own forces, equipment, or materials to supply such portions of the work as are necessary to increase the rate of progress, and Contractor shall deduct the expense, with reasonable overhead and profit, from the subcontract price.

¶24. Correction of the Work: Subcontractor will immediately after notification correct any defective work.

¶25. Cutting and Patching: Subcontractor will cut, patch, and adjust its work so as to properly join with and fit the work of Contractor and other subcontractors.

¶26. Damages for Delay: The project must be constructed according to Contractor's schedule, and be completed in a timely manner as required by the contract documents. Subcontractor recognizes that, in the event Subcontractor delays the completion of the project, Contractor will be vulnerable to delay claims by Owner. Any such delay will also cause additional expense to Contractor, including the expense of manning the job for an extended time.

If Owner should assess damages for delay against Contractor, Contractor will determine the proportion of fault for the delay among Contractor and all subcontractors, and the damages for delay will be distributed between Contractor and Subcontractors accordingly. Contractor's allocation shall be final and binding as long as it is made in good faith.

In addition to distributing the damages for delay that may be assessed by Owner, the Contractor will also assess the damages and expense directly suffered by Contractor, and such damages shall be distributed among Contractor and Subcontractors according to the same principle.

¶27. Damages for Delay: If Subcontractor delays or interferes with the orderly progress of the work by Contractor or other subcontractors, Contractor will determine the monetary amount of resulting damages sustained by Contractor and Subcontractor shall promptly pay the amount thus determined to Contractor.

¶28. Damages for Delay: If the contract between Contractor and Owner contains provisions relative to delay, excuse for delay, claims for extension of time, or damages or liquidated damages for delay, such provisions shall be applicable to Subcontractor. If the prime contract requires Contractor to give written notice to the Owner of claims for extensions of time, then Subcontractor shall give written notice of any delay affecting Subcontractor's work to Contractor in sufficient time to enable Contractor to comply with the requirement. Any provision of the prime contract which would excuse Contractor for delay shall also excuse the Subcontractor. If Contractor suffers damages or liquidated damages for delay caused by Subcontractor, Subcontractor will indemnify and hold harmless Contractor from such damages. Subcontractor will prosecute the work diligently to completion.

¶29. Damages for Delay: Time is of the essence of this agreement. Subcontractor shall provide Contractor with all scheduling information required by Contractor for Subcontractor's work. Subcontractor will commence work within 24 hours after notice to proceed from Contractor, and will prosecute the work with diligence and efficiency in strict accordance with the schedule, and will not delay or interfere with other portions of the work. Should Subcontractor fall behind schedule, Contractor may require Subcontractor to work overtime to catch up, and overtime shall be at Subcontractor's expense.

If the Subcontractor's work is delayed without the fault of Subcontractor, then Contractor shall extend the time for Subcontractor's work to the extent that Owner extends Contractor's time for the work, and the schedule shall be revised accordingly.

Contractor shall not be liable to Subcontractor for damages or compensation for delays or interference caused by Contractor, Owner, or other subcontractors, and Subcontractor's exclusive remedy for such delay or interference shall be an extension of time for performance of Subcontractor's work.

If the contract documents provide for liquidated or other damages for delay, and damages are assessed by Owner against Contractor, the Contractor may assess such damages against Subcontractor in proportion to Subcontractor's share of responsibility for delay. Contractor's assessment shall be final and binding as long as it is made in good faith.

¶30. Default: In the event that Subcontractor appears likely to be unable to complete the work on schedule, or if Subcontractor fails to fully perform its duties under this Subcontract, or if Subcontractor becomes insolvent, or fails to supply sufficient forces to maintain the schedule, or is guilty of any other default under this Subcontract, then Contractor may (a) withhold payment for work performed under this Subcontract or withhold payment of any other obligation of Contractor to Subcontractor, (b) after giving 24 hours written notice to Subcontractor, eject Subcontractor and take over Subcontractor's work and terminate Subcontractor's right to perform under the Subcontract. If Contractor takes over Subcontractor's work, then Contractor will charge Subcontractor for all costs incurred as a result, including reasonable overhead and profit and including attorney's fees and other expenses. If the total amount exceeds the unpaid balance of the Subcontract, then Subcontractor shall pay the difference to Contractor. If the amount is less than the unpaid balance of the Subcontract, the excess shall be paid by Contractor to Subcontractor.

240 SUBCONTRACTS

If Contractor takes over Subcontractor's work, Subcontractor shall permit Contractor to take possession of all materials, equipment, tools, and appliances at the jobsite for the purpose of completing Subcontractor's work. Subcontractor will cooperate with Contractor to facilitate an orderly take-over.

¶31. Design by Subcontractor: Subcontractor will both design and supply all materials, equipment, supplies, and other facilities that are needed to produce a complete operating system. Subcontractor will adhere to the architectural and structural philosophy and details of the project. Subcontractor will submit preliminary drawings and outline specifications to show the essential materials, features, locations, functions, and capacities of the system. The subcontract price includes payment for all things to be furnished and designed by Subcontractor.

¶32. Destruction of the Work: Subcontractor will carry its own insurance to protect it against destruction of or damage to the Subcontractor's work. Subcontractor will be responsible for its work until completion of the entire project and its acceptance by the Owner. Until that time, Subcontractor has the risk of loss. In the event of damage to or destruction of the work, Subcontractor will rebuild its portion of the work without additional compensation, and will look to its own resources or insurance coverage to pay for such rebuilding. Subcontractor will promptly perform rebuilding without additional compensation regardless of the pendency of any claim by Subcontractor against any other party, including Contractor, that such party is liable for damage to or destruction of Subcontractor's work.

¶33. Destruction of the Work: In the event that Subcontractor's work, or any portion thereof, is damaged or destroyed by fire, earthquake, landslide, flood, or similar peril that is not the fault of Subcontractor, then the Subcontractor shall be compensated for the cost of rebuilding by an equitable adjustment to the subcontract price, and an extension of time shall be granted.

¶34. Equal Employment Opportunity: Subcontractor will comply with all applicable statutes, laws, and regulations regarding equal employment opportunity, affirmative action, minority employment, employment of women, minority contracting, and the like.

¶35. Execution Clause: This Subcontract is dated and effective _____. The Subcontract will not be binding until each party has in its possession a copy executed by the other party.

¶36. Final Payment: The final payment (exclusive of the retention) will be due when the Subcontractor's work has been completed and accepted by Contractor and Owner. The making and acceptance of final payment constitutes a waiver of all claims by Contractor against Subcontractor for obvious defects in the work (but not for latent defects), and also constitutes a waiver of any claims by Subcontractor against Contractor for compensation for extra work or for compensation or damages of any kind claimed by Subcontractor because of the activities of Contractor in connection with the project.

¶37. Indemnity: Each party will indemnify the other party, and will hold the other party harmless from claims, litigation, expense, and loss, including attorney's fees, suffered by the other party and caused by the misconduct, fault, or wrongdoing of the party and arising out of or related to the parties' performance of the work called for by this Subcontract. If the parties are both at fault, then the obligation to indemnify shall be proportionate to fault.

¶38. Indemnity: Subcontractor will indemnify Contractor and Owner, and hold them harmless against claims, liability, litigation, loss, and expense, including attorney's fees, suffered by Contractor or Owner as a result of Subcontractor's performance or nonperformance of the work required by this Subcontract. Subcontractor is obliged to indemnify Contractor and Owner under this paragraph for all events caused or partly caused by Subcontractor's negligence, wrongdoing, or other fault even if Contractor or Owner, or Contractor and Owner, should also be partially at fault. This indemnity provision shall not, however, apply to claims, liability, litigation, loss, or expense caused solely by the fault of Contractor or Owner or Contractor and Owner. Subcontractor's obligation under this indemnity provision shall extend to the acts and omissions of Subcontractor's agents, employees, and sub-subcontractors.

¶39. Indemnity: Subcontractor will indemnify and hold Contractor and Owner harmless from claims, demands, liabilities, judgments, liens, encumbrances, costs and expenses, including attorney's fees, arising out of or in connection with the obligations of Subcontractor under this Subcontract, or the operations and work conducted by Subcontractor or its agents, employees, and sub-subcontractors. This indemnity agreement shall apply without regard to whether or not Contractor or Owner, or Contractor and Owner, are actively or passively negligent in respect to the claim, demand, loss, or liability. Subcontractor will provide the defense of any such claims, and will employ counsel who is satisfactory to Contractor or Owner for that purpose. Contractor and Owner may defend such claims at Subcontractor's expense. Subcontractor shall not provide indemnity against claims, liability, loss, or expense, when shown by the final judgment of a court of competent jurisdiction to have been caused by the sole negligence or sole misconduct of Contractor or Owner.

¶40. Insolvency: If either party to this Subcontract should become insolvent, or encounter financial problems that prevent the party from fully and efficiently performing its contractual obligations, then the other party may terminate the insolvent party's performance under this Subcontract, and the terminated party shall be responsible for the payment of all expense, damage, and loss sustained by the terminating party as a result of the termination.

¶41. Insolvency: If Subcontractor should become insolvent, or encounter financial difficulties which impair the ability of Subcontractor to perform its obligations under this Subcontract fully and efficiently, then Contractor may, upon written notice, terminate Subcontractor's performance under this Subcontract, and Subcontractor shall pay to Contractor the amount of loss or damage sustained by Contractor as a result of the termination.

¶42. Insolvency: If the Contractor should be in doubt as to Subcontractor's solvency, or if Contractor believes Subcontractor is in financial difficulties which impair Subcontractor's ability to efficiently and fully to perform its obligations under this Subcontract, then Contractor may demand from Subcontractor reasonable written assurances, supported by detailed financial statements, of Subcontractor's ability to perform. If Subcontractor does not deliver reasonable written assurances, or if such assurances leave Contractor in reasonable doubt as to Subcontractor's ability to diligently, promptly, and efficiently perform the subcontract work, then Contractor may terminate Subcontractor's performance under this Subcontract, and Subcontractor will pay to Contractor all damages, losses, and expenses sustained by Contractor as a result of the termination.

¶43. Inspection and Testing: Subcontractor, at its own expense, will facilitate any inspection and testing required by the contract documents, Contractor, Owner, Architect, or any public agency. If it is necessary to do so for such inspection and testing, Subcontractor will remove and replace, at its own expense, those portions of Subcontractor's work necessary to perform such inspections and testing. If inspections or testing are required because of the improper performance by Subcontractor of its work, then the inspection and testing fees shall be paid by Subcontractor.

¶44. Inspection and Testing: Subcontractor will pay all fees incurred for inspection and testing of Subcontractor's work. Subcontractor will, at its own expense, make all portions of the work easily accessible to inspectors and testing agencies, and will, if necessary, at its own expense, remove any portions of the work that need to be removed to facilitate inspection and testing.

¶45. Insurance: Contractor will provide "wrap-up" liability insurance for this project, insuring Subcontractor and all other subcontractors on the project against liability for property damage and bodily injury. In computing the Subcontract price, and in computing the cost of change orders, Subcontractor shall not charge for liability insurance premiums. The limits of liability for bodily injury and property damage shall not be less than $1,000,000 each. Subcontractor and Contractor waive any right of subrogation against each other that may arise out of bodily injury or property damage that is covered by the wrap-up insurance to the extent that it is valid and collectible. On demand, Contractor will supply Subcontractor with a copy of the wrap-up insurance policy. Contractor makes no representations to Subcontractor as to the policy coverage, but Subcontractor shall judge such policy coverage for itself.

¶46. Insurance: Before Contractor makes any payment to Subcontractor under this Subcontract, and before Subcontractor performs any work on the project, Subcontractor will deliver to Contractor certificates of insurance, which name the Contractor and Owner as additional insureds, signed by hand, showing that Subcontractor has the coverages required by this paragraph.

(a) Liability Insurance: Comprehensive general liability insurance, with broad form coverage, which includes coverages for settlement, collapse, underground hazards, completed operations, products liability, and liability assumed by contract will be provided by Subcontractor. The certificate will provide that the insurance may not be cancelled or modified without 30 days prior written notice by the insurance carrier to Contractor. The certificate will name Contractor and the Owner as additional named insureds under the policy, and will provide that the coverage afforded by the policy is primary, and that any other insurance of Contractor covering the same risk or risks is excess and non-contributory. The insurance shall have a limit of not less than $1,000,000 for bodily injury and a limit of not less than $1,000,000 for property damage.

(b) Automobile Insurance: Subcontractor shall provide Contractor with a certificate showing that it has in force comprehensive automobile liability insurance covering all owned and non-owned vehicles with limits of not less than $1,000,000 for bodily injury, and not less than $1,000,000 for property damage. The certificate of insurance for comprehensive automobile liability shall be in the same form as required above for comprehensive general liability.

(c) Workers' Compensation: Subcontractor shall supply to Contractor a certificate showing that Subcontractor is in compliance with state requirements for workers' compensation insurance. The certificate shall provide that the insurance may not be cancelled without 30 days prior notice to Contractor.

¶47.   Insurance for Builder's Risk: Owner or Contractor will provide builder's risk insurance covering the entire project, and the interests of all subcontractors therein. At the request of Subcontractor, Contractor or Owner will supply a copy of the policy to Subcontractor. In the event of damage to or destruction of Subcontractor's work, Owner or Contractor will look to the builder's risk insurance for compensation, and Subcontractor will be paid equitable compensation for the rebuilding of any damage to or destruction of Subcontractor's work. The insurance shall apply even if the damage to or destruction of Subcontractor's work is caused by Subcontractor. Owner, Contractor, and Subcontractor waive any right of subrogation against each other to the extent that damage to or destruction of work is covered by valid and collectible insurance.

¶48.   Interest: Payments overdue from Contractor to Subcontractor will bear interest at the rate provided in the contract documents for overdue payments from Owner to Contractor. In the event there is no such provision in the agreement between Owner and Contractor, overdue payments shall bear interest at the legal rate.

¶49. Interest: Overdue payments from Contractor to Subcontractor shall bear interest at two points above the prime rate generally charged by commercial banks at the time the overdue payment is due in the state where the project is located.

¶50. Interest: Payments overdue from Contractor to Subcontractor shall bear interest at the highest rate permitted by law.

¶51. Interest: Payments overdue from Contractor to Subcontractor shall bear interest at 1½ per cent per month. If such a rate of interest is unlawful, then such payments shall bear interest at the highest lawful rate.

¶52. Investigation by Subcontractor: Subcontractor has carefully examined and understands this Subcontract and the other contract documents, and has investigated the nature, locality and site of the work and the conditions and difficulties under which it is to be performed. Subcontractor enters this agreement on the basis of its own examination, investigation and evaluation of all such matters, and not in reliance on the opinions or representations of Contractor or Owner. If there are any inconsistencies between the contract documents or ambiguities in any contract document, Subcontractor shall bring such inconsistencies or ambiguities to the attention of Contractor before the execution of this Subcontract; otherwise, Subcontractor shall be bound by Contractor's resolution of such inconsistencies or ambiguities.

¶53. Joint Checks: If Contractor receives information, or has reason to believe, that Subcontractor has not paid for any work, equipment, or materials incorporated into the project, then Contractor reserves the right to make payments to Subcontractor in the form of checks payable jointly to Subcontractor and its workers, suppliers, or sub-subcontractors. By endorsing any such joint check, each worker, supplier, or sub-subcontractor endorser acknowledges that it has been paid the full face amount of the check for work performed on the project covered by this Subcontract.

¶54. Mechanic's Lien Releases: No payment will be made by Contractor to Subcontractor until Subcontractor has provided to Contractor properly executed mechanic's lien releases on forms approved by Contractor and its counsel. The releases will acknowledge payment in full for all work, equipment, or materials supplied to the project prior to the cut-off date of Subcontractor's application for payment. Subcontractor will further supply, if Contractor requests as a condition to each progress payment, evidence in the form of invoices and cancelled checks to show that all such payments have been made.

¶55. Mechanic's Lien Releases: Contractor will make no payment to Subcontractor until Subcontractor has supplied mechanic's lien releases, properly executed, on a form approved by Contractor and its counsel. The releases will be such as to show that Subcontractor has fully paid for all work, materials, and equipment supplied to the project through the cut-off date of Subcontractor's application for payment for the previous month. Subcontractor will hold all funds received from Contractor in trust to pay for work, equipment, and materials supplied to Subcontractor in the performance of the work, and will not be entitled to retain any payments for its own use until all such payments have been made.

¶56. Mechanic's Lien Rights Are Waived: Subcontractor, in consideration of the award of this Subcontract, does hereby waive all right to enforce payment by asserting a claim of mechanic's lien, or by asserting a claim against any construction fund or payment bond. Subcontractor will require all suppliers, materialmen, and sub-subcontractors to execute documents similarly waiving any such rights.

¶57. Mutual Responsibility of Subcontractors: Subcontractor accepts mutual responsibility, along with Contractor and all other subcontractors on the project, for the prompt, efficient, and coordinated progress of the work. Subcontractor will keep itself informed as to the progress of Contractor and other subcontractors, and will coordinate its operations with Contractor and other subcontractors so as to facilitate the progress of the work. In the event of conflict between subcontractors as to access to work areas, coordination, or scheduling, the orders of the Contractor shall be followed.

¶58. No Binding Agreement Without Signatures: This Subcontract shall constitute a binding agreement only when it has been signed by both parties, and when each party has possession of a copy signed by the other party. Any work performed by Subcontractor before both parties have received signed copies of the Subcontract shall be performed as a volunteer, at Subcontractor's expense.

¶59. No Damages for Delay: Subcontractor will complete all work required under this Subcontract on or before _____. In the event that Subcontractor is obstructed or delayed in its performance of its work by Contractor or Owner, Subcontractor will be entitled to a reasonable extension of time. It is agreed that the extension of time will be Subcontractor's sole and exclusive remedy for such obstruction or delay, and that in no event will the Subcontractor be entitled to recover damages from Contractor or Owner for any such obstruction or delay.

¶60. No Damages for Delay: If Subcontractor is obstructed or delayed in the performance of its work by acts of Contractor or Owner, Subcontractor shall be entitled to a reasonable extension of time, provided that, as a condition precedent to such an extension being granted, Subcontractor has provided Contractor with a written notice of the delay within ten days after the commencement of the delay. Such an extension of time shall be Subcontractor's exclusive remedy, and under no circumstances shall Subcontractor be entitled to monetary damages or other compensation for such obstruction or delay.

¶61. Nonaward: In the event that Contractor does not receive an award of the prime contract from Owner, then this Subcontract shall be void.

¶62. No Other Agreement: This Subcontract, and the contract documents referred to in this Subcontract, constitute the entire agreement between the parties. No communication between Contractor and Subcontractor, whether oral or written, before the execution of this Subcontract, shall be referred to in order to explain, modify, expand, or extend this Subcontract or the contract documents. No communication between Contractor and Subcontractor after the execution of this Subcontract, whether oral or written, shall extend or modify the contract documents. This Subcontract and the contract documents incorporated in it are the sole expression of the agreement between the parties.

¶63. Notices: Any notice permitted or required by the contract documents shall be given to Contractor or Subcontractor at the address contained on this Subcontract. Notice will be deemed received by the other party in the ordinary course of the mail. Either party may change its address for purposes of notice under the contract documents at any time, but such a change shall be effective only if it is made in writing to the other party.

¶64. Offsetting Accounts: If Subcontractor is indebted to Contractor on any other job or for any other reason, Contractor may offset such indebtedness against any payments earned under this Subcontract.

¶65. Payment Not Approval: It is not to be inferred from the fact that Contractor makes payments to Subcontractor under this agreement that Contractor accepts, or has approved, any work performed by Subcontractor. Contractor may not waive its right to insist on full compliance by Subcontractor with all the requirements of the contract documents except in a written document, approved in writing by Owner, and specifying the precise things accepted by Contractor.

¶66. Payment of Fringe Benefits: Before Subcontractor is entitled to any progress payment, it will present to Contractor evidence satisfactory to Contractor that will show that Subcontractor has made all of its required contributions to pension, health and welfare, vacation, apprenticeship, and other trust funds established under collective bargaining agreements. If required, Subcontractor will permit Contractor to audit its payroll accounts to satisfy itself that such payments have been made.

¶67. Payment of Fringe Benefits: Subcontractor will make all health and welfare, pension, vacation, and apprenticeship fund contributions and similar payments required under any such agreement. At the request of Coantractor, Subcontractor will furnish evidence satisfactory to Contractor that such payments have been made. Contractor may eject Subcontractor from the job or rescind this Subcontract if Subcontractor, or Subcontractor's subcontractors, are listed by the administrative office of a health and welfare, pension, vacation, apprenticeship, or similar fund as being delinquent in payment, whether such delinquencies arise out of work performed under this Subcontract or not. Contractor may pay any amounts that Contractor believes are due to such administrative funds, and Subcontractor shall reimburse Contractor for such disbursements.

¶68. Payment of Retention: The 10 per cent retention shall be paid 35 days after Notice of Completion has been recorded.

¶69. Payment of Retention: The retention shall be paid 35 days after completion of the entire project.

¶70. Payment of Retention: When 50 per cent of the project has been completed, provided Contractor is satisfied with Subcontractor's progress and performance, no more retention will be withheld, so that the total retention at the end of the project will be 5 per cent.

¶71. Payment of Retention: Provided Contractor is satisfied with Subcontractor's progress and performance, when the project is 50 per cent complete, the retention will be reduced to 5 per cent, and Contractor will remit to Subcontractor the portion of the retention that is in excess of 5 per cent. Thereafter, a 5 per cent retention will be withheld from each progress payment. The retention will be paid 35 days after recording of the Notice of Completion.

¶72. Payment Schedule: Within 15 days after the execution of this Subcontract, Subcontractor shall supply a schedule of values for its work in form and amounts satisfactory to Contractor and Owner, dividing the work into components for billing purposes.

On or before the 25th day of each month, Subcontractor shall deliver to Contractor an application for payment showing the percentages of completion and value of each item of work completed to that date. Applications for payment must be accompanied by mechanic's lien releases properly executed by all persons who have supplied work, equipment or materials to Subcontractor or its subcontractors. The form of lien release shall be satisfactory to Contractor and its counsel. As soon as Contractor has received payment from Owner based on Subcontractor's application for payment, Contractor will pay Subcontractor 90 per cent of the amount earned by Subcontractor for the pay period.

¶73. Payment Schedule: Contractor will make payments to Subcontractor as follows:

_____ when _____;
_____ when _____;
_____ when _____;

_____ when _____ ;
_____ when _____ ;
_____ when _____ ;
_____ when _____ .

The final payment will be made when all of Subcontractor's work has been completed and accepted by Contractor, Owner, and Architect. The retention shall be paid 35 days after completion of the entire project.

¶74. <u>Payment Schedule:</u>   Before commencement of the work, Subcontractor will provide Contractor with a schedule of values, approved by Contractor, Owner, and Architect, that breaks down the values of the component parts of Subcontractor's work for billing purposes. On the 20th day of every month, Subcontractor will submit to Contractor an application for payment, specifying the percentage of completion of each item. The percentages of completion are subject to approval by Contractor, Owner, and Architect. Contractor will pay Subcontractor one business day after Contractor receives payment from Owner. Payments are subject to a 10 per cent retention. The retention will be paid 35 days after recording of the Notice of Completion of the entire project.

¶75. <u>Payment Schedule:</u>   Subcontractor will submit to Contractor an application for payment monthly in time for Contractor to include Subcontractor's application for payment in Contractor's monthly billing to Owner. Subcontractor's application for payment will specify the percentages of completion and values of the various portions of Subcontractor's work. Payment will be made by Contractor to Subcontractor immediately upon receipt of payment from Owner, less a 10 per cent retention which will be paid to Subcontractor 35 days after the completion of the entire project.

¶76. <u>Payment to Subcontractor Conditioned on Payment by Owner:</u>   Subcontractor understands that all payments to Subcontractor will be made only from a special fund, namely, from payments made by Owner to Contractor in respect of work performed by Subcontractor. No payments will be made to Subcontractor unless that fund comes into existence. It is therefore an express condition precedent to Contractor's obligation to make any payment to Subcontractor that the Contractor shall first have been paid by Owner for the work performed by Subcontractor. This paragraph shall not excuse Contractor from paying Subcontractor in the event that Owner refuses payment to Contractor because of reasons that are not connected with Subcontractor's work.

¶77. <u>Performance and Payment Bond:</u>   Before commencing work on the project, Subcontractor will supply to Contractor a performance and payment bond, naming Contractor and Owner as joint obligees. The bonds will be in form satisfactory to Contractor and its counsel. The penalty amount of the bonds shall be 100 per cent of the Subcontract price. The bonds will guarantee that Subcontractor will perform all things to be performed on its part under the Subcontract, and will pay for all work, labor, materials, and equipment supplied to

Subcontractor and its subcontractors for the project. The bonds will be issued by a surety company authorized to do business in this state, and by a company that is satisfactory to Contractor. The performance bond will incorporate by reference this Subcontract, and will guarantee the performance of all change orders issued by Contractor regardless of whether the surety has notice of, or consents to, such changes.

¶78. Performance and Payment Bond: Contractor, at any time during the progress of the work, may require Subcontractor to provide a performance and payment bond, issued by a surety company and in a form satisfactory to Contractor. Contractor will pay the bond premium, provided it is a reasonable and standard premium, and not a substandard market premium. The payment bond will guarantee that all persons who supply work, equipment, or materials to the project on behalf of Subcontractor will be paid. The performance bond will guarantee that Subcontractor will perform the Subcontract and any change orders that are issued by Contractor. Each bond will be in an amount equal to 100 per cent of the Subcontract price.

¶79. Picketing: If Subcontractor's presence on the job should cause picketing, boycott, or other concerted action by any union, Contractor may terminate Subcontractor's performance by written notice, and Subcontractor will be paid a fair proportion of the Subcontract price based upon the percentage of completion of the work.

¶80. Picketing: If picketing should occur on the jobsite, Contractor may employ a reserved gate system. In such event, Subcontractor will take such measures, including the posting of a watchman at the neutral gate, to make certain that all of its personnel, workers, suppliers, and materialmen utilize no gate other than the one designated for them by Contractor. In the event that Subcontractor or its workers or suppliers should contaminate the neutral gate, Subcontractor will pay Contractor liquidated damages of $_____ per day until reestablishment of the neutral gate. It is agreed that contamination of the neutral gate would cause Contractor economic damage in the form of delay and lost productivity, but that such damages would be extremely difficult and impracticable to compute, and the parties have therefore agreed that $_____ per day is a reasonable approximation of Contractor's actual damages in such event.

¶81. Picketing: Should there be picketing at the jobsite, and should Contractor or Owner establish a reserved gate for use by Subcontractor, its employees, material suppliers, and subcontractors, Subcontractor shall carefully enforce the proper use of the reserved gate, as instructed by the Contractor, and will continue the proper performance of its work without interruption or delay.

¶82. Picketing or Other Labor Action: Regardless of whether Subcontractor is a union signatory, in the event that picketing, strikes, or labor disputes develop on the project because of the presence of Subcontractor or its subcontractors or suppliers, Contractor shall have the following cumulative rights: (a) to deny Subcontractor access to the jobsite until the labor dispute has been resolved, and Contractor shall not be liable for any damages incurred by Subcontractor as a result, (b) to eject Subcontractor from the jobsite and terminate Subcontractor's performance under this Subcontract, in which event Subcontractor shall be paid the reasonable value, as measured by the Subcontract price, of work performed and actually installed up to the time of such termination, and (c) to take reasonably necessary steps to place the labor dispute before the National Labor Relations Board for resolution. All costs and expenses, including attorney's fees and delay damages, incurred by Owner or Contractor as a result of labor disputes caused by Subcontractor's presence on the job shall be charged to Subcontractor.

¶83. Protection of the Work: Subcontractor will at all times protect its own work and the work of others from damage by collapse, fire, windstorm, rain, hail, or any other cause. If Subcontractor's work is damaged, Subcontractor will immediately repair the damage at its own expense.

¶84. Quality of the Work: All materials and equipment shall be as specified and all work shall be performed by Subcontractor in a first-class and workmanlike manner.

¶85. Reasonable Assurances: If Contractor should be in doubt as to Subcontractor's ability to perform and complete the work on schedule and as required by the contract documents, the Contractor shall ask the Subcontractor for reasonable written assurances. Subcontractor shall promptly supply such reasonable written assurances, including, if required by Contractor, reasonable financial information as to the solvency of Subcontractor. Failure to supply such reasonable written assurances within ten days will be an event of default, such as to justify Contractor in ejecting Subcontractor from the project. Subcontractor will pay Contractor all damages, losses, and expenses sustained by Contractor as a result of the termination.

¶86. Release Schedule: The project consists of _____ housing units. The work is to be performed in _____ phases. Each phase consists of approximately _____ units. Subcontractor will not commence work on any phase until authorized in writing to do so by Contractor. If Contractor is dissatisfied with Subcontractor's work, Contractor may award any phase to another Subcontractor, and the Subcontract price will be reduced accordingly. If for any reason Contractor does not go forward with production of any phase, or if Contractor decides to delay the production of any phase indefinitely, then Contractor may, by written order, delete that phase from the Subcontract. Subcontractor will commence work on each phase within three days after notice to do so.

¶87. Reliance on Proposal: This Subcontract document, when signed by Subcontractor and delivered to Contractor, constitutes a proposal to perform the work according to the terms of the Subcontract. Contractor is entitled to rely on this proposal in preparing its own proposal to the Owner. If the Owner accepts Contractor's proposal, then Subcontractor is bound by this Subcontract document, even though it may not have been signed by Contractor. Contractor will sign this Subcontract within a reasonable time after award by Owner.

¶88. Repossession: If Contractor fails to pay for equipment or materials installed by Subcontractor, Subcontractor may remove such equipment and materials from the project, doing as little damage as possible to the remainder of the project.

¶89. Responsibility of Individual Signatory: The individual who signs this Subcontract on behalf of Subcontractor is personally financially responsible for the performance of this Subcontract work.

¶90. Right to Stop Work: In the event of any disagreement between Contractor and Subcontractor as to the scope of the work, scheduling, equipment, materials, or any other disagreement, Subcontractor will not stop work or reduce progress, but will continue with the prompt and diligent prosecution of the work.

¶91. Right to Stop Work: If Subcontractor is not promptly paid for any work performed by Subcontractor, then Subcontractor has the right to stop work, and may suspend its performance until all payments that are due have been received.

¶92. Right to Stop Work: In the event that Owner or Contractor shall suspend the prosecution of the project, Subcontractor will promptly demobilize, and will hold itself in readiness to resume operations when ordered to do so by Contractor.

¶93. Risk of Loss: All equipment, materials, and completed and uncompleted work are at the risk of Subcontractor until the entire project has been completed and accepted by the Owner. Subcontractor will provide its own insurance covering such risk, and will not be excused from performance of this Subcontract by damage to or destruction of its equipment, materials, or partially or fully completed work.

¶94. Safety: Subcontractor will familiarize itself with Contractor's safety program, and will promptly comply with all safety instructions issued by Contractor. Subcontractor will strictly enforce safety requirements in its work force, and will hold tailgate safety meetings with all workers at least weekly.

¶95. Scheduling: Subcontractor has examined, and approves of, the preliminary schedule. During the progress of the work, Subcontractor will promptly supply to Contractor all scheduling information required by Contractor. Subcontractor will promptly review and comply with all revised schedules issued by Contractor. Subcontractor will employ overtime, if necessary, to comply with the Contractor's scheduling requirements. No extra compensation will be paid to

Subcontractor for overtime in the absence of written agreement by Contractor to reimburse such overtime.

¶96. Scope of the Work: Subcontractor will supply all work, equipment, tools, and materials necessary to produce a complete and operating project, and will perform all work customarily performed by Subcontractor's trade whether or not so specified in the contract documents. It will be conclusively presumed that all work performed by Subcontractor falls within the scope of the work called for by this Subcontractor unless Subcontractor notifies Contractor in writing, before the commencement of such work, that it considers such work to be extra. If Contractor requires Subcontractor to do work that Subcontractor believes to be outside the scope of Subcontractor's work, Subcontractor will promptly notify Contractor in writing, but will not delay or impede the progress of the work. Subcontractor will promptly perform the work as ordered by Contractor, and the dispute will be settled later.

¶97. Security for Payment: Subcontractor will not commence work until Contractor has supplied information satisfactory to Subcontractor as to the source of payment for Subcontractor's work. If Subcontractor becomes doubtful as to Contractor's ability to pay for the work, Contractor will provide, upon demand by Subcontractor, reasonable security for payment.

¶98. Shop Drawings: Within three weeks from the date of this Subcontract, Subcontractor will submit shop drawings, samples, templates, and material lists, and will take any action needed to provide for anchorage, embedded items, long-lead-time orders, and the like. Subcontractor will check the drawings and advise Contractor in writing if any item to be furnished by Subcontractor will not fit the space provided, or if any special sequence of construction is necessary. Subcontractor will maintain as-built drawings up to date at all times. By submitting any process or item of equipment or material as an "equal", Subcontractor guarantees to Contractor and Owner that the item can be installed without hinderance to other trades, and will perform in a satisfactory manner as to capacity, serviceability, ease of maintenance and repair, function, and aesthetics.

¶99. Subcontracting by Subcontractor: Subcontractor will not subcontract any of its work without the advance written consent of Contractor.

¶100. Substitutions: If Subcontractor recommends any changes or substitutions, then Subcontractor guarantees (1) the substitution is equal in quality, serviceability, durability, capacity, maintainability, and appearance, and (2) the item can be installed and activated without adverse impact on the work of Contractor or any other trades.

¶101. Successors and Assigns: This Subcontract is binding upon, and fully enforceable against, the successors and assigns of both parties.

¶102. Superintendent: Subcontractor will assign _____ as its superintendent. The superintendent will not be changed without the written consent of Contractor. If Contractor becomes dissatisfied with a superintendent, Subcontractor will promptly replace the superintendent.

¶103. Taxes: Subcontractor will pay all income, excise, sales, use, and other taxes levied by any authority on Subcontractor's work, equipment, or materials.

¶104. Termination for Convenience: Contractor, by paying Subcontractor the sum of $500.00, may terminate this Subcontract, and Subcontractor's performance thereunder, at any time, for Contractor's own convenience.

¶105. Time is of the Essence: Time is of the essence of this Subcontract.

¶106. Union Contractor: Subcontractor is signatory to a collective bargaining agreement with _____, and, will remain so until the work required by this Subcontract is complete. Subcontractor will perform all of its obligations under the collective bargaining agreement, and will promptly make all wage and fringe benefit payments that it is obliged to make.

¶107. Union Subcontractor: Subcontractor is required to be a signatory to a collective bargaining agreement with the appropriate union, and it shall remain in full force and effect covering the employees of Subcontractor and of any other firm used by Subcontractor to perform the work. Subcontractor will abide by all terms of the collective bargaining agreement, and will require that any firm employed by Subcontractor about the work shall abide by its terms. Failure to do so shall be a material breach of this Subcontract, entitling Contractor to eject Subcontractor from the job or rescind this Subcontract.

¶108. Unit Prices: The following unit prices will apply for additions to the work:

_____
_____
_____

For deletions from the work, the following unit prices will apply:

_____
_____
_____
_____.

¶109. Warranty: Subcontractor warrants that all work, materials, and equipment supplied by Subcontractor will be suitable for its intended use, and as specified. Promptly upon notification by Owner or Contractor, for a period of one year after the completion of the project, Subcontractor will repair or replace materials, equipment, or work that has become in any way defective.

Subcontractor will remain responsible, after the expiration of one year, for defects caused by a failure to perform as required by the contract documents.

¶110. <u>Warranty:</u> Subcontractor warrants its work and materials against defects. All work and materials will be as called for in the contract documents. If the contract between Contractor and Owner contains warranty provisions, Subcontractor will comply with those provisions at no expense to Owner or Contractor.

If no warranty is provided in the contract between Contractor and Owner, then Subcontractor shall guarantee its work for one year after completion of the project, and, promptly upon notice from Owner or Contractor, shall repair defective work.

¶111. <u>Warranty:</u> Subcontractor guarantees its work, materials, and equipment for a period of one year after the completion of the project, and will promptly repair any defects. Subcontractor will also repair any defects that occur after the expiration of one year as a result of Subcontractor's failure to comply with the requirements of the contract documents.

¶112. <u>Withdrawal of Proposal:</u> This Subcontract, when signed by Subcontractor, becomes a proposal for the performance of the work. The proposal will remain open for ten days after the Subcontract date, at which time it automatically terminates.

¶113. <u>Withdrawal of Proposal:</u> This form of Subcontract, when signed by Subcontractor, becomes a proposal that will remain open for 30 days, and that will continue to remain open during that period unless terminated, in writing, by Subcontractor.

AGC Document No. 600 - Subcontract

§6.07 General Comments

Subcontractors, with good reason, usually view a long form of subcontract with healthy skepticism. The contract form that is most beneficial to the subcontractor is a short one. The payment clause is short. The rest of the clauses in a form of subcontract may often, or usually, be used as a device to justify nonpayment.

AGC Document 600, being long, is no exception.

§6.07 AGC DOCUMENT NO. 600   255

FORM 6-5   AGC Document No. 600 - Subcontract for Building Construction (1984)

THE ASSOCIATED GENERAL CONTRACTORS OF AMERICA

SUBCONTRACT FOR BUILDING CONSTRUCTION

TABLE OF ARTICLES

1. AGREEMENT
2. SCOPE OF WORK
3. SCHEDULE OF WORK
4. CONTRACT PRICE
5. PAYMENT
6. CHANGES, CLAIMS AND DELAYS
7. CONTRACTOR'S OBLIGATIONS
8. SUBCONTRACTOR'S OBLIGATIONS
9. SUBCONTRACT PROVISIONS
10. RECOURSE BY CONTRACTOR
11. LABOR RELATIONS
12. INDEMNIFICATION
13. INSURANCE
14. ARBITRATION
15. CONTRACT INTERPRETATION
16. SPECIAL PROVISIONS

This Agreement has important legal and insurance consequences. Consultation with an attorney and insurance consultant is encouraged with respect to its completion or modification and particularly when used with other than AIA A201 General Conditions of the Contract for Construction, August 1976 edition.

AGC DOCUMENT NO. 600   •   SUBCONTRACT FOR BUILDING CONSTRUCTION   August 1984

©Associated General Contractors of America

TABLE OF CONTENTS

ARTICLE 1
Agreement

ARTICLE 2—Scope of Work
2.1 Subcontractor's Work.
2.2 Contract Documents.
2.3 Conflicts.

ARTICLE 3—Schedule of Work
3.1 Time is of Essence.
3.2 Duty to be Bound.
3.3 Schedule Changes.
3.4 Priority of Work.

ARTICLE 4—Contract Price

ARTICLE 5—Payment
5.1 General Provisions.
5.1.1 Schedule of Values.
5.1.2 Architect Verification.
5.1.3 Payment Use Restriction.
5.1.4 Payment Use Verification.
5.1.5 Partial Lien Waivers and Affidavits.
5.1.6 Subcontractor Payment Failure.
5.1.7 Payment Not Acceptance.
5.2 Progress Payments.
5.2.1 Application.
5.2.2 Retainage/Security.
5.2.3 Time of Application.
5.2.4 Stored Materials.
5.2.5 Time of Payment.
5.2.6 Payment Delay.
5.3 Final Payment.
5.3.1 Application.
5.3.2 Requirements.
5.3.3 Time of Payment.
5.3.4 Final Payment Delay.
5.4 Late Payment Interest.

ARTICLE 6—Changes, Claims and Delays
6.1 Changes.
6.2 Claims Relating To Owner.
6.3 Claims Relating To Contractor.
6.4 Delay.
6.5 Liquidated Damages.

ARTICLE 7—Contractor's Obligations
7.1 Obligations Derivative.
7.2 Authorized Representative.
7.3 Storage Allocation.
7.4 Timely Communications.
7.5 Non-Contracted Services.

ARTICLE 8—Subcontractor's Obligations
8.1 Obligations Derivative.
8.2 Responsibilities.
8.3 Temporary Services.
8.4 Coordination.
8.5 Authorized Representative.
8.6 Provision for Inspection.
8.7 Safety and Cleanup.
8.8 Protection of the Work.
8.9 Permits, Fees and Licenses.
8.10 Assignment.
8.11 Non-Contracted Services.

ARTICLE 9—Subcontract Provisions
9.1 Layout Responsibility and Levels.
9.2 Workmanship.
9.3 Materials Furnished by Others.
9.4 Substitutions.
9.5 Use of Contractor's Equipment.
9.6 Contract Bond Review.
9.7 Owner Ability to Pay.
9.8 Privity.
9.9 Subcontract Bond.
9.10 Warranty.

ARTICLE 10—Recourse by Contractor
10.1 Failure of Performance.
10.1.1 Notice to Cure.
10.1.2 Termination by Contractor.
10.1.3 Use of Subcontractor's Equipment.
10.2 Bankruptcy.
10.2.1 Termination Absent Cure.
10.2.2 Interim Remedies.
10.3 Suspension by Owner.
10.4 Termination by Owner.
10.5 Termination for Convenience.
10.6 Wrongful Exercise.

ARTICLE 11—Labor Relations

ARTICLE 12—Indemnification
12.1 Subcontractor's Performance.
12.2 No Limitation Upon Liability.
12.3 Architect Exclusion.
12.4 Compliance with Laws.
12.5 Patents.

ARTICLE 13—Insurance
13.1 Subcontractor's Insurance.
13.2 Minimum Limits of Liability.
13.3 Number of Policies.
13.4 Cancellation, Renewal or Modification.
13.5 Waiver of Rights.
13.6 Endorsement.

ARTICLE 14—Arbitration
14.1 Agreement to Arbitrate.
14.2 Notice of Demand.
14.3 Award.
14.4 Work Continuation and Payment.
14.5 No Limitation of Rights or Remedies.
14.6 Same Arbitrators.
14.7 Exceptions.

ARTICLE 15—Contract Interpretation
15.1 Inconsistencies and Omissions.
15.2 Law and Effect.
15.3 Severability and Waiver.
15.4 Attorney's Fees.
15.5 Titles.
15.6 Entire Agreement.

ARTICLE 16—Special Provisions
16.1 Precedence.
16.2 Scope of Work.
16.3 Common Temporary Services.
16.4 Other Special Provisions.
16.5 Contract Documents.

§6.07 AGC DOCUMENT NO. 600   257

SUBCONTRACT FOR BUILDING CONSTRUCTION

ARTICLE 1
AGREEMENT

This Agreement made this _____ day of _____, 19___, and effective the _____ day of _____, 19___, by and between _____,

hereinafter called the Contractor and _____,

hereinafter called the Subcontractor, to perform part of the Work on the following Project:

PROJECT:

OWNER:

ARCHITECT:

CONTRACTOR:

SUBCONTRACTOR:

CONTRACT PRICE:

Notice to the parties shall be given at the above addresses.

ARTICLE 2
SCOPE OF WORK

2.1 SUBCONTRACTOR'S WORK. The Contractor employs the Subcontractor as an independent contractor, to perform the work described in Article 16. The Subcontractor shall perform such work (hereinafter called the "Subcontractor's Work") under the general direction of the Contractor and in accordance with this Agreement and the Contract Documents.

2.2 CONTRACT DOCUMENTS. The Contract Documents which are binding on the Subcontractor are as set forth in Article 16.5.

Upon the Subcontractor's request the Contractor shall furnish a copy of any part of these documents.

2.3 CONFLICTS. In the event of a conflict between this Agreement and the Contract Documents, this Agreement shall govern, except as follows:

AGC DOCUMENT NO. 600   •   SUBCONTRACT FOR BUILDING CONSTRUCTION   •   August 1984   3
©Associated General Contractors of America

ARTICLE 3

SCHEDULE OF WORK

3.1 TIME IS OF ESSENCE. Time is of the essence for both parties, and they mutually agree to see to the performance of their respective work and the work of their subcontractors so that the entire Project may be completed in accordance with the Contract Documents and the Schedule of Work. The Contractor shall prepare the Schedule of Work and revise such schedule as the Work progresses.

3.2 DUTY TO BE BOUND. Both the Contractor and the Subcontractor shall be bound by the Schedule of Work. The Subcontractor shall provide the Contractor with any requested scheduling information for the Subcontractor's Work. The Schedule of Work and all subsequent changes thereto shall be submitted to the Subcontractor in advance of the required performance.

3.3 SCHEDULE CHANGES. The Subcontractor recognizes that changes will be made in the Schedule of Work and agrees to comply with such changes subject to a reservation of rights arising hereunder.

3.4 PRIORITY OF WORK. The Contractor shall have the right to decide the time, order and priority in which the various portions of the Work shall be performed and all other matters relative to the timely and orderly conduct of the Subcontractor's Work.

The Subcontractor shall commence its work within _____ days of notice to proceed from the Contractor and if such work is interrupted for any reason the Subcontractor shall resume such work within two working days from the Contractor's notice to do so.

ARTICLE 4

CONTRACT PRICE

The Contractor agrees to pay to the Subcontractor for the satisfactory performance of the Subcontractor's Work the sum of _____

_____
Dollars ($ _____) in accordance with Article 5, subject to additions or deductions per Article 6.

ARTICLE 5

PAYMENT

5.1 GENERAL PROVISIONS

5.1.1 SCHEDULE OF VALUES. The Subcontractor shall provide a schedule of values satisfactory to the Contractor and the Owner no more than fifteen (15) days from the date of execution of this Agreement.

5.1.2 ARCHITECT VERIFICATION. Upon request the Contractor shall give the Subcontractor written authorization to obtain directly from the Architect the percentage of completion certified for the Subcontractor's Work.

5.1.3. PAYMENT USE RESTRICTION. No payment received by the Subcontractor shall be used to satisfy or secure any indebtedness other than one owed by the Subcontractor to a person furnishing labor or materials for use in performing the Subcontractor's Work.

5.1.4 PAYMENT USE VERIFICATION. The Contractor shall have the right at all times to contact the Subcontractor's subcontractors and suppliers to ensure that the same are being paid by the Subcontractor for labor or materials furnished for use in performing the Subcontractor's Work.

5.1.5 PARTIAL LIEN WAIVERS AND AFFIDAVITS. When required by the Contractor, and as a prerequisite for payment, the Subcontractor shall provide, in a form satisfactory to the Owner and the Contractor, partial lien or claim waivers and affidavits from the Subcontractor, and its sub-subcontractors and suppliers for the completed Subcontractor's Work. Such waivers may be made conditional upon payment.

5.1.6 SUBCONTRACTOR PAYMENT FAILURE. In the event the Contractor has reason to believe that labor, material or other obligations incurred in the performance of the Subcontractor's Work are not being paid, the Contractor shall give written notice of such claim or lien to the Subcontractor and may take any steps deemed necessary to insure that any progress payment shall be utilized to pay such obligations.

If upon receipt of said notice, the Subcontractor does not:
(a) supply evidence to the satisfaction of the Contractor that the monies owing to the claimant have been paid; or
(b) post a bond indemnifying the Owner, the Contractor, the Contractor's surety, if any, and the premises from such claim or lien;

then the Contractor shall have the right to retain out of any payments due or to become due to the Subcontractor a reasonable amount to protect the Contractor from any and all loss, damage or expense including attorney's fees arising out of or relating to any such claim or lien until the claim or lien has been satisfied by the Subcontractor.

5.1.7 PAYMENT NOT ACCEPTANCE. Payment to the Subcontractor is specifically agreed not to constitute or imply acceptance by the Contractor or the Owner of any portion of the Subcontractor's Work.

5.2 PROGRESS PAYMENTS

5.2.1 APPLICATION. The Subcontractor's progress payment application for work performed in the preceding payment period shall be submitted to the Contractor per the terms of this Agreement and specifically Articles 5.1.1, 5.2.2, 5.2.3, and 5.2.4 for approval of the Contractor and _____.

The Contractor shall forward, without delay, the approved value to the Owner for payment.

5.2.2 RETAINAGE/SECURITY. The rate of retainage shall not exceed the percentage retained from the Contractor's payment by the Owner for the Subcontractor's Work provided the Subcontractor furnishes a bond or other security to the satisfaction of the Contractor.

If the Subcontractor has furnished such bond or security; its work is satisfactory and the Contract Documents provide for reduction of retainage at a specified percentage of completion, the Subcontractor's retainage shall also be reduced when the Subcontractor's Work has attained the same percentage of completion and the Contractor's retainage for the Subcontractor's Work has been so reduced by the Owner

However, if the Subcontractor does not provide such bond or security, the rate of retainage shall be ____%.

5.2.3 TIME OF APPLICATION. The Subcontractor shall submit progress payment applications to the Contractor no later than the _____ day of each payment period for work performed up to and including the _____ day of the payment period indicating work completed and, to the extent allowed under Article 5.2.4 materials suitably stored during the preceding payment period.

5.2.4 STORED MATERIALS. Unless otherwise provided in the Contract Documents, and if approved in advance by the Owner, applications for payment may include materials and equipment not incorporated in the Subcontractor's Work but delivered and suitably stored at the site or at some other location agreed upon in writing. Approval of payment application for such stored items on or off the site shall be conditioned upon submission by the Subcontractor of bills of sale and applicable insurance or such other procedures satisfactory to the Owner and Contractor to establish the Owner's title to such materials and equipment or otherwise protect the Owner's and Contractor's interests therein, including transportation to the site.

5.2.5 TIME OF PAYMENT. Progress payments to the Subcontractor for satisfactory performance of the Subcontractor's Work shall be made no later than seven (7) days after receipt by the Contractor of payment from the Owner for such Subcontractor's Work.

5.2.6 PAYMENT DELAY. If for any reason not the fault of the Subcontractor, the Subcontractor does not receive a progress payment from the Contractor within seven (7) days after the date such payment is due, as defined in Article 5.2.5, then the Subcontractor, upon giving an additional seven (7) days written notice to the Contractor, and without prejudice to and in addition to any other legal remedies, may stop work until payment of the full amount owing to the Subcontractor has been received. To the extent obtained by the Contractor under the Contract Documents, the contract price shall be increased by the amount of the Subcontractor's reasonable costs of shut-down, delay, and start-up, which shall be effected by appropriate Change Order.

If the Subcontractor's Work has been stopped for thirty (30) days because the Subcontractor has not received progress payments as required hereunder, the Subcontractor may terminate this Agreement upon giving the Contractor an additional seven (7) days written notice.

5.3 FINAL PAYMENT

5.3.1 APPLICATION. Upon acceptance of the Subcontractor's Work by the Owner, the Contractor, and if necessary, the Architect, and upon the Subcontractor furnishing evidence of fulfillment of the Subcontractor's obligations in accordance with the Contract Documents and Article 5.3.2, the Contractor shall forward the Subcontractor's application for final payment without delay.

5.3.2 REQUIREMENTS. Before the Contractor shall be required to forward the Subcontractor's application for final payment to the Owner, the Subcontractor shall submit to the Contractor:

(a) an affidavit that all payrolls, bills for materials and equipment, and other indebtedness connected with the Subcontractor's Work for which the Owner or his property or the Contractor or the Contractor's surety might in any way be liable, have been paid or otherwise satisfied;

(b) consent of surety to final payment, if required;

(c) satisfaction of required closeout procedures; and

(d) other data if required by the Contractor or Owner, such as receipts, releases, and waivers of liens to the extent and in such form as may be designated by the Contractor or Owner.

Final payment shall constitute a waiver of all claims by the Subcontractor relating to the Subcontractor's Work, but shall in no way relieve the Subcontractor of liability for the obligations assumed under Article 9.10 hereof, or for faulty or defective work appearing after final payment.

5.3.3 TIME OF PAYMENT. Final payment of the balance due of the contract price shall be made to the Subcontractor:

(a) upon receipt of the Owner's waiver of all claims related to the Subcontractor's Work except for unsettled liens, unknown defective work, and non-compliance with the Contract Documents or warranties; and

(b) within seven (7) days after receipt by the Contractor of final payment from the Owner for such Subcontractor's Work.

5.3.4 FINAL PAYMENT DELAY. If the Owner or its designated agent does not issue a Certificate for Final Payment or the Contractor does not receive such payment for any cause which is not the fault of the Subcontractor, the Contractor shall promptly inform the Subcontractor in writing. The Contractor shall also diligently pursue, with the assistance of the Subcontractor, the prompt release by the Owner of the final payment due for the Subcontractor's Work. At the Subcontractor's request and joint expense, to the extent agreed upon in writing, the Contractor shall institute all reasonable legal remedies to mitigate the damages and pursue full payment of the Subcontractor's application for final payment including interest thereon.

5.4 LATE PAYMENT INTEREST. To the extent obtained by the Contractor under the Contract Documents, progress payments or final payment due and unpaid under this Agreement shall bear interest from the date payment is due at the rate provided in the Contract Documents, or, in the absence thereof, at the legal rate prevailing at the place of the Project.

ARTICLE 6
CHANGES, CLAIMS AND DELAYS

6.1 CHANGES. When the Contractor so orders in writing, the Subcontractor, without nullifying this Agreement, shall make any and all changes in the Work which are within the general scope of this Agreement.

Adjustments in the contract price or contract time, if any, resulting from such changes shall be set forth in a Subcontract Change Order pursuant to the Contract Documents.

No such adjustment shall be made for any such changes performed by the Subcontractor that have not been so ordered by the Contractor.

6.2 CLAIMS RELATING TO OWNER. The Subcontractor agrees to make all claims for which the Owner is or may be liable in the manner provided in the Contract Documents for like claims by the Contractor upon the Owner.

Notice of such claims shall be given by the Subcontractor to the Contractor within one (1) week prior to the beginning of the Subcontractor's Work or the event for which such claim is to be made, or immediately upon the Subcontractor's first knowledge of the event, whichever shall first occur, otherwise, such claims shall be deemed waived.

The Contractor agrees to permit the Subcontractor to prosecute said claim, in the name of the Contractor, for the use and benefit of the Subcontractor in the manner provided in the Contract Documents for like claims by the Contractor upon the Owner.

6.3 CLAIMS RELATING TO CONTRACTOR. The Subcontractor shall give the Contractor written notice of all claims not included in Article 6.2 within five (5) days of the beginning of the event for which claim is made; otherwise, such claims shall be deemed waived.

All unresolved claims, disputes and other matters in question between the Contractor and the Subcontractor not relating to claims included in Article 6.2 shall be resolved in the manner provided in Article 14 herein.

6.4 DELAY. If the progress of the Subcontractor's Work is substantially delayed without the fault or responsibility of the Subcontractor, then the time for the Subcontractor's Work shall be extended by Change Order to the extent obtained by the Contractor under the Contract Documents and the Schedule of Work shall be revised accordingly.

The Contractor shall not be liable to the Subcontractor for any damages or additional compensation as a consequence of delays caused by any person not a party to this Agreement unless the Contractor has first recovered the same on behalf of the Subcontractor from said person, it being understood and agreed by the Subcontractor that, apart from recovery from said person, the Subcontractor's sole and exclusive remedy for delay shall be an extension in the time for performance of the Subcontractor's Work.

6.5 LIQUIDATED DAMAGES. If the Contract Documents provide for liquidated or other damages for delay beyond the completion date set forth in the Contract Documents, and are so assessed, then the Contractor may assess same against the Subcontractor in proportion to the Subcontractor's share of the responsibility for such delay. However the amount of such assessment shall not exceed the amount assessed against the Contractor.

ARTICLE 7
CONTRACTOR'S OBLIGATIONS

7.1 OBLIGATIONS DERIVATIVE. The Contractor binds itself to the Subcontractor under this Agreement in the same manner as the Owner is bound to the Contractor under the Contract Documents.

7.2 AUTHORIZED REPRESENTATIVE. The Contractor shall designate one or more persons who shall be the Contractor's authorized representative(s) a) on-site and b) off-site. Such authorized representative(s) shall be the only person(s) the Subcontractor shall look to for instructions, orders and/or directions, except in an emergency.

7.3 STORAGE ALLOCATION. The Contractor shall allocate adequate storage areas, if available, for the Subcontractor's materials and equipment during the course of the Subcontractor's Work.

7.4 TIMELY COMMUNICATIONS. The Contractor shall transmit, with reasonable promptness, all submittals, transmittals, and written approvals relating to the Subcontractor's Work.

7.5 NON-CONTRACTED SERVICES. The Contractor agrees, except as otherwise provided in this Agreement, that no claim for non-contracted construction services rendered or materials furnished shall be valid unless the Contractor provides the Subcontractor notice:
  (a) prior to furnishing of the services or materials, except in an emergency affecting the safety of persons or property;
  (b) in writing of such claim within three days of first furnishing such services or materials; and
  (c) the written charges for such services or materials no later than the fifteenth (15th) day of the calendar month following that in which the claim originated.

ARTICLE 8

SUBCONTRACTOR'S OBLIGATIONS

8.1 OBLIGATIONS DERIVATIVE. The Subcontractor binds itself to the Contractor under this Agreement in the same manner as the Contractor is bound to the Owner under the Contract Documents.

8.2 RESPONSIBILITIES. The Subcontractor shall furnish all of the labor, materials, equipment, and services, including, but not limited to, competent supervision, shop drawings, samples, tools, and scaffolding as are necessary for the proper performance of the Subcontractor's Work.

The Subcontractor shall provide a list of proposed sub-subcontractors, and suppliers, be responsible for taking field dimensions, providing tests, ordering of materials and all other actions as required to meet the Schedule of Work.

8.3 TEMPORARY SERVICES. The Subcontractor shall furnish all temporary services and/or facilities necessary to perform its work, except as provided in Article 16. Said article also identifies those common temporary services (if any) which are to be furnished by this subcontractor.

8.4 COORDINATION. The Subcontractor shall:
  (a) cooperate with the Contractor and all others whose work may interfere with the Subcontractor's Work;
  (b) specifically note and immediately advise the Contractor of any such interference with the Subcontractor's Work; and
  (c) participate in the preparation of coordination drawings and work schedules in areas of congestion.

8.5 AUTHORIZED REPRESENTATIVE. The Subcontractor shall designate one or more persons who shall be the authorized Subcontractor's representative(s) a) on-site and b) off-site. Such authorized representative(s) shall be the only person(s) to whom the Contractor shall issue instructions, orders or directions, except in an emergency.

8.6 PROVISION FOR INSPECTION. The Subcontractor shall notify the Contractor when portions of the Subcontractor's Work are ready for inspection. The Subcontractor shall at all times furnish the Contractor and its representatives adequate facilities for inspecting materials at the site or any place where materials under this Agreement may be in the course of preparation, process, manufacture or treatment.

The Subcontractor shall furnish to the Contractor in such detail and as often as required, full reports of the progress of the Subcontractor's Work irrespective of the location of such work.

8.7 SAFETY AND CLEANUP. The Subcontractor shall follow the Contractor's clean-up and safety directions, and
  (a) at all times keep the building and premises free from debris and unsafe conditions resulting from the Subcontractor's Work; and
  (b) broom clean each work area prior to discontinuing work in the same.

If the Subcontractor fails to immediately commence compliance with such safety duties or commence cleanup duties within 24 hours after receipt from the Contractor of written notice of noncompliance, the Contractor may implement such safety or cleanup measures without further notice and deduct the cost thereof from any amounts due or to become due the Subcontractor.

8.8 PROTECTION OF THE WORK. The Subcontractor shall take necessary precautions to properly protect the Subcontractor's Work and the work of others from damage caused by the Subcontractor's operations. Should the Subcontractor cause damage to the Work or property of the Owner, the Contractor or others, the Subcontractor shall promptly remedy such damage to the satisfaction of the Contractor, or the Contractor may so remedy and deduct the cost thereof from any amounts due or to become due the Subcontractor.

8.9 PERMITS, FEES AND LICENSES. The Subcontractor shall give adequate notices to authorities pertaining to the Subcontractor's Work and secure and pay for all permits, fees, licenses, assessments, inspections and taxes necessary to complete the Subcontractor's Work in accordance with the Contract Documents.

To the extent obtained by the Contractor under the Contract Documents, the Subcontractor shall be compensated for additional costs resulting from laws, ordinances, rules, regulations and taxes enacted after the date of the Agreement.

8.10 ASSIGNMENT. The Subcontractor shall not assign this Agreement nor its proceeds nor subcontract the whole nor any part of the Subcontractor's Work without prior written approval of the Contractor which shall not be unreasonably withheld. See Article 16.4 for sub-subcontractors and suppliers previously approved by the Contractor.

8.11 NON-CONTRACTED SERVICES. The Subcontractor agrees, except as otherwise provided in this Agreement, that no claim for non-contracted construction services rendered or materials furnished shall be valid unless the Subcontractor provides the Contractor notice:

(a) prior to furnishing of the services or materials, except in an emergency affecting the safety of persons or property;

(b) in writing of such claim within three days of first furnishing such services or materials; and

(c) the written charge for such services or materials to the contractor no later than the fifteenth day (15th) of the calendar month following that in which the claim originated.

ARTICLE 9

SUBCONTRACT PROVISIONS

9.1 LAYOUT RESPONSIBILITY AND LEVELS. The Contractor shall establish principal axis lines of the building and site whereupon the Subcontractor shall lay out and be strictly responsible for the accuracy of the Subcontractor's Work and for any loss or damage to the Contractor or others by reason of the Subcontractor's failure to set out or perform its work correctly. The Subcontractor shall exercise prudence so that actual final conditions and details shall result in perfect alignment of finish surfaces.

9.2 WORKMANSHIP. Every part of the Subcontractor's Work shall be executed in strict accordance with the Contract Documents in the most sound, workmanlike, and substantial manner. All workmanship shall be of the best of its several kinds, and all materials used in the Subcontractor's Work shall be furnished in ample quantities to facilitate the proper and expeditious execution of the work, and shall be new except such materials as may be expressly provided in the Contract Documents to be otherwise.

9.3 MATERIALS FURNISHED BY OTHERS. In the event the scope of the Subcontractor's Work includes installation of materials or equipment furnished by others, it shall be the responsibility of the Subcontractor to examine the items so provided and thereupon handle, store and install the items with such skill and care as to ensure a satisfactory and proper installation. Loss or damage due to acts of the Subcontractor shall be deducted from any amounts due or to become due the Subcontractor.

9.4 SUBSTITUTIONS. No substitutions shall be made in the Subcontractor's Work unless permitted in the Contract Documents and only then upon the Subcontractor first receiving all approvals required under the Contract Documents for substitutions. The Subcontractor shall indemnify the Contractor for any increased costs incurred by the Contractor as a result of such substitutions, whether or not the Subcontractor has obtained approval thereof.

9.5 USE OF CONTRACTOR'S EQUIPMENT. The Subcontractor, its agents, employees, subcontractors or suppliers shall not use the Contractor's equipment without the express written permission of the Contractor's designated representative.

If the Subcontractor or any of its agents, employees, suppliers or lower tier subcontractors utilize any machinery, equipment, tools, scaffolding, hoists, lifts or similar items owned, leased, or under the control of the Contractor, the Subcontractor shall be liable to the Contractor as provided in Article 12 for any loss or damage (including personal injury or death) which may arise from such use, except where such loss or damage shall be found to have been due solely to the negligence of the Contractor's employees operating such equipment.

9.6 CONTRACT BOND REVIEW. The Contractor's Payment Bond for the Project, if any, may be reviewed and copied by the Subcontractor.

9.7 OWNER ABILITY TO PAY. The Subcontractor shall have the right to receive from the Contractor information relative to the Owner's financial ability to pay for the Work.

9.8 PRIVITY. Until final completion of the Project, the Subcontractor agrees not to perform any work directly for the Owner or any tenants thereof, or deal directly with the Owner's representatives in connection with the Project, unless otherwise directed in writing by the Contractor. All work for this Project performed by the Subcontractor shall be processed and handled exclusively by the Contractor.

9.9 SUBCONTRACT BOND. If a Performance and Payment Bond is not required of the Subcontractor under

Article 16, then within the duration of this Agreement, the Contractor may require such bonds and the Subcontractor shall provide same.

Said bonds shall be in the full amount of this Agreement in a form and by a surety satisfactory to the Contractor.

The Subcontractor shall be reimbursed without retainage for cost of same simultaneously with the first progress payment hereunder.

The reimbursement amount for the bonds shall not exceed the manual rate for such subcontractor work.

Retainage reduction provisions of Article 5.2.2 shall not apply when bonds are furnished under the terms of this Article.

In the event the Subcontractor shall fail to promptly provide such requested bonds, the Contractor may terminate this Agreement and re-let the work to another Subcontractor and all Contractor costs and expenses incurred thereby shall be paid by the Subcontractor.

9.10 WARRANTY. The Subcontractor warrants its work against all deficiencies and defects in materials and/or workmanship and as called for in the Contract Documents.

The Subcontractor agrees to satisfy such warranty obligations which appear within the guarantee or warranty period established in the Contract Documents without cost to the Owner or the Contractor.

If no guarantee or warranty is required of the Contractor in the Contract Documents, then the Subcontractor shall guarantee or warranty its work as described above for the period of one year from the date(s) of substantial completion of all or a designated portion of the Subcontractor's Work or acceptance or use by the Contractor or Owner of designated equipment, whichever is sooner.

The Subcontractor further agrees to execute any special guarantees or warranties that shall be required for the Subcontractor's Work prior to final payment.

ARTICLE 10

RECOURSE BY CONTRACTOR

10.1 FAILURE OF PERFORMANCE

10.1.1 NOTICE TO CURE. If the Subcontractor refuses or fails to supply enough properly skilled workers, proper materials, or maintain the Schedule of Work, or it fails to make prompt payment for its workers, sub-subcontractors or suppliers, disregards laws, ordinances, rules, regulations or orders of any public authority having jurisdiction, or otherwise is guilty of a material breach of a provision of this Agreement, and fails within three (3) working days after receipt of written notice to commence and continue satisfactory correction of such default with diligence and promptness, then the Contractor, without prejudice to any rights or remedies, shall have the right to any or all of the following remedies:

(a) supply such number of workers and quantity of materials, equipment and other facilities as the Contractor deems necessary for the completion of the Subcontractor's Work, or any part thereof which the Subcontractor has failed to complete or perform after the aforesaid notice, and charge the cost thereof to the Subcontractor, who shall be liable for the payment of same including reasonable overhead, profit and attorney's fees;

(b) contract with one or more additional contractors to perform such part of the Subcontractor's Work as the Contractor shall determine will provide the most expeditious completion of the total Work and charge the cost thereof to the Subcontractor;

(c) withhold payment of any monies due the Subcontractor pending corrective action to the extent required by and to the satisfaction of the Contractor and _____; and

(d) in the event of an emergency affecting the safety of persons or property, the Contractor may proceed as above without notice.

10.1.2 TERMINATION BY CONTRACTOR. If the Subcontractor fails to commence and satisfactorily continue correction of a default within three (3) working days after receipt by the Subcontractor of the notice issued under Article 10.1.1, then the Contractor may, in lieu of or in addition to Article 10.1.1, issue a second written notice, by certified mail, to the Subcontractor and its surety, if any. Such notice shall state that if the Subcontractor fails to commence and continue correction of a default within seven (7) working days after receipt by the Subcontractor of the notice, the Contractor may terminate this Agreement and use any materials, implements, equipment, appliances or tools furnished by or belonging to the Subcontractor to complete the Subcontractor's Work. The Contractor also may furnish those materials, equipment and/or employ such workers or Subcontractors as the Contractor deems necessary to maintain the orderly progress of the Work.

All of the costs incurred by the Contractor in so performing the Subcontractor's Work, including reasonable overhead, profit and attorney's fees, shall be deducted from any monies due or to become due the Subcontractor. The Subcontractor shall be liable for the payment of any amount by which such expense may exceed the unpaid balance of the subcontract price.

10.1.3 USE OF SUBCONTRACTOR'S EQUIPMENT. If the Contractor performs work under this Article or sublets such work to be so performed, the Contractor and/or the persons to whom work has been sublet shall have the right to take and use any materials, implements, equip-

264 SUBCONTRACTS

ment, appliances or tools furnished by, belonging or delivered to the Subcontractor and located at the Project.

10.2 BANKRUPTCY

10.2.1 TERMINATION ABSENT CURE. Upon the appointment of a receiver for the Subcontractor or upon the Subcontractor making an assignment for the benefit of creditors, the Contractor may terminate this Agreement upon giving three (3) working days written notice, by certified mail, to the Subcontractor and its surety, if any. If an order for relief is entered under the bankruptcy code with respect to the Subcontractor, the Contractor may terminate this Agreement by giving three (3) working days written notice, by certified mail, to the Subcontractor, its trustee, and its surety, if any, unless the Subcontractor, the surety, or the trustee:

(a) promptly cures all defaults;
(b) provides adequate assurances of future performance;
(c) compensates the Contractor for actual pecuniary loss resulting from such defaults; and
(d) assumes the obligations of the Subcontractor within the statutory time limits.

10.2.2 INTERIM REMEDIES. If the Subcontractor is not performing in accordance with the Schedule of Work at the time of entering an order for relief, or at any subsequent time, the Contractor, while awaiting the decision of the Subcontractor or its trustee to reject or to accept this Agreement and provide adequate assurance of its ability to perform hereunder, may avail itself of such remedies under this Article as are reasonably necessary to maintain the Schedule of Work.

The Contractor may offset against any sums due or to become due the Subcontractor all costs incurred in pursuing any of the remedies provided hereunder, including, but not limited to, reasonable overhead, profit and attorney's fees.

The Subcontractor shall be liable for the payment of any amount by which such expense may exceed the unpaid balance of the contract price.

10.3 SUSPENSION BY OWNER. Should the Owner suspend the Prime Contract or any part of the Prime Contract which includes the Subcontractor's Work, the Contractor shall so notify the Subcontractor in writing and upon receipt of said notice the Subcontractor shall immediately suspend the Subcontractor's Work.

In the event of such Owner suspension, the Contractor's liability to the Subcontractor is limited to the extent of the Contractor's recovery on the Subcontractor's behalf under the Contract Documents. The Contractor agrees to cooperate with the Subcontractor, at the Subcontractor's expense, in the prosecution of any Subcontractor claim arising out of an Owner suspension and to permit the Subcontractor to prosecute said claim, in the name of the Contractor, for the use and benefit of the Subcontractor.

10.4 TERMINATION BY OWNER. Should the Owner terminate the Prime Contract or any part of the Prime Contract which includes the Subcontractor's Work, the Contractor shall so notify the Subcontractor in writing and upon receipt of said notice, this Agreement shall also be terminated and the Subcontractor shall immediately stop the Subcontractor's Work.

In the event of such Owner termination, the Contractor's liability to the Subcontractor is limited to the extent of the Contractor's recovery on the Subcontractor's behalf under the Contract Documents.

The Contractor agrees to cooperate with the Subcontractor, at the Subcontractor's expense, in the prosecution of any Subcontractor claim arising out of the Owner termination and to permit the Subcontractor to prosecute said claim, in the name of the Contractor, for the use and benefit of the Subcontractor, or assign the claim to the Subcontractor.

10.5 TERMINATION FOR CONVENIENCE. The Contractor may order the Subcontractor in writing to suspend, delay, or interrupt all or any part of the Subcontractor's Work for such period of time as may be determined to be appropriate for the convenience of the Contractor.

The Subcontractor shall notify the Contractor in writing within ten (10) working days after receipt of the Contractor's order of the effect of such order upon the Subcontractor's Work, and the contract price or contract time shall be adjusted by Subcontract Change Order for any increase in the time or cost of performance of this Agreement caused by such suspension, delay, or interruption.

No claim under this Article shall be allowed for any costs incurred more than ten (10) working days prior to the Subcontractor's notice to the Contractor.

Neither the contract price nor the contract time shall be adjusted under this Article for any suspension, delay or interruption to the extent that performance would have been so suspended, delayed, or interrupted by the fault or negligence of the Subcontractor.

10.6 WRONGFUL EXERCISE. If the Contractor wrongfully exercises any option under this Article, the Contractor shall be liable to the Subcontractor solely for the reasonable value of work performed by the Subcontractor prior to the Contractor's wrongful action, including reasonable overhead and profit, less prior payments made, and attorney's fees.

ARTICLE 11

LABOR RELATIONS

(Insert here any conditions, obligations or requirements relative to labor relations and their effect on the project. Legal counsel is recommended.)

ARTICLE 12

INDEMNIFICATION

12.1 SUBCONTRACTOR'S PERFORMANCE. To the fullest extent permitted by law, the Subcontractor shall indemnify and hold harmless the Owner, the Architect, the Contractor (including its affiliates, parents and subsidiaries) and other contractors and subcontractors and all of their agents and employees from and against all claims, damages, loss and expenses, including but not limited to attorney's fees, arising out of or resulting from the performance of the Subcontractor's Work provided that

(a) any such claim, damage, loss, or expense is attributable to bodily injury, sickness, disease, or death, or to injury to or destruction of tangible property (other than the Subcontractor's Work itself) including the loss of use resulting therefrom, to the extent caused or alleged to be caused in whole or in any part by any negligent act or omission of the Subcontractor or anyone directly or indirectly employed by the Subcontractor or anyone for whose acts the Subcontractor may be liable, regardless of whether it is caused in part by a party indemnified hereunder.

(b) such obligation shall not be construed to negate, or abridge, or otherwise reduce any other right or obligation of indemnity which would otherwise exist as to any party or person described in this Article 12.

12.2 NO LIMITATION UPON LIABILITY. In any and all claims against the Owner, the Architect, the Contractor (including its affiliates, parents and subsidiaries) and other contractors or subcontractors, or any of their agents or employees, by any employee of the Subcontractor, anyone directly or indirectly employed by the Subcontractor or anyone for whose acts the Subcontractor may be liable, the indemnification obligation under this Article 12 shall not be limited in any way by any limitation on the amount or type of damages, compensation or benefits payable by or for the Subcontractor under worker's or workmen's compensation acts, disability benefit acts or other employee benefit acts.

12.3 ARCHITECT EXCLUSION. The obligations of the Subcontractor under this Article 12 shall not extend to the liability of the Architect, its agents or employees, arising out of (a) the preparation or approval of maps, drawings, opinions, reports, surveys, Change Orders, designs or specifications, or (b) the giving of or the failure to give directions or instructions by the Architect, its agents or employees provided such giving or failure to give is the primary cause of the injury or damage.

12.4 COMPLIANCE WITH LAWS. The Subcontractor agrees to be bound by, and at its own cost, comply with all federal, state and local laws, ordinances and regulations (hereinafter collectively referred to as "laws") applicable to the Subcontractor's Work including, but not limited to, equal employment opportunity, minority business enterprise, women's business enterprise, disadvantaged business enterprise, safety and all other laws with which the Contractor must comply according to the Contract Documents.

The Subcontractor shall be liable to the Contractor and the Owner for all loss, cost and expense attributable to any acts of commission or omission by the Subcontractor, its employees and agents resulting from the failure to comply therewith, including, but not limited to, any fines, penalties or corrective measures.

12.5 PATENTS. Except as otherwise provided by the Contract Documents, the Subcontractor shall pay all royalties and license fees which may be due on the inclusion of any patented materials in the Subcontractor's Work. The Subcontractor shall defend all suits for claims for infringement of any patent rights arising out of the Subcontractor's Work, which may be brought against the Contractor or Owner, and shall be liable to the Contractor and Owner for all loss, including all costs, expenses, and attorney's fees.

ARTICLE 13

INSURANCE

13.1 SUBCONTRACTOR'S INSURANCE. Prior to start of the Subcontractor's Work, the Subcontractor shall procure for the Subcontractor's Work and maintain in force Worker's Compensation Insurance, Employer's Liability Insurance, Comprehensive General Liability Insurance and all insurance required of the Contractor under the Contract Documents except as follows:

The Contractor, Owner and Architect shall be named as additional insureds on each of these policies except for Worker's Compensation.

This insurance shall include contractual liability insurance covering the Subcontractor's obligations under Article 12.

266 SUBCONTRACTS

13.2 MINIMUM LIMITS OF LIABILITY. The Subcontractor's Comprehensive General and Automobile Liability Insurance, as required by Article 13.1, shall be written with limits of liability not less than the following:

A. Comprehensive General Liability including completed operations

    1. Bodily Injury $_____ Each Occurrence

                        $_____ Aggregate

    2. Property Damage $_____ Each Occurrence

                        $_____ Aggregate

B. Comprehensive Automobile Liability

    1. Bodily Injury $_____ Each Person

                        $_____ Each Occurrence

    2. Property Damage $_____ Each Occurrence

13.3 NUMBER OF POLICIES. Comprehensive General Liability Insurance and other liability insurance may be arranged under a single policy for the full limits required or by a combination of underlying policies with the balance provided by an Excess or Umbrella Liability Policy.

13.4 CANCELLATION, RENEWAL OR MODIFICATION. The Subcontractor shall maintain in effect all insurance coverage required under this Agreement at the Subcontractor's sole expense and with insurance companies acceptable to the Contractor.

All insurance policies shall contain a provision that the coverages afforded thereunder shall not be cancelled or not renewed, nor restrictive modifications added, until at least thirty (30) days prior written notice has been given to the Contractor unless otherwise specifically required in the Contract Documents.

Certificates of Insurance, or certified copies of policies acceptable to the Contractor shall be filed with the Contractor prior to the commencement of the Subcontractor's Work.

In the event the Subcontractor fails to obtain or maintain any insurance coverage required under this Agreement, the Contractor may purchase such coverage and charge the expense thereof to the Subcontractor, or terminate this Agreement.

13.5 WAIVER OF RIGHTS. The Contractor and Subcontractor waive all rights against each other and the Owner, the Architect, separate contractors, and all other subcontractors for loss or damage to the extent covered by Builder's Risk or any other property or equipment insurance, except such rights as they may have to the proceeds of such insurance; provided, however, that such waiver shall not extend to the acts of the Architect listed in Article 12.3.

Upon written request of the Subcontractor, the Contractor shall provide the Subcontractor with a copy of the Builder's Risk policy of insurance or any other property or equipment insurance in force for the Project and procured by the Contractor. The Subcontractor shall satisfy itself as to the existence and extent of such insurance prior to commencement of the Subcontractor's Work.

If the Owner or Contractor have not purchased Builder's Risk insurance for the full insurable value of the Subcontractor's Work less a reasonable deductible, then Subcontractor may procure such insurance as will protect the interests of the Subcontractor, its subcontractors and their subcontractors in the Work, and, by appropriate Subcontract Change Order, the cost of such additional insurance shall be reimbursed to the Subcontractor.

If not covered under the Builder's Risk policy of insurance or any other property or equipment insurance required by the Contract Documents, the Subcontractor shall procure and maintain at the Subcontractor's own expense property and equipment insurance for portions of the Subcontractor's Work stored off the site or in transit, when such portions of the Subcontractor's Work are to be included in an application for payment under Article 5.

13.6 ENDORSEMENT. If the policies of insurance referred to in this Article require an endorsement to provide for continued coverage where there is a waiver of subrogation, the owners of such policies will cause them to be so endorsed.

ARTICLE 14

ARBITRATION

14.1 AGREEMENT TO ARBITRATE. All claims, disputes and matters in question arising out of, or relating to, this Agreement or the breach thereof, except for claims which have been waived by the making or acceptance of final payment, and the claims described in Article 14.7, shall be decided by arbitration in accordance with the Construction Industry Arbitration Rules of the American Arbitration Association then in effect unless the parties mutually agree otherwise. This agreement to arbitrate shall be specifically enforceable under the prevailing arbitration law.

14.2 NOTICE OF DEMAND. Notice of the demand for arbitration shall be filed in writing with the other party to this Agreement and with the American Arbitration

Association. The demand for arbitration shall be made within a reasonable time after written notice of the claim, dispute or other matter in question has been given, and in no event shall it be made after the date of final acceptance of the Work by the Owner or when institution of legal or equitable proceedings based on such claim, dispute or other matter in question would be barred by the applicable statute of limitations, whichever shall first occur. The location of the arbitration proceedings shall be the city of the Contractor's headquarters or _____

_____
_____.

14.3 AWARD. The award rendered by the arbitrator(s) shall be final and judgment may be entered upon it in accordance with applicable law in any court having jurisdiction.

14.4 WORK CONTINUATION AND PAYMENT. Unless otherwise agreed in writing, the Subcontractor shall carry on the Work and maintain the Schedule of Work pending arbitration, and, if so, the Contractor shall continue to make payments in accordance with this Agreement.

14.5 NO LIMITATION OF RIGHTS OR REMEDIES. Nothing in this Article shall limit any rights or remedies not expressly waived by the Subcontractor which the Subcontractor may have under lien laws or payment bonds.

14.6 SAME ARBITRATORS. To the extent not prohibited by their contracts with others, the claims and disputes of the Owner, Contractor, Subcontractor and other subcontractors involving a common question of fact or law shall be heard by the same arbitrator(s) in a single proceeding.

14.7 EXCEPTIONS. This agreement to arbitrate shall not apply to any claim:
(a) of contribution or indemnity asserted by one party to this Agreement against the other party and arising out of an action brought in a state or federal court or in arbitration by a person who is under no obligation to arbitrate the subject matter of such action with either of the parties hereto; or does not consent to such arbitration; or
(b) asserted by the Subcontractor against the Contractor if the Contractor asserts said claim, either in whole or part, against the Owner and the contract between the Contractor and Owner does not provide for binding arbitration, or does so provide but the two arbitration proceedings are not consolidated, or the Contractor and Owner have not subsequently agreed to arbitrate said claim, in either case of which the parties hereto shall so notify each other either before or after demand for arbitration is made.

In any dispute arising over the application of this Article 14.7, the question of arbitrability shall be decided by the appropriate court and not by arbitration.

ARTICLE 15

CONTRACT INTERPRETATION

15.1 INCONSISTENCIES AND OMISSIONS. Should inconsistencies or omissions appear in the Contract Documents, it shall be the duty of the Subcontractor to so notify the Contractor in writing within three (3) working days of the Subcontractor's discovery thereof. Upon receipt of said notice, the Contractor shall instruct the Subcontractor as to the measures to be taken and the Subcontractor shall comply with the Contractor's instructions.

15.2 LAW AND EFFECT. This Agreement shall be governed by the law of the state of _____

15.3 SEVERABILITY AND WAIVER. The partial or complete invalidity of any one or more provisions of this Agreement shall not affect the validity or continuing force and effect of any other provision. The failure of either party hereto to insist, in any one or more instances, upon the performance of any of the terms, covenants or conditions of this Agreement, or to exercise any right herein, shall not be construed as a waiver or relinquishment of such term, covenant, condition or right as respects further performance.

15.4 ATTORNEY'S FEES. Should either party employ an attorney to institute suit or demand arbitration to enforce any of the provisions hereof, to protect its interest in any matter arising under this Agreement, or to collect damages for the breach of the Agreement or to recover on a surety bond given by a party under this Agreement, the prevailing party shall be entitled to recover reasonable attorney's fees, costs, charges, and expenses expended or incurred therein.

15.5 TITLES. The titles given to the Articles of this Agreement are for ease of reference only and shall not be relied upon or cited for any other purpose.

15.6 ENTIRE AGREEMENT. This Agreement is solely for the benefit of the signatories hereto and represents the entire and integrated agreement between the parties hereto and supercedes all prior negotiations, representations, or agreements, either written or oral.

ARTICLE 16
SPECIAL PROVISIONS

16.1 PRECEDENCE. It is understood the work to be performed under this Agreement, including the terms and conditions thereof, is as described in Articles 1 thru 16 herein together with the following Special Provisions, which are intended to complement same. However, in the event of any inconsistency, these Special Provisions shall govern.

16.2 SCOPE OF WORK. All work necessary or incidental to complete the _____
_____
_____
_____
Work for the Project in strict accordance with the Contract Documents and as more particularly, though not exclusively, specified in: _____
_____
_____
_____
_____
_____
with the following additions or deletions:

16.3 COMMON TEMPORARY SERVICES. The following "Project" common temporary services and/or facilities are for use of all project personnel and shall be furnished as herein below noted:

By this subcontractor;

By others;

16.4 OTHER SPECIAL PROVISIONS. (Insert here any special provisions required by this subcontract.)

16.5 CONTRACT DOCUMENTS. (List applicable contract documents including specifications, drawings, addenda, modifications and exercised alternates. Identify with general description, sheet numbers and latest date including revisions.)

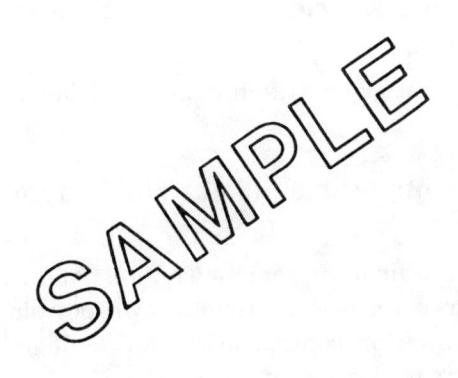

IN WITNESS WHEREOF, the parties hereto have executed this Agreement under seal, the day and year first above written.

_____ _____
Subcontractor   Contractor

By _____ By _____
   (Title)   (Title)

AGC DOCUMENT NO. 600 • SUBCONTRACT FOR BUILDING CONSTRUCTION • August 1984 15
©Associated General Contractors of America

§6.08 Comment: Article 3.2. Schedule

This paragraph contains a seldom-enunciated provision that both the contractor and the subcontractor are bound by the schedule of the work.

§6.09 Comment: Article 5.2.2 Retainage/Security

The prime contractor may retain more from the subcontractor than the owner does from the prime contractor unless subcontractor posts a bond.

§6.10 Comment: Article 5.3. Claims Relating to Contractor

Subcontractor must given written notice of claims within five days.

§6.11 Comment: Article 5.3.4. Final Payment Delay

If the owner delays final payment for a reason not the fault of subcontractor, the contractor may nevertheless withhold payment from subcontractor. At the expense of subcontractor, contractor will pursue litigation against the owner for subcontractor's final payment.

§6.12 Comment: Article 12.1. Indemnification

The parenthetical phrase "(other than Subcontractor's work itself.)" should be stricken. In the first place, subcontractor should indemnify against claims made against contractor or owner for property damage, whether the property damage is to the subcontractor's work or not. In the second place, if subcontractor is required to provide such indemnity, then subcontractor's insurance company (under comprehensive general liability insurance coverage) may likewise be required to provide such indemnity. Some liability policies are worded and construed by the courts so as not to provide coverage for damage to work performed by the named insured; but some policies are not so worded, and in some instances the courts have held that damage to the work of the named insured is covered in spite of exclusionary language.

§6.13 Comment: Article 13.5. Waiver of Rights

This Article requires the subcontractor to make a sophisticated analysis of the owner's builder's risk insurance to determine whether it, the subcontractor, in turn, should purchase supplementary insurance.

AGC Document No. 603 - Subcontract (Short Form)

§6.14 General Comments

The following form, being short, does not give as many advantages to the prime contractor as is the usual case when a longer form is used.

FORM 6-7 AGC Document No. 603 - Subcontract (Short Form) (1987)

THE ASSOCIATED GENERAL CONTRACTORS OF AMERICA

SUBCONTRACT (SHORT FORM)

TABLE OF ARTICLES

1. CONTRACT PAYMENT
2. SCOPE OF WORK
3. SCHEDULE OF WORK
4. CHANGES
5. FAILURE OF PERFORMANCE
6. INSURANCE
7. INDEMNIFICATION
8. WARRANTY
9. SPECIAL PROVISIONS

This document conforms to the high standards for AGC documents and is recommended for use only where the covered work is of small dollar amount and will be completed within a relatively short period of time. For all other work, AGC recommends its comprehensive *Subcontract for Building Construction* (AGC-600).

This document has important legal and insurance consequences. AGC encourages consultation with an attorney and insurance consultant when completing or modifying this document.

AGC DOCUMENT NO. 603 • SUBCONTRACT (SHORT FORM) • 1987   MASTER INDEX NO. 1-1-0-37.4
© Copyright 1987, The Associated General Contractors of America

Special Instructions

AGREEMENT: In the Agreement section above Article 1, the first blanks should be filled in with the current day, month, and year. The second set of date blanks should be filled in with the day, month, and year when the subcontract is to become effective. Both sets of blanks should be filled in, even if the two dates are identical, so there is no confusion over what the parties intend with respect to the effective date.

The legal name of the contractor firm should be filled in the blank before "(Contractor)," and the legal name of the subcontractor firm in the following blank.

After "Project," fill in the name and address of the project where the subcontract work will be performed. After "Owner," fill in the owner's legal business name and address. Similarly, after "Architect," "Contractor," and "Subcontractor," fill in the names of the business firms, the firms' addresses, and the telephone numbers.

ARTICLE 1: Fill in the dollar amount in words in the blank before the word "Dollars." Use numbers to fill in the same amount after the "$" in parentheses. The rate of retainage should be filled in in numbers before the "%" symbol on the next line.

ARTICLE 2: Fill in the first blank with the general term for the work to be performed (for example, roofing or mechanical work). In the second blank, fill in the titles of specific documents containing the description.

ARTICLE 9: Insert any other special requirements agreed to by the parties. For example: bonds furnished by subcontractor; liquidated damages; governmental authority requirements; termination provisions; project work conditions or labor relations; dispute resolution procedures (including attorneys fee provisions); time limits; lien waivers; payment affidavits; or insurance requirements.

SIGNATURES: The top-level lines should be filled in with the legal names of the contractor and subcontractor business firms. The second-level lines should be filled in with the signatures of the persons representing each firm, with each person's name and business title typed or printed below the signature line. The subcontractor's federal tax identification number should be typed or printed in numbers on the last line.

§6.14 AGC DOCUMENT NO. 603   275

JOB NO.: _____   ACCOUNT CODE: _____

DATE: _____

SUBCONTRACT
(SHORT FORM)

This agreement is made this _____ day of _____ 19 ____, and effective the _____ day of _____ 19 ____, by and between _____ (Contractor) and _____ (Subcontractor) to perform the Work identified in Article 2 in accordance with the Project's Contract Documents.

PROJECT:
OWNER:
ARCHITECT:
CONTRACTOR:
SUBCONTRACTOR:

ARTICLE 1

CONTRACT PAYMENT. The Contractor agrees to pay Subcontractor for satisfactory performance of Subcontractor's Work the sum of _____ Dollars ($ _____).

Progress payments, less retainage of _____ %, shall be made to Subcontractor for Work satisfactorily performed no later than seven (7) days after receipt by Contractor of payment from Owner for Subcontractor's Work. Final payment of the balance due shall be made to Subcontractor no later than seven (7) days after receipt by Contractor of final payment from Owner for Subcontractor's Work. These payments are subject to receipt of such lien waivers, affidavits, warranties and guarantees required by the Contract Documents or Contractor.

ARTICLE 2

SCOPE OF WORK. Subcontractor agrees to commence Subcontractor's Work herein described upon notification by Contractor, and to perform and complete such Work in accordance with Contract Documents and under the general direction of Contractor in accord with Contractor's schedule. This shall include all work necessary or incidental to complete the:

_____

Work for the Project as more particularly, though not exclusively specified in _____

_____

_____

ARTICLE 3

SCHEDULE OF WORK. Time is of the essence. Subcontractor shall provide Contractor with any requested scheduling information of Subcontractor's Work. The Schedule of Work, including that of this Subcontract shall be prepared by Contractor and may be revised as the Work progresses.

Subcontractor recognizes that changes may be made in the Schedule of Work and agrees to comply with such changes without additional compensation.

Subcontractor shall coordinate its work with all other contractors, subcontractors, and suppliers on the Project so as not to delay or damage their performance, work, or the Project.

ARTICLE 4

CHANGES. Contractor, without nullifying this Agreement, may direct Subcontractor in writing to make changes to Subcontractor's Work. Adjustment, if any, in the contract price or contract time resulting from such changes shall be set forth in a Subcontract Change Order pursuant to the Contract Documents.

ARTICLE 5

FAILURE OF PERFORMANCE. Should Subcontractor fail to satisfy contractual deficiencies within three (3) working days from receipt of Contractor's written notice, then the Contractor, without prejudice to any right or remedies, shall have the right to take whatever steps it deems necessary to correct said deficiencies and charge the cost thereof to Subcontractor, who shall be liable for payment of same, including reasonable overhead, profit and attorneys fees.

ARTICLE 6

INSURANCE. Prior to the start of Subcontractor's Work, Subcontractor shall procure and maintain in force for the duration of the Work, Worker's Compensation Insurance, Employer's Liability Insurance, Comprehensive General Liability Insurance and all insurance required of Contractor under the Contract Documents. Contractor, Owner and Architect shall be named as additional insureds on each of these policies, except for Worker's Compensation.

ARTICLE 7

INDEMNIFICATION. To the fullest extent permitted by law, Subcontractor shall indemnify and hold harmless Owner, Architect, Architect's consultants, and Contractor from all damages, losses, or expenses, including attorneys fees, from any claims or damages for bodily injury, sickness, disease, or death, or from claims for damage to tangible property, other than the Work itself. This indemnification shall extend to claims resulting from performance of this Subcontract and shall apply only to the extent that the claim or loss is caused in whole or in part by any negligent act or omission of Subcontractor or any of its agents, employees, or subcontractors. This indemnity shall be effective regardless of whether the claim or loss is caused in some part by a party to be indemnified. The obligation of Subcontractor under this Article shall not extend to claims or losses that are primarily caused by the Architect, or Architect's consultant's performance or failure to perform professional responsibilities.

ARTICLE 8

WARRANTY. Subcontractor warrants its work against all deficiencies and defects in materials and/or workmanship and agrees to satisfy same without cost to Owner or Contractor for a period of one (1) year from the date of Substantial Completion of the Project or per Contract Documents, whichever is longer.

ARTICLE 9

SPECIAL PROVISIONS. (Insert any special provisions required by this Subcontract).

In witness whereof, the parties have executed this Agreement under Seal, the day and year first written above.

_____ _____
SUBCONTRACTOR (FIRM NAME)   CONTRACTOR (FIRM NAME)

_____ _____
BY (Type or print signer's name and title)   BY (Type or print signer's name and title)

Subcontractor's Federal Tax ID Number _____

© Copyright 1987 Associated General Contractors of America (AGC No. 603)

AGC Standard Form 605 - Standard Subbid Proposal

§6.15 General Comments

This form has been developed by the AGC along with several national subcontractor associations, including NECA and SMACCNA.

The use of such a standard proposal form should be encouraged, because its use will help to eliminate potential disputes and misunderstandings in work that is bid competitively.

Most subcontractors would prefer to deliver bids by telephone, and within the last half hour before bid opening time, to avoid bid shopping by the general contractor. In such a case, the actual amount of the bid can be left blank, but the subcontractor can submit the printed form in advance because the information on the printed form is not of a confidential nature.

The form has the virtue of making clear what addenda are taken into account for the bid, and of providing that the subcontractor is responsible for all work not specifically excluded.

FORM 6-8 AGC Standard Form 605 - Standard Subbid Proposal

STANDARD SUBBID PROPOSAL

(Developed as a guide by The Associated General Contractors of America, The National Electrical Contractors Association, The Mechanical Contractors Association of America. The Sheet Metal and Air Conditioning Contractors National Association and The National Association of Plumbing-Heating-Cooling Contractors.)

SUBCONTRACTOR _____ Project _____

Address _____ Location _____

_____ _____

GENERAL CONTRACTOR _____ A&E _____

Address _____

_____ Bid Time & Date _____

_____ Subbid Time & Date _____

Type of work (including specification sections) _____

(List the category(ies) this proposal will cover, such as plumbing, heating, air conditioning and ventilation, electrical and elevators.)

This proposal includes furnishing all materials and performing all work in the category(ies) listed above, as required by the plans, specifications, general and special conditions and addenda _____,

(Here list addenda by number)

Identify work to be **excluded** by specification paragraph otherwise the subcontractor will be responsible for all work in the above category(ies) required by the specifications and plans.

If this proposal, including prices, is accepted, the subcontractor agrees to enter into a subcontract and, if required, furnish performance and payment bonds from _____

(Name of surety company or agency)

guaranteeing full performance of the work and payment of all costs incident thereto. The cost of the bond is **not** included in this proposal.

This proposal will remain in effect and will not be withdrawn by the subcontractor for a period of 30 days or for the same period of time required by the contract documents for the general contractor in regard to the prime bid, plus 15 days, whichever period is longer.

Subcontractor _____

By _____ (Title)

BASE BID _____

ALTERNATES

	Add	Deduct
1.	$	$
2.	$	$
3.	$	$
4.	$	$
5.	$	$
6.	$	$
7.	$	$
8.	$	$

AGC STANDARD FORM 605

Design-Build Subcontracts 7

Introduction to Design-Build Subcontracts

§7.01 General Comments

AGC Document No. 450 - Standard Design-Build Subcontract - Subcontractor Not Providing Design

§7.02 General Comments
      FORM 7-1   AGC Document No. 450 - Standard Design-Build Subcontract Agreement with Subcontractor Not Providing Design (1983)

AGC Document No. 450-1 - Standard Design-Build Subcontract - Subcontractor Providing Design

§7.03 General Comments
      FORM 7-2   AGC Document No. 450-1 - Standard Design-Build Agreement with Subcontractor Providing Design (1983)

AGC Document No. 430 - Conditions between Contractor and Subcontractor for Design-Build

§7.04 General Comments
      FORM 7-3   AGC Document No. 430 - Conditions between Contractor and Subcontractor for Design-Build (1982)

Revisions to AGC Document No. 430

§7.05 General Comments
      FORM 7-4   Revisions to AGC Document 430 (with Comments)

Introduction to Design-Build Subcontracts

§7.01 General Comments

An examination of the AGC forms of **Design-Build Subcontract** gives us an opportunity to consider two more variations on the theme of cost-effective construction technique. Ingenious parties may mix and match the elements of fixed price, cost plus, guaranteed maximum price, construction management, conventional contracting, conventional subcontracting, and design-build subcontracting to adopt the formula that is most suitable to particular circumstances.

As is discussed at length in **§2.04,** a design-build contract enables the owner to take advantage of a contractor's knowledge of currently cost-effective construction materials, equipment, systems and techniques. The owner also secures the advantage of a **single point of responsibility.** The contractor who employs the architect/engineer has no legal right to complain to the owner of defective drawings and specifications, whether the defects are real or partly imagined.

In contrast, the construction management philosophy reflected in AGC Document No. 500 (**FORM 3-1**) involves the contractor in the project design phase, yet the architect/engineer, acting on behalf of the owner, retains overall responsibility for design.

A true design-build subcontract imposes on a subcontractor the responsibility for design of the systems to be installed by the subcontractor. A design-build subcontract may be used either in conjunction with a design-build prime contract, or as an element in a conventional construction program in which the architect/engineer retains ultimate responsibility for design. More commonly, though, the design-build subcontract is a part of a program in which the prime contractor also assumes design-build responsibility.

Of the two AGC Design-Build Subcontract forms displayed in this chapter, one is a conventional subcontract to be used when the prime contractor has assumed design-build responsibility (AGC Document No. 450), and the other is a true design-build subcontract in which the subcontractor takes responsibility for the design of its portion of the work (AGC Document 450-1).

The maximum advantages of the design-build philosophy will be attained by the owner who employs a design-build contractor, who in turn employs design-build subcontractors. Perhaps the greatest efficiencies and economies that can be realized through the employment of design-build are those associated with sub-trades. Construction systems, equipment and techniques evolve rapidly. The first to deal with them are the subcontractors who devote their professional lives to the mastery of their trades.

It stands to reason that it would be difficult for an owner to assemble a combination of architects, engineers, and consultants to design a project who would have such intimate knowledge of all the specialties and trades involved in the project as to equal the combined knowledge of the specialty contractors within their own areas of expertise.

One who might wish to take a casual look at the specialized nature of construction knowledge could thumb through a book of ASTM's (American Society for Testing and Materials), which are published in multiple volumes that resemble New York telephone books. To master all the scientific and technical knowledge associated with the subject of concrete alone would require a lifetime of professional study. Roofing, waterproofing, stone masonry, glazing, caulking, soils engineering, excavation, compaction, structural steel, and tile setting all have their secrets and complexities that can be fully understood only after a professional lifetime of ardent study and practice.

This fact is attested by the very existence of shop drawings. Theoretically, an architect working with consulting specialists and engineers should be able to draw and specify every element of a construction project in perfect detail, leaving no need for interpretation and no room for misinterpretation. (In reality, the only way to do this would be to build a full size model: but then the project would be finished!) It is because of the inability of architects and engineers to master all small details of the various specialties and trades that shop drawings are required. Who prepares them? The trade contractors. Therefore, every subcontract that requires shop drawings is, to that degree, a design-build subcontract.

The owner must recognize and guard against potential disadvantages of the design-build subcontract that can occur because the owner, and perhaps the design-build prime contractor, may unknowingly accept elements proposed by the design-build subcontractor which cheapen the job in ways that do not advance the interests of the owner. The best protection against this eventuality is also the best protection against everything else that might go wrong on a construction project: the employment of only experienced and reputable persons and companies.

AGC Document No. 450 - Standard Design-Build Subcontract - Subcontractor Not Providing Design

§7.02 General Comments

The nomenclature of this form is inept because it is not truly a design-build subcontract, but a conventional subcontract form to be employed by a design-build contractor.

The great advantages of design-build are efficiency and economy: efficiency because the design employed will likely be a familiar one that experience shows can be installed without difficulties, conflicts, or delays; economy because the selected design can be installed efficiently.

The greatest danger of inefficiency, delay, and cost overrun occurs within the sub-trades. Therefore, the greater advantages of the design-build philosophy may be attained by the employment of design-build subcontractors.

Thus, it is to be assumed that in most cases, where the design-build philosophy is employed, Document No. 450-1, rather than Document No. 450, will be used.

282 DESIGN-BUILD SUBCONTRACTS

Document No. 450 is little more than a vehicle to identify the project and the contract documents and provide a location at which the parties may place their signatures. AGC Document No. 430 is incorporated into the subcontract, whether attached or not. The form includes a requirement that the subcontractor follow the project schedule and a perfunctory injunction against unapproved extras, but the real meat is in Document No. 430.

FORM 7-1 AGC Document No. 450 - Standard Design-Build Subcontract Agreement with Subcontractor Not Providing Design (1983)

AIA copyrighted material has been reproduced with the permission of the American Institute of Architects under license number 90153. Permission expires December 31, 1991.

This document is intended for use as a "consumable" (consumables are further defined by Senate Report 94-473 on the Copyright Act of 1976). This document is not intended to be used as "model language" (language taken from an existing document and incorporated, without attribution, into a newly-created document). Rather, it is a standard form which is intended to be modified by appending separate amendment sheets and/or fill in provided blank spaces.

DESIGN-BUILD SUBCONTRACTS

THE ASSOCIATED GENERAL CONTRACTORS

STANDARD DESIGN-BUILD SUBCONTRACT AGREEMENT WITH SUBCONTRACTOR NOT PROVIDING DESIGN

This Document shall be used in conjunction with AGC Document 430 — Conditions Between Contractor and Subcontractor for Design-Build.

This Agreement made at _____
this _____ day of _____, 19___, by and between _____,
hereinafter referred to as the Contractor, and _____, hereinafter referred to as the
Subcontractor, to perform part of the Work on the following Project:

PROJECT:

OWNER:

Certain provisions of this document have been derived, with modifications, from the following document published by The American Institute of Architects: AIA Document A201, General Conditions, © 1976. Usage of AIA language, with the permission of AIA, does not imply AIA endorsement or approval of this document. Further reproduction of copyrighted AIA materials without separate written permission from AIA is prohibited.

AGC DOCUMENT NO. 460 • STANDARD DESIGN-BUILD SUBCONTRACT AGREEMENT WITH SUBCONTRACTOR PROVIDING DESIGN • January 1983
© 1986, Associated General Contractors of America.

ARTICLE 1
SCOPE OF WORK

1.1 The Contractor employs the Subcontractor as an independent contractor to construct a part of the Project for which the Contractor has contracted with the Owner. The Subcontractor's portion of the Project, hereinafter referred to as the "Work," is set out in Exhibit A attached hereto. The Subcontractor agrees to perform such Work under the general direction of the Contractor and subject to the final approval of the Owner, in accordance with the Subcontract Documents. This Agreement and the Subcontract Documents incorporated herein represent the entire agreement between the parties and supercede all prior negotiations, representations, or agreements.

1.2 The Subcontract Documents, hereinafter referred to as the "Subcontract," include this Agreement, the Conditions Between Contractor and Subcontractor for Design Build [AGC Document 430], and documents set forth therein, all of which are more specifically identified in Exhibit B attached hereto. If any provisions of such documents conflict with the terms of this Agreement, the terms of this Agreement shall control. The Subcontractor binds himself to the Contractor for the performance of Subcontractor's Work in the same manner as the Contractor is bound to the Owner for such performance under Contractor's contract with the Owner.

1.3 In the performance of his Work, Subcontractor will:

.1 Furnish all labor and materials, along with competent supervision, shop drawings and samples, tools, equipment, scaffolding, permits and fees necessary for the construction of the Work; and,

.2 Give all notices and comply with all applicable laws, building codes, ordinances, regulations and orders of any public authority bearing on the design and construction of the Work under this Agreement.

ARTICLE 2
PROJECT SCHEDULE

2.1 Subcontractor will commence, and thereafter prosecute his Work in accordance with the Project Schedule so as not to cause any delays or interference with the completion of the Project or in the obtaining of payments by the Contractor from the Owner or the final acceptance of the Project by the Owner. If the Subcontractor does not commence the Work in accordance with the Project Schedule, or if at any time the Work is not performed in accordance with such schedule, the Subcontractor agrees, upon three (3) days' written notice from the Contractor, to provide the necessary personnel and supply such equipment, materials, overtime work, workers and other devices and facilities as necessary so as to expedite the Work. Such notice, once given, shall continue in effect until the Work specified therein has been fully completed, even though the Subcontractor has initially acted under the notice but has failed to continue to do so until complete performance thereof. Subcontractor shall work overtime, at the direction of Contractor without additional cost to Contractor if such overtime work is necessary to cure delinquency in maintaining the Project Schedule and such delinquency is due to delays by Subcontractor.

ARTICLE 3
CHANGES IN THE WORK

3.1 The Contractor may order changes in the Work consistent with the provisions of the Conditions Between Contractor and Subcontractor for Design-Build and within the general scope of this Agreement, consisting of additions, deletions or other revisions.

3.2 No claims for extra work or changes will be recognized or paid unless prior approval has been obtained in writing from the Contractor.

ARTICLE 4
GENERAL PROVISIONS

4.1 The Work performed under this Agreement is subject to the approval of the Contractor and Owner.

AGC DOCUMENT NO. 450 • STANDARD DESIGN-BUILD SUBCONTRACT AGREEMENT WITH SUBCONTRACTOR NOT PROVIDING DESIGN • January 1983
© 1986, Associated General Contractors of America.

4.2 If the Work, or any portion thereof is not acceptable, the Subcontractor shall be responsible for the cost of remedying unaccepted Work, whether such remedial Work is performed by the Subcontractor or by any other entity at the request of the Contractor or Owner.

ARTICLE 5

CONTRACT SUM AND PAYMENTS

5.1 The Contractor agrees to pay to the Subcontractor for the satisfactory completion of Subcontractor's Work the Contract Sum of _____ ($_____) in monthly payments of _____ percent of the work performed in any preceding month, in accordance with estimates prepared by the Subcontractor and approved by the Contractor. Payment of the approved portion of the Subcontractor's monthly estimate and final payment shall be conditioned upon receipt by the Contractor of his payment from the Owner.

5.2 Subcontractor shall provide with his monthly applications for payment completed lien waivers and affadavits from his subcontractors and suppliers in a form satisfactory to the Owner and Contractor. Approval and payment of Subcontractor's monthly estimate is specifically agreed not to constitute or imply acceptance by the Contractor or Owner of any portion of the Subcontractor's Work. Final payment shall not constitute acceptance of defective work.

5.3 The Subcontractor agrees and covenants that money received for the performance of this Agreement shall be used solely for the benefit of persons and firms supplying labor, materials, supplies, tools machines, equipment, plant or services exclusively for this Project in connection with this Agreement and having the right to assert liens or other claims against the land improvements, or funds involved in this Project or against any bond or other security posted by Contractor or Owner; that any money paid to the Subcontractor pursuant to this Agreement shall immediately become and constitute a trust fund for the benefit of said persons and firms, and shall not in any instance be diverted by the Subcontractor to any other purpose until all obligations and claims arising hereunder have been fully discharged.

5.4 The Contractor may deduct from any amounts due or to become due to the Subcontractor any sum or sums owing by the Subcontractor to the Contractor; and in the event of any breach by the Subcontractor of any provision or obligation of this Subcontract, or in the event of the assertion by other parties of any claim or lien against the Owner, the Contractor, Contractor's Surety, or the premises upon which the Work was performed, which claim or lien arises out of the Subcontractor's performance of this Agreement, the Contractor shall have the right, but is not required, to retain out of any payments due or to become due to the Subcontractor an amount sufficient to completely protect the Contractor from any and all loss, damage, or expense therefrom, until the claim or lien has been adjusted by the Subcontractor to the satisfaction of the Contractor. This paragraph shall be applicable even though the Subcontractor has posted a 100% labor and material payment bond and a performance bond.

5.5 Final payment will be made when the completed project is accepted by the Owner; the Subcontractor has submitted completed lien waivers and affidavits from his subcontractors and suppliers in a form and to the extent required by the Owner and Contractor; and the Contractor has received final payment from the Owner.

ARTICLE 6

INSURANCE

6.1 The Subcontractor shall, within _____ days of signing this Agreement, but before performing any Work, provide the Contractor with certificates of insurance indicating coverage for Comprehensive General Liability, Comprehensive Auto Liability, claims under workers compensation, disability benefit, and other similar employee benefit acts which are applicable to the work to be performed in accordance with the Conditions Between Contractor and Subcontractor for Design-Build [AGC Document 430] for the following limits:

Comprehensive General Liability		Comprehensive Auto	
Bodily Injury	$_____	Bodily Injury	$_____
Property Damage	$_____	Property Damage	$_____
	Workers' Compensation	$ Legal Limit	

AGC DOCUMENT NO. 450 • STANDARD DESIGN BUILD SUBCONTRACT AGREEMENT WITH SUBCONTRACTOR NOT PROVIDING DESIGN • January 1983
© 1986, Associated General Contractors of America.

6.2 The Builders Risk Insurance contains a deductible of $_____. Each insured shall bear his loss within the deductible unless the Contractor's Agreement with the Owner provides that the Owner shall bear any such loss.

ARTICLE 7
MISCELLANEOUS PROVISIONS

7.1 Governing Law: This Agreement shall be governed by the law in effect at the location of the Project.

IN WITNESS WHEREOF the parties hereto have executed this Agreement under seal, the day and year first above written.

_____
SUBCONTRACTOR

By_____

ATTEST:

_____

_____
CONTRACTOR

By_____
(Title)

ATTEST:

_____

EXHIBIT A

The Subcontractor's Work on this Project shall consist of the following portions of the Project:

EXHIBIT B

The Contract Documents include:

1. The Agreement Between the Owner and Contractor dated _____.

2. The General, Special and Supplementary Conditions identified as:

3. The Project Schedule dated _____

4. The following drawings, specifications, and criteria:

5. The Contract Sum includes the following allowances:

AGC Document No. 450-1 - Standard Design-Build Subcontract - Subcontractor Providing Design

§7.03 General Comments

This subcontract is intended to secure the full benefits of the design-build philosophy by employing the subcontractor not only to construct, but also to design, the part of the project consisting of the subcontractor's trade or specialty.

Again, AGC Document No. 430 is incorporated whether it is attached or specially referred to or not.

In Article 1.3 the subcontractor agrees to furnish properly licensed and qualified architects or engineers to perform architectural and engineering services for the design of the subcontractor's portion of the work. One might infer from this language that the subcontractor would go into the market to employ independent architects or engineers. Such is seldom the case. Most subcontractors with design-build capabilities have architects or engineers on their staffs and thus can readily perform, with their own resources, the design requirements of the contract.

In Article 5 the contractor and subcontractor agree on the contract sum and the method of payment. Article 6 provides for placement of a schedule of insurance, including coverage limits and amount of deductible.

The appropriateness of Article 6.3 will require research for a specific subcontractor and a specific insurance market. Errors and omissions coverage may not be available to a design-build subcontractor.

FORM 7-2 AGC Document No. 450-1 - Standard Design-Build Agreement with Subcontractor Providing Design (1983)

AIA copyrighted material has been reproduced with the permission of the American Institute of Architects under license number 90153. Permission expires December 31, 1991.

This document is intended for use as a "consumable" (consumables are further defined by Senate Report 94-473 on the Copyright Act of 1976). This document is not intended to be used as "model language" (language taken from an existing document and incorporated, without attribution, into a newly-created document). Rather, it is a standard form which is intended to be modified by appending separate amendment sheets and/or fill in provided blank spaces.

THE ASSOCIATED GENERAL CONTRACTORS

STANDARD DESIGN-BUILD SUBCONTRACT AGREEMENT WITH SUBCONTRACTOR PROVIDING DESIGN

SAMPLE

This Document shall be used in conjunction with AGC Document 430 — Conditions Between Contractor and Subcontractor for Design Build.

THIS AGREEMENT made at _____ this _____ day of _____, 19____ by and between _____, hereinafter referred to as the Contractor, and _____, hereinafter referred to as the Subcontractor, to perform part of the Work on the following Project:

PROJECT:

OWNER:

Certain provisions of this document have been derived, with modifications, from the following document published by The American Institute of Architects: AIA Document A201, General Conditions, © 1976. Usage of AIA language, with the permission of AIA, does not imply AIA endorsement or approval of this document. Further reproduction of copyrighted AIA materials without separate written permission from AIA is prohibited.

AGC DOCUMENT NO. 450-1 • STANDARD DESIGN-BUILD SUBCONTRACT AGREEMENT WITH SUBCONTRACTOR PROVIDING DESIGN • January 1983
© 1986, Associated General Contractors of America.

ARTICLE 1

SCOPE OF WORK

1.1 The Contractor employs the Subcontractor as an independent contractor, to design and construct a part of the Project for which the Contractor has contracted with the Owner. The Subcontractor's portion of the Project, hereinafter referred to as the "Work," is set out in Exhibit A attached hereto. The Subcontractor agrees to perform such Work under the general direction of the Contractor and subject to the final approval of the Owner, in accordance with the Subcontract Documents. This Agreement and the Subcontract Documents incorporated herein represent the entire agreement between the parties and supercede all prior negotiations, representations, or agreements.

1.2 The Subcontract Documents, hereinafter referred to as the "Subcontract," include this Agreement, the Conditions Between Contractor and Subcontractor for Design-Build [AGC Document 430], and documents set forth therein, all of which are more specifically indentified in Exhibit B attached hereto. If any provisions of such documents conflict with the terms of this Agreement, the terms of this agreement shall control. The Subcontractor binds himself to the Contractor for the performance of Subcontractor's Work in the same manner as the Contractor is bound to the Owner for such performance under Contractor's contract with the Owner.

1.3 In the performance of his Work, Subcontractor will:

.1 Furnish by properly licensed and qualified architects or engineers all necessary professional architectural and engineering design services for the design of the Work;

.2 Furnish all labor and materials, along with competent supervision, shop drawings and samples, tools, equipment, scaffolding permits and fees necessary for the construction of the Work;

.3 Give all notices and comply with all applicable laws, building codes, ordinances, regulations and orders of any public authority bearing on the design and construction of the Work under this Agreement; and,

.4 The Subcontractor shall submit for the Contractor's approval in accordance with the Project Schedule, design development documents, working drawings, specified shop drawings and samples, and data and specifications of materials proposed to be incorporated in the Work. The Subcontractor shall provide copies of approved drawings in the form and quantity specified by the Contractor. Subcontractor shall advise Contractor and other affected trades of all design development changes in a timely manner so as to preclude additional costs and conflicts with work of others on the Project. Subcontractor shall be liable for the extra costs incurred for failure to provide such timely notice.

ARTICLE 2

PROJECT SCHEDULE

2.1 Subcontractor will commence, and thereafter prosecute his Work in accordance with the Project Schedule so as not to cause any delays or interference with the completion of the Project or in the obtaining of payments by the Contractor from the Owner or the final acceptance of the Project by the Owner. If the Subcontractor does not commence the Work in accordance with the Project Schedule, or if at any time the Work is not performed in accordance with such schedule, the Subcontractor agrees, upon three (3) days' written notice from the Contractor, to provide the necessary personnel to complete the design and supply such equipment, materials, overtime work, workers and other devices and facilities as necessary so as to expedite the Work. Such notice, once given, shall continue in effect until the Work specified therein has been fully completed, even though the Subcontractor has initially acted under the notice but has failed to continue to do so until complete performance thereof. Subcontractor shall work overtime, at the direction of Contractor without additional cost to Contractor if such overtime work is necessary to cure delinquency in maintaining the Project Schedule and such delinquency is due to delays by Subcontractor.

ARTICLE 3

CHANGES IN THE WORK

3.1 The Contractor may order changes in the Work consistent with the provisions of the Conditions Between Contractor and Subcontractor for Design-Build and within the general scope of this Agreement, consisting of additions, deletions or other revisions.

294 DESIGN-BUILD SUBCONTRACTS

3.2 No claims for extra work or changes will be recognized or paid unless prior approval has been obtained in writing from the Contractor.

ARTICLE 4

GENERAL PROVISIONS

4.1 The Work performed under this Agreement is subject to the approval of the Contractor and Owner.

4.2 If the Work, or any portion thereof is not acceptable, the Subcontractor shall be responsible for the cost of remedying unaccepted Work, whether such remedial Work is performed by the Subcontractor or by any other entity at the request of the Contractor or Owner.

ARTICLE 5

CONTRACT SUM AND PAYMENTS

5.1 The Contractor agrees to pay to the Subcontractor for the satisfactory completion of Subcontractor's Work the Contract Sum of _____ ($_____) in monthly payments of _____ percent of the work performed in any preceding month, in accordance with estimates prepared by the Subcontractor and approved by the Contractor. Payment of the approved portion of the Subcontractor's monthly estimate and final payment shall be conditioned upon receipt by the Contractor of his payment from the Owner.

5.2 Subcontractor shall provide with his monthly applications for payment completed lien waivers and affidavits from his subcontractors and suppliers in a form satisfactory to the Owner and Contractor. Approval and payment of Subcontractor's monthly estimate is specifically agreed not to consititute or imply acceptance by the Contractor or Owner of any portion of the Subcontractor's Work. Final payment shall not constitute acceptance of defective work.

5.3 The Subcontractor agrees and covenants that money reserved for the performance of this Agreement shall be used solely for the benefit of persons and firms supplying labor, materials, supplies, tools machines, equipment, plant or services exclusively for this Project in connection with this Agreement and having the right to assert liens or other claims against the land improvements, or funds involved in this Project or against any bond or other security posted by Contractor or Owner; that any money paid to the Subcontractor pursuant to this Agreement shall immediately become and constitute a trust fund for the benefit of said persons and firms, and shall not in any instance be diverted by the Subcontractor to any other purpose until all obligations and claims arising hereunder have been fully discharged.

5.4 The Contractor may deduct from any amounts due or to become due to the Subcontractor any sum or sums owing by the Subcontractor to the Contractor; and in the event of any breach by the Subcontractor of any provision or obligation of this Subcontract, or in the event of the assertion by other parties of any claim or lien against the Owner, the Contractor, Contractor's Surety, or the premises upon which the Work was performed, which claim or lien arises out of the Subcontractor's performance of this Agreement, the Contractor shall have the right, but is not required, to retain out of any payments due or to become due to the Subcontractor an amount sufficient to completely protect the Contractor from any and all loss, damage, or expense therefrom, until the claim or lien has been adjusted by the Subcontractor to the satisfaction of the Contractor. This paragraph shall be applicable even though the Subcontractor has posted a 100% labor and material payment bond and a performance bond.

5.5 Final payment will be made when the completed project is accepted by the Owner; the Subcontractor has submitted completed lien waivers and affidavits from his subcontractors and suppliers in a form and to the extent required by the Owner and Contractor; and the Contractor has received final payment from the Owner.

ARTICLE 6
INSURANCE

6.1 The Subcontractor shall, within _____ days of signing this Agreement, but before performing any Work, provide the Contractor with certificates of insurance indicating coverage for Comprehensive General Liability, Comprehensive Auto Liability, claims under Workers compensation, disability benefit, and other similar employee benefit acts which are applicable to the work to be performed in accordance with the Conditions Between Contractor and Subcontractor for Design-Build [AGC Document 430] for the following limits:

Comprehensive General Liability		Comprehensive Auto	
Bodily Injury	$_____	Bodily Injury	$_____
Property Damage	$_____	Property Damage	$_____

Workers' Compensation $ Legal Limit

6.2 The Builders Risk Insurance contains a deductible of $_____. Each insured shall bear his loss within the deductible unless the Contractor's Agreement with the Owner provides that the Owner shall bear any such loss.

6.3 The Subcontractor shall, within _____ days of the same time period, furnish a certificate of insurance in the amount of $_____ to protect himself and the Contractor from claims arising out of the performance of professional services caused by any errors, omissions, or negligent acts for which he is legally liable.

ARTICLE 7
MISCELLANEOUS PROVISIONS

7.1 Governing Law: This Agreement shall be governed by the law in effect at the location of the Project.

IN WITNESS WHEREOF the parties hereto have executed this Agreement under seal, the day and year first above written.

```
                                        _____
                                        SUBCONTRACTOR
                                        By_____
                                                      (Title)
ATTEST:
_____

                                        _____
                                        CONTRACTOR
                                        By_____
                                                      (Title)
ATTEST:
_____
```

EXHIBIT A

The Subcontractor's Work on this Project shall consist of the following portions of the Project:

EXHIBIT B

The Contract Documents include:

1. The Agreement Between the Owner and Contractor dated _____.

2. The General, Special and Supplementary Conditions identified as:

3. The Project Schedule dated _____

4. The following drawings, specifications, and criteria:

5. The Contract Sum includes the following allowances:

AGC Document No. 430 - Conditions between Contractor and Subcontractor for Design-Build

§7.04 General Comments

As may be properly assumed with all AGC documents, No. 430 adequately provides for the protection of the contractor's interests. Therefore, the contractor or practitioner who is motivated to protect the interests of the subcontractor will wish to refer to **FORM 7-4** for clauses appropriate to that purpose.

As with other AGC documents, this author apprehends that difficulties may be encountered in the event of damage to or destruction of the work, and in the event of defective construction by the subcontractor, unless the liability and property insurance provisions of Document No. 430 are revised.

FORM 7-3 AGC Document No. 430 - Conditions between Contractor and Subcontractor for Design-Build (1982)

AIA copyrighted material has been reproduced with the permission of the American Institute of Architects under license number 90153. Permission expires December 31, 1991.

This document is intended for use as a "consumable" (consumables are further defined by Senate Report 94-473 on the Copyright Act of 1976). This document is not intended to be used as "model language" (language taken from an existing document and incorporated, without attribution, into a newly-created document). Rather, it is a standard form which is intended to be modified by appending separate amendment sheets and/or fill in provided blank spaces.

DESIGN-BUILD SUBCONTRACTS

THE ASSOCIATED GENERAL CONTRACTORS

CONDITIONS BETWEEN CONTRACTOR AND SUBCONTRACTOR FOR DESIGN-BUILD

INSTRUCTIONS FOR CONTRACTOR

1. This document is intended to be used with AGC Document No. 450, Standard Design-Build Subcontract Agreement With Subcontractor Not Providing Design, or AGC Document No. 450-1, Standard Design-Build Subcontract Agreement With Subcontractor Providing Design, as the Conditions Between the Contractor and Subcontractor. These conditions govern the obligations of the Subcontractors and in addition establish the general procedures for the administration of construction. These Conditions Between Contractor and Subcontractor differ from those in AGC Form No. 410, Standard Form of Design-Build Agreement and General Conditions Between Owner and Contractor.

2. In all cases your attorney should be consulted to advise you on their use and any modifications.

3. Nothing contained herein is intended to conflict with local, state or federal laws or regulations.

4. It is recommended all insurance matters be reviewed with your insurance consultant and carrier such as implications of errors and omission liability, completed operations, and waiver of subrogation.

5. Each article should be reviewed by the Contractor as to the applicability to a given project and contractual conditions.

6. Special conditions and terms for the project or the subcontracts should cover the following:

   — subcontractor retainages
   — payment schedules
   — insurance limits
   — builder's risk deductible, if any.

7. If the Owner does not provide Builder's Risk Insurance, Paragraph 12.2 will need to be modified.

Certain provisions of this document have been derived, with modifications, from the following document published by The American Institute of Architects: AIA Document A201, General Conditions, © 1976 Usage of AIA language, with the permission of AIA, does not apply AIA endorsement or approval of this document. Further reproduction of copyrighted AIA materials without separate written permission from AIA is prohibited.

AGC DOCUMENT NO. 430 • CONDITIONS BETWEEN CONTRACTOR AND SUBCONTRACTOR FOR DESIGN-BUILD • January 1982
Associated General Contractors of America

THE ASSOCIATED GENERAL CONTRACTORS

CONDITIONS BETWEEN CONTRACTOR AND SUBCONTRACTOR FOR DESIGN-BUILD

TABLE OF CONTENTS

ARTICLES	PAGE
1 Contract Documents	1
2 Owner	2
3 Architect/Engineer	2
4 Contractor	3
5 Subcontractors	4
6 Sub-Subcontractors	8
7 Separate Subcontracts	8
8 Miscellaneous Provisions	9
9 Time	11
10 Payments and Completion	12
11 Protection of Persons and Property	14
12 Insurance	15
13 Changes in the Work	17
14 Uncovering and Correction of Work	18
15 Termination of the Contract	19

Certain provisions of this document have been derived, with modifications, from the following document published by The American Institute of Architects: AIA Document A201, General Conditions. ©1976 Usage of AIA language, with the permission of AIA, does not apply AIA endorsement or approval of this document. Further reproduction of copyrighted AIA materials without separate written permission from AIA is prohibited.

AGC DOCUMENT NO. 430 • CONDITIONS BETWEEN CONTRACTOR AND SUBCONTRACTOR FOR DESIGN-BUILD • January 1982
Associated General Contractors of America

ARTICLE 1
CONTRACT DOCUMENTS

1.1 DEFINITIONS

1.1.1 THE CONTRACT DOCUMENTS

The Subcontract Documents(hereinafter referred to as the Subcontract) consist of the Contract between the Contractor and the Subcontractor, the Subcontract Conditions (including any Supplementary Conditions), the Drawings (and Criteria if the drawings are not complete), the Specifications, all Addenda issued prior to execution of the Contract, and all Modifications issued after the execution of the contract. A Modification is (1) a written amendment to the Contract signed by both parties, (2) a written interpretation issued by the Architect/Engineer pursuant to Subparagraph 3.2.2; or (3) a written order for a minor change in the Work issued on the Owner's behalf pursuant to Subparagraph 13.4. In addition, the Subcontractor assumes toward the Contractor all the obligations and responsibilities which the Contractor assumes toward the Owner under the Agreement between the Owner and the Contractor. A copy of the pertinent parts of the Agreement will be made available on request. The Contract Documents do not include Bidding or Proposal Documents such as the Advertisement or Invitation To Bid, Requests for Proposals, sample forms, Subcontractors Bid or Proposal, or portions of Addenda relative to any of these, or any other documents other than those set forth in this subparagraph unless specifically set forth in the Agreement with the Subcontractor.

1.1.2 THE SUBCONTRACT

The Subcontract forms the contract with the Subcontractor. This contract represents the entire and integrated agreement and supersedes all prior negotiations, representations, or agreements, either written or oral. The Contract may be amended or modified only by a Modification as defined in Subparagraph 1.1.1.

1.1.3 THE WORK

The Work comprises the completed construction and any design required by the Subcontractor's Contract and includes all labor necessary to produce such construction required of the Contractor or a particular Subcontractor, and all materials and equipment incorporated or to be incorporated in such construction.

1.1.4 THE PROJECT

The Project is the total design and construction to be performed under the Agreement between the Owner and Contractor of which the Work is a part.

1.2 EXECUTION, CORRELATION AND INTENT

1.2.1 By executing the Subcontract, each Subcontractor represents that he has visited the site, familiarized himself with the local conditions under which the Work is to be performed and correlated his observations with the requirements of the Subcontract.

1.2.2 The intent of the Subcontract is to include all items necessary for the proper execution and completion of the Work. The documents constituting the Subcontract are complementary, and what is required by any one shall be as binding as if required by all. Work not covered in the Subcontract will not be required unless it is consistent therewith and is reasonably inferable therefrom as being necessary to produce the intended results. Words and abbreviations in the Subcontract which have well-known technical or trade meanings are used in accordance with such recognized meanings.

1.2.3 The organization of the Specifications into divisions, sections and articles, and the arrangements of Drawings shall not control the Contractor in dividing the Work among Subcontractors or in establishing the extent of Work to be performed by any trade.

1.3 OWNERSHIP AND USE OF DOCUMENTS

1.3.1 Unless otherwise provided in the Subcontract, the Subcontractor will be furnished, free of charge, all copies of Drawings and Specifications reasonably necessary for the execution of the Work.

1.3.2 All Drawings, Specifications and copies thereof furnished by the Contractor are and shall remain his property. They are to be used only with respect to this Project and are not to be used on any other project. With the exception of one contract set for each party, such documents are to be returned or suitably accounted for to the Contractor on request at the completion of the Work. Submission or distribution to meet official regulatory requirements or for other purposes in connection with the Project is not to be construed as publication in derogation of the Contractor's common law copyright or other reserved rights.

ARTICLE 2
OWNER

2.1 DEFINITION

2.1.1 The Owner is the person or entity identified as such in the Subcontract and is referred to as if singular in number and masculine in gender. The term Owner means the Owner or his authorized representative.

2.2 INFORMATION AND SERVICES REQUIRED OF THE OWNER

2.2.1 The Owner will furnish all surveys describing the physical characteristics, legal limitations and utility locations for the site of the Project, and a legal description of the site.

2.2.2 Except as provided in Subparagraph 5.7.1 the Owner will secure and pay for necessary approvals, easements, assessments and charges required for the construction, use, or occupancy of permanent structures or permanent changes in existing facilities.

2.2.3 Information or services under the Owner's control will be furnished by the Owner with reasonable promptness to avoid delay in the orderly progress of the Work.

2.2.4 The Owner shall forward all instructions to the Subcontractors through the Contractor.

ARTICLE 3
ARCHITECT/ENGINEER

3.1 DEFINITION

3.1.1 The Architect/Engineer is the person lawfully licensed to practice architecture or engineering or an entity lawfully practicing architecture or engineering and identified as such in the Agreement between the Owner and Contractor and is referred to as if singular in number and masculine in gender. The term Architect/Engineer means the Architect/Engineer or his authorized representative.

3.1.2 Nothing contained in the Contract Documents shall create any contractual relationship between the Architect/Engineer and any Subcontractor.

3.2 ARCHITECT/ENGINEER'S DUTIES DURING CONSTRUCTION

3.2.1 The Architect/Engineer shall at all times have access to the Work wherever it is in preparation and progress. When directed by the Contractor, the Subcontractor shall provide facilities for such access so the Architect/Engineer may perform his functions under these conditions.

3.2.2 The Architect/Engineer will be the interpreter of the requirements of the Drawings and Specifications. The Architect/Engineer will, within a reasonable time, render such interpretations as are necessary for the proper execution of the progress of the Work.

3.2.3 All interpretations of the Architect/Engineer shall be consistent with the intent of and reasonably inferable from the Subcontract and will be in writing or in the form of drawings. All requests for interpretations shall be directed through the Contractor. Neither the Architect/Engineer nor the Contractor will be liable to the Subcontractor for the result of any interpretation or decision rendered in good faith in such capacity.

3.2.4 The Architect/Engineer's decisions in matters relating to artistic effect will be final if consistent with the intent of the Subcontract.

3.2.5 The Architect/Engineer will have authority to reject Work which does not conform to the Subcontract. Whenever, in his opinion, he considers it necessary or advisable for the implementation of the intent of the Subcontract, he will have authority to require special inspection or testing of the Work in accordance with Subparagraph 8.7.2 whether or not such Work be then fabricated, installed or completed. However, neither the Architect/Engineer's authority to act under this Subparagraph 3.2.5, nor any decision made by him in good faith either to exercise or not to exercise such authority, shall give rise to any duty or responsibility of the Architect/Engineer to the Subcontractor, any Sub-Subcontractor, any of their agents or employees, or any other person performing any of the Work.

3.2.6 The Architect/Engineer will review and approve or take other appropriate action upon Subcontractor's submittals such as Shop Drawings, Product Data and Samples, but only for conformance with the design concept of the Work and with the information in the Subcontract. Such action shall be taken with reasonable promptness so as to cause no delay. The Architect/Engineer's approval of a specific item shall not indicate approval of an assembly of which the item is a component.

3.2.7 The Architect/Engineer along with the Contractor will conduct inspections to determine the dates of Substantial Completion and final completion.

3.2.8 The Architect/Engineer will communicate with the subcontractors through the Contractor.

ARTICLE 4

CONTRACTOR

4.1 DEFINITION

4.1.1 The Contractor is the person or entity which has entered into an agreement with the Owner to design and construct the Project and is referred to throughout the Subcontract as if singular in number and masculine in gender. The Contractor is authorized to enter into agreements with subcontractors to perform the Work necessary to complete the Project and to perform some of the construction with his own forces. The term Contractor means the Contractor acting through his authorized representative.

4.2 ADMINISTRATION OF THE CONTRACT

4.2.1 The Contractor will provide the general administration of the Project as herein described.

4.2.2 The Contractor shall have the responsibility to supervise and coordinate the Work of all Subcontractors.

4.2.3 The Contractor shall prepare and update all Construction Schedules and shall direct the Work with respect to such schedules.

4.2.4 The Contractor shall have authority to reject Work which does not conform to the Subcontract and to require any Special Inspection and Testing in accordance with Subparagraph 8.7.2.

4.2.5 The Contractor will prepare and issue Change Orders to the Subcontractors in accordance with Article 13.

4.2.6 The Contractor along with the Architect/Engineer will conduct inspections to determine the dates of Substantial Completion and final completion, and will receive and review written warranties and related documents required by the Subcontract and assembled by the Subcontractor.

4.3 CONTRACTOR'S RIGHT TO STOP THE WORK

4.3.1 If the Subcontractor fails to correct defective Work as required by Paragraph 14.2 or persistently fails to carry out the Work in accordance with the Contract Documents, the Contractor may order the Subcontractor to stop the Work, or any portion thereof, until the cause for such order has been eliminated.

4.3.2 If the Subcontractor defaults or neglects to carry out the Work in accordance with the Subcontract and fails within seven days after receipt of written notice from the Contractor to commence and continue correction of such default or neglect with diligence and promptness, the Contractor may, by written notice, and without prejudice to any other remedy he or the Owner may have, make good such deficiencies, or exercise any of the options he has in 15.2.1. In such case an appropriate Change Order shall be issued deducting from the payments then or thereafter due the Subcontractor the cost of correcting such deficiencies, including compensation for the Architect/Engineer's and Contractor's additional services made necessary by such default, neglect or failure.

ARTICLE 5

SUBCONTRACTORS

5.1 DEFINITION

5.1.1 A Subcontractor is the person or entity identified as such in the Agreement between the Contractor and a Subcontractor and is referred to throughout the Subcontract as if singular in number and masculine in gender. The term Subcontractor means the Subcontractor or his authorized representative.

5.2 REVIEW OF CONTRACT DOCUMENTS

5.2.1 The Subcontractor shall carefully study and compare the documents within the Subcontract and shall at once report to the Contractor any error, inconsistency or omission he may discover. The Subcontractor shall not be liable to the Owner, the Contractor or the Architect/Engineer for any damage resulting from any such errors, inconsistencies or omissions.

5.3 SUPERVISION AND CONSTRUCTION PROCEDURES

5.3.1 The Subcontractor shall supervise and direct the Work, using his best skill and attention. He shall be solely responsible for all construction means, methods, techniques, sequences and procedures and for coordinating all portions of the Work under the Subcontract subject to the overall coordination of the Contractor.

5.3.2 The Subcontractor shall be responsible to the Contractor for the acts and omissions of his employees and all his Sub-subcontractors and their agents and employees and other persons performing any of the Work under a contract with the Subcontractor.

5.3.3 The Subcontractor shall not be relieved from his obligations to perform the work in accordance with the Subcontract by inspections, tests or approvals required or performed by persons other than the Subcontractor.

5.4 LABOR AND MATERIALS

5.4.1 Unless otherwise specifically provided in the Subcontract, the Subcontractor shall provide and pay for all labor, materials, equipment, tools, construction equipment and machinery, transportation, and other facilities and services necessary for the proper execution and completion of the Work.

5.4.2 The Subcontractor shall at all times enforce strict discipline and good order among his employees and shall not employ on the Work any unfit person or anyone not skilled in the task assigned to him.

5.5. WARRANTY

5.5.1 The Subcontractor warrants to the Owner and the Contractor that all materials and equipment furnished under this Contract will be new unless otherwise specified, and that all Work will be of good quality, free from faults and defects and in conformance with the Subcontract. All Work not so conforming to these requirements, including substitutions not properly approved and authorized, may be considered defective. If required by the Contractor, the Subcontractor shall furnish satisfactory evidence as to the kind and quality of materials and equipment. This warranty is not limited by the provisions of Paragraph 14.2. Warranties required by the Contract Documents shall commence on the Date of Substantial Completion of the Project as established by the Certificate of Substantial Completion between the Contractor and the Owner.

5.6 TAXES

5.6.1 The Subcontractor shall pay all sales, consumer, use and other similar taxes for the Work or portions thereof provided by the Subcontractor which are legally enacted at the time bids or proposals are received, whether or not yet effective, for which he is legally liable.

5.7 PERMITS, FEES AND NOTICES

5.7.1 Unless otherwise provided in the Subcontract, the Subcontractor shall secure and pay for all permits, governmental fees, licenses and inspections necessary for the proper execution and completion of the Work, which are customarily secured after execution of the contract and which are legally required at the time bids or proposals are received.

5.7.2 The Subcontractor shall give all notices and comply with all laws, ordinances, rules, regulations and orders of any public authority bearing on the performance of the Work.

5.7.3 Unless otherwise provided in the Subcontract, it is not the responsibility of the Subcontractor to make certain that the Subcontract is in accordance with applicable laws, statutes, building codes and regulations except to the extent he has contracted to provide part of the design. If the Subcontractor observes that any of the Subcontract Documents are at variance therewith in any respect, he shall promptly notify the Contractor in writing, and any necessary changes shall be by appropriate Modification.

5.7.4 If the Subcontractor performs any Work knowing it to be contrary to such laws, ordinances, rules and regulations, and without such notice to the Contractor, he shall assume full responsibility therefor and shall bear all costs attributable thereto.

5.8 ALLOWANCES

5.8.1 The Contract Sum as defined in Paragraph 10.1.1 includes all allowances. Items covered by these allowances shall be supplied for such amounts and by such persons as the Contractor may direct.

5.8.2 Unless otherwise provided in the Subcontract:

.1 These allowances shall cover the cost to the Subcontractor, less any applicable trade discount, of the materials and equipment required by the allowance delivered at the site, and all applicable taxes;

.2 The Subcontractor's costs for unloading and handling on the site, labor, installation costs, overhead, profit and other expenses contemplated for the original allowance shall be included in the Contract Sum and not in the allowance;

.3 Whenever the cost is more than or less than the allowance, the Contract Sum shall be adjusted accordingly by Change Order, the amount of which will recognize changes, if any, in handling costs on the site, labor, installation costs, overhead, profit and other expenses.

5.9 SUPERINTENDENT

5.9.1 The Subcontractor shall employ a competent superintendent and necessary assistants who shall be in attendance at the Project site during the progress of the Work. The superintendent shall be satisfactory to the Contractor, and shall not be changed except with the consent of the Contractor, unless the superintendent proves to be unsatisfactory to the Subcontractor or ceases to be in his employ. The superintendent shall represent the Subcontractor and all communications given to the superintendent shall be as binding as if given to the Subcontractor. Important communications shall be confirmed in writing. Other communications shall be so confirmed on written request in each case.

5.10 PROGRESS SCHEDULE

5.10.1 The Subcontractor, immediately after being awarded the Contract, shall prepare and submit for the Contractor's information an estimated progress schedule for the Work. The progress schedule shall be related to the entire Project and shall provide for expeditious and practicable execution of the Work. This schedule shall indicate the dates for the starting and completion of the various stages of construction, shall be revised as required by the conditions of the Work, and shall be subject to the Contractor's approval.

5.11 DRAWINGS AND SPECIFICATIONS AT THE SITE

5.11.1 The Subcontractor shall maintain at the site for the Contractor one copy of all Drawings, Specifications, Addenda, Change Orders and other Modifications, in good order and marked currently to record all changes made during construction. These Drawings, marked to record all changes during construction, and approved Shop Drawings, Product Data and Samples shall be delivered to the Contractor for the Owner upon completion of the Work.

5.12 SHOP DRAWINGS, PRODUCT DATA AND SAMPLES

5.12.1 Shop Drawings are drawings, diagrams, schedules and other data especially prepared for the Work by the Subcontractor or any Subsubcontractor, manufacturer, supplier or distributor to illustrate some portion of the Work.

5.12.2 Product Data are illustrations, standard schedules, performance charts, instructions, brochures, diagrams and other information furnished by the Subcontractor to illustrate a material, product or system for some portion of the Work.

5.12.3 Samples are physical examples which illustrate materials, equipment or workmanship and establish standards by which the Work will be judged.

5.12.4 The Subcontractor shall review, approve and submit through the Contractor with reasonable promptness and in such sequence as to cause no delay in the Work or in the work of any separate contractor, all Shop Drawings, Product Data and Samples required by the Subcontract.

5.12.5 By approving and submitting Shop Drawings, Product Data and Samples, the Subcontractor represents that he has determined and verified all materials, field measurements, and field construction criteria related thereto, or will do so, and that he has checked and coordinated the information contained within such submittals with the requirements of the Work under the Subcontract.

5.12.6 The Contractor, if he finds such submittals to be in order will forward them to the Architect/Engineer. If the Contractor finds them not to be complete or in proper form, he may return them to the Subcontractor for correction or completion.

5.12.7 The Subcontractor shall not be relieved of responsibility for any deviation from the requirements of the Subcontract by the Architect/Engineer's approval of Shop Drawings, Product Data or Samples under Subparagraph 3.2.6 unless the Subcontractor has specifically informed the Architect/Engineer and Contractor in writing of such deviation at the time of submission and the Architect/Engineer has given written approval to the specific deviation. The Subcontractor shall not be relieved from responsibility for errors or omissions in the Shop Drawings, Product Data or Samples by the Architect/Engineer's approval thereof.

5.12.8 The Subcontractor shall direct specific attention, in writing or on resubmitted Shop Drawings, Product Data or Samples, to revisions other than those requested by the Architect/Engineer or Contractor on previous submittals.

5.12.9 No portion of the Work requiring submission of a Shop Drawing, Product Data or Sample shall be commenced until the submittal has been approved by the Architect/Engineer. All such portions of the Work shall be in accordance with approved submittals.

5.13 USE OF SITE

5.13.1 The Subcontractor shall confine operations at the site to areas designated by the Contractor, permitted by law, ordinances, permits and the Subcontract and shall not unreasonably encumber the site with any materials or equipment.

5.14 CUTTING AND PATCHING OF WORK

5.14.1 The Subcontractor shall be responsible for all cutting, fitting or patching that may be required to complete the Work or to make its several parts fit together properly. He shall provide protection of existing Work as required.

5.14.2 The Subcontractor shall not damage or endanger any portion of the Work or the work of the Contractor or any separate contractors or subcontractors by cutting, patching or otherwise altering any work, or by excavation. The Subcontractor shall not cut or otherwise alter the work of the Contractor or any separate contractor except with the written consent of the Contractor and of such separate contractor. The Subcontractor shall not unreasonably withhold from the Contractor or any separate contractor his consent to cutting or otherwise altering the Work.

5.15 CLEANING UP

5.15.1 The Subcontractor at all times shall keep the premises free from accumulation of waste materials or rubbish caused by his operations. At the completion of the Work he shall remove all his waste materials and rubbish from and about the Project as well as all his tools, construction equipment, machinery and surplus materials.

5.15.2 If the Subcontractor fails to clean up within 24 hours after receipt of notice of noncompliance from the Contractor, the Contractor may do so and the cost thereof shall be charged to the Subcontractor.

5.16 COMMUNICATIONS

5.16.1 The Subcontractor shall forward all communications to the Owner and Architect/Engineer through the Contractor.

5.17 ROYALTIES AND PATENTS

5.17.1 The Subcontractor shall pay all royalties and license fees for materials, methods and systems incorporated in the Work. He shall defend all suits or claims for infringement of any patent rights and shall save the Owner and Contractor harmless from loss on account thereof, except that the Owner shall be responsible for all such loss when a particular design, process or the product of a particular manufacturer or manufacturers is specified by the Owner. If the Subcontractor has reason to believe that the design, process or product specified is an infringement of a patent, he shall be responsible for such loss unless he promptly gives such information to the Contractor.

5.18 INDEMNIFICATION

5.18.1 To the fullest extent permitted by law, the Subcontractor shall indemnify and hold harmless the Owner, the Contractor and the Architect/Engineer and their agents and employees from and against all claims, damages, losses, and expenses including but not limited to, attorneys' fees, arising out of or resulting from the performance of the Work, provided that any such claim, damage, loss or expense (1) is attributable to bodily injury, sickness, disease or death, or to injury to or destruction of tangible property (other than the Work itself) including the loss of use resulting therefrom, and (2) is caused in whole or in part by any negligent act or omission of the Subcontractor, any Sub-subcontractor, anyone directly or indirectly employed by any of them or anyone for whose acts any of them may be liable, regardless of whether or not it is caused in part by a party indemnified hereunder. Such obligations shall not be construed to negate, abridge or otherwise reduce any other right or obligation of indemnity which would otherwise exist as to any party or person described in this Paragraph 5.18.

5.18.2 In any and all claims against the Owner, the Contractor or the Architect/Engineer or any of their agents or employees by any employee of the Subcontractor, any Sub-subcontractor, anyone directly or indirectly employed by any of them or anyone for whose acts any of them may be liable, the indemnification obligation under this Paragraph 5.18 shall not be limited in any way by any limitation on the amount or type of damages, compensation or benefits payable by or for the Subcontractor or any Sub-subcontractor under workers' or workmen's compensation acts, disability benefit acts or other employee benefit acts.

5.18.3 The obligations of the Subcontractor under this Paragraph 5.18 shall not extend to the liability of the Architect/Engineer, his agents or employees arising out of (1) the preparation or approval of maps, drawings, opinions, reports, surveys, designs or specifications, or (2) the giving of or the failure to give directions or instruction by the Architect/Engineer, his agents or employees provided such giving or failure to give is the primary cause of the injury or damage.

ARTICLE 6
SUB-SUBCONTRACTORS

6.1 DEFINITION

6.1.1 A Sub-subcontractor is a person or entity who has a direct contract with the Subcontractor to perform any of the Work at the site. The term Sub-subcontractor is referred to throughout the Subcontract as if singular in number and masculine in gender and means a Sub-subcontractor or his authorized representative.

6.2 AWARDS OF SUB-SUBCONTRACTS AND OTHER CONTRACTS FOR PORTIONS OF THE WORK

6.2.1 Unless otherwise required by the Subcontract or in the Bidding or Proposal Documents, the Subcontractor shall furnish to the Contractor in writing, for acceptance by the Contractor in writing, the names of the persons or entities (including those who are to furnish materials or equipment fabricated to a special design) proposed for each of the principal portions of the Work. The Contractor will promptly reply to the Subcontractor in writing if the Contractor, after due investigation, has reasonable objection to any such proposed person or entity. Failure of the Contractor to reply promptly shall constitute notice of no reasonable objection.

6.2.2 The Subcontractor shall not contract with any such proposed person or entity to whom the Contractor has made reasonable objection under the provisions of Subparagraph 6.2.1. The Subcontractor shall not be required to contract with anyone to whom he has a reasonable objection.

6.2.3 If the Contractor refuses to accept any person or entity on a list submitted by the Subcontractor in response to the requirements of these conditions, the Subcontractor shall submit an acceptable substitute; however, no increase in the Contract Sum shall be allowed for any such substitution.

6.2.4 The Subcontractor shall make no substitution for any Sub-subcontractor, person or entity previously selected if the Contractor makes reasonable objection to such substitution.

6.3 SUB-SUBCONTRACTUAL RELATIONS

6.3.1 By an appropriate agreement, written where legally required for validity, the Subcontractor shall require each Sub-subcontractor, to the extent of the work to be performed by the Sub-subcontractor, to be bound to the Subcontractor by the terms of the Subcontract and to assume toward the Subcontractor all the obligations and responsibilities which the Subcontractor, by the Subcontract, assumes toward the Owner, the Contractor or the Architect/Engineer. Said agreement shall preserve and protect the rights of the Owner, the Contractor and the Architect/Engineer under the Subcontract with respect to the Work to be performed by the Sub-subcontractor so that the subcontracting thereof will not prejudice such rights, and shall allow to the Sub-subcontractor, unless specifically provided otherwise in the Subcontractor — Sub-subcontractor agreement, the benefit of all rights, remedies and redress against the Subcontractor that the Subcontractor, by these Documents, has against the Contractor. Where appropriate, the Subcontractor shall require each Sub-subcontractor to enter into similar agreements with his Sub-subcontractors. The Subcontractor shall make available to each proposed Sub-subcontractor, prior to the execution of the Sub-subcontract, copies of the Subcontract to which the Sub-subcontractor will be bound by this Paragraph 6.3, and shall identify to the Sub-subcontractor any terms and conditions of the proposed Sub-subcontract which may be at variance with the appropriate parts of the Subcontract. Each Sub-subcontractor shall similarly make copies of parts of the Subcontract available to his Sub-subcontractors.

ARTICLE 7

SEPARATE SUBCONTRACTS

7.1 MUTUAL RESPONSIBILITY OF SUBCONTRACTORS

7.1.1 The Subcontractor shall afford the Contractor and other subcontractors reasonable opportunity for the introduction and storage of their materials and equipment and the execution of their work, and shall connect and coordinate his Work with others under the general direction of the Contractor.

7.1.2 If any part of the Subcontractor's Work depends, for proper execution or results, upon the Work of the Contractor or any separate subcontractor, the Subcontractor shall, prior to proceeding with the Work, promptly report to the Contractor any apparent discrepancies or defects in such Work that render it unsuitable for such proper execution and results. Failure of the Subcontractor so to report shall constitute an acceptance of the other subcontractor's or the Contractor's Work as fit and proper to receive his Work, except as to defects which may subsequently become apparent in such work by others.

7.1.3 Any costs caused by defective or ill-timed work shall be borne by the party responsible therefor.

7.1.4 Should the Subcontractor wrongfully cause damage to the Work or property of the Owner or to other work on the site, the Subcontractor shall promptly remedy such damage as provided in Subparagraph 11.2.5.

310　DESIGN-BUILD SUBCONTRACTS

7.1.5 Should the Subcontractor wrongfully cause damage to the work or property of any separate subcontractor or other contractor, the Subcontractor shall, upon due notice, promptly attempt to settle with the other contractor by agreement, or otherwise resolve the dispute. If such separate contractor sues the Owner or the Contractor or initiates an arbitration proceeding against the Owner or Contractor on account of any damage alleged to have been caused by the Subcontractor, the Owner or Contractor shall notify the Subcontractor who shall defend such proceedings at the Subcontractor's expense, and if any judgment or award against the Owner or Contractor arises therefrom, the Subcontractor shall pay or satisfy it and shall reimburse the Owner or Contractor for all attorneys' fees and court or arbitration costs which the Owner or Contractor has incurred.

7.2 CONTRACTOR'S RIGHT TO CLEAN UP

7.2.1 If a dispute arises between the separate subcontractors as to their responsibility for cleaning up as required by Paragraph 5.15, the Contractor may clean up and charge the cost thereof to the subcontractors responsible therefor as the Contractor shall determine to be just.

ARTICLE 8
MISCELLANEOUS PROVISIONS

8.1 GOVERNING LAW

8.1.1 The Subcontract shall be governed by the law of the place where the Project is located.

8.2 SUCCESSORS AND ASSIGNS

8.2.1 The Contractor and the Subcontractor each binds himself, his partners, successors, assigns and legal representatives to the other party hereto and to the partners, successors, assigns and legal representatives of such other party in respect to all covenants, agreements and obligations contained in the Subcontract. Neither party to the Contract shall assign the Contract or sublet it as a whole without the written consent of the other.

8.3 WRITTEN NOTICE

8.3.1 Written notice shall be deemed to have been duly served if delivered in person to the individual or member of the firm or entity or to an officer of the corporation for whom it was intended, or if delivered at or sent by registered or certified mail to the last business address known to him who gives the notice.

8.4 CLAIMS FOR DAMAGES

8.4.1 Should either party to the Subcontract suffer injury or damage to person or property because of any act or omission of the other party of his employees, agents or others for whose acts he is legally liable, claim shall be made in writing to such other party within a reasonable time after the first observance of such injury or damage.

8.5 PERFORMANCE BOND AND LABOR AND MATERIAL PAYMENT BOND

8.5.1 The Contractor shall have the right to require the Subcontractor to furnish bonds in a form and with a corporate surety acceptable to the Contractor covering the faithful performance of the Subcontract and the payment of all obligations arising thereunder if and as required in the Subcontract.

8.6 RIGHTS AND REMEDIES

8.6.1 The duties and obligations imposed by the Subcontract shall be in addition to and not a limitation of any duties, obligations and rights otherwise imposed by law. However, the remedies provided in the Subcontract shall be the sole remedies available with respect to monetary claims either party may have against the other. Moreover, when the Subcontractor makes a claim against the Contractor for additional time or money and the Contractor presents that claim to or asserts that claim against the Owner, the Subcontractor shall be bound by the determination of the Owner, an award of arbitration, or a judgment of a court of record on such claim. The Contractor shall afford the Subcontractor reasonable opportunity to either present such claim himself or to assist the Contractor in the presentation of such claim to the Owner, an arbitration tribunal or a court of record. Subcontractor shall bear his proportionate share of Contractor's cost in pursuing such claim. Nothing herein,

AGC DOCUMENT NO. 430 • CONDITIONS BETWEEN CONTRACTOR AND SUBCONTRACTOR FOR DESIGN BUILD • JANUARY 1982 however, shall obligate the Contractor to initiate an arbitration proceeding or intitiate a claim in any court if the Contractor reasonably determines that the cost of pursuing the claim further is not justified or that the merits of the claim do not justify its further pursuit.

8.6.2 No action or failure to act by the Contractor, Architect/Engineer or Subcontractor shall constitute a waiver of any right or duty afforded any of them under the Subcontract, nor shall any such action or failure to act constitute an approval of or acquiescence in any breach thereunder, except as may be specifically agreed in writing.

8.7 TESTS

8.7.1 If the Subcontract, laws, ordinances, rules, regulations or orders of any public authority having jurisdiction require any portion of the Work to be inspected, tested or approved, the Subcontractor shall give the Architect/Engineer timely notice of its readiness so the Architect/Engineer and Contractor may observe such inspection, testing, or approval. The Subcontractor shall bear all costs of such inspections, tests or approvals unless otherwise provided.

8.7.2 If the Architect/Engineer or Contractor determines that any Work requires special inspection, testing or approval which Subparagraph 8.7.1 does not include, he will, through the Contractor, instruct the Subcontractor to order such special inspection, testing or approval and the Subcontractor shall give notice as in Subparagraph 8.7.1. If such special inspection or testing reveals a failure of the Work to comply with the requirements of the Subcontract, the Subcontractor shall bear all costs thereof, including compensation for the Architect/Engineer's and Contractor's additional services made necessary by such failure. If the work complies, the Contractor shall bear such costs and an appropriate Change Order shall be issued.

8.7.3 Required certificates of inspection, testing or approval shall be secured by the Subcontractor and promptly delivered by him through the Contractor to the Architect/Engineer.

8.7.4 If the Architect/Engineer or Contractor is to observe the inspections, tests or approvals required by the Subcontract, he will do so promptly and, where practicable, at the source of supply.

8.8 ARBITRATION

8.8.1 All claims, disputes and other matters in question arising out of, or relating to this Subcontract or the breach thereof, except as set forth in Subparagraph 3.2.4 with respect to the Architect/Engineer's decisions on matters relating to artistic effect, and except for claims which have been waived by the making or acceptance of final payment provided by Subparagraphs 10.8.4 and 10.8.5, shall be decided by arbitration in accordance with the Construction Industry Arbitration Rules of the American Arbitration Association then obtaining unless the parties mutually agree otherwise. This agreement to arbitrate shall be specifically enforceable under the prevailing arbitration law. The award rendered by the arbitrators shall be final, and judgment may be entered upon it in accordance with applicable law in any court having jurisdiction thereof.

8.8.2 Notice of the demand for arbitration shall be filed in writing with the other party to the Subcontract and with the American Arbitration Association. The demand for arbitration shall be made within a reasonable time after the claim, dispute or other matter in question has arisen, and in no event shall it be made after the date when institution of legal or equitable proceedings based on such claim, dispute or other matter in question would be barred by the applicable statute of limitations.

8.8.3 The Subcontractor shall carry on the Work and maintain the progress schedule during any arbitration proceedings, unless otherwise agreed by him and the Contractor in writing.

8.8.4 All claims which are related to or dependent upon each other shall be heard by the same arbitrator or arbitrators even though the parties are not the same unless a specific contract prohibits such consolidation.

8.8.5 These provisions relating to mandatory arbitration shall not be applicable to a claim asserted in an action in a state or federal court by a person who is under no obligation to arbitrate such claim with either of the parties to this Agreement insofar as the parties to this Agreement may desire to assert any rights of indemnity or contribution with respect to the subject matter of such action. These provisions shall also not be applicable to any claim the Subcontractor may wish to assert against the Contractor if the Contractor desires to assert that claim, either in whole or part, over against the Owner and the Agreement between the Owner and Contractor does not provide for binding arbitration or does so provide but the two arbitration proceedings cannot be consolidated. In such a case, the Contractor shall notify the Subcontractor either before or after demand for arbitration is made of Contractor's desire to assert the claim against the Owner. In such a case, the Subcontractor shall not proceed by arbitration but in a state or federal court which has jurisdiction over both the Contractor and the Owner. If a dispute arises over the application of these provisions, the question of arbitrability shall be decided by the appropriate court and not by an arbitrator.

ARTICLE 9

TIME

9.1 DEFINITIONS

9.1.1 The Contract Time is the period of time allotted in the Subcontract for the Substantial Completion of the Work as defined in Subparagraph 9.1.3 including authorized adjustments thereto.

9.1.2 The date of commencement of the Work is the date established in a notice to proceed. If there is no notice to proceed, it shall be the date of the Subcontract or such other date as may be established therein.

9.1.3 The Date of Substantial Completion of the Work or designated portion thereof is the Date certified by the Architect/Engineer when construction is sufficiently complete, in accordance with the Subcontract, so the Owner can occupy or utilize the Work or designated portion thereof for the use for which it is intended.

9.1.4 The term day as used in the Subcontract shall mean calendar day unless otherwise specifically designated.

9.2 PROGRESS AND COMPLETION

9.2.1 All time limits stated in the Contract Documents are of the essence of the Contract.

9.2.2 The Subcontractor shall begin the Work on the date of commencement as defined in Subparagraph 9.1.2. He shall carry the Work forward expeditiously with adequate forces and shall achieve Substantial Completion within the Contract Time.

9.3 DELAYS AND EXTENSIONS OF TIME

9.3.1 If the Subcontractor is delayed at any time in the progress of the Work by any act or neglect of the Owner, Contractor, or the Architect/Engineer, or by any employee of either, or by any separate contractor employed by the Owner, or by changes ordered in the Work, or by labor disputes, fire, unusual delay in transportation, adverse weather conditions not reasonably anticipatable, unavoidable casualties or any causes beyond the Subcontractor's control, or by delay authorized by the Owner or the Contractor pending arbitration, or by any other cause which the Contractor determines may justify the delay, then the Contract Time shall be extended by Change Order for such reasonable time as the Contractor may determine.

9.3.2 Any claim for extension of time shall be made in writing to the Contractor no more than twenty days after the commencement of the delay; otherwise it shall be waived. In the case of a continuing cause of delay only one claim is necessary. The Subcontractor shall provide an estimate of the probable effect of such delay on the progress of the Work.

9.3.3 If no agreement is made stating the dates upon which interpretations as set forth in Subparagraph 3.2.2 shall be furnished, then no claim for delay shall be allowed on account of failure to furnish such interpretations until fifteen days after written request is made for them, and not then unless such claim is reasonable.

9.3.4 It shall be recognized by the Subcontractor that he may reasonably anticipate that as the job progresses, the Contractor will be making changes in and updating Construction Schedules pursuant to the authority given him in Subparagraph 4.2.3. Therefore, no claim for an increase in the Contract Sum for either acceleration or delay will be allowed for extensions of time pursuant to this paragraph 9.3 or for other changes in Construction Schedules which are of the type ordinarily experienced in projects of similar size and complexity.

9.3.5 This Paragraph 9.3 does not exclude the recovery of damages for delay by either party under other provisions of the Contract Documents.

ARTICLE 10

PAYMENTS AND COMPLETION

10.1 CONTRACT SUM

10.1.1 The Contract Sum is stated in the agreement between the Contractor and the Subcontractor including adjustments thereto and is the total amount payable to the Subcontractor for the performance of the Work under the Subcontract.

10.2 SCHEDULE OF VALUES

10.2.1 Before the first Application for Payment, the Subcontractor shall submit to the Contractor a schedule of values allocated to the various portions of the Work prepared in such form and supported by such data to substantiate its accuracy as the Contractor may require. This schedule, when accepted by the Contractor, shall be used only as a basis for the Subcontractor's Applications for Payment.

10.3 APPLICATIONS FOR PAYMENT

10.3.1 At least ten days before the date for each progress payment established in the Subcontractor's Agreement, the Subcontractor shall submit to the Contractor an itemized Application for Payment, notarized if required, supported by such data substantiating the Subcontractor's right to payment as the Owner or the Contractor may require, and reflecting such retainage as provided in the Subcontract.

10.3.2 Unless otherwise provided, payments will be made on account of materials or equipment not incorporated in the Work but delivered and suitably stored at the site and, if approved in advance by the Contractor, payments may similarly be made for materials or equipment stored at some other location agreed upon in writing. Payments made for materials or equipment stored on or off the site shall be conditioned upon submission by the Subcontractor of bills of sale or such other procedures satisfactory to the Contractor to establish the Owner's title to such materials or equipment or otherwise protect the Owner's interest, including applicable insurance and transportation to the site for those materials and equipment stored off the site.

10.3.3 The Subcontractor warrants that title to all Work, materials and equipment covered by an Application for Payment will pass to the Owner either by incorporation in the construction or upon the receipt of payment by the Subcontractor, whichever occurs first, free and clear of all liens, claims, security interests or encumbrances, hereinafter referred to in this Article 10 as "liens;" and that no Work, materials or equipment covered by an Application for Payment will have been acquired by the Subcontractor, or by any other person performing the Work at the site or furnishing materials and equipment for the Project, subject to an agreement under which an interest therein or an encumbrance thereon is retained by the seller or otherwise imposed by the Subcontractor or such other person. All Subcontractors and Sub-subcontractors agree that title will so pass upon their receipt of payment from the Subcontractor.

10.4 PROGRESS PAYMENTS

10.4.1 If the Subcontractor has made Application for Payment as above, the Contractor will, with reasonable promptness but not more than seven days after the receipt of payment from the Owner make payment in accordance with the Subcontract.

10.4.2 No approval of an application for a progress payment, nor any progress payment, nor any partial or entire use or occupancy of the Project by the Owner, shall constitute an acceptance of any Work not in accordance with the Subcontract.

10.4.3 The Subcontractor shall promptly pay each Sub-subcontractor upon receipt of payment out of the amount paid to the Subcontractor on account of such Sub-subcontractor's Work, the amount to which said Sub-subcontractor is entitled, reflecting the percentage actually retained, if any, from payments to the Subcontractor on account of such Sub-subcontractor's Work. The Subcontractor shall, by an appropriate agreement with each Sub-subcontractor, also require each Sub-subcontractor to make payments to his subcontractors in a similar manner.

314 DESIGN-BUILD SUBCONTRACTS

10.5 PAYMENTS WITHHELD

10.5.1 The Contractor may decline to approve an Application for Payment if in his opinion the Application is not adequately supported. If the Subcontractor and Contractor cannot agree on a revised amount, the Contractor shall process the Application for the amount he deems appropriate. The Contractor may also decline to approve any Applications for Payment or, because of subsequently discovered evidence or subsequent inspections, he may nullify in whole or in part any approval previously made to such extent as may be necessary in his opinion because of:

.1   defective work not remedied;

.2   third party claims filed or reasonable evidence indicating probable filing of such claims;

.3   failure of the Subcontractor to make payments properly to Sub-subcontractors or for labor, materials or equipment;

.4   reasonable evidence that the Work cannot be completed for the unpaid balance of the Contract Sum;

.5   damage to the Contractor, the Owner or another contractor working at the Project;

.6   reasonable evidence that the Work will not be completed within the Contract time; or

.7   persistent failure to carry out the Work in accordance with the Subcontract.

10.5.2 When the above grounds in Subparagraph 10.5.1 are removed, payment shall be made for amounts withheld because of them.

10.6 FAILURE OF PAYMENT

10.6.1 If the Subcontractor is not paid within seven days after payment to the Contractor by the Owner, then the Subcontractor may, upon seven days additional written notice to the Contractor, stop the work until payment of the amount owing has been received. The Contract Sum shall be increased by the amount of the Subcontractor's reasonable costs of shutdown, delay and start-up, which shall be effected by appropriate Change Order in accordance with Paragraph 13.3.

10.7 FINAL COMPLETION AND FINAL PAYMENT

10.7.1 Upon receipt of written notice that the Work is ready for final inspection and acceptance and upon receipt of a final Application for Payment, the Architect/Engineer and Contractor will promptly make such inspection and, when they find the Work acceptable under the Subcontract and the Contract fully performed, the Contractor will promptly approve final payment.

10.7.2 Neither the final payment nor the remaining retainage percentage shall become due until the Subcontractor submits to the Contractor (1) an affidavit that all payrolls, bills for materials and equipment, and other indebtedness connected with the Work for which the Owner or his property might in anywaybe responsible, have been paid or otherwise satisfied, (2) consent of surety, if any, to final payment and (3), if required by the Owner, other data establishing payment or satisfaction of all such obligations, such as receipts, releases and waivers of liens arising out of the Subcontract, to the extent and in such form as may be designated by the Owner. If any Sub-subcontractor refuses to furnish a release or waiver required by the Owner or Contractor, the Subcontractor may furnish a bond satisfactory to the Owner and Contractor to indemnify them against any such lien. If any such lien remains unsatisfied after all payments are made, the Subcontractor shall refund to the Owner or Contractor all moneys that the latter may be compelled to pay in discharging such lien, including all costs and reasonable attorneys' fees.

10.7.3 If, after Substantial Completion of the Work, final completion thereof is materially delayed through no fault of the Subcontractor or by the issuance of Change Orders affecting final completion, and the Contractor so confirms, the Owner or Contractor shall, upon certification by the Contractor, and without terminating the Contract, make payment of the balance due for that portion of the Work fully completed and accepted. If the remaining balance for Work not fully completed or corrected is less than the retainage stipulated in the Subcontract, and if bonds have been furnished as provided in Paragraph 8.5, the written consent of the surety to the payment of the balance due for that portion of the Work fully completed and accepted shall be submitted by the Subcontractor to the Contractor prior to certification of such payment. Such payment shall be made under the terms and conditions governing final payment, except that it shall not constitute a waiver of claims.

10.7.4 The making of final payment shall constitute a waiver of all claims by the Contractor except those arising from:

.1 unsettled liens;

.2 faulty or defective Work appearing after Substantial Completion;

.3 failure of the Work to comply with the requirements of the Subcontract; or

.4 terms of any special warranties required by the Subcontract.

10.7.5 The acceptance of final payment shall constitute a waiver of all claims by the Subcontractor except those previously made in writing and identified by the Subcontractor as unsettled at the time of the Final Application for Payment.

ARTICLE 11

PROTECTION OF PERSONS AND PROPERTY

11.1 SAFETY PRECAUTIONS AND PROGRAMS

11.1.1 The Subcontractor shall be responsible for initiating, maintaining and supervising all safety precautions and programs in connection with the Work.

11.1.2 If the Subcontractor fails to maintain the safety precautions required by law or directed by the Contractor, the Contractor may take such steps as necessary and charge the Subcontractor therefor.

11.1.3 The failure of the Contractor to take any such action shall not relieve the Subcontractor of his obligations in Subparagraph 11.1.1.

11.2 SAFETY OF PERSONS AND PROPERTY

11.2.1 The Subcontractor shall take all reasonable precautions for the safety of, and shall provide all reasonable protection to prevent damage, injury or loss to:

.1 all employees on the Work and all other persons who may be affected thereby;

.2 all the Work and all materials and equipment to be incorporated therein, whether in storage on or off the site, under the care, custody or control of the Subcontractor or any of his Sub-subcontractors or Sub-subsubcontractors; and

.3 other property at the site or adjacent thereto, including trees, shrubs, lawns, walks, pavements, roadways, structures and utilities not designated for removal, relocation or replacement in the course of construction.

11.2.2 The Subcontractor shall give all notices and comply with all applicable laws, ordinances, rules, regulations and lawful orders of any public authority bearing on the safety of persons or property or their protection from damage, injury or loss.

11.2.3 The Subcontractor shall erect and maintain, as required by existing conditions and progress of the Work, all reasonable safeguards for safety and protection, including posting danger signs and other warnings against hazards, promulgating safety regulations and notifying owners and users of adjacent utilities. If the Subcontrator fails to so comply he shall, at the direction of the Contractor, remove all forces from the Project without cost or loss to the Owner or Contractor, until he is in compliance.

11.2.4 When the use or storage of explosives or other hazardous materials or equipment is necessary for the execution of the Work the Subcontractor shall exercise the utmost care and shall carry on such activities under the supervision of properly qualified personnel.

316 DESIGN-BUILD SUBCONTRACTS

11.2.5 The Subcontractor shall promptly remedy all damage or loss (other than damage or loss insured under Paragraphs 12.2 and 12.3) to any property referred to in Clauses 11.2.1.2 and 11.2.1.3 caused in whole or in part by the Subcontractor, his Sub contractors, his Sub-subcontractors, or anyone directly or indirectly employed by any of them or by anyone for whose acts any of them may be liable and for which the Subcontractor is responsible under Clauses 11.2.1.2 and 11.2.1.3, except damage or loss attributable to the acts or omissions of the Owner or Architect/Engineer or anyone directly or indirectly employed by either of them or by anyone for whose acts either of them may be liable, and not attributable to the fault or negligence of the Subcontractor. The foregoing obligations of the Subcontractor are in addition to his obligation under Paragraph 7.1.5.

11.2.6 The Subcontractor shall designate a responsible member of his organization at the site whose duty shall be the prevention of accidents. This person shall be the Subcontractor's superintendent unless otherwise designated by the Subcontractor in writing to the Contractor.

11.2.7 The Subcontractor shall not load or permit any part of the Work to be loaded so as to endanger its safety.

11.3 EMERGENCIES

11.3.1 In any emergency affecting the safety of persons or property, the Subcontractor shall act, at his discretion, to prevent threatened damage, injury or loss. Any additional compensation or extension of time claimed by the Subcontractor on account of emergency work shall be determined as provided in Article 13 for Changes in the Work.

ARTICLE 12
INSURANCE

12.1 SUBCONTRACTOR'S LIABILITY INSURANCE

12.1.1 The Subcontractor shall purchase and maintain such insurance as will protect him from claims set forth below which may arise out of or result from the Subcontractor's operations under the Subcontract, whether such operations be by himself or by any of his Sub subcontractors or by anyone directly or indirectly employed by any of them, or by anyone for whose acts any of them may be liable:

.1 claims under workers' compensation, disability benefit and other similar employee benefit acts which are applicable to the work to be performed;

.2 claims for damages because of bodily injury, occupational sickness or disease, or death of his employees under any employer's liability law including, if applicable, those required under maritime or admiralty law for wages, maintenance, and cure;

.3 claims for damages because of bodily injury, sickness or disease, or death of any person other than his employees;

.4 claims for damages insured by usual personal injury liability coverage which are sustained (1) by any person as a result of an offense directly or indirectly related to the employment of such person by the Subcontractor, or (2) by any other person;

.5 claims for damages other than to the work itself because of injury to or destruction of tangible property, including loss of use resulting therefrom; and

.6 claims for damages because of bodily injury or death of any person or property damage arising out of the ownership, maintenance or use of any motor vehicle including those not owned by the Subcontractor.

12.1.2 The insurance required by Subparagraph 12.1.1 shall be written for not less than any limits of liability specified in the Contract Documents, or required by law, whichever is greater.

AGC DOCUMENT NO. 430 • CONDITIONS BETWEEN CONTRACTOR AND SUBCONTRACTOR FOR DESIGN-BUILD • JANUARY 1982

12.1.3 The insurance required by Subparagraph 12.1.1 shall include premises-operations (including explosion, collapse and underground coverage), elevators, independent contractors, products and completed operations, and contractual liability insurance (on a "blanket basis" designating all written contracts), all including broad form property damage coverage. Liability insurance may be arranged under Comprehensive General Liability policies for the full limits required or by a combination of underlying policies for lesser limits with the remaining limits provided by an Excess or Umbrella Liability Policy. The insurance required by Paragraph 12.1.1 shall include contractual liability insurance applicable to the Subcontractor's liability under Paragraph 5.18.

12.1.4 The foregoing policies shall contain a provision that coverages afforded under the policies will not be cancelled or not renewed until at least sixty days' prior written notice has been given to the Contractor. Certificates of Insurance acceptable to the Contractor shall be filed with the Contractor prior to commencement of the Work. Upon request, the Subcontractor shall allow the Contractor to examine the actual policies.

12.2 PROPERTY INSURANCE

12.2.1 Unless otherwise provided, the Owner will purchase and maintain property insurance upon the entire Work at the site to the full insurable value thereof. This insurance shall include the interests of the Owners, the Contractor, the Subcontractors, and Sub-subcontractors in the Work and shall insure against the perils of fire and extended coverage, and shall include "all risk" insurance for physical loss or damage.

12.2.2 The Owner will effect and maintain such boiler and machinery insurance as may be necessary and/or required by law. This insurance shall include the interest of the Owner, the Contractor, the Subcontractors, and Sub-subcontractors in the Work.

12.2.3 Any loss insured under Paragraph 12.2 is to be adjusted with the Owner and Contractor and made payable to the Owner and Contractor as trustees for the insureds, as their interests may appear, subject to the requirements of any applicable mortgagee clause.

12.2.4 The Owner, the Contractor, the Architect/Engineer, the Subcontractor, and his Sub-subcontractors waive all rights against each other and any other contractor or subcontractor engaged in the project for damages caused by fire or other perils to the extent covered by insurance provided under Paragraph 12.2, or any other property or consequential loss insurance applicable to the Project, equipment used in the Project, or adjacent structures, except such rights as they may have to the proceeds of such insurance. If any policy of insurance requires an endorsement to maintain coverage with such waivers, the owner of such policy will cause the policy to be so endorsed. The Owner and contractor will require, by appropriate agreement, written where legally required for validity, similar waivers in favor of the Subcontractor and Sub-subcontractors by any separate contractor and his subcontractors. The policies shall be endorsed to provide waivers of subrogation.

12.2.5 The Owner and Contractor shall deposit in a separate account any money received as trustees, and shall distribute it in accordance with such agreement as the parties in interest may reach, or in accordance with an award by arbitration in which case the procedure shall be as provided in Paragraph 8.8. If after such loss no special agreement is made, replacement of damaged work shall be covered by an appropriate Change Order.

12.2.6 The Owner and Contractor as trustees shall have power to adjust and settle any loss with the insurers unless one of the parties in interest shall object in writing within five days after the occurrence of loss to the Owner's and Contractor's exercise of this power, and if such objection be made, arbitrators shall be chosen as provided in Paragraph 8.8. The Owner and Contractor as trustees shall, in that case, make settlement with the insurers in accordance with the directions of such arbitrators. If distribution of the insurance proceeds by arbitration is required, the arbitrators will direct such distribution.

12.2.7 If the Owner finds it necessary to occupy or use a portion or portions of the Work prior to Substantial Completion thereof, such occupancy shall not commence prior to a time mutually agreed to by the Owner and Contractor and to which the insurance company or companies providing the property insurance have consented by endorsement to the policy or policies. This insurance shall not be cancelled or lapsed on account of such partial occupancy. Consent of the Contractor and of the insurance company or companies to such occupancy or use shall not be unreasonably withheld.

318 DESIGN-BUILD SUBCONTRACTS

ARTICLE 13

CHANGES IN THE WORK

13.1 CHANGE ORDERS

13.1.1 A Change Order is a written order to the Subcontractor signed by the Contractor, issued after the execution of the Subcontract, authorizing a Change in the Work or an adjustment in the Contract Sum or the Contract Time. The Contract Sum and the Contract Time may be changed only by Change Order. A Change Order signed by the Subcontractor indicates his agreement therewith, including the adjustment in the Contract Sum or the Contract Time.

13.1.2 The Contractor, without invalidating the Contract, may order Changes in the Work within the general scope of the Subcontract consisting of additions, deletions or other revisions, the Contract Sum and the Contract Time being adjusted accordingly. All such changes in the Work shall be authorized by Change Order, and shall be performed under the applicable conditions of the Subcontracts.

13.1.3 The cost or credit to the Contractor resulting from a Change in the Work shall be determined in one or more of the following ways:

.1   by mutual acceptance of a lump sum properly itemized and supported by sufficient substantiating data to permit evaluation; or

.2   by unit prices stated in the Subcontract or subsequently agreed upon; or

.3   by cost to be determined in a manner agreed upon by the parties and a mutually acceptable fixed or percentage fee; or

.4   by the method provided in Subparagraph 13.1.4.

13.1.4 If none of the methods set forth in Clauses 13.1.3.1, 13.1.3.2 or 13.1.3.3 is agreed upon, the Subcontractor, provided he receives a written order signed by the Contractor, shall promptly proceed with the Work involved. The cost of such Work shall be determined by the Contractor on the basis of the reasonable expenditures and savings of those performing the Work attributable to the change, including, in the case of an increase in the Contract Sum, a reasonable allowance for overhead and profit. In such case, and also under Clauses 13.1.3.3 and 13.1.3.4 above, the Subcontractor shall keep and present, in such form as the Contractor may prescribe, an itemized accounting together with appropriate supporting data for inclusion in a Change Order. Unless otherwise provided in the Subcontract, cost shall be limited to the following: cost of materials, including sales tax and cost of delivery, cost of labor, including social security, old age and unemployment insurance, and fringe benefits required by agreement or custom; workers' or workmen's compensation insurance; bond premiums; rental value of equipment and machinery; and the additional costs of supervision and field office personnel directly attributable to the change. Pending final determination of cost, payments on account shall be made as determined by the Contractor. The amount of credit to be allowed by the Subcontractor for any deletion or change which results in a net decrease in the Contract Sum will be the amount of the actual net cost as confirmed by the Contractor. When both additions and credits covering related Work or substitutions are involved in any one change, the allowance for overhead and profit shall be figured on the basis of the net increase, if any, with respect to that change.

13.1.5 If unit prices are stated in the Subcontract or subsequently agreed upon, and if the quantities originally contemplated are so changed in a proposed Change Order that application of the agreed unit prices to the quantities of Work proposed will cause substantial inequity to the Owner, the Contractor, or the Subcontractor, the applicable unit prices shall be equitably adjusted.

13.2 CONCEALED CONDITIONS

13.2.1 Should concealed conditions encountered in the performance of the Work below the surface of the ground or should concealed or unknown conditions in an existing structure be at variance with the conditions indicated by the Subcontract or should unknown physical conditions below the surface of the ground or should concealed or unknown conditions in an existing structure of an unusual nature, differing materially from those ordinarily encountered and generally recognized as inherent in work of the character provided for in this Subcontract, be encountered, the Contract Sum shall be equitably adjusted by Change Order upon claim by either party made within twenty days after the first observance of the conditions.

13.3 CLAIMS FOR ADDITIONAL COST

13.3.1 If the Subcontractor wishes to make a claim for an increase in the Contract Sum, he shall given the Contractor written notice thereof within twenty days after the occurrence of the event giving rise to such claim. This notice shall be given by the Subcontractor before proceeding to execute the Work, except in an emergency endangering life or property in which case the Subcontractor shall proceed in accordance with Paragraph 11.3. No such claim shall be valid unless so made. Any change in the Contract Sum resulting from such claim shall be authorized by Change Order.

13.3.2 If the Subcontractor claims that additional cost is involved because of, but not limited to, (1) any written interpretation issued pursuant to Subparagraph 3.2.2, (2) any order by the Contractor to stop the Work pursuant to Paragraph 4.3 where the Subcontractor was not at fault, or (3) any written order for a minor change in the Work issued pursuant to Paragraph 13.4, the Subcontractor shall make such claim as provided in Subparagraph 13.3.1.

13.4 MINOR CHANGES IN THE WORK

13.4.1 The Owner will have authority to order through the Contractor minor changes in the Work not involving an adjustment in the Contract Sum or an extension of the Contract Time and not inconsistent with the intent of the Subcontract. Such changes shall be effected by written order and such changes shall be binding on the Owner, the Contractor and the Subcontractor. The Subcontractor shall carry out such written orders promptly.

ARTICLE 14

UNCOVERING AND CORRECTION OF WORK

14.1 UNCOVERING OF WORK

14.1.1 If any portion of the Work should be covered contrary to the request of the Contractor or Architect/Engineer, or to requirements specifically expressed in the Subcontract, it must, if required in writing by the Contractor, be uncovered for their observation and replaced, at the Subcontractor's expense.

14.1.2 If any other portion of the Work has been covered which the Contractor or the Architect/Engineer has not specifically requested to observe prior to being covered, the Architect/Engineer or Contractor may request to see such Work and it shall be uncovered by the Subcontractor. If such Work be found in accordance with the Subcontract, the cost of uncovering and replacement shall, by appropriate Change Order, be charged to the Contractor. If such Work be found not in accordance with the Subcontract, the Subcontractor shall pay such costs unless it be found that this condition was caused by a separate subcontractor employed as provided in Article 7, and in that event the separate subcontractor shall be responsible for the payment of such costs.

14.2 CORRECTION OF WORK

14.2.1 The Subcontractor shall promptly correct all Work rejected by the Architect/Engineer or the Contractor as defective or as failing to conform to the Subcontract whether observed before or after Substantial Completion and whether or not fabricated, installed or completed. The Subcontractor shall bear all costs of correcting such rejected Work, including compensation for the Architect/Engineer's and/or Contractor's additional services made necessary thereby.

14.2.2 If, within one year after the Date of Substantial Completion of Work or designated portion thereof, or within one year after acceptance by the Owner of designated equipment or within such longer period of time as may be prescribed by law or by the terms of any applicable special warranty required by the Subcontract, any of the Work is found to be defective or not in accordance with the Subcontract, the Subcontractor shall correct it promptly after receipt of a written notice from the Owner or Contractor to do so unless the Owner or Contractor has previously given the Subcontractor a written acceptance of such condition. This obligation shall survive the termination of the Subcontract. The Owner or Contractor shall give such notice promptly after discovery of the condition.

14.2.3 The Subcontractor shall remove from the site all portions of the Work which are defective or non-conforming and which have not been corrected under Subparagraphs 14.2.1, 5.5.1 and 14.2.2 unless removal has been waived by the Owner.

14.2.4 If the Subcontractor fails to correct defective or non-conforming Work as provided in Subparagraphs 5.5.1, 14.2.1 and 14.2.2, the Owner or Contractor may correct it in accordance with Subparagraph 4.3.2.

14.2.5 If the Subcontractor does not proceed with the correction of such defective or non-conforming Work within a reasonable time fixed by written notice from the Contractor, the Owner or Contractor may remove it and may store the materials or equipment at the expense of the Subcontractor. If the Subcontractor does not pay the cost of such removal and storage within ten days thereafter, the Owner or Contractor may upon ten additional days' written notice sell such Work at auction or at private sale and shall account for the net proceeds thereof, after deducting all the costs that should have been borne by the Subcontractor, including compensation for the Contractor's additional services made necessary thereby. If such proceeds of sale do not cover all costs which the Subcontractor should have borne, the difference shall be charged to the Subcontractor, and an appropriate Change Order shall be issued. If the payments then or thereafter due the Subcontractor are not sufficient to cover such amount, the Subcontractor shall pay the difference to the Owner or Contractor.

14.2.6 The Subcontractor shall bear the cost of making good all work of the Contractor, other Subcontractors and other contractors destroyed or damaged by such removal or correction.

14.3 ACCEPTANCE OF DEFECTIVE OR NONCONFORMING WORK

14.3.1 If the Owner or Contractor prefers to accept defective or non-conforming Work, he may do so instead of requiring its removal and correction, in which case a Change Order will be issued to reflect reduction in the Contract Sum where appropriate and equitable. Such adjustment shall be effected whether or not final payment has been made.

ARTICLE 15

TERMINATION OF THE CONTRACT

15.1 TERMINATION BY THE SUBCONTRACTOR

15.1.1 If the Work should be stopped for a period of thirty days by the Subcontractor because of failure to receive payment in accordance with the Subcontract, then the Subcontractor may, upon seven additional days' written notice to the Contractor, terminate the Subcontract and recover from the Contractor payment for all Work executed and for any proven loss sustained upon any materials, equipment, tools, construction equipment and machinery, including reasonable profit and damages.

15.2 TERMINATION BY THE CONTRACTOR

15.2.1 If, after being notified of any of the following failures to perform, the Subcontractor continues to fail to commence his Work; continues to fail, except in cases for which extension of time is provided, to supply enough properly skilled workmen or proper materials; continues to fail to make prompt payment to Sub-subcontractors or for materials or labor; continues to fail to perform his Work in accordance with the Drawings and Specifications; continues to disregard laws, ordinances, rules, regulations or orders of any public authority having jurisdiction; or continues to be otherwise guilty of a substantial violation of a provision of the Subcontract; then the Contractor shall, without prejudice to any other right or remedy and after giving the Subcontractor and his Surety, if any, three day's written notice, have the right to any one or any combination of the following remedies: (1) supply such number of workers and quantity of material, equipment and other facilities as the Contractor deems advisable for the completion of the Work, or any part thereof which Subcontractor has failed to complete or perform after the aforesaid notice, and charge the cost thereof to the Subcontractor, who shall be liable for the payment of same; (2) contract with one or more additional contractors to perform such part of the completion of the Work as Contractor shall determine will provide the most expeditious completion of the total Work and charge the cost thereof to the Subcontractor, who shall be liable for the payment of same; or (3) terminate the Subcontract and use any materials, implements, equipment, appliances or tools furnished by or belonging to Subcontractor in completing the Work, or, at its option, itself or through a subcontractor or subcontractors furnish any such labor, material, implements, equipment, appliances or tools, in whole or in part, necessary for the completion of the Work, and charge the cost thereof to the Subcontractor, who shall be liable for the payment of same. The Subcontract shall be terminated, unless the Contractor subsequently otherwise agrees, upon the appointment of a receiver of the Subcontractor by reason of his insolvency or upon the Subcontractor making an assignment for the benefit of creditors. If Subcontractor files a petition under the Bankuptcy Code, the Subcontract shall terminate under (3) above if the Subcontractor or his trustee rejects the contract or, when not performing in accordance with the Project Schedule, is unable to give adequate assurance that he will complete the Subcontract in accordance with the Project Schedule. If Subcontractor is not performing in accordance with the Project Schedule at the time of filing such petition or at any subsequent time, the Contractor may, while awaiting the Subcontractor or his trustee to reject the Subcontract or to accept and provide adequate assurance of his ability to perform, avail himself of such remedies under (1) and (2) above as are reasonably necessary to maintain the Project Schedule. Contractor may offset all costs incurred by it in the pursuance of any of the remedies provided in the preceding sentences, together with Contractor's reasonable overhead and direct job expenses incurred in pursuing such remedy or remedies, including without limitation, its attorneys' fees, and, at Contractor's discretion, a reasonable profit not to exceed six percent (6%), against any sums due or to become due hereunder. Subcontractor shall be liable for the payment of any amount by which such costs may exceed the unpaid balance of the Contract Sum.

15.2.2 If the unpaid balance of the Contract Sum exceeds the cost of finishing the Work, including compensation for the Contractor's additional services made necessary thereby, such excess shall be paid to the Subcontractor. If such costs exceed the unpaid balance, the Subcontractor shall pay the difference to the Contractor.

15.2.3 The Contractor has the option to terminate his Agreement with the Owner if the Work is stopped for a period of thirty days under an order of any court or other public authority having jurisdiction, or as a result of an act of government, such as a declaration of a national emergency making materials unavailable, or from the failure of the Owner to make payment. If the Contractor exercises such option he may then terminate the subcontracts with the Subcontractors and the Subcontractors shall be entitled to recover such amounts for his proven losses as the Contractor may be able to recover from the Owner.

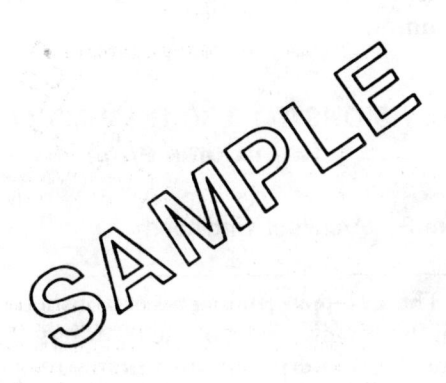

Revisions to AGC Document No. 430

§7.05 General Comments

Most of the proposed revisions following are intended to give additional protection to the interests of the subcontractor.

It is the author's view that the revisions to insurance language proposed in **FORM 7-4**, ¶¶4, 10, and 11 should be adopted to conform to an insurance program that basically is beneficial to all parties (owner, contractor, subcontractor) at the expense of the insurance industry without additional offseting premium.

FORM 7-4 Revisions to AGC Document 430 (with Comments)

REVISIONS TO AGC DOCUMENT 430
(with Comments)

¶1. **First:** **Article 3.** Architect/Engineer.

> Comment: The architect/engineer is established in Article 3 as the interpreter of the requirements of the drawings and specifications, who will render such interpretations within a reasonable time. The architect/engineer has authority to reject work and approve or disapprove submittals and shop drawings.
>
> The appropriateness of this language where the subcontractor supplies the design for its own work needs special consideration. Arrangements should be made for the architect/engineer to review and approve the total design originally submitted by the subcontractor so as to avoid the possibility of unpleasant surprises in the event that the architect/engineer cannot agree with the design philosophy of the architect or engineer who is employed by the subcontractor.

¶2. **Second:** **Article 5.2.1.** Errors and Omissions. If Subcontractor supplies the design, the last sentence should be annulled.

> Comment: The last sentence of this Article provides that the subcontractor is not liable for errors and omissions in the contract documents.

¶3. **Third:** **Article 5.3.3.** Inspection and Testing. Article 5.3.3 should be annulled.

Comment: The provision that the subcontractor is not relieved from its obligation to perform in accordance with the contract documents by inspections, tests, or approvals given by the owner, testing agency, architect, or contractor looks plausible in print, but it can lead to an unfair result. If the owner employs a testing lab or an inspecting agency, the subcontractor in practice is usually required to conform to the requirements imposed by the lab or the agency and should probably be able to assume that if the lab or the agency is satisfied, then the owner has received what the owner is entitled to receive.

For example, suppose that the testing lab employed by the owner approves the rebar and its placement, but, unknown to the subcontractor, they do not comply with the contract documents. In practice, the subcontractor relies on the testing lab to determine compliance. The testing lab is employed by the owner, so should not the subcontractor be entitled to rely on that approval? If not, the subcontractor would have to employ its own engineer or testing lab to check up on the tests and inspections performed by the lab employed by the owner. This is not customary; it would seem absurd.

The subcontractor of a particular trade, therefore, would probably be justified in requiring the annulment of Article 5.3.3. The application of the article is unobjectionable where inspections are occasional or cursory. For work done under continuous inspection, however, such as soils compaction and structural concrete pours, the subcontractor should be able to rely on the testing lab employed by the owner to set the standard of performance.

¶4. **Fourth: Article 5.18.1.** Liability Insurance. The parenthetical phrase "(other than the Work itself)" should be deleted.

Comment: The subcontractor should be required to provide a broad form endorsement to its comprehensive general liability insurance policy and to provide coverage for liability assumed by contract. "Liability assumed by contract" means, in insurance lingo, an indemnity agreement.

It is in the interest of owner, contractor, and subcontractor that the subcontractor's insurance policy have the broadest possible scope, so that damages to property will be paid for by insurance rather than by the subcontractor. A subcontractor's insurance policy will always cover damage to work performed by other subcontractors. Under many broad form endorsements, even physical damage to the subcontractor's own work is covered.

¶5. Fifth: Article 8.1.1. Choice of Law. Either omit the choice of law clause, or provide language such as the following: "This choice of law clause shall not be interpreted so as to avoid the application of the Federal Arbitration Act to disputes arising under this Subcontract."

Comment: A choice of law provision such as the one contained in Article 8.1.1 can have unexpected consequences with respect to the enforceability of an arbitration agreement. See *Volt Information Sciences, Inc v Board of Trustees of the Leland Stanford Junior University,* 489 US 468 (1989). In the *Volt* case, the end result of the able. Therefore, parties who wish to be sure of their ability to enforce an arbitration clause in spite of the inability to join all parties in the arbitration who might have an interest in it should either omit the choice of law clause, or provide language such as above.

¶6. Sixth: Article 8.6.1. Pass Through Provision.

Comment: The effect of this article is to make a subcontractor's claim against the contractor for additional time or money depend upon the contractor's ability to recover such additional time or money from the owner. A subcontractor will resist the inclusion of this article in the subcontract document, because there are many occasions on which the subcontractor may have a just claim against a contractor even though the contractor has no such just claim against the owner. On other occasions, a subcontractor may have a strong claim against the contractor who in turn has a weak claim against the owner. A subcontractor will resist joining its fate with that of the contractor.

¶7. Seventh: Article 8.8. Arbitration.

Comment: Generally speaking, both subcontractors and contractors have much to gain from arbitration as opposed to litigation and, unless the circumstances are unusual, they should support the inclusion of arbitration clauses in their contracts. Such an unusual situation does arise, however, where the subcontract has an arbitration clause and the prime contract does not. This situation is appropriately dealt with, from the standpoint of the prime contractor, in Article 8.8.

¶8. Eighth: Article 12.1.1.4. Personal Injury Insurance.

Comment: There is no good reason for the subcontractor to be required to carry personal injury insurance. *Personal injury,* in insurance lingo, does not refer to bodily injury, but to such injuries as are sustained from false advertising, invasion of privacy, and the like. The author does not perceive the need for the contractor to require the subcontractor to have such insurance.

¶9. Ninth: Article 12.1.1.5. The words "other than to the Work itself" should be stricken. See the comment to ¶4 above.

¶10. Tenth: Article 12.1.5. Insurance. Article 12.1.5 is added to read as follows:

> **12.1.5** The comprehensive general liability policy of subcontractor will be endorsed to name Owner and Contractor as additional insureds, and to provide that, with respect to claims and losses arising out of the operations of Subcontractor, the insurance of Subcontractor shall be primary to any insurance provided by Owner or Contractor. Subcontractor shall deliver copies of such endorsements to Contractor before commencing work on the jobsite.

¶11. Eleventh: Article 12.2. Property Insurance. Article 12.2 should be annulled.

> Comment: The philosophy of Article 12.2 is that the project will be covered by property insurance, only one premium will be paid, but the interests of owner, contractor, and all subcontractors and sub-subcontractors will be thereby protected. This attempts to spread the benefits of the insurance too far. In most cases, construction is funded by a construction loan, and the mortgage or deed of trust provides that the mortgagee or beneficiary has the right to take possession of insurance proceeds and use them to satisfy the owner's indebtedness. In the event of a fire or similar casualty, the project usually stops for several months and during that time the amount of the construction loan escalates because of accumulating interest. By the time the fire insurance proceeds are available, the construction lender takes so much of the insurance proceeds (usually all of them), that there is nothing left over to protect the interests of contractor and subcontractors.
>
> Now the contractor, unless it has included a provision excusing further performance in the event of casualty, will be required to rebuild at the contractor's expense, but will not have proceeds of insurance to finance the rebuilding. Therefore, for adequate protection, the contractor will either need to write a clause into the contract excusing further performance in the event of a casualty, or buy its own builder's risk insurance.

Whether exactly the same considerations apply to a subcontractor or not is a nice question. A subcontractor would be excused by the doctrine of impossibility from wiring a building, for example, that did not exist. But if the contractor rebuilds the building, is the subcontractor required to rewire the building without additional compensation? From the provisions of Article 12.2, one would infer yes, the subcontractor is required to rebuild, for otherwise, why would the subcontractor have an insurable interest in the continued existence of the building, as is assumed by the very presence of Article 12.2?

Therefore, contractor and subcontractor should either (1) provide that further performance is excused in the event of a casualty, or (2) provide their own builder's risk insurance.

Purchase Orders

8

Introduction to Purchase Orders

§8.01 Purchase Orders in the Construction Industry
§8.02 Special Rules for Commercial Transactions

Purchase Order Forms

§8.03 General Comments
      FORM 8-1   Short Form Purchase Order
      FORM 8-2   Long Form Purchase Order

Alternate Purchase Order Provisions

§8.04 General Comments
      FORM 8-3   Alternate Purchase Order Provisions

Alternate Purchase Order Forms

      FORM 8-4   Short Form Purchase Order - Another Version
      FORM 8-5   Short Form Purchase Order - Another Version
      FORM 8-6   Long Form Purchase Order - Another Version

Introduction to Purchase Orders

§8.01   Purchase Orders in the Construction Industry

Purchase orders, or the lack of them, cause problems that infrequently come to the attention of the practitioner of construction law, and seldom rise to a level of such significance as to be found among reported cases. One has the impression that the paperwork side of purchasing is little emphasized in most construction offices. This practitioner has had occasion in the course of studying a construction dispute to review the contents of a purchase order only a scant number of times.

The building materials most likely to cause construction disputes seem to be waterproofing materials, roofing materials, glue-lam beams, air conditioning equipment, curtainwall systems and paint. Concrete and plaster cause many construction disputes, but the fault usually seems to be in the application of the product rather than the product itself. Imported soils are a building material, but the author has never seen a purchase order for soils. Fault is usually in the processing of the material rather than in the material itself.

These observations are interesting in view of the fact that, in most trades, a large percentage of the cost of the work (often more than half) is absorbed by building equipment and materials that are **buy-out, off the shelf** items. From such considerations it could easily be argued that purchase orders are just as important as contracts and subcontracts. Although experience does not in any way support such a bold assertion, a particular case may turn upon the wording of a purchase order; therefore, purchase order forms are deserving of space in this work, and also deserving of the consideration of the contractor, subcontractor, and practitioner.

Not much bargaining may occur as to the phraseology of a particular purchase order, because, in effect, the wording may be imposed on the purchaser by the seller. A subcontractor purchasing ready mix concrete is not given much opportunity to bargain with the supplier as to the contents of a purchase order. One who orders air conditioning equipment or switch gear from a Fortune 500 company may not have much leverage to bargain about legal phraseology. The purchaser is pretty much left to rely upon the reputation of the supplier and its product in the optimistic assumption that no problems will occur so long as the product is delivered undamaged and on time.

There are times when it may not be easy to draw the line between an item that should be acquired by purchase order and one that should be acquired by contract. For example, vocabulary and sentence structure would suggest that marble or granite is just another building material to be purchased like lumber or concrete block. Yet in many cases, the granite or marble is specially selected, cut, sized, polished, and shipped to meet a construction program and schedule for a particular building. Therefore, all the considerations that apply to any other subcontract are applicable to the granite or marble, right down to the preparation of shop drawings, erection schedules, and fabrication criteria.

§8.02 Special Rules for Commercial Transactions

Purchases of materials fall under the legal rubric **sales** rather than **contracts,** and are controlled by the provisions of the Uniform Commercial Code as adopted, with variations, by state legislatures. The law as it pertains to the interpretation and enforcement of contracts has been developed by courts, over centuries, as common law. The law of sales has had a different history. It originated partly to facilitate commercial transactions between merchants in different nations, and was eventually codified in a series of codes developed from customs, traditions, and practices formalized as rules of **law merchant.** In transactions governed by the Uniform Commercial Code, many legal rules that would apply to a construction contract are altered or reversed.

In most states, for example, an oral bid given over the telephone by a subcontractor is enforceable, even if it has not been accepted, if the contractor relied on it in making its prime bid to the owner. The legal doctrine under which this occurs is called *promissory estoppel.*

But if the oral telephone bid is from a merchant (a seller of goods), rather than a contractor, in most states the doctrine of promissory estoppel would not apply, and the bid could be enforced only if confirmed in writing within a few days.

Under rules of contract law, a contract cannot be formed by an acceptance that varies the terms of the offer. Under law merchant, however, as reflected in the Uniform Commercial Code, an offeree may qualify acceptance by inserting new, commercially reasonable, terms, and new terms become a part of the contract if not explicitly rejected by the offeror.

Under the Uniform Commercial Code, sales contracts in excess of a few hundred (or thousand) dollars (depending on the state) must be supported by a writing to be enforceable. An oral order, or a telephone order, is binding in most states only for a few days unless confirmed by one party or the other in writing. The written confirmation may be enforceable even if it varies the terms of the original order, if the variation is commercially reasonable and not rejected by the other side. The logical routine to be followed by a contractor ordering materials, therefore, is to confirm the order in writing within a few days, and at the same time ask the seller to sign the contractor's form of purchase order.

Purchase Order Forms

§8.03 General Comments

The author has drafted a short form **(FORM 8-1)** and a long form **(FORM 8-2)** purchase order, each of which is complete within itself and may be modified by insertion of selected alternate provisions **(FORM 8-3)**.

The reader interested in the subject may scan the two forms and the alternate provisions to become acquainted with the types of material that should be considered for inclusion in any form of purchase order to be developed for a particular party to use as a standard form.

FORM 8-1   Short Form Purchase Order

The most potent provision in this purchase order form is the requirement that material will be manufactured and delivered so as to comply with the contract documents.

The other terms are considered minimal for the adequate protection of buyer.

330 PURCHASE ORDERS

SHORT FORM PURCHASE ORDER

¶1. This Purchase Order is between _____, Buyer, and _____, Seller. Buyer has contracted for performance of a project described as _____. SHIP MATERIAL TO _____ on or before _____.

¶2. All material will be manufactured and delivered so as to comply with the contract documents under which Buyer is bound to perform on behalf of the project Owner. The full contract documents are available for inspection by Seller, and are incorporated herein by this reference.

¶3. Seller will supply the following material at the following price, in accordance with the terms of this Purchase Order.

_____
_____
_____
_____
_____
_____

¶4. Deliveries: Deliveries will be in accordance with Buyer's schedule, in proper order for assembly and installation, FOB jobsite, spotted as instructed by Buyer's superintendent.

¶5. Risk of Loss: Risk of loss will be on Seller until Buyer moves material from its point of delivery.

¶6. Warranty: Seller warrants that material is in compliance with the contract documents and is of merchantable quality, fit for its intended purpose, new, and free from defects. For a period of one year after the completion of the entire project, Seller will, at the request of Buyer, owner, tenant, or purchaser of the project, at its own expense, promptly repair or replace any defective material.

DATED: _____

_____, Buyer   _____, Seller

By _____   By _____
   (Signature)   (Signature)

FORM 8-2 Long Form Purchase Order

If the seller is willing to sign the buyer's purchase order, the following form gives a very high measure of protection to the interests of the buyer.

LONG FORM PURCHASE ORDER

¶1. This Purchase Order is between _____, Buyer, and _____, Seller.

SHIP TO PROJECT LOCATION AT:_____

____ on or before _____. Material must comply with the following contract documents:

_____
_____
_____ ,

which are incorporated herein by this reference.

¶2. Material and Price: Seller will sell and deliver, and Buyer will purchase, the following material at the following price:

_____
_____
_____

¶3. Delivery: Material will be delivered FOB jobsite at the project location. Material will be spotted by Seller's truck as directed by Buyer's superintendent. Seller must notify Buyer's superintendent of delivery in writing or by telephone at least 24 hours before delivery. Material must not be shipped until Buyer's superintendent has released it for delivery.

¶4. Compliance with Contract Documents: All material will comply with the requirements of the contract documents and with this Purchase Order.

¶5. Compliance with Codes: All material will comply with applicable building and safety codes.

¶6. Risk of Loss: Risk of loss will be with Seller until material, after its delivery, has been moved by Buyer.

¶7. Samples and Mock-Ups: Seller will provide, at its own expense, samples and mock-ups to comply with the requirements of the contract documents.

¶8. Schedule: Seller will comply with the schedule established by the contract documents or as otherwise directed by Buyer. Buyer may change the schedule from time to time to adjust to job conditions.

¶9. Drawings and Operating Manuals: Seller will supply proper operating, training, and maintenance manuals, drawings, and any other documentation that is required by the contract documents.

¶10. Shop Drawings: Shop drawings will be delivered in form, number and in time to comply with the requirements of the contract documents, but no later than four weeks after the date of this Purchase Order.

¶11. Substitutions: No substitution will be permitted without the written consent of Buyer. If Seller proposes any substitution, Seller guarantees that the substitution is equal in quality, capacity, durability, ease of maintenance, and ease of installation to the material originally specified.

¶12. Inspection and Testing: Buyer may inspect and test material at any time. Seller will facilitate Buyer's inspection and testing at the factory, in the warehouse, on the road, and in the field.

¶13. Changes: Buyer, by written order, may delete material to be supplied under this Purchase Order, and the Purchase Order price will be equitably reduced. Buyer may order an increase in material to be supplied at the unit prices stated in the Purchase Order. If no unit prices are stated, Seller will promptly, at the request of Buyer, quote prices, and Buyer will promptly accept or reject the quote.

¶14. Delay: If Seller does not deliver material timely in accordance with the requirements of this Purchase Order, Seller understands Buyer's work will be disrupted and delayed, and Seller will pay Buyer any damages sustained as a result. In the event of delay in delivery of material, Buyer may also incur liability to the Owner of the project, and in that event, Seller will indemnify Buyer against such damages.

¶15. Indemnity: Seller will indemnify Buyer and hold it harmless from claims, losses, damage, and expense, including attorney's fees, caused in whole or in part by the negligence or fault of Seller in performing its duties under this Purchase Order. This indemnity shall be enforceable even if Buyer is partly at fault, but Seller will not indemnify Buyer for losses shown to be occasioned by the sole negligence or fault of Buyer.

¶16. Warranty: Seller warrants that all material supplied under this Purchase Order will be new, first-class, merchantable, fit for the intended purpose, and undamaged. For a period of one year after the occupancy of the project, Seller will at its own expense replace or repair defective material whether at the request of Buyer, Owner, or any subsequent tenant or purchaser of the project. This warranty may be enforced by Owner, tenant, or purchaser.

¶17. Payment: Payment of the Purchase Order price will be made progressively, according to the percentage of completion allowed by the project Owner to Buyer. Buyer will withhold 10 per cent of the price until 35 days after completion of the entire project. No payment will be made until Seller has supplied mechanic's lien releases, properly executed and on a form approved by Buyer and Owner.

¶18. Termination: In the event that Owner terminates the project, Buyer may terminate this Purchase Order by written notice to Seller. Buyer may also terminate this Purchase Order for its own convenience as to items that have not yet been shipped, at any time, by reasonable notice to Seller.

¶19. Time is of the Essence: Time is of the essence of this Purchase Order.

¶20. Arbitration: Any dispute arising out of or related to this Purchase Order or its performance or interpretation will be decided under the Construction Industry Rules of the American Arbitration Association, and judgment may be entered on the award. If a party, after due notice, fails to participate in hearings, the award will be made on the basis of evidence introduced by the party who does participate. The arbitrator will award reasonable attorney's fees to the prevailing party.

¶21. Attorney's Fees: In the event of litigation arising out of this Purchase Order, or the performance or interpretation thereof, the court will award reasonable attorney's fees to the prevailing party.

¶22. No Other Agreement: This Purchase Order is the full and final agreement of the parties, and no written or oral communication between the parties before the execution of this Purchase Order will modify or amend the agreement. The Purchase Order may be modified only by a written document signed by both parties.

DATED: _____

_____, Buyer   _____, Seller

By _____   By _____
   (Signature)   (Signature)

Alternate Purchase Order Provisions

§8.04 General Comments

The alternate provisions are arranged in alphabetical order and, in some cases, more than one form is provided for treatment of the same subject.

If the buyer under the purchase order is subject to an arbitration clause, then the first version of the arbitration clause should be used, because it will enable the buyer to involve the seller in the overall arbitration and thus resolve all disputes in one proceeding.

Provisions for inspection and testing, samples, shop drawings, substitution, scheduling, and warranty should be coordinated with the provisions of the project contract documents.

If the job is a union job and the supplier is nonunion, a picketing clause should be included.

FORM 8-3 Alternate Purchase Order Provisions

ALTERNATE PURCHASE ORDER PROVISIONS
PARAGRAPHS ARE IN ALPHABETICAL ORDER

¶1. Approval of Submittals No Waiver: All materials supplied by Seller will comply with the requirements of the contract documents. Buyer's approval will not excuse this requirement unless the submittal clearly, obviously, and explicitly discloses the particular portions of the submittal that deviate from the requirements of the contract documents.

¶2. Arbitration: If the contract documents include an arbitration provision that requires or permits Buyer to arbitrate disputes, Seller, at demand of Buyer, will become a party to such arbitration proceedings and be bound by the award. If, because of objections by other parties for other reasons, Seller cannot become a party to the proceedings, then Seller will present its arguments and evidence in the name of Buyer, with Buyer's cooperation, at the expense of Seller, and Seller will be bound by the award. If the contract documents do not contain such an arbitration clause, any dispute between Buyer and Seller arising out of the performance of this Purchase Order shall be decided in accordance with the Construction Industry Rules of the American Arbitration Association, and judgment will be entered on the award. The arbitrator will award reasonable attorney's fees to the prevailing party. If a party after due notice fails to participate in a hearing, the hearing will be held ex parte, and the award will be based on evidence produced by the party who does participate.

¶3. Arbitration: Any dispute arising out of or related to this Purchase Order or the interpretation thereof shall be decided by arbitration under the Construction Industry Rules of the American Arbitration Association, and judgment will be entered on the award. If a party after due notice fails to appear at a hearing, the hearing will proceed ex parte and the arbitrator will make an award based on evidence presented by the party who does appear and participate.

¶4. Arbitration: Any dispute arising out of or related to the performance of this Purchase Order or the interpretation thereof shall be decided by arbitration, and judgment will be entered on the award. A party demanding arbitration will notify the other party in writing of its claim, and will designate its arbitrator. The other party will designate its arbitrator in writing within ten days, and the two arbitrators will jointly select a neutral arbitrator within ten days, otherwise the neutral arbitrator will be appointed by the court. The award will be signed by at least two arbitrators. The arbitrators are empowered to award attorney's fees to the prevailing party.

¶5. Attached Identification: Each item of material supplied under this Purchase Order will have, securely attached, appropriate identification sufficient to enable Buyer to associate the item with its description both in the contract documents and on this Purchase Order, identify its location on the project, and its proper sequence of installation.

¶6. Attorney's Fees: In the event of arbitration or litigation arising out of or related to this Purchase Order or the material furnished under it, the arbitrator or court will award reasonable attorney's fees to the prevailing party.

¶7. Attorney's Fees: In the event of litigation related to the interpretation or performance of this Purchase Order, the court will award reasonable attorney's fees to the prevailing party.

¶8. Changes: Buyer may by written notice change or delete items of material or equipment to be supplied under this Purchase Order. In the event of a deletion of material, the dollar amount of the Purchase Order will be equitably reduced. Seller will promptly in writing quote prices for added or changed material which Buyer will promptly and in writing accept or reject.

§9. Changes: If Owner or Architect should order changes that affect material to be provided under this Purchase Order, Buyer will notify Seller in writing. For deletions, the Purchase Order price will be equitably reduced. If Buyer orders different material, Seller will promptly, in writing, quote prices and Buyer will promptly, in writing, accept or reject them.

¶10. Compliance with Codes: Seller is familiar with all building and other codes that apply to material supplied under this Purchase Order. Seller assures Buyer that the materials supplied by Seller will comply with such codes. Buyer relies on Seller's expertise to give such assurance.

¶11. Conditioned on Approval: The effectiveness of this Purchase Order as to any item of material is conditioned on its approval by Owner. Seller will process shop drawings promptly to expedite approval.

¶12. Contract Documents: Items to be supplied under this Purchase Order will conform to the requirements of the contract documents, which are identified as _____. The portions of the contract documents that are applicable to the description, installation, scheduling, inspection, testing, warranty, guarantee, quantity, quality, and physical characteristics of material to be supplied under this Purchase Order are incorporated herein by this reference.

¶13. Delay: If Seller fails to deliver material promptly at the times called for in this Purchase Order, the operations of Buyer will be delayed and disrupted. Seller will compensate Buyer for all damages suffered because of delay.

¶14. Delay: The contract documents under which the project is to be constructed provide that Buyer is liable for damages in the event that the progress of the project is delayed or disrupted. If Seller fails to deliver material on time, it will indemnify and hold harmless Buyer against all damages for delay under the contract documents, and will also reimburse Buyer for its damages suffered because of such delay.

¶15. Delay: If Seller does not supply material on time, Buyer will sustain damages that would be extremely difficult and impractical to compute. It is therefore agreed that Seller will pay Buyer the sum of $_____ for every day of delay in delivering material under this Purchase Order, as liquidated damages and not as a penalty.

¶16. Description of Material: Seller will supply Buyer with the following material:

_____
_____
_____
_____

All material will be new, undamaged, and of first-class merchantable quality.

¶17. Description of Material: All material supplied under this Purchase Order will be new, undamaged, and of first-class merchantable quality.

¶18. Destination: Material will be delivered FOB jobsite, at jobsite locations designated by Buyer. Jobsite address is:

_____
_____
_____
_____

¶19. Destination: Material will be delivered by Seller's carrier to the following destination:

_____
_____
_____
_____

¶20. Destination: Material will be delivered by Seller's carrier FOB to Buyer's warehouse located at:

_____
_____

¶21. Destination: Material will be delivered on Seller's trucks FOB jobsite at locations within the jobsite to be pointed out by Buyer to Seller, in proper sequence for efficient unloading and utilization. Before shipping material, Seller will obtain approval by telephone from Buyer for delivery. The jobsite is located at: _____

_____

_____

¶22. Indemnity: Seller will indemnify Buyer and hold it harmless from claims, liability, loss or damage, including attorney's fees, actually or allegedly caused or contributed to by any defect in material, delay in furnishing material, breach of contract, or negligent or wrongful act of Seller. The obligation to indemnify will apply if the claim, liability, loss or damage is partly caused or contributed to by the fault or negligence of Buyer. This indemnity agreement shall not apply to claims, liability, loss, or damage caused by the sole fault or negligence of Buyer.

¶23. Indemnity: Seller will indemnify Buyer and hold it harmless against all claims, liability, loss or damage, including attorney's fees, arising out of or related to material covered by this Purchase Order, or acts or omissions of Seller in carrying out this Purchase Order if such claim, liability, loss, or damage is caused, or alleged to be caused, by the fault or negligence of Seller.

¶24. Indemnity: Each party will indemnify the other party against all claims, liability, loss or damage, including attorney's fees, sustained and caused, in whole or in part, by the negligence or wrongdoing of the other party.

¶25. Inspection and Testing: Buyer may inspect and test material at any time. Seller will facilitate Buyer's inspection and testing which may take place at the factory, in the warehouse, on the road, or in the field.

¶26. Manuals Related to Material: Seller will separately deliver to Buyer all operating and installation manuals, and all technical data applicable to the material.

¶27. Measurement and Fitting: Seller will make measurements both from the contract documents and in the field to insure that material supplied under this Purchase Order will fit its designated location at the project. Material that does not fit will be promptly replaced or modified at no expense to Buyer.

¶28. No Other Agreement: This Purchase Order contains the entire contract, and it will not be modified by any prior quote or written or oral communication between the parties before the time this Purchase Order is executed.

¶29. No Other Agreement: This Purchase Order contains the entire contract, and may not be interpreted or modified by reference to written or oral communications prior to its execution. Its terms may not be changed except by a written document signed by both parties.

¶30. Notice Before Delivery: Seller will not deliver material without a minimum of 24 hours notice to Buyer. Notice may be written or by telephone. If delivery times proposed by Seller are inconvenient to the Buyer, Seller will modify its shipping schedule.

¶31. Offsetting Accounts: Buyer may offset against the price of this Purchase Order the amounts of any obligations of Seller to Buyer, whether arising out of this or any other project.

¶32. Packaging Protection and Storage: Seller will supply adequate protective packaging, will protect materials from damage and inclement weather, and will provide proper storage.

¶33. Payment: Payment is due _____ days after delivery, provided that Seller has complied with all its obligations under this Purchase Order, and has supplied Buyer with properly executed mechanic's lien releases, in form satisfactory to Buyer and Owner of the project.

¶34. Payment: Payment is due _____ days after delivery. Buyer will withhold _____ per cent of the price until material is installed, tested, and operating.

¶35. Payment: Payment is due _____ days after delivery. Buyer will withhold a retention of 10 per cent of the purchase price until 35 days after the completion of the entire project.

¶36. Payment: Payment is due _____ days after delivery. Buyer will withhold a retention of 10 per cent until Seller has delivered 100 per cent of material.

¶37. Payment: The contract documents call for payments to Buyer to be measured by the percentage of completion of various portions of the work. Buyer will pay Seller the same percentage of the purchase price as is allowed to Buyer under the contract documents at the times when those percentages are approved for payment by Owner.

¶38. Picketing: In the event of picketing at the jobsite, Seller will follow the instructions of Buyer as to delivery and unloading of material.

¶39. Picketing: If there is picketing at the jobsite, Seller will follow the instructions of Buyer as to scheduling of deliveries at unusual times, offloading, transshipment, and other such matters. Buyer will reimburse Seller for additional expense incurred as a result of such conditions.

¶40. Releases: Before Buyer makes any payment under this Purchase Order, Seller will furnish Buyer with properly executed mechanic's lien releases, in form satisfactory to Buyer and Owner.

¶41. Removal of Defective Material: Seller will promptly remove any material that Buyer designates as nonconforming or defective.

¶42. Replacement of Defective Material: Seller will promptly replace defective material so as to avoid disrupting Buyer's schedule.

¶43. Risk of Loss: Seller shall bear the risk of loss of or damage to material until delivery to and acceptance by Buyer.

¶44. Risk of Loss: Seller will bear the risk of loss of or damage to material until such time as Buyer takes actual possession of material by moving it from the point of delivery.

¶45. Sales Tax: Material supplied under this Purchase Order is subject to sales tax of _____ per cent, which will be added to the purchase price and paid by Buyer.

¶46. Sales Tax: Sales taxes will be paid by Buyer.

¶47. Sales Tax: This Purchase Order is not subject to sales tax.

¶48. Sales Tax: This Purchase Order is not subject to sales tax. Buyer's resale number is _____.

¶49. Samples: Before delivery of any material, Seller will provide samples to Buyer for its examination, testing, and approval. The materials delivered shall comply with the approved samples.

¶50. Samples and Mock-Ups: If the contract documents call for samples and mock-ups, Seller will provide them at no increase in the Purchase Order price.

¶51. Samples and Mock-Ups: The contract documents call for samples at Paragraph _____ and for mock-ups at Paragraph _____. Seller will provide samples and mock-ups to comply with those paragraphs at no additional cost. The materials supplied shall comply with the approved mock-up and samples.

¶52. Schedule: Buyer's construction schedule may be modified from time to time in order to conform to job conditions. Seller will keep itself informed as to schedule revisions, and will accelerate or delay deliveries so as to comply with the schedule.

¶53. Sequence of Deliveries: Seller will schedule its deliveries in proper sequence and so as to enable Buyer to process the material efficiently into the project.

¶54. Shop Drawings: Within _____ days after the execution of this Purchase Order, Seller will supply Buyer with shop drawings that comply with the requirements of the contract documents.

¶55. Shop Drawings: Seller will supply shop drawings in time and form to comply with the requirements of the contract documents.

¶56. Shop Drawings: Seller's shop drawings are required under Paragraph _____ of the contract documents. Seller will submit its shop drawings in time and form to comply with the requirements of the contract documents.

¶57. Start-Up, Testing and Instruction: Seller will start up and adequately test its equipment, and will instruct Buyer and Owner as to proper operation and maintenance.

¶58. Substitutions: Seller will make no substitutions without the written consent of Buyer.

¶59. Substitutions: If Seller recommends a substitution, Seller guarantees that the substituted material is at least equal in appearance, durability, function, capacity, and ease of maintenance to the specified material. Seller will make no substitution without prior written consent of Buyer.

¶60. Termination: Buyer may terminate this Purchase Order as to future deliveries at any time, and the Purchase Order price will be adjusted accordingly.

¶61. Termination: Buyer may terminate this Purchase Order at any time without cause, for its own convenience, upon payment to Seller the sum of $500.00.

¶62. Time is of the Essence: Time is of the essence of this Purchase Order.

¶63. Times for Delivery: Material will be delivered according to the following schedule:

_____
_____
_____

¶64. Unloading Directions: When making deliveries, Seller will report to Buyer's superintendent at the jobsite, and will follow his unloading instructions.

¶65. Union Drivers: Material will be delivered by union drivers.

¶66. <u>Warranty:</u> Seller warrants that all material will be new, of merchantable quality, free of defects and damage. Seller will repair or replace defective material, at no expense to Buyer or Buyer's customer, for a period of one year after the completion of the project.

¶67. <u>Warranty:</u> Seller warrants that all material supplied under this Purchase Order will be new, merchantable, of first-class quality, and undamaged. This warranty may be enforced by Buyer, and all persons to whom any portion of the project may be rented or transferred. For a period of _____ years after completion of the entire project, Seller will promptly and at its own expense repair or replace any defective material. Seller will comply with Buyer's policy, which is to satisfy the customer in all cases where a warranty claim is plausible, even though questionable.

¶68. <u>Warranty:</u> The contract documents provide for warranties at Paragraph _____. Seller extends to Buyer and the other parties mentioned in the warranty provisions of the contract documents the same warranties and will perform replacement and repair work as provided in the contract documents.

¶69. <u>Warranty:</u> Seller has studied the contract documents and has reviewed their provisions with respect to warranties. The warranty provisions of the contract documents apply in favor of Buyer to the material covered by this Purchase Order.

¶70. <u>Warranty:</u> Before final payment under this Purchase Order Seller will sign and deliver to Owner a form of warranty that guarantees Owner that the material supplied under this Purchase Order is of merchantable quality and free from defects, and that Seller will, for a period of one year after the completion of the entire project, at its own expense, promptly repair or replace any defective material.

¶71. <u>Warranty:</u> Before final payment under this Purchase Order, Seller will sign and deliver to owner a form of warranty that complies with the requirements of the contract documents. Seller will thereafter, upon the request of Owner, promptly repair or replace any defective material as provided in the contract documents.

Alternate Purchase Order Forms

FORM 8-4 Short Form Purchase Order - Another Version

Purchase Order

Date _____

TO:

PURCHASE ORDERS

SHIP TO:

Purchase Order No. _____

Above purchase order number MUST appear on all inquiries, invoices, packing slips and shipping documents.

Render all invoices in TRIPLICATE

Job _____

_____

Ship via:

F.O.B.

Freight Terms:

SHIP THE FOLLOWING ITEMS AND DO THE WORK IN STRICT ACCORDANCE WITH THE PLANS AND SPECIFICATIONS:

Price:

Terms:

Delivery Date(s) Required:

ALL TERMS AND CONDITIONS AS SET FORTH ON REVERSE SIDE ARE PART OF THIS PURCHASE ORDER.

ACCEPTED: _____   _____
           Supplier   Purchaser

By: _____   _____
     Title   Title

Date: _____

General Conditions

All material and equipment furnished under this order shall be guaranteed by the Seller to the Purchaser and Owner to be fit and sufficient for the purpose intended, and that they are merchantable, of good material and workmanship and free from defects, and Seller agrees to replace without charge to Purchaser or Owner said material and equipment, or remedy any defects latent or patent not due to ordinary wear and tear or due to improper use or maintenance, which may develop within one year from date of acceptance by the Owner, or within the guarantee period set forth in applicable plans and specifications, whichever is longer. The warranties herein are in addition to those implied by law.

The Seller and all material and equipment furnished under this order shall be subject to the approval of the Owners, architect, engineer, or the Purchaser, and Seller shall furnish the required number of submittal data or samples for said approval. In the event approval is not obtained the order may be cancelled by Purchaser with no liability on the part of Purchaser.

All material and equipment furnished hereunder shall be in strict compliance with plans, specifications, and general conditions applicable to the contract of Purchaser with the Owner or another contractor, and Seller shall be bound thereby in the performance of this contract.

The materials and equipment covered by this order, whether in a deliverable state or otherwise, shall remain the property of the Seller until delivered to a designated site and actually received by the Purchaser, and any damage to the material and equipment or loss of any kind occasioned in transit shall be borne by the Seller, notwithstanding the manner in which the goods are shipped or who pays the freight or other transportation costs.

The Seller hereby agrees to indemnify and save harmless the Purchaser from and against all claims, liability, loss, damage or expense, including attorneys' fees by reason of any actual or alleged infringement of letters patent or any litigation based thereon covering any article purchased hereunder.

Time is of the essence of this contract. Should the Supplier for any reason fail to make deliveries as required hereunder to the satisfaction of the Purchaser, or if the materials are not satisfactory to the Owner, Architect, Engineer, or Purchaser, the Purchaser shall be at liberty to purchase the materials elsewhere, and any excess in cost of same over the price herein provided shall be chargeable to and paid by the Supplier on demand. Should any delay on the part of the Supplier or defects or nonconformance of the materials or equipment with the plans and specifications occasion loss, damage or expense including consequential damages to the Owner or to the Purchaser, the Supplier shall indemnify the Owner and the Purchaser against such loss, damage or expense including attorneys' fees. If for any cause, all or any portion of the materials to be furnished are not delivered at the time or times herein specified, the Purchaser may, at his option, cancel this order as to all or any portion of materials not so delivered.

Seller shall furnish all necessary lien waivers, affidavits, or other documents required to keep the Owner's premises free from liens or claims for liens, arising out of the furnishing of the material or equipment herein, as payments are made from time to time under this order.

All prior representations, conversations or preliminary negotiations shall be deemed to be merged in this order, and no changes will be considered or approved unless this order is modified by an authorized representative of Purchaser in writing.

FORM 8-5   Short Form Purchase Order - Another Version

Purchase Order—Short

PURCHASE ORDER NO. _____ SHIP TO:

TO:

Purchase Order Agreement made this _____ day of _____, 19____, between _____ located at _____ ("Contractor") and _____ located at _____ ("Vendor")

Contractor has entered a contract ("Prime Contract") with _____ ("Principal") to furnish certain work, labor, services and equipment necessary for the construction of a _____ ("Project") in accordance with Prime Contract documents including certain Plans and Specifications prepared by _____ ("A/E").

Contractor and Vendor enter this Agreement ("Contract"), incorporating the Prime Contract, and agree as follows:

The Vendor shall provide and furnish all materials, supplies, equipment, services, facilities, administration, etc. for the complete performance and acceptance, in exact accord with and subject to the Prime Contract, the following work:
_____
_____

Total Contract Price $_____

Proper Approval Drawings and Data must be to Contractor no later than _____, 19____. Failure to comply with this schedule may be deemed a breach. Vendor is allowed _____ weeks for completion of work. A firm delivery requirement will be issued by Contractor. Vendor shall insure its work against all risks of loss and damage. No shipment is to be made without release and consent by Contractor. Delivery will be F.O.B. Project at a time and place directed by Contractor. Units must be shipped complete and in the proper sequence. All material delivered to the Project shall have attached identification.

Vendor will furnish notarized certificates of compliance stating that all work is in full compliance with the Prime Contract, as relates to this Contract. Delivery, installation, or erection of equipment shall not be considered complete until all spare parts and approved copies of the instruction, operation, and maintenance manuals are furnished. These manuals shall include drawings of all equipment. Any and all samples, test reports, certificates of compliance, warranties, guarantees, or the like, required by the Prime Contract, shall be furnished at no additional cost. Vendor shall be liable to Contractor as Contractor is liable to the Principal under Prime Contract. Contractor shall not be liable for any delays, suspensions or cost escalations. This Contract may be terminated by Contractor without cause and Vendor shall be entitled to payment only for work performed pro-rata to this Contract price, and in no case to profit on unperformed work.

Materials, supplies, or services covered by this Contract (are) (are not) exempt from Sales Tax.

The Vendor, and any other manufacturer of the work supplied under this Contract, shall indemnify and save harmless the Contractor and Principal, and all persons acting for or on behalf of these parties, from all claims and liability of any nature or kind, including costs, attorney fees, and expenses arising from or occasioned by any breach of this Contract, or by infringement or alleged infringement of patent rights on any invention, process, article, or apparatus, furnished to Contractor or arising from or occasioned by the use thereof. Vendor shall be liable for all damages, costs, and expenses, including Contractor's attorney fees, resulting from any breach of this Contract. Contractor shall pay the total sum of $_____ (including) (excluding) taxes. Vendor shall be entitled to payment, upon payment to Contractor, equal to _____ per cent of the approved amount on the last day of month following delivery and acceptance of the complete unit. Balance on completion of testing, acceptance, compliance with all guarantee and warranty obligations, and payment.

_____   _____
Contractor   Vendor

FORM 8-6   Long Form Purchase Order - Another Version

Purchase Order—Long

PURCHASE ORDER NO. _____   SHIP TO:
TO:
Agreement made this _____ day of _____, 19___, by and between

_____ with its principal place of business located at _____ (hereinafter designated as "Contractor") and _____ _____ with its principal place of business located at _____
(hereinafter desgnated as "Vendor"):

WHEREAS, the Contractor has heretofore entered a contract (hereinafter designated as the "Prime Contract") with _____, (hereinafter designated as the "Principal") to furnish certain work, labor, services and equipment necessary for the construction of a _____
 (hereinafter designated as the "Project") in accordance with Prime Contract documents including certain Plans and Specifications prepared by _____
_____ (hereinafter designated as the "A/E");

WITNESS: The Contractor and Vendor, in consideration of mutual covenants do hereby enter this Agreement, including the Purchase Order Articles of Construction, (hereinafter collectively referred to as "Contract") and agree as follows:

The Vendor shall provide and furnish all materials, supplies, equipment, services, facilities, administration, etc. for the complete performance and acceptance, in exact accord with, and subject to the Prime Contract, the following work:
_____
_____
_____

                            Total Contract Price $_____

This Project is being scheduled on the basis of a progress schedule. Proper Approval Drawings and other Data must be to the Contractor no later than _____, 19_____. Failure to comply with this schedule may be deemed a breach. Vendor shall immediately make all required corrections. Specification Section *MUST* appear on all drawings and correspondence. Vendor is allowed _____ weeks for fabrication and completion of equipment and work after return of approved drawings. A firm delivery requirement will be issued by Contractor. Vendor shall insure its work against all risks of loss and damage. All shippers must notify the jobsite 48 hours before attempting delivery. No shipment is to be made without release and consent by Contractor. Delivery will be F.O.B. Project at a time and place directed by Contractor. Units must be shipped complete and in the proper sequence for installation. No partial shipments will be accepted unless requested and approved in writing. All material delivered to the Project shall have attached identification. Each accessory or component which is shipped "loose" shall be marked or tagged the same as the basic item. Vendor will furnish notarized certificates of compliance stating that all work is in full compliance with the Prime Contract before any material is processed, fabricated or delivered.

Bound instruction manuals, if specified, including parts lists and certifications, to be forwarded within _____ days after receipt of approved drawings. Delivery, installation, or erection of equipment shall not be considered to be _____ percent complete until approved copies of the operation and maintenance manuals are in the hands of the Contractor. These manuals shall include drawings of all equipment, including minor parts and sub-assemblies, in such detail as will permit disassembly of each piece of equipment for maintenance. Parts drawings shall show such fabrication and assembly details as are required to permit disassembly and assembly of the equipment. Vendor shall furnish start-up and instructional service, if specified.

Vendor shall furnish, with each piece of equipment, the complete set of tools recommended by the manufacturer for the servicing of the equipment. Each piece of equipment shall be furnished with the spare parts listed or referenced in the Prime Contract for the equipment, in addition to the standard set of spare parts recommended by the manufacturer of the equipment. The recommended list of spare parts shall be submitted to the A/E prior to the delivery of the equipment. All spare parts shall be plainly tagged and marked for identification and ordering. They shall be treated with suitable preservatives, wrapped and packaged to provide adequate protection during storage.

Any and all samples, test reports, certificates of compliance, warranties, guarantees, or the like, required by the Prime Contract, shall be furnished at no additional cost. Vendor shall be liable to Contractor as Contractor is liable to the Principal under Prime Contract.

Materials, supplies, or services covered by this Contract (are) (are not) exempt from Sales Tax. Tax Exempt Purchase Certificates (are) (are not) attached.

The Vendor and manufacturer of the work supplied under this Contract shall indemnify and save harmless the Contractor, A/E and Principal, and all persons acting for or on behalf of these parties, from all claims and liability of any nature or kind, including costs, attorney fees, expenses arising from or occasioned by any breach of this Contract, or infringement or alleged infringement of patent rights on any invention, process, article, or apparatus, or any part thereof, or arising from or occasioned by the use thereof, including their use by the Principal. Vendor shall be liable for all damages, costs, and expenses, direct and indirect, including Contractor's attorney fees, resulting from any breach of this Contract.

In consideration of the Vendor's performance of this Contract, which incorporates the Purchase Order Articles of Construction and the Prime Contract as a part hereof, the Contractor shall pay the total sum of $_____ (including) (excluding) Taxes. Vendor shall be entitled to payment, upon payment to Contractor, equal to _____ per cent of the approved amount on the last day of month following delivery and acceptance of the complete unit; and, _____ per cent upon acceptance of and payment for the installation. Balance on completion of testing, acceptance, compliance with all guarantee and warranty obligations, and payment to Contractor by Principal.

_____
Vendor

Witnessed: _____ By: _____
Officer

Witnessed: _____ _____
Contractor

PURCHASE ORDER
ARTICLES OF CONSTRUCTION

I These Articles are made part of and are incorporated into the Contract between the Contractor and Vendor. The terms and conditions contained herein shall be binding on Vendor.

II The Prime Contract, including all of its contract documents, is incorporated herein by reference and made an integral part of this Contract. The Prime Contract can be reviewed by the Vendor at the Contractor's principal place of business. The Vendor is bound, responsible, obligated, and liable to the Contractor as the Contractor is bound, responsible, obligated, and liable under the Prime Contract. The term "Contract" as used herein shall include all documents incorporated into and made a part of the Agreement, between the Contractor and Vendor; and any revisions thereto. The term "Architect/Engineer" (hereinafter referred to as "A/E") shall be deemed to be that representative directing the work for the Principal, or any other person authorized by the Prime Contract to direct, judge, approve or reject any matter or thing connected with the performance of the Prime Contract. The Prime Contract and this Contract shall be interpreted together and, in harmony with one another. However, in case of conflict between the Prime Contract and this Contract, this Contract shall govern. The Vendor must call any such conflict or discrepancy to the Contractor's attention, in writing, prior to executing this Contract, for written decision, otherwise the Vendor agrees to be bound by the more onerous provision.

III All work included in the Contract shall be done under the direction of the Contractor, and to the satisfaction of the Contractor, Principal, and A/E. Said work shall be performed in exact accord with the Prime Contract. The work to be performed by the Vendor includes that work specifically set forth in this Contract, as well as any and all other work reasonably necessary to have a properly working and totally acceptable system and Project. All work covered by this Contract shall be performed in a skillful and workmanlike manner with material, equipment, etc. being both new and of the best kind and grade for the exact purpose intended. Said work shall be deemed to include any and all work required to be performed by the Contractor, Principal, A/E or by any judicial or administrative tribunal. The Vendor agrees, without additional compensation, to perform, conform and abide by all decisions issued by the Contractor, when the Contractor has been directed to perform, conform and abide by similar decisions, without additional compensation, issued by the Principal or A/E. The Vendor shall provide, at its own expense, all working drawings, tests, samples, models, guarantees, insurance and delivery services, and all other items necessary for the proper performance of this Contract and acceptance of the Project. The Vendor shall pay for all inspection fees, royalties, and license fees. The Vendor shall make all necessary arrangements and agreements so as not to infringe any patents, trademarks, or copyrights, and shall hold the Contractor, Principal and A/E harmless from any infringement, claim, or suit.

IV The Vendor acknowledges that it has carefully reviewed and examined this Contract with all of its contract documents, and all other documents directly or indirectly relating to the Contract; and the Vendor will not make any claim of the Contractor based upon or arising out of any misunderstanding or misconception on its part of the provisions and requirements of the Prime Contract or this Contract. Any information given or statements made to the Vendor shall not reduce the work to be performed by the Vendor under this Contract. The Vendor acknowledges that it has fully examined and analyzed all conditions that could affect its performance and that no conditions exist which would affect the progress, performance or price of this Contract. The Vendor will perform and furnish any and all work, labor, services, and/or materials, mentioned, shown, depicted, or required in one Contract document and not mentioned, shown, depicted, or required in another document, as if it were clearly mentioned, shown, depicted, or required in all Contract documents. The Vendor shall be required to do all things and be bound by all rulings of the Principal or A/E to the same extent and degree as the Contractor is bound thereto. The Vendor shall be responsible for all its own field measurements where applicable.

V All work, labor, services, and materials to be furnished, supplied, or performed by Vendor must strictly comply with all Federal, State, Local, Municipal, as well as any and all other governing Jurisdictions and Authorities. Laws, Rules, Regulations, Statutes, Ordinances, and Directives (hereinafter designated as "Laws"). All work, labor, services, or materials, in addition to that specifically required by this Contract, but necessary to fully comply with said Laws, will be furnished by Vendor as part of this Contract, without additional compensation.

VI The Vendor shall not be entitled to nor shall it receive any increase or upward adjustment in its Contract price unless said amount and liability are acknowledged, in writing, by an Officer of the Contractor. No alteration, addition, omission or change shall be made in the work, except upon the written Change Order of the Contractor. Any change or adjustment in the Contract price by virtue of such Change Order shall be specifically stated in said Change Order. Change Orders are subject to the terms of these Articles and all other Contract documents. Prior to the issuance of any Change Order, the Contractor may require the Vendor to furnish to the Contractor a detailed breakdown showing the difference in value of the work, labor, services, and materials altered, added omitted or changed by the proposed Change Order. If an agreement as to monetary allowance or other term in the Change Order cannot be reached, the Contractor, by an authorized representative, may direct, in writing, the Vendor to perform the work with the final determination reserved until final completion of this Contract and the Prime Contract. The monetary amount for the performance of any Change Order shall not exceed the allowance set forth in the Vendor's prior price breakdown. Any extension of time needed as a result of a proposed Change Order shall be requested by the Vendor, in writing, prior to the issuance of the Change Order, and shall be incorporated therein. There shall be no other monetary or time allowance, direct or indirect, to the Vendor other than that which is specifically written in the Change Order. Ordinary field modifications which do not substantially increase Vendor's cost of this Contract will be performed without any price adjustment. Where unit prices are stipulated in the Contract, all adjustments, whether increases or decreases shall be made in accordance with said units. Said units shall be deemed to include all general and administrative expenses, overhead, profit, supervision, extended performance time cost factors, and all other direct and indirect expenses. If the Contractor elects the option to direct the Change Order work to be done on a time and material basis, the Vendor shall prepare daily time and material invoices. Said daily time and material invoices shall include only direct out-of-pocket material and labor costs with a maximum total additional mark-up of 10 per cent. The 10 per cent mark-up is deemed to be full compensation for all administrative expenses, overhead, and profit. The Vendor shall in no event receive any compensation or allowance for any Change Order in an amount greater than that which the Contractor actually receives from the Principal, less a reasonable deduction for the Contractor's overhead and profit. No Change Order shall vary, abrogate, avoid, or otherwise affect the terms, conditions, and provisions of this Contract except as specifically set forth in the Change Order.

VII The Contractor may, upon the written request of the Vendor, appeal on behalf of the Vendor from any ruling or decision of the Principal or A/E, or institute any action or proceeding to recover damages by reason of any affirmative claim by the Vendor, or by reason of any deduction or refusal to pay by the Principal for any reason, involving the work or performance of the Vendor. In that event, the Vendor shall pay all costs attributable thereto and shall render all assistance requested by Contractor. The Vendor shall be bound by the determination of the Principal, the A/E, or in the event of an appeal or further action or proceeding, by the determination of same, and shall be entitled only to its proportionate share of any actual net recovery, less overhead and profit to the Contractor, and less the Contractor's expenses and attorney's fees. The Vendor hereby waives and releases any and all claims, causes of actions, and rights to further payment, beyond the Contract amount, except as the Contractor may receive funds or extensions of time from the Principal or A/E.

VIII The Vendor shall provide at its own place of business, at the places of business of its subcontractors and suppliers, and at the Project, sufficient safe and proper facilities for the inspection of the Vendor's work by the Contractor, Principal, A/E, or any other authorized representative. The Vendor must be prepared, at all times, to prove the exact quantities and qualities of the materials and equipment being used. If the Vendor is assigned a storage area for its equipment, material, and tools, it shall not store any item outside of the designated area. The Vendor shall be responsible for the receipt, delivery, unloading, storage, warehousing, protection, insurance, and all other risk of loss relating to any materials or equipment it is to furnish, provide, or have provided to it under this Contract. The Vendor shall be obligated to inspect all material and equipment furnished to it at time of receipt. The Vendor shall be responsible to immediately notify the Contractor, in writing, of any defects or non-conformity in the material or equipment so received. Failure to notify the Contractor shall be deemed an acknowledgment and acceptance of the material as being in accord with this Contract. The Vendor shall be liable for any damages incurred by the Contractor as a result of its failure to so notify the Contractor. It is the Vendor's obligation, upon direction by the Contractor, to take all necessary steps, including but not limited to delivery of samples, tests and reports, guarantees, drawings, manuals, certificates, details, warranties, inspections etc., to obtain any and all required approvals necessary or requested under this Contractor or the Prime Contract. The Vendor shall, within 24 hours after receiving specific written notice from the Contractor, commence to take down and remove any designated portion of its work which is condemned, disapproved, improper, or is questioned as not being in strict compliance and conformity with the requirements of this Contract. The Vendor shall promptly, at its own expense, correct and rectify same. If the Contractor determines that it will accept non-conforming work, the Contractor shall be entitled to a credit for the non-conformity. Any damage prior to final acceptance and payment shall be corrected by the Vendor at its sole expense. Inspection or supervision by the Contractor shall not relieve the Vendor of its obligations.

IX The Vendor shall proceed with each and every part of this Contract in a prompt and diligent manner. The Vendor shall commence, continue, and complete its performance of the Project so as not to delay the Contractor, the Principal, other contractors or subcontractors, completion of this Contract, the Prime Contract, or any portions thereof, and so as to insure completion as directed by the Contractor. Any time specified for the completion of this Contract, or a portion thereof, is a material provision of this Contract, and time is of the essence. The Vendor shall, from time to time, on demand of the Contractor, give adequate evidence to the Contractor to substantiate the planned performance and progress of the Contract and the various parts thereof. If the Vendor should delay or threaten to delay the progress or performance of its contract, or cause any actual or potential damage or liability to the Contractor, the Vendor may be deemed in breach of this Contract, and shall indemnify and hold the Contractor harmless from all liability and costs. The Vendor shall bear the costs of all damages done to others and shall be directly responsible to same for any damages caused by or resulting from acts or omissions of the Vendor. In the event any other vendor, contractor or subcontractor should damage the Vendor, the Vendor shall neither seek nor be entitled to any compensation from the Contractor, but will seek its damages directly from such other party. The Vendor acknowledges that the Contract price is based on the fact that the Contractor is not liable, absent any actual fraud or intentional and active tortious conduct, for any damages or costs due to delays, accelerations, non-performance, interferences with performance, suspensions, or changes in the performance or sequence of the Vendor's work. Should this Contract, in whole or part, be interfered with or delayed, or be suspended in the commencement, prosecution or completion, for reasons beyond the Vendor's control and without its fault or negligence, the Vendor shall be entitled to an extension of time in which to complete its Contract; but, only if it shall have notified, in writing, the Contractor of the cause of delay within two days of the occurance of the event, and provided a similar extension of time, if needed, is alloted to the Contractor by the Principal.

X The Contractor shall not be liable for any loss or casualty incurred or caused by the Vendor. The Vendor shall hold the Contractor, Principal, and A/E harmless from any and all liability, costs, damages, attorney's fees, and expenses from any claims or causes of action of whatsoever nature arising while on or near the Project, or while performing Contract related work, including those claims relating to its subcontractors, suppliers or employees, or by reason of any claim or dispute of any person or entity for damages from any cause directly or indirectly relating to any action or failure to act by the Vendor, its representatives, employees, subcontractors, or suppliers and whether or not it is alleged that the Contractor, Principal or A/E, in any way contributed to the alleged wrongdoing or is liable due to a non-delegable duty. The Vendor will maintain whatever security or insurance the Contractor deems necessary to fully protect the Contractor against any loss or liability.

XI The Vendor shall be responsible for and shall pay any and all taxes, contributions, increased wages and material costs, fees, etc., imposed directly or indirectly on account of its work, labor, material, and services required under or relating to this Contract. At no time shall there by any increase or escalation in the Contract price.

XII The Vendor shall, as part of this Contract, furnish to the Contractor a full and duly executed Performance and Payment Bond issued by a surety company and in such format as is satisfactory to the Contractor. If such is not furnished with this Contract, the Contractor may, at any time prior to or during performance of this Contract, demand that the Vendor furnish same. The cost of said bonds shall be separately itemized and be paid for by the Contractor. The Vendor's failure to deliver satisfactory bonds within ten days after demand may be deemed a material breach of this Contract.

XIII Should the Vendor fail to perform in strict accordance with the Prime Contract or this Contract, become insolvent, unable to or fail to pay its obligations as they mature, or, in any other respect, fail, in the opinion of the Contractor, to properly prosecute and perform any part of its work, or be terminated under any other contract with the Contractor, then the Vendor may be deemed by the Contractor to have breached this Contract. In case of a breach, the Contractor may, at its discretion, terminate this Contract, or any part thereof, by written notice to the Vendor. In case of termination, the Contractor may use any and all materials, equipment, tools, or chattles furnished by or belonging to the Vendor either at or for the Project. The Vendor, on termination, will be deemed to have offered to the Contractor an assignment of all its subcontracts or purchase orders relating to this Project.

XIV The Vendor shall do whatever is necessary in the prosecution of its work to assure harmonious labor relations at the Project.

XV The Vendor shall become entitled to receive progress payments, if included in the Prime Contract, for work performed during the payment periods established in the Prime Contract, based upon a payment breakdown furnished to the Contractor upon return of this executed Contract. Progress payments become payable ten days after such payment has been received by the Contractor. All progress payment requisitions are subject to audit. The estimate by the Principal or A/E of the value of work performed during a payment period or any deduction, offset or counterclaim against the requisitioned amount shall be binding on the Vendor. Progress payments shall not exceed 90 percent of the amount requisitioned, and then paid by the Principal. Final payment shall become payable thirty days after final completion and acceptance of the Prime Contract and receipt of final payment by the Contractor. In no event shall Vendor be entitled to receive any form of payment prior to the Contractor's actual receipt of that payment. Payment is subject to the Contractor's withholding an amount reasonably necessary to protect itself against any liability directly or indirectly relating to this or any other Contract. Payment may be withheld until the Vendor furnishes an affidavit detailing each and every unpaid obligation directly or indirectly relating to that payment and this Contract. Prior to final payment the Vendor shall submit from each and every subcontractor and supplier releases of the Contractor and its Surety, and indicating full payment of all monies due or to become due relating to this Contract. Before any payment is made to the Vendor, it shall prove that the Project is free and clear from all liens and claims. The Contractor's withholding of monies from the Vendor shall be interest free. The acceptance of any payment shall constitute a release of the Contractor from any liability, except retainage, due to any reason, to date. No payment, including final payment, shall be evidence of the performance of this Contract by the Vendor, and payment shalls not be construed as an acceptance of defective or incomplete work.

XVI The Vendor waives, releases, and relinquishes all rights to file any Stop Work Notice, Notice of Intent, Notice of Lien, Mechanic's Lien, or other encumbrance against the Contractor, Surety, Principal, Project, or any monies earned by the Contractor.

XVII The validity, interpretation and performance of this Contract shall be governed by the Laws of the State where the designated principal place of business of the Contractor is located. Titles, captions, or headings to any provision, Article, etc., shall not limit the full contents of same. If any term or provision of this Contract is found invalid, it shall not affect the validity and enforcement of all remaining terms and provisions of the Contract.

XVIII This Contract cannot be changed, modified, altered, or terminated orally.

XIX The Vendor shall be responsible and liable for all costs, disbursements, and expenses, including attorney's fees, incurred by the Contractor as a result of the Vendor's breach of threatened breach of any Article, term, or condition of this Contract.

XX Vendor shall not deal directly with the Principal or A/E without Contractor's written consent.

XXI This Contract is made conditional upon the approval of the Vendor by the Principal or A/E, where such approval is required. However, the Vendor is responsible to maintain and abide by all statements and quotes given to Contractor.

XXII The approval by the Contractor, Principal, or A/E of any submittals of the Vendor shall not relieve it of liability for any deviations from the Prime Contract or this Contract, unless specifically called to the Contractor's attention, in writing, and is then so acknowledged by the Contractor, in writing.

XXIII The Vendor, in addition to all other guarantees and warranties contained in this Contract and the Prime Contract, and not in limitation of the Contractor's other legal rights, warrants and guarantees that its work is in strict and absolute accord with the Contract, and that it shall, for a minimum of one year after the date of final acceptance of the Prime Contract, perform any maintenance or corrective work, without cost, as directed by the Contractor. The Contractor may demand assurance, by bond or otherwise, from the Vendor that it will abide by its guarantee and warranty.

XXIV The Contractor, by written notice, shall have the right to terminate and cancel this Contract, for any cause or for its own convenience. In such event, the Contractor shall pay the Vendor for that work actually performed in an amount proportionate to this Contract price. The Contractor shall not be liable for any other costs, including prospective profits on work not performed. However, if the reason for the termination is due to any default or action by the Principal, A/E or as a result of Court Order or public authority, then the Contractor shall not be liable to the Vendor for any sum greater than that which the Contractor has actually received from the Principal on behalf of the Vendor's performance, less any costs incurred by the Contractor.

XXV The Vendor agrees to incorporate into any subcontracts or purchase orders it has with any other party, all those provisions required by law to be incorporated therein, and all those provisions of this Contract which affect the rights of the Contractor.

9 Joint Venture Agreements

Introduction to Joint Venture Agreements
§9.01 General Comments
§9.02 Rights and Responsibilities
§9.03 Interests of Parties
§9.04 Control of Operations
§9.05 Contributions and Financing
§9.06 Employees of the Joint Venture
§9.07 Insurance

Joint Venture Agreements
    FORM 9-1 Joint Venture Agreement
    FORM 9-2 Joint Venture Agreement - Another Version

Introduction to Joint Venture Agreements

§9.01 General Comments

The joint venture has been defined as a temporary contractual association of independent companies for the purpose of entering into a single business transaction. In the construction industry, the usual purpose of the joint venture is to secure and perform a construction contract for a single project.

Courts apply the law of partnerships to joint ventures to determine the rights and liabilities of the co-venturers among themselves and with respect to third parties. However, the characteristic of temporariness distinguishes a joint venture from a partnership. By utilizing the joint venture form, two independent companies can join together to bid and perform work on a single construction project, and thereafter can return to their original status.

The joint venture approach to a project allows the combination of existing skills of the co-venturers without requiring a drastic restructuring of the venturers' present organizations. The ability to perform a large project without risking capital beyond the individual contractor's means is another advantage which is provided by the joint venture.

Each joint venture agreement must be tailored to the circumstances of the particular project and venturers. The contractual clauses contained in the text are provided for purposes of illustration. Many alternatives are possible, and legal counsel should be consulted both in the planning and drafting of such an agreement.

§9.02 Rights and Responsibilities

This paragraph should specify that the parties to the joint venture agreement do not intend to create a partnership. It is stated plainly that the relationship between the joint venturers is a temporary association confined to the performance of a particular contract.

This paragraph should also state whether or not the joint venturers are permitted to carry on their own businesses contemporaneously with joint venture operations.

§9.03 Interests of Parties

The joint venture agreement must provide a method for allocation of the revenue, profits or losses, and liabilities of the joint venture resulting from the performance of the construction contract. If the parties agree to divide the gross contract price, this paragraph will state the percentage, or lump sum, division of the contract price. If profits or losses are to be allocated among the co-venturers, the formula for such allocation will be set forth in this clause. In addition to specifying interests in the profits and losses of the joint venture, provision may also be made for the venturers' interests in any property and equipment held by the joint venture.

There are many methods for dividing joint venture interests among the co-venturers; however, the most common method is by a fixed percentage allocation among all parties.

The clause dealing with the interests of the parties may also contain a provision whereby the parties agree to indemnify each other against any loss or liability arising out of the joint venture work, in excess of the agreed upon percentage division.

§9.04 Control of Operations

The agreement should establish some mechanism for the centralized control of joint venture operations. One option is designation of one venturer as the joint venture sponsor, having control over the joint venture and performance of the construction contract. More often, the joint venture agreement provides for the establishment of a management committee, consisting of one or more representatives of each joint venturer.

This portion of the agreement either should designate the representatives of the respective venturers who will serve on the management committee, or provide a procedure for their selection. Also, provision should be made for the appointment of alternate representatives to serve when the principal representatives are absent, incapacitated, or otherwise unable to serve.

§9.05 Contributions and Financing

Arrangements for the initial and continued financing of the joint venture must be specified. A decision must be made as to the amount of any initial capital contributions by the co-venturers. Initial contributions are normally specified in the agreement, and are usually in proportion to the percentage interests of the parties.

It is possible that the initial capital contributions of the parties, coupled with the revenues generated by the joint venture throughout the project, will be insufficient to finance the joint venture operations. This potential problem can be dealt with effectively by including in the agreement a clause which requires the parties to remit additional capital contributions to the joint venture in proportion to their respective interests in the joint venture, when and if the management committee determines that additional funds are necessary. Occasions can arise where one venturer is unable to contribute the capital required by the joint venture and specified in the agreement. If any venturer is unable to make a required capital contribution, provision should be made for the remaining venturers to contribute the difference. The agreement can provide for repayment of any advances from the first joint venture revenues available for distribution, with interest from the date the deficiency was advanced. The interest should be charged against the delinquent venturer. Another method of dealing with advances by one party is to provide for a readjustment of the interests of the parties to coincide with the new ratio of invested capital. In such cases, the agreement can provide for a readjustment of the profit percentage only, or of the interest in both profits and losses.

In the opposite case, the joint venture may find that is has excess funds on hand. These excess funds may be distributed at the discretion of the management committee. A distribution will not affect the parties' liability for future losses and expenses of the joint venture.

§9.06 Employees of the Joint Venture

Many construction contractors have established their own pension and profit-sharing plans, while others contribute to jointly administered multi-employer pension and profit-sharing plans created pursuant to the terms of collective bargaining agreements negotiated by the employer or by an employer association and a union. Where a co-venturer has established its own pension or profit-sharing plan, problems may arise if the employees participating in such plans terminate their employment with the co-venturer to become employees of the joint venture.

The most important issues affecting the status of an employee of a joint venturer, who terminates employment with the company to become employed by the joint venture, is whether the employee thereby will incur a one-year break in service. This is defined generally as a period of 12 consecutive months during which the employee has not completed more than 500 hours of service with the employer (IRC §411(1)(6)(A)).

The consequences of a one-year break in service are very unfavorable for the employee. The most immediate consequence is that the employee forfeits accrued but non-vested benefits. This can cause a serious monetary loss to the employee whose interest in the plan is not 100 per cent vested.

In addition, joint venture employees who return to their respective companies after incurring a one-year break in service may find that the resumption of participation in the pension or profit-sharing plan of their employer is delayed. The terms of the pension or profit-sharing plan may provide that the employee must complete a full year of service after return, as a condition for eligibility for the particular plan (IRC §410(a)(5)(C)).

Even after returning to the employ of a venturer, the one-year break in service may continue to have detrimental effects when the number of years of service with the employer are computed for vesting purposes. The plan may require a one-year waiting period before the employee's pre-break and post-break service must be aggregated under the plan; in certain cases, the plan may disregard the employee's pre-break service if the period of absence equals or exceeds the years of service prior to the break.

The problems created by terminating the employee's employment with a company to service the joint venture directly throughout its duration can be alleviated by proper planning. While pension and profit-sharing plans typically include only those persons who are directly in the employ of the legal entity sponsoring the plan, it is possible to provide in the pension and profit-sharing plan involved that persons who are indirectly employed by the company sponsoring the plan, and in particular, those employed by the joint venture, be included in the plan.

Another method of avoiding the problems resulting from termination of employment is through the joint venture agreement. May joint ventures provide that personnel are not the employees of the joint venture, but rather retain their status as employees of the respective joint venturers. Such a provision may eliminate completely the termination of employment problem.

§9.07 Insurance

A construction contracting joint venture needs the same types of insurance coverage as any other contractor, and policies should be secured which protect the joint venture. Each contractor participating in the joint venture should maintain the individual coverage carried prior to entering the joint venture. Before entering in to the joint venture, the advice of an experienced insurance adviser should be sought to establish the joint venture insurance program. The insurance adviser can play a crucial role in recommending adequate insurance protection for the joint venture, as well as in reviewing the sufficiency of the coverage maintained by the individual venturers. Insurance coverage for joint venture participants may often be excluded by individual insurance policies. Endorsements or separate policies to cover joint venture activities may be obtained.

Joint Venture Agreements

FORM 9-1   Joint Venture Agreement

JOINT VENTURE AGREEMENT

¶1.   This JOINT VENTURE AGREEMENT is made _____(Date) between _____ and _____

¶2.   **Purpose**

The parties desire to associate themselves in a Joint Venture for the purpose of securing a contract and performing mechanical construction on an Office Building to serve as a Corporate Headquarters for _____ (the "Construction Contract" and the "Project").

¶3.   **Joint Venture Established**

The parties constitute themselves a Joint Venture for the purpose of performing and completing the Project described above, and for the purpose of furnishing or performing the necessary work, labor, materials, and services in connection with the Project, and for no other purpose. It is expressly understood that nothing contained in this Agreement shall be construed as creating any partnership, or one party the general agent of the other, or in any way preventing or hindering either party from carrying on its respective business or businesses for its own benefit.

¶4.   **Joint and Several Liability**

The Construction Contract shall be made in the name of the Joint Venture for the mutual benefit of the parties hereto, and the obligations under the contract shall be joint and several.

¶5.   **Name and Principal Office**

The name of this Joint Venture shall be _____ JOINT VENTURE. The principal office of the Joint Venture shall be located at the Project, or at such other location as may be agreed upon.

¶6.   **Interests of the Parties**

   a.   The interest of the parties in the Construction Contract, and in any property and equipment acquired in connection with the performance of the Construction Contract, and in monies derived from the performance of the Construction Contract, and the obligations of the parties with respect to any liabilities and losses shall be:

  _____: (Party 1)   50 per cent
  _____: (Party 2)   50 per cent

 b. Each party agrees to indemnify the other against any loss or liability exceeding the proportions stated above, including liability or loss arising out of the execution of any surety bonds or indemnity agreements secured in connection with the Construction Contract.

¶7. Representatives and Management Committee

 a. Each party shall designate a Representative to serve on a Management Committee, who shall have complete responsibility to act on behalf of that party in any matter involving the performance of the Construction Contract by the Joint Venture.

 b. Each party shall also designate an Alternate Representative, who shall serve only when the Principal Representative is absent, or incapacitated, or unable to serve. The Principal and Alternate Representatives shall serve without compensation, or for such compensation from the funds of the Joint Venture as may be agreed upon by the Management Committee.

 c. Subject to the terms of this Agreement, the Management Committee shall have full responsibility and authority for the performance of the Construction Contract, including, but not limited to, assignment of work between the parties, preparation of schedules of work, settlement of disputes with other parties, and any other matters affecting the performance of the Construction Contract. Actions and decisions of the Management Committee shall be by unanimous vote.

 d. Should the Principal or Alternate Representatives cease to serve, the party shall promptly, by written notice, name a successor.

 e. Each representative may at any time replace either the Principal or Alternate Representative by notice in writing.

¶8. Contributions and Financing

 a. The initial capital contribution by each party to the Joint Venture shall be as follows:

  _____: (Party 1)   (Dollar Amount)

_____: (Party 2)   (Dollar Amount)

b. A bank account, or accounts (Joint Venture Account), shall be opened in the name of the Joint Venture.

c. Within five (5) days after the execution of this Agreement, the parties shall each advance pay into the Joint Venture Account, the initial capital contributions specified above.

d. All monies contributed by the parties and all monies received as payment under the Construction Contract or otherwise received by the Joint Venture are to be declared trust funds for the performance of the Construction Contract and for no other purpose, until the Construction Contract has been fully completed, and all obligations of the Joint Venture have been paid or otherwise discharged, or adequate reserves have been established to cover any such obligations. Fidelity bond coverage shall be maintained on all persons who are directly connected with handling Joint Venture funds or the performance of the Construction Contract. The cost of such fidelity bond premiums shall be part of the Construction Costs, as defined below.

e. All payments received by the Joint Venture under the Construction Contract or from others in connection with the Project shall be promptly deposited in the Joint Venture Account and all invoices received by the Joint Venture shall be paid by check drawn on the Joint Venture Account.

f. Checks drawn against the Joint Venture Account shall require the signature of a representative of each party. Each party shall designate an individual or individuals authorized on its behalf to endorse checks deposited to, and to sign checks drawn on, the Joint Venture Account.

g. If the Management Committee determines that any additional funds are required or desirable for carrying out the Construction Contract, or to pay any losses arising from the Construction Contract, or to make good any deficits, then the parties shall within ten (10) days after such determination contribute additional funds pro rata to their percentage interests. Should any party fail to contribute such additional funds in the Joint Venture Account, then the other party advancing such deficiency shall receive interest on the funds advanced at a rate computed at ____ per cent per annum. Such excess funds shall be repaid in full, with interest, from the first monies available for such purpose, and before any other payments are made to the parties. The interest paid for funds thus advanced shall be charged against the party on account of whose failure the said funds were advanced.

h. When the Management Committee determines that the funds in the Joint Venture Account are in excess of the needs of the Project, such excess funds shall be first applied to the return of the parties' capital contributions, until such capital contributions have been entirely repaid, and the balance of such excess shall be distributed to the parties in their respective percentage interests set forth above.

i. Neither party acting alone shall have the power to borrow money on behalf of, or pledge the credit of, the Joint Venture.

¶9. Equipment Rental

A party may rent equipment to the Joint Venture only with the consent of the other party, and with written agreement as to the rental rates.

¶10. Labor

a. The parties shall furnish the labor required to perform the work on the Project in the following proportions:

_____: (Party 1)	50 per cent
_____: (Party 2)	50 per cent

The provision of labor for the Project by the parties shall be in compliance with the terms of any applicable collective bargaining agreements.

b. All expenses incurred in providing labor, including but not limited to salaries, insurance, employee benefits, worker's compensation insurance, public liability insurance, Federal old age taxes, State unemployment taxes, and any other taxes levied by Federal, State, or local authorities, shall be paid directly by the Joint Venture.

¶11. Cost of Construction

The Cost of Construction of the Project shall include: The cost of all subcontracts, labor, material, plant, tools, and equipment purchased or leased (including any of the foregoing items purchased or leased from either of the parties); bonds, insurance, taxes of all types (excepting income); miscellaneous charges; legal fees; consultants' fees; administrative and accounting expenses; liabilities not covered by insurance; and all other expenses and obligations incurred or suffered in performance of the Construction Contract of a nature properly charged as a cost of performance of the Construction Contract under generally accepted accounting principles.

¶12. Project Manager and Assistant Project Manager

The representatives of the respective parties to the Management Committee shall appoint a Project Manager and an Assistant Project Manager for the Project who shall (1) be responsible for the direction and management of the work in accordance with policies and procedures established by the Management Committee, (2) coordinate the work, and (3) be responsible for contact with the General Contractor and other necessary parties in order to perform the work.

The Project Manager shall be appointed by the representative of _____ (Party 1), and the Assistant Project Manager shall be appointed by the representative of _____ (Party 2).

The Project Manager and Assistant Project Manager shall be subject to removal and reappointment by the representative of the party empowered to appoint same; provided, however, that any such removal and reappointment shall be subject to the approval of the Management Committee.

¶13. **Disputes Between the Parties**

a. All disputes between the parties arising out of or related to this Joint Venture Agreement, or the performance thereof, or on matters of policy with respect to the performance of the Construction Contract shall be submitted to an independent arbiter mutually agreed upon by the parties. Unless otherwise mutually agreed by the parties, or unless the arbiter is unwilling or unable to serve, the parties appoint _____ (Name) to act as the independent arbiter with respect to all disputes between the parties.

b. The decision rendered by the independent arbiter, provided for in Subparagraph a, shall be final, conclusive, and binding upon the parties.

c. Notice of submission of the policy dispute to the independent arbiter shall be filed with the other party to this Agreement by the party submitting same. The policy dispute shall be submitted to the independent arbiter within a reasonable time after the dispute has arisen.

d. Disputes shall be resolved in accordance with the Construction Industry Arbitration Rules of the American Arbitration Association, or such rules as may otherwise be mutually agreed upon in writing by the parties and the arbiter.

¶14. **Accounting**

a. One person designated by the Management Committee shall be appointed Treasurer of the Joint Venture. The Treasurer shall keep for the Joint Venture a separate set of full and current books on account, upon such basis as the Management Committee may determine. Such books of accounts shall be kept and maintained as the principal office of the Joint Venture, and, along with all records of the Joint Venture, shall be open for inspection by the parties to the Joint Venture at mutually convenient times.

b. A periodic audit of such books of accounts shall be made by an independent firm of certified public accountants as may be mutually agreed upon by the parties, and a like audit shall be make upon completion of the Construction Contract. With respect to the periodic audits, there shall be included, if requested by the parties, a periodic comparison between the items of cost and the items set up in the estimate of cost. The cost of these audits shall be part of the Construction Costs.

¶15. Insurance

The Joint Venture will effect and maintain insurance to protect itself and the parties from claims arising out of its activities. The Joint Venture shall acquire all necessary bonds, completed operations insurance, commercial general liability insurance, worker's compensation insurance, automobile liability insurance, and in such amounts as the Management Committee believes necessary to protect the Joint Venture. To the extent that any party provides these coverages for the Joint Venture, the party shall be reimbursed for its cost of obtaining same, which payment shall not affect or limit the party's interest in the Joint Venture.

¶16. Bankruptcy, Insolvency, or Liquidation

a. Notwithstanding any other provision contained herein, in the event of the bankruptcy, insolvency, or liquidation of either party, this Joint Venture Agreement shall terminate, and the bankrupt, insolvent, or liquidated party shall share only in the profits earned, or loss, or liability incurred to the date of such bankruptcy, insolvency, or liquidation. The profits earned, or loss, or liability incurred to the date of such bankruptcy, insolvency, or liquidation shall be deemed to bear the same proportion to the total profits earned, or loss, or liability incurred upon the final completion of the Construction Contract. Such share in any profits shall in no event be payable to the bankrupt, insolvent, or liquidated party before the completion of the Construction Contract, the collection of all receipts, and the payment of all liabilities.

b. In the event of the bankruptcy, insolvency, or liquidation of either party, the remaining party, being the one no bankrupt, insolvent, or liquidated, shall be privileged to complete the Construction Contract without incurring liability of any kind to the other party to this Agreement for the profit earned after the date of bankruptcy, insolvency, or liquidation, and such earnings or accruals after such happening shall belong to the surviving party.

¶17. Assignment of Interest

Neither party may assign, pledge, transfer, or hypothecate its interest in this Agreement or in any monies belonging to, or which may accrue to, the Joint Venture in connection with the Construction Contract or any interest in the Joint Venture Account, or in any property, real or personal, loaned to or belonging to, or employed by the Joint Venture, except with the prior written consent of the other party.

¶18. Legal Counsel

The Joint Venture may retain, as and when necessary, legal counsel to be mutually agreed upon for use in connection with any matters of concern to the Joint Venture which may require legal counsel or assistance.

¶19. **Commencement and Termination**

a. This Joint Venture will commence on _____.

b. Except as otherwise provided herein, this Agreement shall remain in full force and effect until terminated by written agreement signed by all parties, or until all of the purposes for which this Joint Venture has been undertaken have been accomplished and completed.

¶20. **Technical Assistance of Each Party**

Except as otherwise provided herein, each party shall make available for the Project such of its personnel, facilities, experience, and records, as may be reasonably necessary or desirable to the end that the Project may be promptly and successfully carried out.

¶21. **Fiscal Year**

The books of account of the Joint Venture shall be maintained on a fiscal year basis. The fiscal year shall begin on _____ and end on _____.

¶22. **Notices**

Any and all notices required or permitted to be given under this agreement will be sufficient if furnished in writing, sent by United States Mail, postage prepaid to the last known residence in the case of an individual, or its principal office in the case of a corporation or other business entity.

¶23. **Binding Agreement**

This Agreement shall be binding upon and inure to the benefit of the parties, their heirs, successors, and assigns as the case may be.

¶24. **Merger**

This Agreement, and the exhibits attached hereto and referenced herein, contain and embody the entire Agreement of the parties, and no representations, inducements, or agreements, oral or otherwise, between the parties not contained or embodied in the Agreement shall be of any force or effect. This Agreement may not be modified or changed, in whole or in part, orally or in any other manner than be agreement in writing, signed by all the parties.

	(Party 1)
(CORPORATE SEAL)	By: _____
	President

ATTEST:

_____
Secretary

	(Party 2)
(CORPORATE SEAL)	By: _____
	President

ATTEST:

_____
Secretary

FORM 9-2   Joint Venture Agreement - Another Version

JOINT VENTURE AGREEMENT

¶1. Recitals: The parties of this Joint Venture Agreement are both licensed union electrical contractors, and they wish to form a joint venture in order to bid work. This Joint Venture Agreement will be applicable only to specified projects that are agreed to in writing in advance by the parties, and each joint venturer will retain its ability to conduct its independent electrical contracting business any place in the world, whether such conduct is or is not in competition with the other joint venturer. The parties therefore constitute themselves a joint venture on the following terms and conditions:

¶2. Name: The name of this joint venture shall be _____.

¶3. Projects: From time to time, one joint venturer will nominate a project to be performed by the Joint Venture in writing. If the other joint venturer agrees to pursue the project in writing, then the Joint Venture will bid or negotiate the Project Contract, and perform the work under the terms of this Joint Venture Agreement. Each party is free to bid all work and carry on all business in competition with the other party, except those projects as to which the parties have reached a written agreement to pursue as a joint venture. Once the parties have agreed to pursue a project as a joint venture, neither shall pursue that project in its individual capacity, without the written consent of the other party.

¶4. Joint Venture License: Before bidding any work as a joint venture, the parties shall obtain a joint venture contractor's license.

¶5. Profits and Losses: The profits and losses of the Joint Venture shall be divided _____ per cent to _____ and _____ per cent to _____.

¶6. Capital: _____ will contribute $_____, and _____ will contribute $_____ to the capital of the Joint Venture. The funds will be utilized to open a Joint Venture bank account. All funds accruing to the Joint Venture, and all costs and expenses of the Joint Venture, will be deposited in and paid out of the Joint Venture bank account, and such other Joint Venture bank accounts as may be established from time to time for the convenience of the Joint Venture. When additional funds are needed to meet the obligations of the Joint Venture, each party will contribute its pro rata share, _____/_____ per cent.

¶7. Joint Venture Manager: _____ (Party 1) will act as the Joint Venture Manager. _____ (Party 1) will consult with _____ (Party 2) to extent practicable as to management decisions, but for the purpose of harmonizing and streamlining the activities of the Joint Venture, the final power of decision shall rest with _____ (Party 1) as to all management questions, except as otherwise provided in this Agreement. _____ (Party 1) will exercise its management powers in good faith and for the benefit of the Joint Venture.

¶8. Designated Representatives: Each party will designate a representative who will have the authority to make all decisions required of the party under this Joint Venture Agreement. In the absence of the Designated Representative, each party will appoint an Alternate Representative. The parties may make substitutions of Designated Representatives and Alternates by written notice to the other party. The initial Designated Representative are as follows:_____ (Party 1), _____, Representative; _____, Alternate; _____ (Party 2), _____, Representative; _____, Alternate.

¶9. Legal Services: _____ (Party 1) will obtain legal services for the Joint Venture through its regularly employed attorneys, their fees to be paid by the Joint Venture.

¶10. Books and Records: _____ (Party 1) will maintain the Joint Venture books and records, both on the job and in its home office. _____ (Party 1) will be responsible for filing the appropriate partnership income tax return, and for supply a copy of the return and its associated forms to _____ (Party 2). _____ (Party 2) will cooperate with _____ (Party 1) in furnishing jobsite records and payroll records that may be necessary to keeping proper books and records. The books and records of the Joint Venture shall at all times be open to inspection by both parties.

¶11. Decisions Requiring Concurrence: The following decisions may not be made alone by either party, but must be made jointly:

(a) Establishment of bid prices and contract prices for projects.

(b) Decisions to bid or negotiate projects.

(c) Approval of contracts documents for projects.

(d) Purchases of any item or group of items costing more than $5,000, and subcontracts that amount to more than $5,000.

(e) Establishment of a change order format.

(f) Establishment of Joint Venture insurance requirements.

¶12. **Working Capital:** It is understood that the Joint Venture will require working capital, and that the need for working capital will fluctuate from time to time. It is anticipated that the initial required working capital will be $_____. At such time as the manager determines that additional working capital is needed, it will issue a call in writing, and the parties will contribute their share, _____/_____ per cent. If either party fails or refuses to respond to a call within ten (10) days, the other party may advance the delinquent share, but is not obligated to do so. Advances made by a party under this paragraph shall be repaid before any profit is distributed to any party. Advances made under this paragraph shall bear interest at three (3) points over the prime rate generally charged by commercial banks in _____ (City) during the period of the advance. The prime rate shall be adjusted from time to time in accordance with commercial banking practice. The party that fails to respond to the call shall also pay to the advancing party any special economic loss that the advancing party may incur in order to obtain the funds that are needed for the advance. If a party fails to respond, and, as a result, the Joint Venture incurs economic loss, then the party who fails to respond to the advance shall reimburse the Joint Venture for such loss.

¶13. **Distributions:** The Manager shall first set aside a sufficient amount of money to establish a reserve for the operations of the Joint Venture. Thereafter, any revenues that are not needed for reserves or operations shall be distributed, at convenient intervals, to the venturers, _____/_____ per cent.

¶14. **Warranty Reserve:** The Manager will establish, on the completion of a project, a reasonable reserve for the performance of pickup, call back, repair, or warranty work. If the reserve needs to be increased, it shall be increased by a call. If the reserve becomes excessive, it shall be reduced by a distribution. The reserve shall be maintained until the expiration of the warranty period for the project.

¶15. **Joint Venture Funds:** All Joint Venture funds shall be kept in bank accounts standing in the name of the Joint Venture. Any surplus funds that are set aside for reserves shall, if commercially expedient, be placed in an interest bearing account, and the interest shall accrue to the Joint Venture.

¶16. **No Interest on Capital:** No interest shall be paid to any joint venturer for capital invested in the Joint Venture.

¶17. **Borrowing:** The Manager is authorized to borrow money at commercially reasonable terms in the name of the Joint Venture. A joint venturer may lend money to the Joint Venture, but only upon terms that receive the written consent of both parties. Neither party shall borrow money from the Joint Venture without the written consent of the other party.

¶18. **Spheres of Responsibility:** Each joint venturer will contribute its services and expertise in all areas. However, the spheres of primary responsibility shall be as follows:
_____ (Party One): _____
_____ .
_____ (Party 2): _____
_____ .

¶19. **Equipment Rental:** In the discretion of the Manager, either party may rent equipment to the Joint Venture at reasonable rates. However, any substantial amount of equipment rental by a party shall be approved in advance by the other party as to rates and terms. As a general rule, and to avoid possible controversy, the Joint Venture will rent equipment from outside sources. In the discretion of the Manager, the Joint Venture shall buy rather than rent equipment. The equipment may be stored at reasonable rates, or rented to outsiders during periods between projects, or may be sold, and the proceeds of the sale distributed to the Joint Venture.

¶20. **Job Costs:** The Joint Venture will reimburse the joint venturers for all job costs incurred by them. Job costs include the cost of labor, materials, equipment, equipment rental, subcontracts, and fringes. The parties will agree, from time to time, in writing, on the percentage figure to be applied against direct labor for payroll taxes, union fringes, worker's compensation insurance, liability insurance, and other similar payroll burdens. The Joint Venture will also reimburse the venturers for the cost of Project Managers, superintendents, and general superintendents furnished to the project for the actual hours of time that are devoted to the project, plus _____ per cent for fringes and payroll costs. If a question should arise about any item charged to the venture by either of the venturers, then the party questioning the cost is entitled to a full review of the books and records of the party questioning the item charged. Charges made by a venturer to the Joint Venture shall be accompanied by detailed backup. In the event that the Joint Venture does not have the resources to pay the charges that are made by a venturer to the Joint Venture, then the Joint Venture shall pay its outside creditors, and shall withhold payment from the venturers on a ____/____ per cent basis.

¶21. **Bonds and Insurance:** _____ (Party 1) will supply bonds and insurance that may be needed by the Joint Venture, and the premiums shall be paid by the Joint Venture. Upon the completion of the project, the Joint Venture shall purchase completed operations insurance, and the premium will be paid by the Joint Venture.

¶22. **Withdrawal or Termination:** Neither joint venturer may withdraw from the Joint Venture or terminates its relationship with the Joint Venture while a project remains incomplete. If a venturer, in spite of the provisions of this Paragraph, should withdraw from, or refuse to participate in, the operations of the Joint Venture, then the remaining joint venturer shall be paid, by the Joint Venture, a management fee equal to 7 per cent of the value of the performed by the Joint Venture after the withdrawal or termination. The management fee shall be paid before any distribution of profits or return of capital to either venturer.

¶23. **Termination:** The Joint Venture may be terminated by written notice from one venturer to another at any time when no project is under negotiation, bidding, or construction, and when all warranty periods have expired. Upon termination, the Joint Venture will pay its debts, including debts to joint venturers, and the remaining assets will be divided on a ____/____ per cent basis.

¶24. **Arbitration:** Any dispute between the joint venturers arising out of this Joint Venture Agreement, or the operation, termination, or dissolution of the Joint Venture, is subject to arbitration in accordance with the rules of the American Arbitration Association. The arbitrators are authorized to appoint a receiver, or an independent accountant, at the expense of the Joint Venture, and are authorized to issue injunctions, restraining orders, and any other provisional remedy that could be ordered by a court of competent jurisdiction. Each joint venturer will make available to the auditors of the other joint venturer any books and records that may be called for, to be used in, or in preparation for, the arbitration proceedings. If a party to the arbitration, after due notice, failed to appear at or participate in a hearing, then the tribunal will make an award based on the evidence that is presented by the party who does appear and participate. The arbitrators are authorized to award a just amount to compensate the party who is justly entitled thereto for the costs, expenses, time, and trouble of arbitration, including reasonable attorneys' fees. Arbitration will be in the _____ office of the American Arbitration Association, unless the American Arbitration Association, for good cause, decides that the hearings should be held elsewhere. The arbitrators shall not enforce the rules of evidence, but will base their decision on the kind of evidence that is usually relied upon by prudent persons in the conduct of their business affairs. The arbitrators will expedite the proceedings, and parties will not be permitted to introduce cumulative, unimportant, unreliable, or dubious evidence, or evidence that has little probative value when compared to the time that is consumed by its introduction. The

American Arbitration Association shall attempt to appoint a tribunal composed of a lawyer, a CPA, and an electrical contractor. In the event that the dispute arises while a project is in progress, the tribunal is authorized to make interlocutory orders, and the parties will comply with those orders to expedite the completion of the project. If a party fails to comply with interlocutory orders issued by the tribunal, the arbitrators are authorized to include in their award an amount to compensate the Joint Venture for the economic loss incurred because of the failure.

¶25. **Assignment:** Neither venturer shall assign its interest in the Joint Venture, or in the capital, profits, or proceeds of the Joint Venture, without the written consent of the other party.

¶26. **Insolvency:** If a petition in bankruptcy should be filed by or against a venturer, or if a venturer should make an assignment for the benefits of creditors, or if a receiver is appointed to take charge of the affairs of a venturer, then the other joint venturer may, but is not required to, eject the insolvent joint venturer from the Joint Venture and continue the project. In such event, the continuing joint venture shall be paid a management fee equal to 7 per cent of the work performed after the termination of the insolvent joint venturer, and the insolvent joint venturer, or the receiver, or trustee in bankruptcy, shall not be entitled to receive any payment until the completion of the project.

DATED: _____

_____
(Party 1)

By _____

_____
(Party 2)

By _____

Index

A

ADDENDUM TO AIA DOCUMENT A111
  Prime contracts §1.27
ADVANTAGES, OWNERS POINT OF VIEW
  Design-build contracts §2.04
AGC DOCUMENT NO. 30, REVISIONS TO
  Design-build subcontracts §7.05
AGC DOCUMENT NO. 410, DESIGN-BUILD AGREEMENT
  Design-build contracts §2.08
AGC DOCUMENT NO. 415, DESIGN-BUILD AGREEMENT
  Design-build contracts §2.07
AGC DOCUMENT NO. 420
  Agreements between contractor and architect §5.02
AGC DOCUMENT NO. 420, REVISIONS TO
  Agreements between contractor and architect §5.03
AGC DOCUMENT NO. 430, CONDITIONS BETWEEN CONTRACTOR AND SUBCONTRACTOR FOR DESIGN-BUILD
  Design-build subcontracts §7.04
AGC DOCUMENT NO. 450, SUBCONTRACTOR NOT PROVIDING DESIGN
  Design-build subcontracts §7.02
AGC DOCUMENT NO. 450-1, SUBCONTRACTOR PROVIDING DESIGN
  Design-build subcontracts §7.03
AGC DOCUMENT NO. 500, GUARANTEED MAXIMUM PRICE
  Construction management contracts §3.01
AGC DOCUMENT NO. 501, AMENDMENT TO OWNER-CONSTRUCTION MANAGER CONTRACT
  Construction management contracts §3.02

373

AGC DOCUMENT NO. 520, GENERAL CONDITIONS FOR TRADE CONTRACTORS
Construction management contracts §3.03
AGC DOCUMENT NO. 600
Subcontracts §§6.07-6.13
AGC DOCUMENT NO. 603
Subcontracts §6.14
AGC STANDARD FORM 605, STANDARD SUBBID PROPOSAL
Subcontracts §6.15
AIA DOCUMENT A107
Prime contracts §1.33
AIA DOCUMENT A201
Prime contracts §1.28
AIA DOCUMENT B141, STANDARD FORM OF AGREEMENT BETWEEN OWNER AND ARCHITECT
Contracts between owners and architects §4.02
ALTERNATE PRIME CONTRACT PROVISIONS
Prime contracts §1.32
ALTERNATE PURCHASE ORDER PROVISIONS
Purchase orders §8.04
ALTERNATES
Prime contracts §1.24
ALTERNATE SUBCONTRACT PROVISIONS
Subcontracts §6.06
APPLICATIONS FOR PAYMENT
Prime contracts §1.13
ARCHITECTS
Contractors and architects, agreements between. See CONTRACTORS AND ARCHITECTS, AGREEMENTS BETWEEN

ARCHITECTS, *continued*
Owners and architects, contracts between. See OWNERS AND ARCHITECTS, CONTRACTS BETWEEN
AUTHOR
See FORMS DRAFTED BY AUTHOR

B

BUILDING CONSTRUCTION
Subcontracts §6.07

C

CHANGES IN WORK
Prime contracts §1.26
CLAIMS
Subcontracts §6.10
COMMERCIAL TRANSACTIONS
Purchase orders §8.02
CONSTRUCTION INDUSTRY
Purchase orders §8.01
CONSTRUCTION MANAGEMENT CONTRACTS
Generally, AGC Document No. 500, construction management agreement, guaranteed maximum price §3.01
AGC Document No. 501, amendment to owner-construction manager contract §3.02
AGC Document No. 520, general conditions for trade contractors §3.03
Prime contracts §1.08
CONCEPT
Design-build contracts §2.01
CONTRACT DOCUMENTS
Prime contracts §1.18

CONTRACTORS
Construction management contracts §§3.01-3.03
Design-build contracts §§2.07, 2.08
Prime contractors. See PRIME CONTRACTORSPrime contracts §§1.09, 1.28, 1.33Subcontracts §6.10

CONTRACTORS AND ARCHITECTS, AGREEMENTS BETWEEN
Generally §5.01
AGC Document No. 420, agreement between contractor and architect §5.02
AGC Document No. 420, revisions to §5.03

CONTRACTS
Owners and architects, contracts between. See OWNERS AND ARCHITECTS, CONTRACTS BETWEEN
Subcontracts. See SUBCONTRACTS

CONTRACT SUM
Prime contracts §1.22

CONTRIBUTIONS AND FINANCING
Joint venture agreements §9.05

CONTROL OF OPERATIONS
Joint venture agreements §9.04

CONVENTIONAL PRIME CONTRACTS
See PRIME CONTRACTS

COST PLUS CONTRACT, AIA DOCUMENT A111
Prime contracts. See PRIME CONTRACTS

COST PLUS PERCENTAGE
Prime contracts §1.30

D

DATE OF COMMENCEMENT
Prime contracts §1.11

DEFINITIONS
Prime contracts §1.01

DELAY
See FINAL PAYMENT DELAY

DESIGN-BUILD CONTRACTS
Generally §2.01
Advantages from owners point of view §2.04
AGC Document No. 410, Design-Build Agreement, guaranteed maximum §2.08
AGC Document No. 415, Design-Build Agreement, lump sum §2.07
Clarifications to AGC Documents Nos. 410 and 415 §2.09
Disadvantages from owners point of view §2.03
Evolution of §2.02
Practical attributes §2.06
Prime contracts §1.06
Process of §2.05

DESIGN-BUILD SUBCONTRACTS
Generally §7.01
AGC Document No. 30, revisions to §7.05
AGC Document No. 430, conditions between contractor and subcontractor for design-build §7.04
AGC Document No. 450, standard design-build subcontract, subcontractor not providing design §7.02
AGC Document No. 450-1, standard design-build subcontract, subcontractor providing design §7.03

DISADVANTAGES, OWNERS POINT OF VIEW
Design-build contracts §2.03

E

EMPLOYEES
    Joint venture agreements §9.06
EVOLUTION OF CONTRACT
    Design-build contracts §2.02

F

FAST TRACK CONTRACTS
    Prime contracts §1.07
FINAL PAYMENT DELAY
    Subcontracts §6.11
FINAL PAYMENTS
    Prime contracts §1.17
FINANCING
    See CONTRIBUTIONS AND FINANCING
FIRST PAGE
    Prime contracts §1.10
FORMS
    Purchase orders §8.03
FORMS DRAFTED BY AUTHOR
    Subcontracts §6.02

G

GUARANTEED MAXIMUM COST
    Prime contracts §1.30
GUARANTEED MAXIMUM PRICE
    Prime contracts §§1.04, 1.23

I

INDEMNIFICATION
    Subcontracts §6.12
INSURANCE
    Joint venture agreements §9.07
INTERESTS OF PARTIES
    Joint venture agreements §9.03

J

JOINT VENTURE AGREEMENTS
    Generally §9.01
    Contributions and financing §9.05
    Control of operations §9.04
    Employees of the joint venture §9.06
    Insurance §9.07
    Interests of parties §9.03
    Rights and responsibilities §9.02

O

OPERATIONS
    See CONTROL OF OPERATIONS
OWNERS
    Construction management contracts §§3.01-3.03
    Design-build contracts §§2.03, 2.04, 2.07, 2.08
    Prime contracts §§1.09, 1.28, 1.33
OWNERS AND ARCHITECTS, CONTRACTS BETWEEN
    Generally §4.01
    AIA Document B141, standard form of agreement between owner and architect §4.02

P

PARTIES
    See INTERESTS OF PARTIES
PARTIES, RELATIONSHIP OF
    Prime contracts §1.21
PAYMENTS
    Applications for payment. See APPLICATIONS FOR PAYMENT
    Final payments. See FINAL PAYMENTS
    Progress payments. See PROGRESS PAYMENTS
PRIME CONTRACTORS
    Subcontracts §6.03

PRIME CONTRACTS
   Addendum to AIA Document A111 §1.27
   AIA Document A107, abbreviated form of agreement between owner and contractor §1.33
   AIA Document A201, general conditions §1.28
   Alternate prime contract provisions §1.32
   Construction management contract §1.08
   Cost plus contract, generally §1.03
   Cost plus contract, AIA Document A111
   –generally §1.20
   –alternates §1.24
   –changes in work §1.26
   –contract sum §1.22
   –guaranteed maximum price §1.23
   –relationship of parties §1.21
   –unit prices §1.25
   Cost plus contract with guaranteed maximum price §1.04
   Cost plus percentage, guaranteed maximum cost §1.30
   Definition §1.01
   Design-build contract §1.06
   Fast track contract §1.07
   Small project, short form §1.31
   "Split savings" contract §1.05
   Stipulated sum, AIA Document A101
   –generally §1.09
   –applications for payment §1.13
   –contract documents §1.18
   –date of commencement §1.11
   –final payment §1.17
   –first page §1.10
   –progress payments §1.16
   –retention §1.15
   –schedule of values §1.14
   –signatures §1.19

PRIME CONTRACTS, *continued*
   –substantial completion §1.12
   Stipulated sum contract, generally §1.02
   Stipulated sum §1.29
PROCESS
   Design-build contracts §2.05
PROGRESS PAYMENTS
   Prime contracts §1.16
PROPOSALS
   Prime contracts §1.31
   Subcontracts §6.05
PURCHASE ORDERS
   Alternate purchase order provisions §8.04
   Commercial transactions, special rules for §8.02
   Construction industry §8.01
   Forms §8.03

R

RETAINAGE/SECURITY
   Subcontracts §6.09
RETENTION
   Prime contracts §1.15
RIGHTS
   See WAIVER OF RIGHTS
RIGHTS AND RESPONSIBILITIES
   Joint venture agreements §9.02

S

SCHEDULE OF VALUES
   Prime contracts §1.14
SCHEDULES
   Subcontracts §6.08
SECURITY
   See RETAINAGE/SECURITY
SIGNATURES
   Prime contracts §1.19
SMALL PROJECTS
   Prime contracts §1.31

"SPLIT SAVINGS" CONTRACT
Prime contracts §1.05
STIPULATED SUM, AIA DOCUMENT A101
Prime contracts. See PRIME CONTRACTS
SUBCONTRACTS
Generally §6.01
AGC Document No. 600 §6.07
AGC Document No. 603, short form §6.14
AGC Document No. 605, standard subbid proposal §6.15
Alternate subcontract provisions §6.06
Building construction §6.07
Claims relating to contractor §6.10
Design-build subcontracts. See DESIGN-BUILD SUBCONTRACTSFinal payment delay §6.11Forms drafted by author §6.02Indemnification §6.12Long form §6.03Proposal and subcontract §6.05
Retainage/security §6.09
Schedule §6.08Short form §6.04
Waiver of rights §6.13

SUBSTANTIAL COMPLETION
Prime contracts §1.12

T

TRANSACTIONS
See COMMERCIAL TRANSACTIONS

U

UNIT PRICES
Prime contracts §1.25

W

WAIVER OF RIGHTS
Subcontracts §6.13
WORK
See CHANGES IN WORK